MCAT®

Psychology and Sociology Review

2nd Edition

The Staff of The Princeton Review

Penguin
Random
House

The Princeton Review
24 Prime Parkway, Suite 201
Natick, MA 01760
E-mail: editorialsupport@review.com

Published in the United States by Penguin Random
House LLC, New York, and in Canada by Random House
of Canada, a division of Penguin Random House Ltd.,
Toronto.

The Princeton Review is not affiliated with Princeton
University.

MCAT is a registered trademark of the Association of
American Medical Colleges, which is not affiliated with
The Princeton Review.

ISBN: 978-1-101-92060-2
ISSN: 2332-8495

Editor: Sarah Litt
Production Artist: Craig Patches
Production Editor: Beth Hanson

Printed in the United States of America on partially
recycled paper.

10   9   8   7   6   5

2nd edition

Editorial
Rob Franek, Senior VP, Publisher
Casey Cornelius, VP Content Development
Mary Beth Garrick, Director of Production
Selena Coppock, Managing Editor
Meave Shelton, Senior Editor
Colleen Day, Editor
Sarah Litt, Editor
Aaron Riccio, Editor
Orion McBean, Editorial Assistant

Random House Publishing Team
Tom Russell, Publisher
Alison Stoltzfus, Publishing Manager
Melinda Ackell, Associate Managing Editor
Ellen Reed, Production Manager
Kristin Lindner, Production Supervisor
Andrea Lau, Designer

CONTRIBUTORS

Nadia L. Johnson, M.A., M.S.
   Senior Author
Rizwan Ahmad, M.A.
   Senior Author

TPR MCAT Psychology and Sociology Team:

Rizwan Ahmad, M.A.
Jon Fowler, M.A.
Nadia L. Johnson, M.A., M.S., Lead Developer
Bikem Ayse Polat
Betsy Walli, M.S., Ph.D.
Judene Wright, M.S., M.A.Ed, Senior Editor

Edited for Production by:

Judene Wright, M.S., M.A.Ed.
   National Content Director, MCAT Program, The Princeton Review

The TPR MCAT Psychology and Sociology Team and Judene would like to thank the following people for their contributions to this book :

Erika C. Castro, B.A., Maria S. Chushak, M.S., Guenevieve O. del Mundo, B.A., B.S., C.C.S., Michelle E. Fox, B.S., Tom Kurtovic, Ali Landreau, B.A., Toni Lupro, Mike Matera, Jennifer A. McDevitt, Paola A. Munoz , M.A., B.A., Jonathan Nasrallah, Shalom Shapiro, Andrew D. Snyder, M.S., M.A., Gordy Steil, M.A., M.F.T., David Stoll, Chelsea K. Wise, M.S., Alexandra Vinson.

Periodic Table of the Elements

1 **H** 1.0																	2 **He** 4.0
3 **Li** 6.9	4 **Be** 9.0											5 **B** 10.8	6 **C** 12.0	7 **N** 14.0	8 **O** 16.0	9 **F** 19.0	10 **Ne** 20.2
11 **Na** 23.0	12 **Mg** 24.3											13 **Al** 27.0	14 **Si** 28.1	15 **P** 31.0	16 **S** 32.1	17 **Cl** 35.5	18 **Ar** 39.9
19 **K** 39.1	20 **Ca** 40.1	21 **Sc** 45.0	22 **Ti** 47.9	23 **V** 50.9	24 **Cr** 52.0	25 **Mn** 54.9	26 **Fe** 55.8	27 **Co** 58.9	28 **Ni** 58.7	29 **Cu** 63.5	30 **Zn** 65.4	31 **Ga** 69.7	32 **Ge** 72.6	33 **As** 74.9	34 **Se** 79.0	35 **Br** 79.9	36 **Kr** 83.8
37 **Rb** 85.5	38 **Sr** 87.6	39 **Y** 88.9	40 **Zr** 91.2	41 **Nb** 92.9	42 **Mo** 95.9	43 **Tc** (98)	44 **Ru** 101.1	45 **Rh** 102.9	46 **Pd** 106.4	47 **Ag** 107.9	48 **Cd** 112.4	49 **In** 114.8	50 **Sn** 118.7	51 **Sb** 121.8	52 **Te** 127.6	53 **I** 126.9	54 **Xe** 131.3
55 **Cs** 132.9	56 **Ba** 137.3	57 ***La** 138.9	72 **Hf** 178.5	73 **Ta** 180.9	74 **W** 183.9	75 **Re** 186.2	76 **Os** 190.2	77 **Ir** 192.2	78 **Pt** 195.1	79 **Au** 197.0	80 **Hg** 200.6	81 **Tl** 204.4	82 **Pb** 207.2	83 **Bi** 209.0	84 **Po** (209)	85 **At** (210)	86 **Rn** (222)
87 **Fr** (223)	88 **Ra** 226.0	89 **†Ac** 227.0	104 **Rf** (261)	105 **Db** (262)	106 **Sg** (266)	107 **Bh** (264)	108 **Hs** (277)	109 **Mt** (268)	110 **Ds** (281)	111 **Rg** (272)	112 **Cn** (285)	113 **Uut** (286)	114 **Fl** (289)	115 **Uup** (288)	116 **Lv** (293)	117 **Uus** (294)	118 **Uuo** (294)

*Lanthanide Series:

58 **Ce** 140.1	59 **Pr** 140.9	60 **Nd** 144.2	61 **Pm** (145)	62 **Sm** 150.4	63 **Eu** 152.0	64 **Gd** 157.3	65 **Tb** 158.9	66 **Dy** 162.5	67 **Ho** 164.9	68 **Er** 167.3	69 **Tm** 168.9	70 **Yb** 173.0	71 **Lu** 175.0
90 **Th** 232.0	91 **Pa** (231)	92 **U** 238.0	93 **Np** (237)	94 **Pu** (244)	95 **Am** (243)	96 **Cm** (247)	97 **Bk** (247)	98 **Cf** (251)	99 **Es** (252)	100 **Fm** (257)	101 **Md** (258)	102 **No** (259)	103 **Lr** (260)

†Actinide Series:

CONTENTS

Register Your

1 Go to **PrincetonReview.com/cracking**

2 You'll see a welcome page where you should register your book or boxed set of books using the ISBN. If you have a book, the ISBN can be found above the bar code on the back cover. If you have a boxed set, the ISBN can be found on the back of the box above the bar code.

3 After placing this free order, you'll either be asked to log in or to answer a few simple questions in order to set up a new Princeton Review account.

4 Finally, click on the "Student Tools" tab located at the top of the screen. It may take an hour or two for your registration to go through, but after that, you're good to go.

NOTE: If you are experiencing book problems (potential content errors), please contact EditorialSupport@review.com with the full title of the book, its ISBN number, and the page number of the error.

Experiencing technical issues? Please email TPRStudentTech@review.com with the following information:

- your full name
- e-mail address used to register the book
- full book title and ISBN
- your computer OS (Mac or PC) and Internet browser (Firefox, Safari, Chrome, etc.)
- description of technical issue

Book Online!

Once you've registered, you can...

- Take 3 full-length practice MCAT exams
- Find useful information about taking the MCAT and applying to medical school
- Check to see if there have been any updates to this edition

Offline Resources

If you are looking for more review or medical school advice, please feel free to pick up these books in stores right now!

- *Medical School Essays That Made a Difference*
- *The Best 167 Medical Schools*
- *The Princeton Review Complete MCAT*

Chapter 1
MCAT Basics

SO YOU WANT TO BE A DOCTOR.

So...you want to be a doctor. If you're like most premeds, you've wanted to be a doctor since you were pretty young. When people asked you what you wanted to be when you grew up, you always answered "a doctor." You had toy medical kits, you bandaged up your dog or cat, and you played "hospital." You probably read your parents' home medical guides for fun.

When you got to high school you took the honors and AP classes. You studied hard, got straight As (or at least really good grades!), and participated in extracurricular activities so you could get into a good college. And you succeeded!

At college you knew exactly what to do. You took your classes seriously, studied hard, and got a great GPA. You talked to your professors and hung out at office hours to get good letters of recommendation. You were a member of the premed society on campus, volunteered at hospitals, and shadowed doctors. All that's left to do now is get a good MCAT score.

Just the MCAT.

Just the most confidence-shattering, most demoralizing, longest and most brutal entrance exam for any graduate program. At about 7.5 hours (including breaks), the MCAT tops the list...even the closest runners up, the LSAT and GMAT, are only about 4 hours long. The MCAT tests significant science content knowledge along with the ability to think quickly, reason logically, and read comprehensively, all under the pressure of a timed exam.

The path to a good MCAT score is not as easy to see as the path to a good GPA or the path to a good letter of recommendation. The MCAT is less about what you know, and more about how to apply what you know...and how to apply it quickly to new situations. Because the path might not be so clear, you might be worried. That's why you picked up this book.

We promise to demystify the MCAT for you, with clear descriptions of the different sections, how the test is scored, and what the test experience is like. We will help you understand general test-taking techniques as well as provide you with specific techniques for each section. We will review the science content you need to know as well as give you an overview of the Psychology/Sociology section of the MCAT section. We'll show you the path to a good MCAT score and help you walk the path.

After all...you want to be a doctor. And we want you to succeed.

WHAT IS THE MCAT...REALLY?

Most test-takers approach the MCAT as though it were a typical college science test, one in which facts and knowledge simply need to be regurgitated in order to do well. They study for the MCAT the same way they did for their college tests, by memorizing facts and details, formulas and equations. And when they get to the MCAT they are surprised...and disappointed.

It's a myth that the MCAT is purely a content-knowledge test. If medical school admission committees want to see what you know, all they have to do is look at your transcripts. What they really want to see, is how you *think*, especially how you think under pressure. That's what your MCAT score will tell them.

The MCAT is really a test of your ability to apply basic knowledge to different, possibly new, situations. It's a test of your ability to reason out and evaluate arguments. Do you still need to know your science content? Absolutely. But not at the level that most test-takers think they need to know it. Furthermore, your science knowledge won't help you on the the Critical Analysis and Reasoning Skills (CARS) section. So how do you study for a test like this?

You study for the science sections by reviewing the basics and then applying them to MCAT practice questions. You study for the Psychology and Sociology section of the MCAT by reading this book, and by studying the people, and world, around you.

The book you are holding will review all the relevant MCAT Psychology and Sociology content you will need for the test, and a little bit more. Plus, it includes questions designed to make you think about the material in a deeper way, along with full explanations to clarify the logical thought process needed to get to the answer. It also comes with access to three full-length online practice exams to further hone your skills. For more information on accessing those online exams, please refer to the "Register Your Book Online!" spread on page viii.

MCAT NUTS AND BOLTS

Overview

The MCAT is a computer-based test (CBT) that is *not* adaptive. Adaptive tests base your next question on whether or not you've answered the current question correctly. The MCAT is *linear*, or *fixed-form*, meaning that the questions are in a predetermined order and do not change based on your answers. However, there are many versions of the test, so that on a given test day, different people will see different versions. The following table highlights the features of the MCAT exam.

Registration	Online via www.aamc.org. Begins as early as six months prior to test date; available up until week of test.
Testing Centers	Administered at Prometric testing sites; smaller, climate-controlled computer testing rooms.
Security	Photo ID with signature, electronic fingerprint, electronic signature verification, assigned seat.
Proctoring	None. Test administrator checks examinee in and assigns seat at computer. All testing instructions are given on the computer.
Frequency of Test	Many times per year distributed over January, April, May, June, July, August, and September.
Format	Exclusively computer based. NOT an adaptive test.
Length of Test Day	7.5 hours
Breaks	Optional 10-minute breaks between sections, with a 30-minute break for lunch.
Section Names	1. Chemical and Physical Foundations of Biological Systems (Chem/Phys) 2. Critical Analysis and Reasoning Skills (CARS) 3. Biological and Biochemical Foundations of Living Systems (Bio/Biochem) 4. Psychological, Social, and Biological Foundations of Behavior (Psych/Soc)
Number of Questions and Timing	59 Chem/Phys questions, 95 minutes 53 CARS questions, 90 minutes 59 Bio/Biochem questions, 95 minutes 59 Psych/Soc questions, 95 minutes
Scoring	Test is scaled. Several forms per administration.
Allowed/Not allowed	No timers. Noise reduction headphones available. Unopened package of foam earplugs OK. Scratch paper and pencils given at start of test and taken at end of test. Locker provided for personal items.
Results: Timing and Delivery	Approximately 30 days. Electronic scores only. Examinees can print official score reports.
Maximum Number of Retakes	As of April 2015, the MCAT can be taken a maximum of three times per year in one year, four times over two years, and seven times over the lifetime of the examinee. An examinee can only be registered for one date at a time.

Registration

Registration for the exam is completed online at www.aamc.org/students/applying/mcat/reserving. The AAMC opens registration for a given test date at least two months in advance of the date, often earlier. It's a good idea to register well in advance of your desired test date to make sure that you get a seat.

Sections

There are four sections on the MCAT exam: Chemical and Physical Foundations of Biological Systems (Chem/Phys), Critical Analysis and Reasoning Skills (CARS), Biological and Biochemical Foundations of Living Systems (Bio/Biochem), and Psychological, Social, and Biological Foundations of Behavior (Psych/Soc). All sections consist of multiple-choice questions.

Section	Concepts Tested	Number of Questions and Timing
Chemical and Physical Foundations of Biological Systems	Basic concepts in chemistry and physics, including biochemistry, scientific inquiry, reasoning, research and statistics skills	59 questions in 95 minutes
Critical Analysis and Reasoning Skills	Critical analysis of information drawn from a wide range of social science and humanities disciplines	53 questions in 90 minutes
Biological and Biochemical Foundations of Living Systems	Basic concepts in biology and biochemistry, scientific inquiry, reasoning, research and statistics skills	59 questions in 95 minutes
Psychological, Social, and Biological Foundations of Behavior	Basic concepts in psychology, sociology, and biology, research methods and statistics.	59 questions in 95 minutes

Most questions on the MCAT (44 in the science sections, all 53 in the CARS section) are passage-based; the science sections have 10 passages each and the CARS section has 9. A passage consists of a few paragraphs of information on which several following questions are based. In the science sections, passages often include graphs, figures, and experiments to analyze. CARS passages come from literature in the social sciences, humanities, ethics, philosophy, cultural studies, and population health, and do not test content knowledge in any way.

Some questions in the science sections are *freestanding questions* (FSQs). These questions are independent of any passage information and appear in several groups of about four to five questions interspersed throughout the passages. About 15 of the questions in the sciences sections are freestanding, and the remainder are passage-based.

Each section on the MCAT is separated by either a 10-minute break or a 30-minute lunch break:

Section	Time
Test center check-in	Varies, can take up to 40 minutes if center is busy.
Tutorial	10 minutes
Chemical and Physical Foundations of Biological Systems	95 minutes
Break	10 minutes
Critical Analysis and Reasoning Skills	90 minutes
Lunch Break	30 minutes
Biological and Biochemical Foundations of Living Systems	95 minutes
Break	10 minutes
Psychological, Social, and Biological Foundations of Behavior	95 minutes
Void Option	5 minutes
Survey	5 minutes

The survey includes questions about your satisfaction with the overall MCAT experience, including registration, check-in, etc., as well as questions about how you prepared for the test.

Scoring

The MCAT is a scaled exam, meaning that your raw score will be converted into a scaled score that takes into account the difficulty of the questions. There is no guessing penalty. All sections are scored from 118–132, with a total scaled score range of 472–528. Because different versions of the test have varying levels of difficulty, the scale will be different from one exam to the next. Thus, there is no "magic number" of questions to get right in order to get a particular score. Plus, some of the questions on the test are considered "experimental" and do not count toward your score; they are just there to be evaluated for possible future inclusion in a test.

At the end of the test (after you complete the Psychological, Social, and Biological Foundations of Behavior section), you will be asked to choose one of the following two options, "I wish to have my MCAT exam scored" or "I wish to VOID my MCAT exam." You have five minutes to make a decision, and if you do not select one of the options in that time, the test will automatically be scored. If you choose the VOID option, your test will not be scored (you will not now, or ever, get a numerical score for this test), medical schools will not know you took the test, and no refunds will be granted. You cannot "unvoid" your scores at a later time.

So, what's a good score? The AAMC is centering the scale at 500 (i.e., 500 will be the 50th percentile), and recommends that application committees consider applicants near the center of the range. To be on the safe side, aim for a total score of around 510. Remember that if your GPA is on the low side, you'll need higher MCAT scores to compensate, and if you have a strong GPA, you can get away with lower MCAT scores. But the reality is that your chances of acceptance depend on a lot more than just your MCAT scores. It's a combination of your GPA, MCAT scores, undergraduate coursework, letters of recommendation, experience related to the medical field (such as volunteer work or research), extracurricular activities, your personal statement, and so on. Medical schools are looking for a complete package, not just good scores and a good GPA.

GENERAL LAYOUT AND TEST TAKING STRATEGIES

Layout of the Test

In each section of the test, the computer screen is divided vertically, with the passage on the left and the range of questions for that passage indicated above (e.g. "Passage 1 Questions 1–5"). The scroll bar for the passage text appears in the middle of the screen. Each question appears on the right, and you need to click "Next" to move to each subsequent question.

In the science sections, the freestanding questions are found in groups of 4–5, interspersed with the passages. The screen is still divided vertically; on the left is the statement "Questions [X–XX] do not refer to a passage and are independent of each other" and each question appears on the right as described above.

CBT Tools

There are a number of tools available on the test, including highlighting, strike-outs, the Mark button, the Review button, the Periodic Table button, and of course, scratch paper. The following is a brief description of each tool.

1) **Highlighting:** This is done in the passage text (including table entries and some equations, but excluding figures and molecular structures) and in the question stems by left-clicking and dragging the mouse across the words you wish to highlight; the selected words will then be highlighted in blue. When you release the mouse, a highlighting icon will appear; clicking on the icon will highlight the selected text in yellow. To remove the highlighting, left-click on the highlighted text.

2) **Strike-outs:** Right-clicking on an answer choice causes the entire text of that choice to be crossed out. The strike-out can be removed by right-clicking again. Left-clicking selects an answer choice; note than an answer choice that is selected cannot be struck out. When you strike out a figure or molecular structure, instead of being crossed out, the image turns grey.

3) **Mark button:** This allows you to flag the question for later review. When clicked, the flag on the "Mark" button turns red and says "Marked."

4) **Review button:** Clicking this button brings up a new screen showing all questions and their status (either "completed," "incomplete," or "marked"). You can choose to: "review all," "review incomplete," or "review marked." You can also double-click any question number to quickly return to that specific question. You can only review questions in the section of the MCAT you are currently taking, but the Review button can be clicked at any time during the allotted time for that section; you do NOT have to wait until the end of the section to click it.

5) **Periodic Table button:** Clicking this button will open a periodic table. Note that the periodic table is large, however it can be resized to see the questions and a portion of the periodic table at the same time.

6) **Scratch paper:** You will be given four pages (8 faces) of scratch paper at the start of the test. You can ask for more at any point during the test, and your first set of paper will be collected before you receive fresh paper. Scratch paper is only useful if it is kept organized; do not give in to the tendency to write on the first available open space! Good organization will be very helpful when/ if you wish to review a question. Indicate the passage number and the range of questions for that passage in a box near the top of your scratch work, and indicate the question you are working on in a circle to the left of the notes for that question. Draw a line under your scratch work when you change passages to keep the work separate. Do not erase or scribble over any previous work. If you do not think it is correct, draw one line through the work and start again. You may have already done some useful work without realizing it.

General Strategy for the Science Sections

Passages vs. FSQs in the Science Sections: What to Start With

Since the questions are displayed on separate screens, it is awkward and time consuming to click through all of the questions up front to find the FSQs. Therefore, go through the section on a first pass and decide whether to do the passage now or to save it for later, basing your decision on the passage text and the first question. Tackle the FSQs as you come upon them. More details are below.

Here is an outline of the procedure:

1) For each passage, write a heading on your scratch paper with the passage number, the general topic, and its range of questions (e.g. "Passage 1, thermodynamics, Q 1–5" or "Passage 2, enzymes, Q 6–9). The passage numbers do not currently appear in the Review screen, thus having the question numbers on your scratch paper will allow you to move through the section more efficiently.

2) Skim the text and rank the passage. If a passage is a "Now," complete it before moving on to the next passage (also see "Attacking the Questions" below). If it is a "Later" passage, first write "SKIPPED" in block letters under the passage heading on your scratch paper and leave room for your work when you come back to complete that passage. (Note that the specific passages you skip will be unique to you; in the Bio/Biochem section, you might choose to do all Biology passages first, then come back for Biochemistry. Or in Chem/Phys you might choose to skip experiment-based or analytical passages. Know ahead of time what type of passage you are going to skip and follow your plan.)

3) Next, click on the "Review" button at the bottom to get to the review screen. Double-click on the first question of the next passage; you'll be able to identify it because you know the range of questions from the passage you just skipped. This will take you to the next passage, where you will repeat steps 1–3.

4) Once you have completed the "Now" passages, go to the review screen and double-click the first question for the first passage you skipped. Answer the questions, and continue going back to the review screen and repeating this procedure for other passages you have skipped.

Attacking the Questions

As you work through the questions, if you encounter a particularly lengthy question, or a question that requires a lot of analysis, you may choose to skip it. This is a wise strategy because it ensures you will tackle all the easier questions first, the ones you are more likely to get right. If you choose to skip the question (or if you attempt it but get stuck), write down the question number on your scratch paper, click the Mark button to flag the question in the Review screen, and move on to the next question. At the end of the passage, click back through the set of questions to complete any that you skipped over the first time through, and make sure that you have filled in an answer for every question.

General Strategy for the CARS Section

Ranking and Ordering the Passages: What to Start With

Ranking: Since the questions are displayed on separate screens, it is awkward and time consuming to click through all of the questions before ranking each passage as Now (an easier passage), Later (a harder passage), or Killer (a passage that you will randomly guess on). Therefore, rank the passage and decide whether or not to do it on the first pass through the section based on the passage text, skimming the first 2–3 sentences.

Ordering: Because of the additional clicking through screens (or, use of the Review screen) that is required to navigate through the section, the "Two-Pass" system (completing the "Now" passages as you find them) is likely to be your most efficient approach. However, if you find that you are continuously making a lot of bad ranking decisions, it is still valid to experiment with the "Three-Pass" approach (ranking all nine passages up front before attempting your first "Now" passage).

Here is an outline of the basic Ranking and Ordering procedure to follow.

1) For each passage, write a heading on your scratch paper with the passage number and its range of questions (e.g. "Passage 1 Q 1–7). The passage numbers do not currently appear in the Review screen, thus having the question numbers on your scratch paper will allow you to move through the section more efficiently.

2) Skim the first 2–3 sentences and rank the passage. If the passage is a "Now," complete it before moving on to the next. If it is a "Later" or "Killer," first write either "Later" or "Killer" and "SKIPPED" in block letters under the passage heading on your scratch paper and leave room for your work if you decide to come back and complete that passage. Then click through each question, marking each one and filling in random guesses, until you get to the next passage.

3) Once you have completed the "Now" passages, come back for your second pass and complete the "Later" passages, leaving your random guesses in place for any "Killer" passages that you choose not to complete. Go to the Review screen and use your scratch paper notes on the question numbers. Double-click on the number of the first question for that passage to go back to that question, and proceed from there. Alternatively, if you have consistently marked all the questions for passages you skipped in your first pass you can use "Review Marked" from the Review screen to find and complete your "Later" passages.

4) Regardless of how you choose to find your second pass passages, unmark each question after you complete it, so that you can continue to rely on the Review screen (and the "Review Marked" function") to identify questions that you have not yet attempted.

Previewing the Questions

The formatting and functioning of the tools facilitates effective previewing. Having each question on a separate screen will encourage you to really focus on that question. Even more importantly, you can now highlight in the question stem (but not in the answer choices).

Here is the basic procedure for previewing the questions:

1) Start with the first question, and if it has lead words referencing passage content, highlight them. You may also choose to jot them down on your scratch paper. Once you reach and preview the last question for the set on that passage, THEN stay on that screen and work the passage (your highlighting appears and stays on every passage screen, and persists through the whole 90 minutes).

2) Once you have worked the passage and defined the Bottom Line—the main idea and tone of the entire passage—work **backward** from the last question to the first. If you skip over any questions as you go (see "Attacking the Questions" below), write down the question number on your scratch paper. Then click **forward** through the set of questions, completing any that you skipped over the first time through. Once you reach and complete the last question for that passage, clicking "Next" will send you to the first question of the next passage. Working the questions from last to first the first time through the set will eliminate the need to click back through multiple screens to get to the first question immediately after previewing, and will also make it easier and more efficient to do the hardest questions last (see "Attacking the Questions" below).

Attacking the Questions

The question types and the procedure for actually attacking each type will be discussed later. However, it is still important **not** to attempt the hardest questions first (potentially getting stuck, wasting time, and discouraging yourself).

So, as you work the questions from last to first (see "Previewing the Questions" above), if you encounter a particularly difficult and/or lengthy question (or if you attempt a question but get stuck) write down the question number on your scratch paper (you may also choose to mark it) and move on backward to the next question. Then click **forward** through the set and complete any that you skipped over the first time through the set, unmarking any questions that you marked that first time through and making sure that you have filled in an answer for every question.

Pacing Strategy for the MCAT

Since the MCAT is a timed test, you must keep an eye on the timer and adjust your pacing as necessary. It would be terrible to run out of time at the end only to discover that the last few questions could have been easily answered in just a few seconds each.

If you complete every question, in the science section you will have about on minute and thirty-five seconds (1:35) per question, and in the CARS section you will have about one minute and forty seconds (1:40) per question (not taking into account time spent reading the passage before answering the questions).

Section	# of Questions in passage	Approximate time (including reading the passage)
Chem/Phys, Bio/Biochem, and Psych/Soc	4	6.5 minutes
	5	8 minutes
	6	9.5 minutes
CARS	5	8.5 minutes
	6	10 minutes
	7	11.5 minutes

When starting a passage in the science sections, make note of how much time you will allot for it, and the starting time on the timer. Jot down on your scratch paper what the timer should say at the end of the passage. Then just keep an eye on it as you work through the questions. If you are near the end of the time for that passage, guess on any remaining questions, make some notes on your scratch paper, mark the questions, and move on. Come back to those questions if you have time.

For the CARS section, keep in mind that many people will maximize their score by *not* trying to complete every question or every passage in the section. A good strategy for test takers who cannot achieve a high level of accuracy on all nine passages is to randomly guess on at least one passage in the section, so that you can spend your time getting a high percentage of the other questions right. To complete all nine CARS passages, you have about ten minutes per passage. To complete eight of the nine, you have about 11 minutes per passage.

To help maximize your number of correct answer choices in any section, do the questions and passages within that section in the order *you* want to do them in. See "General Strategy" above.

Process of Elimination

Process of elimination (POE) is probably the most useful technique you have to tackle MCAT questions. Since there is no guessing penalty, POE allows you to increase your probability of choosing the correct answer by eliminating those you are sure are wrong.

1) Strike out any choices that you are sure are incorrect or that do not address the issue raised in the question.
2) Jot down some notes to help clarify your thoughts if you return to the question.
3) Use the "Mark" button to flag the question for review. (Note, however, that in the CARS section, you generally should not be returning to rethink questions once you have moved on to a new passage.)
4) Do not leave it blank! For the sciences, if you are not sure and you have already spent more than 60 seconds on that question, just pick one of the remaining choices. If you have time to review it at the end, you can always debate the remaining choices based on your previous notes. For CARS, if you have been through the choices two or three times, have re-read the question stem and gone back to the passage and you are still stuck, move on. Do the remaining questions for that passage, take one more look at the question you were stuck on, then pick an answer and move on for good.
5) Special Note: if three of the four answer choices have been eliminated, the remaining choice must be the correct answer. Don't waste time pondering *why* it is correct, just click it and move on. The MCAT doesn't care if you truly understand why it's the right answer, only that you have the right answer selected.
6) More subject-specific information on techniques will be presented in the next chapter.

Guessing

Remember, there is NO guessing penalty on the MCAT. NEVER leave a question blank!

QUESTION TYPES

In the science sections of the MCAT, the questions fall into one of three main categories.

1) Memory questions: These questions can be answered directly from prior knowledge and represent about 25 percent of the total number of questions.
2) Explicit questions: These questions are those for which the answer is explicitly stated in the passage. To answer them correctly, for example, may just require finding a definition, or reading a graph, or making a simple connection. Explicit questions represent about 35 percent of the total number of questions.
3) Implicit questions: These questions require you to apply knowledge to a new situation; the answer is typically implied by the information in the passage. These questions often start "If.... Then...." (for example, "if we modify the experiment in the passage like this, then what result would we expect?"). Implicit style questions make up about 40 percent of the total number of questions.

In the CARS section, the questions fall into four main categories:

1) Specific questions: These either ask you for facts from the passage (Retrieval questions) or require you to deduce what is most likely to be true based on the passage (Inference questions).
2) General questions: These ask you to summarize themes (Main Idea and Primary Purpose questions) or evaluate an author's opinion (Tone/Attitude questions).

3) Reasoning questions: These ask you to describe the purpose of, or the support provided for, a statement made in the passage (Structure questions) or to judge how well the author supports his or her argument (Evaluate questions).

4) Application questions: These ask you to apply new information from either the question stem itself (New Information questions) or from the answer choices (Strengthen, Weaken, and Analogy questions) to the passage.

More detail on question types and strategies can be found in Chapter 2.

TESTING TIPS

Before Test Day

- Take a trip to the test center at least a day or two before your actual test date so that you can easily find the building and room on test day. This will also allow you to gauge traffic and see if you need money for parking or any other unexpected expenses. Knowing this type of information ahead of time will greatly reduce your stress on the day of your test.
- During the week before the test, adjust your sleeping schedule so that you are going to bed and getting up in the morning at the same times as on the day before and morning of the MCAT. Prioritize getting a reasonable amount of sleep during the last few nights before the test.
- Don't do any heavy studying the day before the test. This is not a test you can cram for! Your goal at this point is to rest and relax so that you can go into test day in a good physical and mental condition.
- Eat well. Try to avoid excessive caffeine and sugar. Ideally, in the weeks leading up to the actual test you should experiment a little bit with foods and practice tests to see which foods give you the most endurance. Aim for steady blood sugar levels during the test: sports drinks, peanut-butter crackers, trail mix, etc. make good snacks for your breaks and lunch.

General Test Day Info and Tips

- On the day of the test, arrive at the test center at least a half hour prior to the start time of your test.
- Examinees will be checked in to the center in the order in which they arrive.
- You will be assigned a locker or secure area in which to put your personal items. Textbooks and study notes are not allowed, so there is no need to bring them with you to the test center.
- Your ID will be checked, a digital image of your fingerprint will be taken, and you will be asked to sign in.
- You will be given scratch paper and a couple of pencils, and the test center administrator will take you to the computer on which you will complete the test. You may not choose a computer; you must use the computer assigned to you.
- Nothing, not even your watch, is allowed at the computer station except your photo ID, your locker key (if provided), and a factory sealed packet of ear plugs.
- If you choose to leave the testing room at the breaks, you will have your fingerprint checked again, and you will have to sign in and out.
- You are allowed to access the items in your locker, except for notes and cell phones. (Check your test center's policy on cell phones ahead of time; some centers do not even allow them to be kept in your locker.)
- Don't forget to bring the snack foods and lunch you experimented with in your practice tests.
- At the end of the test, the test administrator will collect your scratch paper and shred it.
- Definitely take the breaks! Get up and walk around. It's a good way to clear your head between sections and get the blood (and oxygen!) flowing to your brain.
- Ask for new scratch paper at the breaks if you use it all up.

Chapter 2
Psychology and Sociology Strategy for the MCAT

2.1 SCIENCE SECTIONS OVERVIEW

There are three science sections on the MCAT:

- Chemical and Physical Foundations of Biological Systems
- Biological and Biochemical Foundations of Living Systems
- Psychological, Social, and Biological Foundations of Behavior

The Chemical and Physical Foundations of Biological Systems section (Chem/Phys) is the first section on the test. It includes questions from General Chemistry (about 30%), Physics (about 25%), Organic Chemistry (about 15%), Biochemistry (about 25%), and Biology (about 5%). Further, the questions often test chemical and physical concepts within a biological setting, for example, pressure and fluid flow in blood vessels. A solid grasp of math fundamentals is required (arithmetic, algebra, graphs, trigonometry, vectors, proportions, and logarithms), however there are no calculus-based questions.

The Biological and Biochemical Foundations of Living Systems section (Bio/Biochem) is the third section on the test. Approximately 65% of the questions in this section come from biology, approximately 25% come from biochemistry, and approximately 10% come from Organic and General Chemistry. Math calculations are generally not required on this section of the test, however a basic understanding of statistics as used in biological research is helpful.

The Psychological, Social, and Biological Foundations of Behavior section (Psych/Soc) is the fourth and final section on the test. About 60% of the questions will be drawn from Psychology, about 30% from Sociology, and about 10% from Biology. As with the Bio/Biochem section, calculations are generally not required, however a basic understanding of statistics as used in research is helpful.

Most of the questions in the science sections (44 of the 59) are passage-based, and each section has ten passages. Passages consist of a few paragraphs of information and include equations, reactions, graphs, figures, tables, experiments, and data. Four to six questions will be associated with each passage.

The remaining 25% of the questions (15 of 59) in each science section are freestanding questions (FSQs). These questions appear in approximately four groups interspersed between the passages. Each group contains four to five questions.

95 minutes are allotted to each of the science sections. This breaks down to approximately one minute and 35 seconds per question.

2.2 SCIENCE PASSAGE TYPES

The passages in the science sections fall into one of three main categories: Information and/or Situation-Presentation, Experiment/Research Presentation, or Persuasive Reasoning.

Information and/or Situation Presentation

These passages either present straightforward scientific information or they describe a particular event or occurrence. Generally, questions associated with these passages test basic science facts or ask you to predict outcomes given new variables or new information. Here is an example of an Information/Situation Presentation passage:

Figure 1 shows a portion of the inner mechanism of a typical home smoke detector. It consists of a pair of capacitor plates which are charged by a 9-volt battery (not shown). The capacitor plates (electrodes) are connected to a sensor device, D; the resistor R denotes the internal resistance of the sensor. Normally, air acts as an insulator and no current would flow in the circuit shown. However, inside the smoke detector is a small sample of an artificially produced radioactive element, americium-241, which decays primarily by emitting alpha particles, with a half-life of approximately 430 years. The daughter nucleus of the decay has a half-life in excess of two million years and therefore poses virtually no biohazard.

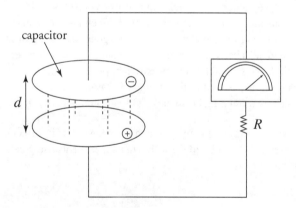

Figure 1   Smoke detector mechanism

The decay products (alpha particles and gamma rays) from the ^{241}Am sample ionize air molecules between the plates and thus provide a conducting pathway which allows current to flow in the circuit shown in Figure 1. A steady-state current is quickly established and remains as long as the battery continues to maintain a 9-volt potential difference between its terminals.

However, if smoke particles enter the space between the capacitor plates and thereby interrupt the flow, the current is reduced, and the sensor responds to this change by triggering the alarm. (Furthermore, as the battery starts to, "die out," the resulting drop in current is also detected to alert the homeowner to replace the battery.)

$$C = \varepsilon_0 \frac{A}{d}$$

Equation 1

where ε_0 is the universal permittivity constant, equal to 8.85 $\times 10^{-32}$ $C^2/(N \cdot m^2)$. Since the area A of each capacitor plate in the smoke detector is 20 cm2 and the plates are separated by a distance d of 5 mm, the capacitance is 3.5×10^{-12} F = 3.5 pF.

Experiment/Research Presentation

These passages present the details of experiments and research procedures. They often include data tables and graphs. Generally, questions associated with these passages ask you to interpret data, draw conclusions, and make inferences. Here is an example of an Experiment/Research Presentation passage:

The development of sexual characteristics depends upon various factors, the most important of which are hormonal control, environmental stimuli, and the genetic makeup of the individual. The hormones that contribute to the development include the steroid hormones estrogen, progesterone, and testosterone, as well as the pituitary hormones FSH (follicle-stimulating hormone) and LH (luteinizing hormone).

To study the mechanism by which estrogen exerts its effects, a researcher performed the following experiments using cell culture assays.

Experiment 1:

Human embryonic placental mesenchyme (HEPM) cells were grown for 48 hours in Dulbecco's Modified Eagle's Medium (DMEM), with media change every 12 hours. Upon confluent growth, cells were exposed to a 10 mg per mL solution of green fluorescent-labeled estrogen for 1 hour. Cells were rinsed with DMEM and observed under confocal fluorescent microscopy.

Experiment 2:

HEPM cells were grown to confluence as in Experiment 1. Cells were exposed to Pesticide A for 1 hour, followed by the 10 mg/mL solution of labeled estrogen, rinsed as in Experiment 1, and observed under confocal fluorescent microscopy.

Experiment 3:

Experiment 1 was repeated with Chinese Hamster Ovary (CHO) cells instead of HEPM cells.

Experiment 4:

CHO cells injected with cytoplasmic extracts of HEPM cells were grown to confluence, exposed to the 10 mg/mL solution of labeled estrogen for 1 hour, and observed under confocal fluorescent microscopy.

The results of these experiments are given in Table 1.

Table 1 Detection of Estrogen (+ indicates presence of Estrogen)

Experiment	Media	Cytoplasm	Nucleus
1	+	+	+
2	+	+	+
3	+	+	+
4	+	+	+

After observing the cells in each experiment, the researcher bathed the cells in a solution containing 10 mg per mL of a red fluorescent probe that binds specifically to the estrogen receptor only when its active site is occupied. After 1 hour, the cells were rinsed with DMEM and observed under confocal fluorescent microscopy. The results are presented in Table 2.

The researcher also repeated Experiment 2 using Pesticide B, an estrogen analog, instead of Pesticide A. Results from other researchers had shown that Pesticide B binds to the active site of the cytosolic estrogen receptor (with an affinity 10,000 times greater than that of estrogen) and causes increased transcription of mRNA.

Table 2 Observed Fluorescence and Estrogen Effects (G = green, R = red)

Experiment	Media	Cytoplasm	Nucleus	Estrogen effects observed?
1	G only	G and R	G and R	Yes
2	G only	G only	G only	No
3	G only	G only	G only	No
4	G only	G and R	G and R	Yes

Based on these results, the researcher determined that estrogen had no effect when not bound to a cytosolic, estrogen-specific receptor.

Persuasive Reasoning

These passages typically present a scientific phenomenon along with a hypothesis that explains the phenomenon, and may include counter-arguments as well. Questions associated with these passages ask you to evaluate the hypothesis or arguments. Persuasive Reasoning passages in the science sections of the MCAT tend to be less common than Information Presentation or Experiment-based passages. Here is an example of a Persuasive Reasoning passage:

Two theoretical chemists attempted to explain the observed trends of acidity by applying two interpretations of molecular orbital theory. Consider the pK_a values of some common acids listed along with the conjugate base:

acid	pK_a	conjugate base
H_2SO_4	< 0	HSO_4-
H_2CrO_4	5.0	$HCrO_4-$
H_2PO_4	2.1	H_2CrO_4-
HF	3.9	F–
HOCl	7.8	ClO–
HCN	9.5	CN–
HIO_3	1.2	IO_3-

Recall that acids with a pK_a < 0 are called strong acids, and those with a pKa > 0 are called weak acids. The arguments of the chemists are given below.

Chemist #1:

"The acidity of a compound is proportional to the polarization of the H—X bond, where X is some nonmetal element.

Complex acids, such as H_2SO_4, $HClO_4$, and HNO_3 are strong acids because the H—O bonding electrons are strongly drawn towards the oxygen. It is generally true that a covalent bond weakens as its polarization increases. Therefore, one can conclude that the strength of an acid is proportional to the number of electronegative atoms in that acid."

Chemist #2:

"The acidity of a compound is proportional to the number of stable resonance structures of that acid's conjugate base. H_2SO_4, $HClO_4$, and HNO_3 are all strong acids because their respective conjugate bases exhibit a high degree of resonance stabilization."

MAPPING A PASSAGE

"Mapping a passage" refers to the combination of on-screen highlighting and scratch paper notes that you take while working through a passage. Typically, good things to highlight include the overall topic of a paragraph, familiar terms, unusual terms, italicized terms, numerical values, hypothesis, and experimental results. Scratch paper notes can be used to summarize the paragraphs and to jot down important facts and connections that are made when reading the passage. More details on passage mapping will be presented in section 2.5.

2.3 SCIENCE QUESTION TYPES

Questions in the science sections are generally one of three main types: Memory, Explicit, or Implicit.

Memory Questions

These questions can be answered directly from prior knowledge, with no need to reference the passage or question text. Memory questions represent approximately 25 percent of the science questions on the MCAT. Usually, Memory questions are found as FSQs, but they can also be tucked into a passage. Here's an example of a Memory question:

Which of the following acetylating conditions will convert diethylamine into an amide at the fastest rate?

A) Acetic acid / HCl
B) Acetic anhydride
C) Acetyl chloride
D) Ethyl acetate

Explicit Questions

Explicit questions can be answered primarily with information from the passage, along with prior knowledge. They may require data retrieval, graph analysis, or making a simple connection. Explicit questions make up approximately 35–40 percent of the science questions on the MCAT; here's an example (taken from the Information/Situation Presentation passage above):

The sensor device D shown in Figure 1 performs its function by acting as:

A) an ohmmeter.
B) a voltmeter.
C) a potentiometer.
D) an ammeter.

Implicit Questions

These questions require you to take information from the passage, combine it with your prior knowledge, apply it to a new situation, and come to some logical conclusion. They typically require more complex connections than do Explicit questions, and may also require data retrieval, graph analysis, etc. Implicit questions usually require a solid understanding of the passage information. They make up approximately 35–40 percent of the science questions on the MCAT; here's an example (taken from the Experiment/Research Presentation passage above):

If Experiment 2 were repeated, but this time exposing the cells first to Pesticide A and then to Pesticide B before exposing them to the green fluorescent-labeled estrogen and the red fluorescent probe, which of the following statements will most likely be true?

A) Pesticide A and Pesticide B bind to the same site on the estrogen receptor.
B) Estrogen effects would be observed.
C) Only green fluorescence would be observed.
D) Both green and red fluorescence would be observed.

2.4 PSYCHOLOGY AND SOCIOLOGY ON THE MCAT

This section will test your content knowledge of psychological, biological, and sociological factors that shape human thought, perception, behavior, attitude, and learning. Furthermore, you will be expected to have a basic understanding of mental illness, social structure, and global disparities in health, health care, and social class. The MCAT will test your knowledge and application of these subjects at approximately the level that you would be expected to understand them in an introductory psychology class (one semester), introductory sociology class (one semester), and an introductory biology class (two semesters, though you should be prepared for more advanced physiology concepts, like you would see on the MCAT Biological and Biochemical Foundations of Living Systems section). The application of this material is potentially vast; passages can discuss anything from the specifics about a psychological research study to the complexities of studying population dynamics, to the nuances of an unusual neurological disease. Additionally, questions on the Psych/Soc section will require you to demonstrate your scientific inquiry, reasoning, and understanding of basic research and statistical methods as applied to concepts in the psychological, sociological, and biological sciences. Overall, this section is designed to test your knowledge and application of the behavioral, biological, and social determinants of health and wellness.

The science sections of the MCAT have 10 passages and 15 freestanding questions (FSQs). On the Psych/Soc section, introductory biology will comprise approximately 10% of the questions, introductory sociology concepts will comprise roughly 30% of the questions, and introductory psychology concepts will comprise about 60% of the questions.

2.5 TACKLING A PSYCH/SOC PASSAGE

In order to complete all of the passages and freestanding questions on the Psych/Soc section, it will be important to tackle this section strategically. An understanding about the types of passages you will encounter should help you accomplish this.

Experiment/Research Presentation

This type of passage on the Psych/Soc section will typically present some information about a relevant topic, and also present the details behind an experiment relating to that topic. Data will be presented in tables, graphs, and/or figures. These passages are challenging because they require an understanding of the reasoning and logic behind the experiment and research, the ability to analyze the results and form conclusions, and a basic understanding of statistics.

Information/Situation Presentation

This type of passage will generally present a basic concept with additional detail (that goes well beyond an introductory-level understanding) or a novel concept (like a rare neurological disease) that extrapolates information from more basic information. In order to tackle these passages, first, do not panic if you see information that you've never heard about! Rather, look for concepts that parallel what you *do* know about. For example, if you see a question about a rare neurological disorder, look for information that applies to your basic knowledge of the nervous system.

2.5

However, in order to answer passage questions and freestanding questions effectively and efficiently, you *will* need to know your basics. Don't waste time staring at a passage or question wondering, "Should I know this?" Instead, with a solid foundation in the basic core knowledge, you will be confident that you are *not* expected to know about this random, rare disease, and rather will find information in the passage and/or apply core concepts.

READING A PSYCH/SOC PASSAGE

Although tempting, try not to get too bogged down in reading all of the little details in a passage. While it is easy to get lost in the science or the glut of background information in a passage, it isn't necessary to read every nuance.

For Experiment/Research Presentation passages, you will need to read more closely/carefully. You will likely have questions concerning the experimental design and/or the data and results. Therefore, invest a little more time reading so you understand the experiment and the outcomes, but don't worry about completely absorbing the results until you see what types of questions are asked.

For Information/Situation Presentation passages, you will not need to read as closely or as carefully. These can be skimmed to get a general sense of where the information is located within the passage. Furthermore, these passages may contain a fair amount of detailed information that you may not need, so save your time—don't bother reading all of the details until you come to a question that asks about them, then go back and read more closely.

Advanced Reading Skills

To improve your ability to read and glean information from a passage, you need to practice. Be critical when you read the content; watch for vague areas or holes in the passage that aren't explained clearly. Remember that information about new topics will be woven throughout the passage; you may need to piece together information from several paragraphs and a figure to get the whole picture.

After you've read, highlighted, and mapped a passage (more on this in a bit) stop and ask yourself the following questions:

- What was this passage about? What was the conclusion or main point?
- Was there a paragraph that was mostly background?

- Were there paragraphs or figures that seemed useless?
- What information was found in each paragraph? Why was that paragraph there?
- Are there any holes in the story?
- What extra information could I have pulled out of the passage? What inferences or conclusions could I make?
- If something unique was explained or mentioned, what might be its purpose?
- What am I *not* being told?
- Can I summarize the purpose and/or results of the experiment in a few sentences?
- Were there any comparisons in the passage?

2.5

This takes a while at first, but eventually becomes second nature and you will start doing it as you are reading the passage. If you have a study group you are working with, consider doing this as an exercise with your study partners. Take turns asking and answering the questions above. Having to explain something to someone else not only solidifies your own knowledge, but helps you see where you might be weak.

MAPPING A PSYCH/SOC PASSAGE

Mapping a Psych/Soc passage is a combination of highlighting and scratch paper notes that can help you organize and understand the passage information.

Resist the temptation to highlight everything (everyone has done this: You're reading a psychology textbook with a highlighter, and then look back and realize that the whole page is yellow!). Restrict your highlighting to a few things:

- the main theme of a paragraph.
- an unusual or unfamiliar term that is defined specifically for that passage (e.g., something that is italicized).
- statements that either support the main theme or contradict the main theme.
- list topics: sometimes lists appear in paragraph form within a passage. Highlight the general topic of the list.

Scratch paper should be organized. Make sure the passage number and the range of questions for that passage appears at the top of your scratch paper notes. For each paragraph, note "P1," "P2," etc., on the scratch paper, and jot down a few notes about that paragraph. Try to translate science-y jargon into your own words using everyday language (this is particularly useful for experiments). Also, make sure to jot down simple relationships (e.g., the relationship between two variables).

Pay attention to figures and tables to see what type of information they contain. Don't spend a lot of time analyzing at this point, but do jot down on your scratch paper "Fig 1" and a brief summary of the data. Also, if you've discovered a list in the passage, note its topic and location down on your scratch paper.

2.5

Let's take a look at how we might highlight and map a practice passage:

Psychotic disorders—most notably schizophrenia and bipolar disorder with psychotic features—affect approximately 2% of Americans. These disorders are extremely manageable with psychotropic medications—to relieve symptoms such as hallucinations and delusions—and behavioral therapy, such as social skills training and hygiene maintenance.

However, individuals with psychotic disorders have the lowest level of medication compliance, as compared to individuals with mood or anxiety disorders. Antipsychotic medications can have extremely negative side effects, including uncontrollable twitching of the face or limbs, blurred vision, and weight gain, among others. They also must be taken frequently, and at high doses, in order to be effective. While relatively little is known about the reasons for noncompliance, studies do suggest that in Schizophrenia, age of schizophrenia diagnosis and medication compliance is positively correlated. Evidence also suggests that medication noncompliance is disproportionally prevalent in individuals of a low socioeconomic status (SES) due to issues such as homelessness, lack of insurance benefits, and lack of familial or social support.

Researchers were interested to see how drug education might affect compliance or noncompliance with psychotropic medications based on patient socioeconomic status. In a study of 1200 mentally ill individuals in the Los Angeles metro area, researchers measured baseline psychotropic medication compliance, then provided patients with a free educational seminar on drug therapy, and then measured psychotropic medication compliance six months later. The one-day, 8-hour seminar included information on positive effects of psychotropic medication, side effects of psychotropic medication, psychotropic medication interactions with other substances such as alcohol and non-prescribed drugs, and information on accessing MediCare benefits. Compliance was measured by number of doses of prescribed psychotropic medication that the patients took in a week, over the course of 12 weeks, as compared to the number of doctor-recommended doses per week. Compliance was measured using a self-report questionnaire.

Results indicated that post-seminar, mentally ill patients from middle or upper class backgrounds (Upper and Middle SES) were significantly more compliant with their psychotropic medication regimens than prior to the seminar. However, no significant differences were found in patients at or below the poverty level (Lower SES). Table 1 displays psychotropic medication compliance by SES and disorder.

Disorder	SES	Pre-Seminar Compliance	Post-Seminar Compliance
Bipolar I	Upper	60%	73%
	Middle	57%	61%
	Lower	25%	27%
Schizophrenia	Upper	53%	65%
	Middle	51%	62%
	Lower	22%	26%

Table 1   Psychotropic Medication Compliance by Socioeconomic Status (SES) and Disorder

2.5

Analysis and Passage Map

This passage is an Experiment/Research Presentation passage and starts with an introduction to the topic, psychotic disorders (specifically schizophrenia and bipolar disorder). This is primarily a background information paragraph and can be skimmed quickly, with a few specific words/phrases highlighted.

The second paragraph starts with "however" indicating a change in direction. The first paragraph said that schizophrenia is easily managed with drugs and therapy, but the second paragraph indicates that that isn't the whole story—in fact, the main topic of the passage is presented—medication noncompliance, particularly in low socioeconomic (SES) individuals.

The third paragraph presents relevant information about the study conducted to determine the impact of drug education on medication noncompliance in various SES groups. It is important to highlight the key features of the study here—what is it looking at, and how is data collected. You do not necessarily need to highlight every single detail, but understand the basic premise of the study.

The final paragraph describes the results of the study, and presents the data in Table 1. The paragraph provides you with the significant finding that is demonstrated by the data in the table—while upper and middle SES individuals demonstrated an increased medication compliance after the drug education treatment, low SES individuals did not.

Here is what your scratch paper should look like:

> *P1—psychotic disorders are manageable with medication and therapy*
> *P2—but medication compliance is a big problem, especially for low SES*
> *P3—STUDY: medication compliance by SES before and after a drug education seminar*
> *P4—RESULTS: medication compliance increases for upper and middle SES, no improvement for low SES*
> *Table 1—medication compliance by SES for schizophrenia and bipolar I*

One more thing about passages on the MCAT: you can do the passages in any order you want to. There are no bonus points for taking the test in order. Therefore, tackle the passages that you are most comfortable with first, and save the harder ones for last (see "General Strategy" in Chapter 1 for more information on how to move around efficiently in the test).

2.6 TACKLING THE QUESTIONS

Questions on the Psych/Soc section mimic the three typical science question types: Memory, Explicit, and Implicit.

Memory Questions in the Psych/Soc Section

Memory questions are exactly what they sound like: They test your knowledge of some specific fact or concept. While Memory questions are typically found as freestanding questions, they can also be tucked into a passage. The questions, aside from requiring memorization, do not generally cause problems for students because they are similar to the types of questions that would appear on a typical college psychology or sociology exam. Below are two examples of Memory questions, taken from the passage above:

1. What is one "positive" symptom of schizophrenia?

    A) Catatonia
    B) Weight gain
    C) Flattened affect
    D) Auditory or visual hallucinations

2. Bipolar disorder involves periods of mania and depression, and for some, episodes of hypomania. Hypomania, a state that is less severe than mania, is characterized by "feeling good/high" and increased well-being and productiveness. Which of the mechanisms is most likely involved with the hypomanic episodes experienced by individuals diagnosed with bipolar disorder?

    A) Increased dopamine in the brain
    B) Decreased stimulation of the enteric plexus
    C) Increased activation of the posterior pituitary
    D) Decreased serotonin in the central nervous system

These are Memory questions because, even though they are associated with the passage, you could have answered them (and should be able to answer them) without reading the passage. It is important that you recognize them as a Memory questions so you don't go back to the passage and waste time looking for answers that are not there! There is no specific "trick" to answering Memory questions; either you know the correct answer or you don't.

If you find that you are missing a fair number of Memory questions, it is a sure sign that you do not know the content well enough. Go back and review.

Solutions for the questions above are:

1. **D** A "positive" symptom of schizophrenia is an addition to, excess of, or distortion of normal functions; auditory or visual hallucinations are positive symptoms of the illness (choice D is correct). A "negative" symptom of schizophrenia is a diminishment or absence of normal function; catatonia (lack or responsiveness to stimuli) and flattened affect (lack of emotion) are both negative symptoms (choice A and choice C are wrong). Weight gain is often a side effect of psychotropic medications, not a symptom of schizophrenia (choice B is wrong).

2. **A** Dopamine is the primary neurotransmitter involved with the "reward centers" of the brain; since hypomania is characterized by "feeling good/high," it can reasonably be concluded that an increase of dopamine in the brain could produce this effect (choice A is correct). The enteric plexus or enteric nervous system is a portion of the autonomic nervous system that controls the gastrointestinal tract; decreased stimulation of the enteric nervous system would not produce any of the characteristics of hypomania described (choice B is wrong). The posterior pituitary is responsible for producing oxytocin, a hormone that controls lactation and uterine contractions, and vasopressin, a hormone that controls how much water the kidneys resorb; therefore, increased activation of the posterior pituitary would not produce any of the characteristics of hypomania described (choice C is wrong). Serotonin is a neurotransmitter with widespread effects in the brain; a decrease of serotonin in the brain has been shown to produce symptoms of depression, not hypomania (choice D is wrong).

Explicit Questions in the Psych/Soc section

True, pure Explicit questions are rare in the Psych/Soc section. A purely Explicit question can be answered with only information in the passage. Below is an example of a pure Explicit question from the passage above:

3. What is the incidence of psychotic disorders in the American population?

A) 1%
B) 2%
C) 4%
D) Unknown

Referring back to the first paragraph of the passage, it clearly states that "Psychotic disorders—most notably schizophrenia and bipolar disorder with psychotic features—affect approximately 2% of Americans;" therefore, choice **B** is correct.

2.6

However, more often on the Psych/Soc section, Explicit questions are more of a blend of Explicit and Memory; they require not only retrieval of passage information, but also recall of some relevant information. They usually do not require in-depth analysis or connections. Here is an example of a common type of Explicit question:

2.6

4. Based on the design of the study described in the passage, what limits the researchers' abilities to draw conclusions about the causal relationship between socioeconomic status and psychotropic medication compliance?

A) Age at first diagnosis was not measured.
B) Participants were not randomly assigned to socioeconomic status.
C) The sample contained only Los Angeles metro area residents.
D) Severity of symptoms were not measured.

To answer this question, you first need to retrieve information from the passage about the study's experimental design (from paragraph 3). You also need to recall some information about experimental design, and what sort of factors limit a researcher's ability to infer a causal relationship.

Here is the solution to the question above:

4. **B** Causation is extremely difficult to determine when experimenting with humans, particularly because all of the variables in a given experiment must by controlled by the researcher, and subjects must be randomly assigned to experimental and control groups. Therefore, random assignment of subjects to a group (in this case, a socioeconomic status group) is one of the many variables that should have been controlled for in order to determine a causal relationship between socioeconomic status and psychotropic medication compliance (choice B is correct). While age at first diagnosis and symptom severity are important variables that could have been measured, neither specifically limits the researchers' abilities to draw conclusions about the causal relationship between socioeconomic status and psychotropic medication compliance (choices A and D are wrong). The fact that the sample only contained participants from the Los Angeles metro area limits the researchers' ability to draw conclusions about how their results might apply to the general population, not about causality (choice C is wrong).

A final subgroup in the Explicit question category are graph or data interpretation questions. These questions will either ask you to take graphical information from the passage and convert it into a text answer, or will ask you to take text from the passage and convert it into a graph. Below is an example from the passage above:

5. Which of the following graphs would best illustrate the relationship between age of schizophrenia diagnosis and medication compliance described in the passage?

A)

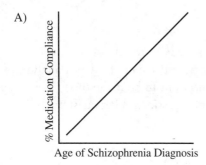

B)

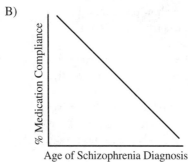

C)

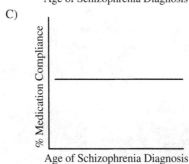

D)

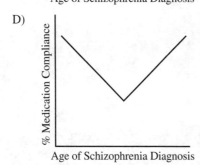

2.6

The passage states, in the second paragraph, that "…studies do suggest that in Schizophrenia, age of schizophrenia diagnosis and medication compliance is positively correlated." Therefore, as age of diagnosis increases, so does compliance. Therefore, a graphical representation should look like the figure in choice **A**.

If you find you are missing Explicit questions, practice your passage mapping. Make sure you aren't missing the critical items in the passage that lead you to the right answer. Slow down a little; take an extra 15 to 30 seconds per passage to read or think about it more carefully.

Implicit Questions

Implicit questions require the most thought. These require recall not only of Psych/Soc content information but also information gleaned from the passage, and a more in-depth analysis of how the two relate. Implicit questions require more analysis and connections to be made than Explicit questions. Often they take the form "If…then…." Below is an example of a classic Implicit question, based on the passage above:

6. If the experiment described in the passage were repeated, but instead of testing how drug education affects compliance, researchers measured how incentives affect compliance in low SES schizophrenics. The low SES schizophrenia group was broken into two groups. Group A received an incentive every time they took their medication for seven consecutive days while Group B received an incentive every two weeks, regardless of compliance level. Based on operant conditioning principles, what results should the researchers see?

A) No difference in compliance levels from the first study.
B) Group A's compliance should be higher than Group B's compliance.
C) Group B's compliance should be higher than Group A's compliance.
D) Both groups should demonstrate increased compliance from the first study but it is impossible to tell which group's compliance is expected to be higher.

To answer this question, conclusions have to be drawn about the experiment described in the passage, and the new experiment described in the question stem, and then applied to your content knowledge about reward schedules in operant conditioning. Many, many more connections need to be made than when answering an Explicit question. A detailed explanation for this question is below:

6. **B** According to the question, Group A is receiving an incentive on a fixed-ratio schedule (after every seven consecutive days of medication compliance) and Group B is receiving an incentive on a fixed-interval schedule (every two weeks, regardless of compliance). According to operant conditioning principles, a fixed-ratio schedule should produce a high rate of desired behavior (in this case, medication compliance), while a fixed-interval schedule produces a steady rate of response that tends to increase closer to the reward, but is not nearly as frequent as what is expected from a fixed-ratio reward schedule (choice B is correct; choice C is wrong). Based on operant conditioning principles, rewarding desired behavior should increase behavior (choice A is wrong), and applying a fixed-ratio and fixed-interval reward schedule should increase behavior in predictable ways (choice D is wrong).

2.6

If you find that you are missing a lot of Implicit questions, first of all, make sure that you are using POE aggressively. Second, go back and review the explanations for the correct answer, and figure out where your logic went awry. Did you miss an important fact in the passage? Did you forget the relevant Psych/Soc content? Did you follow the logical train of thought to the right answer? Once you figure out where you made your mistake, you will know how to correct it.

2.7   SUMMARY OF THE APPROACH TO PSYCHOLOGY AND SOCIOLOGY

How to Map the Passage and Use Scratch Paper

1) The passage should not be read like textbook material, with the intent of learning something from every sentence (science majors especially will be tempted to read this way). Passages should be read to get a feel for the type of questions that will follow, and to get a general idea of the location of information within the passage.

2) Highlighting—Use this tool sparingly, or you will end up with a passage that is completely covered in yellow highlighter! Highlighting in a Psych/Soc passage should be used to draw attention to a few words that demonstrate one of the following:
   - The main theme of a paragraph
   - An unusual or unfamiliar term that is defined specifically for that passage (e.g., something that is italicized)
   - Statements that either support the main theme or counteract the main theme
   - List topics (see below)
   - Relationships

3) Pay brief attention to figures and experiments, noting only what information they deal with. Do not spend a lot of time analyzing at this point.

4) For each passage, start by noting the passage number, the general topic, and the range of questions on your scratch paper. You can then work between your scratch paper and the review screen to easily get to the questions you want (see Chapter 1).

5) For each paragraph, note "P1," "P2," etc. on the scratch paper and jot down a few notes about that paragraph. Try to translate psych/soc jargon into your own words using everyday language. Especially note down simple relationships (e.g., the relationship between two variables).

6) Lists—Whenever a list appears in paragraph form, jot down on the scratch paper the paragraph and the general topic of the list. It will make returning to the passage more efficient and help to organize your thoughts.

7) Scratch paper is only useful if it is kept organized! Make sure that your notes for each passage are clearly delineated and marked with the passage number and question range. This will allow you to easily read your notes when you come back to a review a marked question. Resist the temptation to write in the first available blank space as this makes it much more difficult to refer back to your work.

Psych/Soc Question Strategies

1) Remember that the content in Psychology and Sociology is broad but not necessarily super deep, so don't panic if something seems completely unfamiliar. Understand the basic content well, find the basics in the unfamiliar topic, and apply them to the question.

2) Process of Elimination is paramount! The strikeout tool allows you to eliminate answer choices; this will improve your chances of guessing the correct answer if you are unable to narrow it down to one choice.

3) Answer the straightforward questions first (typically the memory questions). Leave questions that require analysis of experiments and graphs for later. Take the test in the order YOU want. Make sure to use your scratch paper to indicate questions you skipped.

4) Make sure that the answer you choose actually answers the question, and isn't just a true statement.

5) Try to avoid answer choices with extreme words such as "always," "never," etc. In psych/soc, there is almost always an exception and answers are rarely black-and-white.

6) I-II-III questions: always work between the I-II-III statements and the answer choices. Unfortunately, it is not possible to strike out the Roman numerals, but this is a great use for scratch paper notes. Once a statement is determined to be true (or false) strike out answer choices which do not contain (or do contain) that statement.

7) LEAST/EXCEPT/NOT questions: Don't get tricked by these questions that ask you to pick that answer that doesn't fit (the incorrect or false statement). It's often good to use your scratch paper and write a T or F next to answer choices A–D. The one that stands out as different is the correct answer!

8) Again, don't leave any question blank.

A Note About Flashcards

For most of the exams you've taken previously, flashcards were likely very helpful. This was because those exams mostly required you to regurgitate information, and flashcards are pretty good at helping you memorize facts. However, the most challenging aspect of the MCAT is not that it requires you to memorize the fine details of content knowledge, but that it requires you to apply your basic scientific knowledge to unfamiliar situations: flashcards alone may not help you there.

Flashcards can be beneficial if your basic content knowledge is deficient in some area. For example, if you don't know the stages of Erikson's psychosocial model of development, flashcards can certainly help you memorize these facts. Or, maybe you are unsure of the functions of the different brain regions. You might find that flashcards can help you memorize these. But unless you are trying to memorize basic facts in your personal weak areas, you are better off doing and analyzing practice passages than carrying around a stack of flashcards.

Chapter 3
Biological Foundations of Behavior

All human behavior has a biological foundation; psychological, sociological, and biological drivers influence how we perceive and respond to our environment. The ability to receive and process sensory information is dependent on several specialized cells, receptors, and biochemical pathways. The mechanisms of sensation can be understood largely from a biological perspective. The way we perceive, interpret, and respond to sensory information, however, can be infinitely more complex. It is important to keep a psychological, social, and cultural perspective in mind when understanding perception and behavior. This chapter covers the biological foundations of behavior, including the nervous system and endocrine system, as well as some of the genetic and environmental factors that play a role in behavior.

3.1 NEURONAL STRUCTURE AND FUNCTION

Neurons are specialized cells that transmit and process information from one part of the body to another. This information takes the form of electrochemical impulses known as **action potentials**. The action potential is a localized area of depolarization of the plasma membrane that travels in a wave-like manner along an axon. When an action potential reaches the end of an axon at a synapse, the signal is transformed into a chemical signal with the release of neurotransmitter into the synaptic cleft, a process called **synaptic transmission** (Section 7.2). The information of many synapses feeding into a neuron is integrated to determine whether that neuron will in turn fire an action potential. In this way the action of many individual neurons is integrated to work together in the nervous system as a whole.

Structure of the Neuron

The basic functional and structural unit of the nervous system is the **neuron** (Figure 1). The structure of these cells is highly specialized to transmit and process **action potentials**, the electrochemical signals of the nervous system (Figure 3). Neurons have a central cell body, the **soma**, which contains the nucleus and is where most of the biosynthetic activity of the cell takes place. Slender projections, termed **axons** and **dendrites**, extend from the cell body. Neurons have only one axon (as long as a meter in some cases), but most possess many dendrites. Neurons with one dendrite are termed **bipolar**; those with many dendrites are **multipolar**. Neurons generally carry action potentials in one direction, with dendrites receiving signals and axons carrying action potentials away from the cell body. Axons can branch multiple times and terminate in **synaptic knobs** that form connections with target cells. When action potentials travel down an axon and reach the synaptic knob, chemical messengers are released and travel across a very small gap called the **synaptic cleft** to the target cell. The nature of the action potential and the transmission of signals across the synaptic cleft are key aspects of nervous system function. [In Figure 1, in what direction does an action potential travel in the axon shown?[1] What's the difference between a neuron and a nerve?[2]]

---

[1] Action potentials travel from the cell body down the axon, or from left to right in Figure 1.

[2] A neuron is a single cell. A nerve is a large bundle of many different axons from different neurons.

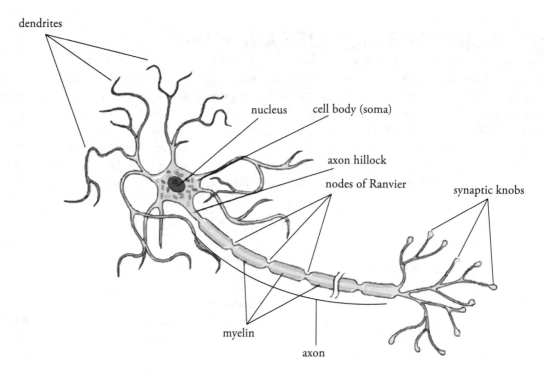

Figure 1 A Multipolar Neuron

- A motor protein called *kinesin* is one of several different proteins that drive movement of vesicles and organelles along microtubules in axons. Kinesin specifically drives anterograde movement (movement from the soma toward the axon terminus). If a kinesin inhibitor is added to neurons in culture, what is the likely result?[3]
    A) Spontaneous action potentials
    B) Cell division
    C) Accumulation of material in the synaptic knob
    D) Atrophy of axons

The Action Potential

The Resting Membrane Potential

The **resting membrane potential** is an electric potential across the plasma membrane of approximately −70 millivolts (mV), with the interior of the cell negatively charged with respect to the exterior of the cell. Two primary membrane proteins are required to establish the resting membrane potential: the Na⁺/K⁺

---

[3] A large amount of biosynthetic activity takes place in the cell body, and materials are transported from the cell body down the axon to its end by kinesin. The correct answer is **D**. If material cannot be transported through the axon from the cell body, the axon will atrophy. Note that although this may not immediately be apparent, choices A, B, and C should have been easily eliminated; kinesin has nothing to do with action potentials, neurons in general do not divide (and inhibiting kinesin should not change this), and the inhibition of kinesin would prevent materials from accumulating at the synaptic knobs.

ATPase and the potassium leak channels. The **Na⁺/K⁺ ATPase** pumps three sodium ions out of the cell and two potassium ions into the cell with the hydrolysis of one ATP molecule. [What form of transport is carried out by the Na⁺/K⁺ ATPase?[4]] The result is a sodium gradient with high sodium outside of the cell and a potassium gradient with high potassium inside the cell. **Leak channels** are channels that are open all the time, and that simply allow ions to "leak" across the membrane according to their gradient. Potassium leak channels allow potassium, but no other ions, to flow down their gradient out of the cell. The combined loss of many positive ions through Na⁺/K⁺ ATPases and the potassium leak channels leaves the interior of the cell with a net negative charge, approximately 70 mV more negative than the exterior of the cell; this difference is the resting membrane potential. Note that there are very few sodium leak channels in the membrane (the ratio of K⁺ leak channels to Na⁺ leak channels is about 100:1), so the cell membrane is virtually impermeable to sodium.

- Are neurons the only cells with a resting membrane potential?[5]
- If the potassium leak channels are blocked, what will happen to the membrane potential?[6]
- What would happen to the membrane potential if sodium ions were allowed to flow down their concentration gradient?[7]

The resting membrane potential establishes a negative charge along the interior of axons (along with the rest of the neuronal interior). Thus, the cells can be described as **polarized**; negative on the inside and positive on the outside. An action potential is a disturbance in this membrane potential, a wave of **depolarization** of the plasma membrane that travels along an axon. Depolarization is a change in the membrane potential from the resting membrane potential of approximately –70 mV to a less negative, or even positive, potential. After depolarization, **repolarization** returns the membrane potential to normal. The change in membrane potential during passage of an action potential is caused by movement of ions into and out of the neuron through ion channels. The action potential is therefore not strictly an electrical impulse, like electrons moving in a copper telephone wire, but an electro*chemical* impulse.

Depolarization

Key proteins in the propagation of action potentials are the **voltage-gated sodium channels** located in the plasma membrane of the axon. In response to a change in the membrane potential, these ion channels open to allow sodium ions to flow down their gradient into the cell and depolarize that section of membrane. [What is the effect of opening the voltage-gated sodium channels on the membrane potential?[8]] These channels are opened by depolarization of the membrane from the resting potential of –70 mV to a **threshold potential** of approximately –50 mV. Once this threshold is reached, the channels are opened fully, but below the threshold they are closed and do not allow the passage of any ions through the channel. When the channels open, sodium flows into the cell, down its concentration gradient, depolarizing that section of the membrane to about +35 mV before inactivating. Some of the sodium ions flow down the

---

[4] The Na⁺/K⁺ ATPase uses ATP to drive transport against a gradient; this is primary active transport.

[5] No. All cells have the resting membrane potential. Neurons and muscle tissue are unique in using the resting membrane potential to generate action potentials.

[6] The flow of potassium out of the cell makes the interior of the cell more negatively charged. Blocking the potassium leak channels would reduce the magnitude of the resting membrane potential, making the interior of the cell less negative.

[7] Sodium ions would flow into the cell and reduce the potential across the plasma membrane, making the interior of the cell less negative and even relatively positive if enough ions flow into the cell.

[8] Sodium (positively charged) flows into the cell, down its concentration gradient, making the interior of the cell less negatively charged, or even positively charged.

interior of the axon, slightly depolarizing the neighboring section of membrane. When the depolarization in the next section of membrane reaches threshold, those voltage-gated sodium channels open as well, passing the depolarization down the axon (Figure 2). [If an action potential starts at one end of an axon, can it run out of energy and not reach the other end?[9]]

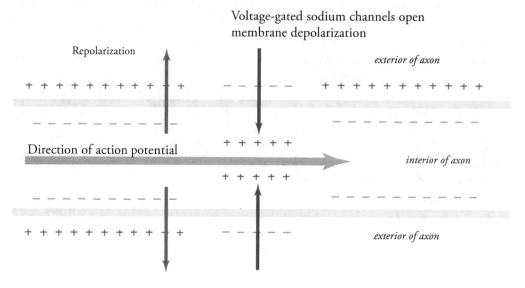

Figure 2   The Action Potential is a Wave of Membrane Depolarization

- Which one of the following can cause the interior of the neuron to have a momentary positive charge?[10]
    A)   Opening of potassium leak channels
    B)   Activity of the Na^+/K^+ ATPase
    C)   Opening of voltage-gated sodium channels
    D)   Opening of voltage-gated potassium channels

- Given the above description, which of the following best describes the response of voltage-gated sodium channels to a membrane depolarization from −70 mV to −60 mV?[11]
    A)   All of the channels open fully.
    B)   50% of the channels open fully.
    C)   All of the channels open 50%.
    D)   None of the channels open.

---

[9]   No, it cannot. Action potentials are continually renewed at each point in the axon as they travel. Assuming there are enough voltage-gated channels, once an action potential starts, it will propagate without a change in amplitude (size) until it reaches a synapse.

[10]   Choices A, B, and D all make the interior of the cell more negative. C is the answer. Voltage-gated sodium channels can make the interior of the cell momentarily positive during passage of an action potential.

[11]   Voltage-gated sodium channels require a threshold depolarization to open. A depolarization below the threshold will produce essentially no response, while a depolarization greater than or equal to the threshold will cause all of the channels to open fully. This is called an **all-or-none** response. The correct answer is **D**. The depolarization is less than the threshold, so there is no response.

Repolarization

With the opening of voltage-gated sodium channels, sodium flows into the cell and depolarizes the membrane to positive values. As the wave of depolarization passes through a region of membrane, however, the membrane does not remain depolarized (Figure 3).

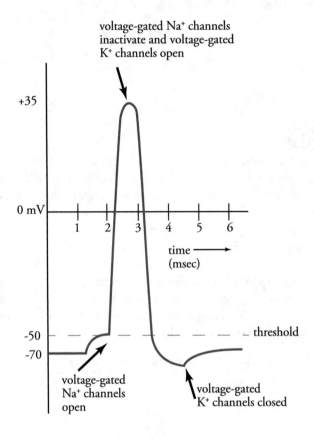

Figure 3   The Action Potential at a Single Location

After depolarization, the membrane is **repolarized**, re-establishing the original resting membrane potential. A number of factors combine to produce this effect:

1) Voltage-gated sodium channels inactivate very quickly after they open, shutting off the flow of sodium into the cell. The channels remain **inactivated** until the membrane potential nears resting values again.

2) Voltage-gated potassium channels open more slowly than the voltage-gated sodium channels and stay open longer. Voltage-gated potassium channels open in response to membrane depolarization. As potassium leaves the cell down its concentration gradient, the membrane potential returns to negative values, actually overshooting the resting potential by about 20 mV (to about –90 mV). At this point the voltage-gated potassium channels close.

3) Potassium leak channels and the Na⁺/K⁺ ATPase continue to function (as they always do) to bring the membrane back to resting potential. These factors alone would repolarize the membrane potential even without the voltage-gated potassium channels, but it would take a lot longer.

- If a toxin prevents voltage-gated sodium channels from closing, which of the following will occur?[12]
    - I. Voltage-gated potassium channels will open but not close.
    - II. The membrane will not repolarize to the normal resting membrane potential.
    - III. The Na⁺/K⁺ ATPase will be inactivated.

    - A) I only
    - B) II only
    - C) I and II only
    - D) II and III only

Saltatory Conduction

The axons of many neurons are wrapped in an insulating sheath called **myelin** (Figure 4). The myelin sheath is not created by the neuron itself, but by cells called **Schwann cells**[13], a type of glial cell, that exist in conjunction with neurons, wrapping layers of specialized membrane around the axons. No ions can enter or exit a neuron where the axonal membrane is covered with myelin. [Would an axon be able to conduct action potentials if its entire length were wrapped in myelin?[14]] There is no membrane depolarization and no voltage-gated sodium channels in regions of the axonal plasma membrane that are wrapped in myelin. There are periodic gaps in the myelin sheath however, called **nodes of Ranvier** (Figures 1, 4, and 5). Voltage-gated sodium and potassium channels are concentrated in the nodes of Ranvier in myelinated axons. Rather than impeding action potentials, the myelin sheath dramatically speeds the movement of action potentials by forcing the action potential to jump from node to node. This rapid jumping conduction in myelinated axons is termed **saltatory conduction**.

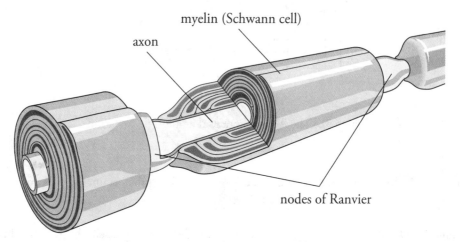

myelin (Schwann cell)

axon

nodes of Ranvier

Figure 4   A Schwann Cell Wrapping an Axon with Myelin

---

[12] **Item I is true:** Voltage-gated potassium channels are normally closed by the repolarization of the membrane, so if the membrane is not repolarized, they will not close. **Item II is true:** Sodium ions will continue to flow into the cell, even as the Na⁺/K⁺ ATPase works to pump them out. This will prevent the repolarization of the membrane. **Item III is false:** The Na⁺/K⁺ ATPase will work harder than ever. The answer is **C**.

[13] Schwann cells are found in the peripheral nervous system (PNS). In the central nervous system (CNS) myelination of axons is accomplished via similar cells called oligodendrocytes.

[14] No. The action potential requires the movement of ions across the plasma membrane to create a wave of depolarization.

- Which one of the following is true concerning myelinated and unmyelinated axons?[15]
    A) The amount of energy consumed by the Na⁺/K⁺ ATPase is much less in myelinated axons than in unmyelinated axons.
    B) Myelinated axons can conduct many more action potentials per second than can unmyelinated axons.
    C) The size of action potential depolarization is much greater in myelinated axons than in unmyelinated axons.
    D) Voltage-gated potassium channels do not play a role in repolarization in unmyelinated axons.

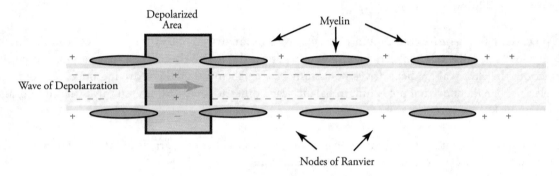

Figure 5   Propagation of the AP in a Myelinated Axon (cross section)

Glial Cells

As mentioned above, the myelin sheath is formed by a type of glial cell called a Schwann cell. However, Schwann cells are not the only type of glial cell. **Glial cells** are specialized, non-neuronal cells that typically provide structural and metabolic support to neurons (Table 1). Glia maintain a resting membrane potential but do not generate action potentials.

Cell Type	Location	Primary Functions
Schwann cells	PNS	Form myelin—increase speed of conduction of APs along axon
Oligodendrocytes	CNS	Form myelin—increase speed of conduction of APs along axon
Astrocytes	CNS	Guide neuronal development Regulate synaptic communication via regulation of neurotransmitter levels
Microglia	CNS	Remove dead cells and debris
Ependymal cells	CNS	Produce and circulate cerebrospinal fluid

Table 1   Types of Glial Cells and Their Functions

[15] Since the area of membrane that is conducting is much less in myelinated axons, Na⁺/K⁺ ATPase only works to maintain the resting potential in the nodes of Ranvier, whereas in unmyelinated axons the Na⁺/K⁺ ATPase hydrolyzes ATP to maintain the resting potential across the entire membrane (choice **A** is correct). The length of the refractory period (and hence the frequency of action potentials) is based on the characteristics of the voltage-gated sodium and potassium channels, which do not change (choice B is false). The size of depolarization in an action potential does not vary greatly; action potentials are an all-or-nothing response (choice C is false). Voltage-gated potassium channels are the same in both neurons (choice D is false).

Equilibrium Potentials

During the action potential, the movement of Na^+ and K^+ ions across the membrane through the voltage-gated channels is *passive*; driven by gradients. The **equilibrium potential** is the membrane potential at which this driving force (the gradient) does not exist; in other words, there would be no net movement of ions across the membrane. Note that the equilibrium potential is specific for a particular ion. For example, the Na^+ equilibrium potential is *positive*, approximately +50 mV. Na^+ ions are driven inward by their concentration gradient. However, if the interior of the cell is too positive, the positively-charged ions are repelled; in other words, the *electrical* gradient would drive sodium *out*. These forces, the chemical gradient driving sodium in and the electrical gradient driving sodium out balance each other at about +50 mV, so this is the equilibrium potential for Na^+.

K^+, however, has a *negative* equilibrium potential. K^+ ions are driven outward by their concentration gradient. However if the interior of the cell is too negative, the positively-charged ions cannot escape the attraction; the electrical gradient drives potassium *in*. The chemical gradient driving potassium out and the electrical gradient driving potassium in balance each other at about −90 mV, so this is the equilibrium potential for K^+.

The equilibrium potential for any ion is based on the electrochemical gradient for that ion across the membrane, and can be predicted by the **Nernst equation**:

$$E_{ion} = \frac{RT}{zF} \ln \frac{[X]_{outside}}{[X]_{inside}}$$

where E_{ion} is the equilibrium potential for the ion, R is the universal gas constant, T is the temperature (in Kelvin), z is the valence of the ion, F is Faraday's constant, and $[X]$ is the concentration of the ion on each side of the plasma membrane. Note that the relative concentrations of the ion on each side of the membrane create the *chemical* gradient, while the valence (charge of the ion) helps determine the *electrical* gradient.

Note that the fact that the resting membrane potential is −70 mV reflects both the differences in the equilibrium potentials for Na^+ and K^+, and also the relative numbers of leak channels for these two ions. If the cell were completely permeable to K^+, the resting potential would be about −90 mV. The fact that the resting potential is *very close* to the K^+ equilibrium potential indicates that there are a large number of K^+ leak channels in the membrane; the cell at rest is almost completely permeable to potassium. However, the resting potential is slightly more positive than −90 mV, indicating that there are a few Na^+ leak channels allowing Na^+ in. Not very many Na^+ leak channels, though, otherwise the resting potential would be much more positive—closer to the Na^+ equilibrium potential. (This is in fact what we see when the cell *does* become completely permeable to Na^+ at the beginning of the action potential; the membrane potential shoots upward to +35 mV.)

The Refractory Period

Action potentials can pass through a neuron extremely rapidly, thousands each second, but there is an upper limit to how soon a neuron can conduct an action potential after another has passed. The passage of one action potential makes the neuron nonresponsive to membrane depolarization and unable to transmit another action potential, or **refractory**, for a short period of time. There are two phases of the refractory period, caused by two different factors. During the **absolute refractory period**, a neuron will not fire another action potential no matter how strong a membrane depolarization is induced. During this time, the voltage-gated sodium channels have been *inactivated* (not the same as *closed*) after depolarization. They will not be able to be opened again until the membrane potential reaches the resting potential and the Na^+ channels have returned to their "closed" state. During the **relative refractory period**, a neuron can be induced to transmit an action potential, but the depolarization required is greater than normal because the membrane is **hyperpolarized**. When repolarization occurs, there is a brief period in which the membrane potential is more negative than the resting potential (Figure 3) caused by voltage-gated potassium channels that have not closed yet. Because it is further from threshold, a greater stimulus is required to open the voltage-gated sodium channels to start an action potential. [If a fruit fly mutant is found that has voltage-gated potassium channels that shut more quickly after repolarization, how would this affect the refractory period in the fly?[16]]

3.2   SYNAPTIC TRANSMISSION

A **synapse** is a junction between the axon terminus of a neuron and the dendrites, soma, or axon of a second neuron. It can also be a junction between the axon terminus of a neuron and an organ. There are two types of synapses: electrical and chemical. **Electrical synapses** occur when the cytoplasms of two cells are joined by gap junctions. If two cells are joined by an electrical synapse, an action potential will spread directly from one cell to the other. Electrical synapses are not common in the nervous system although they are quite important in propagating action potentials in smooth muscle and cardiac muscle. In the nervous system, **chemical synapses** are found at the ends of axons where they meet their target cell; here, an action potential is converted into a chemical signal. The following steps are involved in the transmission of a signal across a chemical synapse in the nervous system (Figure 6), as well as at the junctions of neurons with other cell types, such as skeletal muscle cells:

1) An action potential reaches the end of an axon, the synaptic knob.
2) Depolarization of the presynaptic membrane opens voltage-gated calcium channels.
3) Calcium influx into the presynaptic cell causes exocytosis of neurotransmitter stored in secretory vesicles.
4) Neurotransmitter molecules diffuse across the narrow synaptic cleft (small space between cells).
5) Neurotransmitter binds to receptor proteins in the postsynaptic membrane. These receptors are ligand-gated ion channels.
6) The opening of these ion channels in the postsynaptic cell alters the membrane polarization.
7) If the membrane depolarization of the postsynaptic cell reaches the threshold of voltage-gated sodium channels, an action potential is initiated.
8) Neurotransmitter in the synaptic cleft is degraded and/or removed to terminate the signal.

---

[16] The absolute refractory period would not be altered, since this is due to the inability of voltage-gated sodium channels to open. However, the relative refractory period would be decreased.

Presynaptic Neuron
1. Voltage-gater calcium channels open.
2. Influx of calcium.
3. Exocytosis of secretory vesicle.
4. Release of neurotransmitter into synaptic cleft.

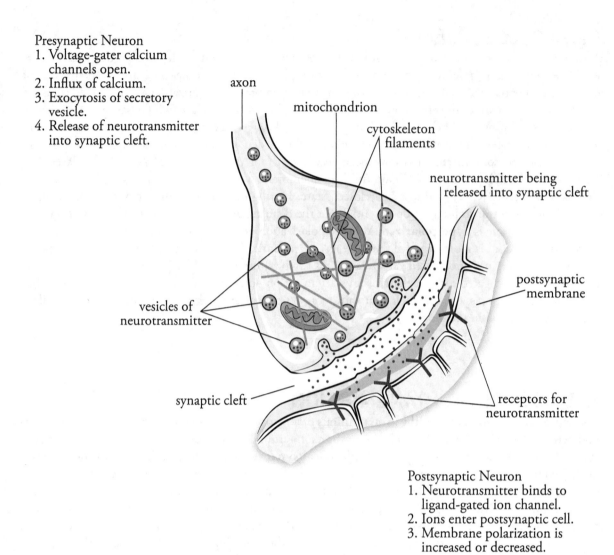

Postsynaptic Neuron
1. Neurotransmitter binds to ligand-gated ion channel.
2. Ions enter postsynaptic cell.
3. Membrane polarization is increased or decreased.

Figure 6 A Typical Synapse

An example of a chemical synapse that is commonly used is the **neuromuscular junction** between neurons and skeletal muscle. The neurotransmitter that is released at the neuromuscular junction is **acetylcholine** (**ACh**). When an action potential reaches such a synapse, acetylcholine is released into the synaptic cleft. The acetylcholine binds to the acetylcholine receptor on the surface of the postsynaptic cell membrane. When acetylcholine binds to its receptor, the receptor opens its associated sodium channel, allowing sodium to flow down a gradient into the cell, depolarizing the postsynaptic cell membrane. Meanwhile, acetylcholine in the synaptic cleft is degraded by the enzyme **acetylcholinesterase** (**AChE**).

There are several different neurotransmitters and neurotransmitter receptors. Some of the other neurotransmitters are **gamma-aminobutyric acid (GABA)**, **serotonin**, **dopamine**, and **norepinephrine**. If a neurotransmitter, such as acetylcholine, opens a channel that depolarizes the postsynaptic membrane, the neurotransmitter is termed **excitatory**. Other neurotransmitters, however, have the opposite effect, making the postsynaptic membrane potential more negative than the resting potential, or hyperpolarized. Neurotransmitters that induce hyperpolarization of the postsynaptic membrane are termed **inhibitory.** (Note, however, that ultimately it is not the *neurotransmitter* that determines the effect on the postsynaptic cell, it is the *receptor* for that neurotransmitter and its associated ion channel. The same neurotransmitter can be excitatory in some cases and inhibitory in others.) Postsynaptic neurons may have many different receptors, allowing them to respond to many different neurotransmitters.

- If a neurotransmitter causes the entry of chloride into the postsynaptic cell, is the neurotransmitter excitatory or inhibitory?[17]

- If an inhibitor of acetylcholinesterase is added to a neuromuscular junction, then the postsynaptic membrane will:[18]
    A) be depolarized by action potentials more frequently.
    B) be depolarized longer with each action potential.
    C) be resistant to depolarization.
    D) spontaneously depolarize.

- Signals can be sent in only one direction through synapses such as the neuromuscular junction. Which of the following best explains unidirectional signaling at synapses between neurons?[19]
    A) Neurotransmitter is always degraded by the postsynaptic cell or in the synaptic cleft.
    B) Only the presynaptic cell has vesicles of neurotransmitters.
    C) Axons can propagate action potentials in only one direction.
    D) Only the postsynaptic cell has a resting membrane potential

---

[17] Chloride ions are negatively charged. The entry of chloride ions into the cell will make the postsynaptic potential more negative, or hyperpolarized, so the neurotransmitter is inhibitory.

[18] **B is the correct answer.** If acetylcholinesterase is inhibited, acetylcholine will remain in the synaptic cleft longer, and acetylcholine-gated sodium channels will remain open longer with each action potential that reaches the synapse. If the sodium channels are open longer, the depolarization of the postsynaptic membrane will last longer.

[19] Signaling is unidirectional because only the presynaptic cell has vesicles of neurotransmitter that are released in response to action potentials, and only the postsynaptic neuron has receptors that bind neurotransmitter to either depolarize or hyperpolarize the cell (choice **B** is correct). The degradation of neurotransmitter is irrelevant to the direction of signal propagation (choice A is wrong), axons are capable of propagating action potentials in both directions (even though this is not what they normally do; choice C is wrong), and all cells have a resting membrane potential (choice D is wrong).

3.2

Summation

Once an action potential is initiated in a neuron, it will propagate to the end of the axon at a speed and magnitude of depolarization that do not vary from one action potential to another. The action potential is an "**all-or-nothing**" event. The key regulated step in the nervous system is whether or not a neuron will fire an action potential. Action potentials are initiated when the postsynaptic membrane reaches the threshold depolarization (about –50 mV) required to open voltage-gated sodium channels. The postsynaptic depolarization caused by the release of neurotransmitter by one action potential at one synapse is not generally sufficient to induce this degree of depolarization. A postsynaptic neuron has many different neurons with synapses leading to it, however, and each of these synapses can release neurotransmitter many times per second. The "decision" by a postsynaptic neuron whether to fire an action potential is determined by adding the effect of all of the synapses impinging on a neuron, both excitatory and inhibitory. This addition of stimuli is termed **summation**.

Excitatory neurotransmitters cause postsynaptic depolarization, or **excitatory postsynaptic potentials** (**EPSPs**), while inhibitory neurotransmitters cause **inhibitory postsynaptic potentials** (**IPSPs**). One form of summation is **temporal summation**, in which a presynaptic neuron fires action potentials so rapidly that the EPSPs or IPSPs pile up on top of each other. If they are EPSPs, the additive effect might be enough to reach the threshold depolarization required to start a postsynaptic action potential. If they are IPSPs, the postsynaptic cell will hyperpolarize, moving further and further away from threshold, effectively becoming inhibited. The other form of summation is **spatial summation**, in which the EPSPs and IPSPs from all of the synapses on the postsynaptic membrane are summed at a given moment in time. If the total of all EPSPs and IPSPs causes the postsynaptic membrane to reach the threshold voltage, an action potential will be fired.

- In which one of the following ways can a presynaptic neuron increase the intensity of signal it transmits?[20]
  A) Increase the size of presynaptic action potentials
  B) Increase the frequency of action potentials
  C) Change the type of neurotransmitter it releases
  D) Change the speed of action potential propagation

---

[20] A neuron cannot change the size of action potentials it transmits, but it can increase the *number* of action potentials it transmits in a given amount of time (the *frequency* of action potentials). The increased frequency of action potentials will add up through temporal summation in the postsynaptic cell to produce an increased response (choice **B** is correct). Action potentials are all-or-nothing once they are started. The magnitude of membrane depolarization during propagation of the action potential does not change (choice A is wrong). A neuron does not change the neurotransmitters it releases (choice C is wrong), and the speed of propagation cannot be varied from one action potential to the next (choice D is wrong).

3.3 FUNCTIONAL ORGANIZATION OF THE HUMAN NERVOUS SYSTEM

The nervous system must receive information, decide what to do with it, and cause muscles or glands to act upon that decision. Receiving information is the **sensory** function of the nervous system (carried out by the peripheral nervous system, or **PNS**), processing the information is the **integrative** function (carried out by the central nervous system, or **CNS**), and acting on it is the **motor** function (also carried out by the PNS).[21] **Motor neurons** carry information from the nervous system toward organs which can act upon that information, known as **effectors**. [What are the two types of effectors?[22]] Notice that "motor" neurons do not lead only "to muscle." Motor neurons, which carry information away from the central nervous system and innervate effectors, are called **efferent** neurons (remember, efferents go to effectors). **Sensory neurons**, which carry information toward the central nervous system, are called **afferent** neurons.

Reflexes

The simplest example of nervous system activity is the **reflex**. This is a direct motor response to sensory input which occurs without conscious thought. In fact, it usually occurs without any involvement of the brain at all. In the simplest example, a sensory neuron transmits an action potential to a synapse with a motor neuron in the spinal cord, which causes an action to occur. For example, in the **muscle stretch reflex**, a sensory neuron detects stretching of a muscle (Figure 7). The sensory neuron has a long dendrite and a long axon, which transmits an impulse to a motor neuron cell body in the spinal cord. The motor neuron's long axon synapses with the muscle that was stretched and causes it to contract. That is why the quadriceps (thigh) muscle contracts when the patellar tendon is stretched by tapping with a reflex hammer. A reflex such as this one, involving only two neurons and one synapse, is known as a **monosynaptic reflex arc**.

Something else also happens when a physician taps the patellar tendon. Not only does the quadriceps *contract*, but the hamstring also *relaxes*. If it did not, the leg would not be able to extend (straighten). The sensory neuron (that detects stretch) synapses with not only a motor neuron for the quadriceps, but also with an **inhibitory interneuron**. This is a short neuron which forms an inhibitory synapse with a motor neuron innervating the hamstring muscle. When the sensory neuron is stimulated by stretch, it stimulates both the quadriceps motor neuron and the inhibitory interneuron to the hamstring motor neuron. As a result, the quadriceps contracts and the hamstring relaxes. An interneuron is the simplest example of the integrative role of the nervous system. Concurrent relaxation of the hamstring and contraction of the quadriceps is an example of **reciprocal inhibition**.

- If a reflex occurs without the involvement of the brain, how are we aware of the action?[23]

---

[21] More detailed information about the anatomy and functions of the CNS and PNS will be presented later in this chapter.

[22] Muscles and glands.

[23] Two ways: First, the sensory neuron also branches to form a synapse with a neuron leading to the brain. Second, other sensory information is received after the action is taken.

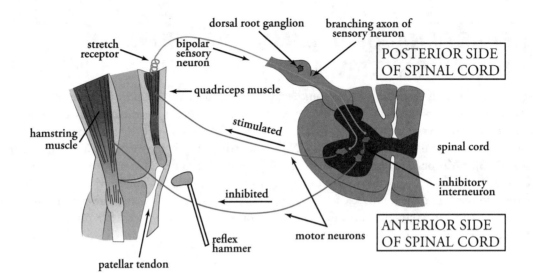

Figure 7   The Muscle Stretch Reflex

Large-Scale Functional Organization

The peripheral nervous system can be subdivided into several functional divisions (Figure 8). The portion of this system concerned with conscious sensation and deliberate, voluntary movement of skeletal muscle is the **somatic** division. The portion concerned with digestion, metabolism, circulation, perspiration, and other involuntary processes is the **autonomic** division. The somatic and autonomic divisions both include afferent and efferent functions, although the sources of sensory input and the target of efferent nerves are different. The efferent portion of the autonomic division is further split into two subdivisions: *sympathetic* and **parasympathetic**. When the sympathetic system is activated, the body is prepared for "fight or flight." When the parasympathetic system is activated, the body is prepared to "rest and digest." Table 2 summarizes the main effects of the autonomic system. Notice that many sympathetic effects result from release of epinephrine[24] into the bloodstream by the adrenal medulla. The parasympathetic system prepares you to rest and digest food.

---

[24] In Greek, "epi" means upon or on top of, and "nephr" refers to the kidney (as in nephron, the microscopic functional unit of the kidney); hence epinephrine is "the hormone secreted by the gland on top of the kidney." Another name for epinephrine is adrenaline. In Latin, "ad" also means upon, and "renal" likewise refers to the kidney. The gland which secretes epinephrine is the adrenal gland.

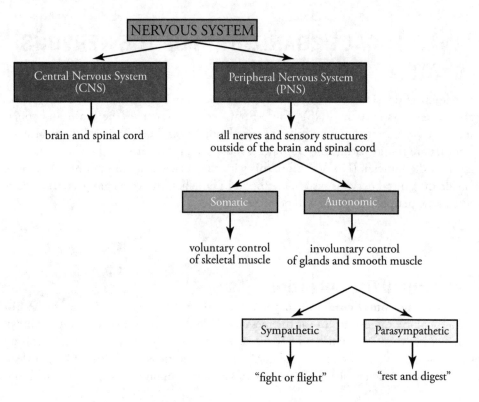

Figure 8   Overall Organization of the Nervous System

Organ or System	Parasympathetic: rest and digest	Sympathetic: fight or flight
digestive system: glands	stimulation	inhibition
motility	stimulation (stimulates digestion)	inhibition (inhibits digestion)
sphincters	relaxation	contraction
urinary system: bladder	contraction (stimulates urination)	relaxation (inhibits urination)
urethral sphincter	relaxation (stimulates urination)	contraction (inhibits urination)
bronchial smooth muscle	constriction (closes airways)	relaxation (opens airways)
cardiovascular system:		
heart rate and contractility	decreased	increased
blood flow to skeletal muscle	—	increased
skin	—	sweating and general vasoconstriction; emotional vasodilation (blushing)
eye: pupil	constriction	dilation
muscles controlling lens	near vision accommodation	accommodation for far vision
adrenal medulla	—	release of epinephrine
genitals	erection / lubrication	ejaculation / orgasm

Table 2   Effects of the Autonomic Nervous System

3.4   ANATOMICAL ORGANIZATION OF THE NERVOUS SYSTEM

The main anatomical division of the nervous system is between the **central nervous system** (**CNS**) and the **peripheral nervous system** (**PNS**). The central nervous system is the brain and spinal cord. The peripheral nervous system includes all other axons, dendrites, and cell bodies. The great majority of neuronal cell bodies are found within the central nervous system. Sometimes they are bunched together to form structures called **nuclei.** (Don't confuse this with the nucleic-acid-containing nuclei of cells.) Somas located outside the central nervous system are found in bunches known as **ganglia.** The anatomy of both the central and the peripheral system will be presented.

CNS Anatomical Organization

The CNS includes the **spinal cord** and the brain. The brain has three subdivisions: the **hindbrain** (or the rhombencephalon), the **midbrain** (or the mesencephalon), and the **forebrain** (or the prosencephalon). These four regions of the CNS (which will be discussed individually below) perform increasingly complex functions. The entire CNS (brain and spinal cord) floats in **cerebrospinal fluid** (**CSF**), a clear liquid that serves various functions such as shock absorption and exchange of nutrients and waste with the CNS.

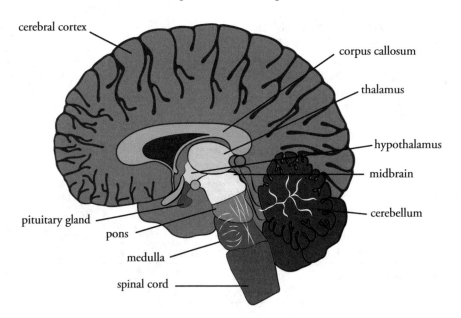

Figure 9   Organization of the CNS (cross-section of the brain)

1) The spinal cord is connected to the brain and is protected by the CSF and the vertebral column. It is a pathway for information to and from the brain. Most sensory data is relayed to the brain for integration, but the spinal cord is also a site for information integration and processing. The spinal cord is responsible for simple spinal reflexes (like the muscle stretch reflex) and is also involved in primitive processes such as walking, urination, and sex organ function.

2) The hindbrain includes the medulla, the pons, and the cerebellum.
   - The **medulla** (or medulla oblongata) is located below the pons and is the area of the brain that connects to the spinal cord. It functions in relaying information between other areas of the brain, and regulates vital autonomic functions such as blood pressure and digestive functions (including vomiting). Also, the respiratory rhythmicity centers are found here.
   - The **pons** is located below the midbrain and above the medulla oblongata. It is the connection point between the brain stem and the cerebellum (see below). The pons controls some autonomic functions and coordinates movement; it plays a role in balance and antigravity posture.
   - The **cerebellum** (or "little brain") is located behind the pons and below the cerebral hemispheres. It is an integrating center where complex movements are coordinated. An instruction for movement from the forebrain must be sent to the cerebellum, where the billions of decisions necessary for smooth execution of the movement are made. Damage to the cerebellum results in poor hand-eye coordination and balance. Both the cerebellum and the pons receive information from the vestibular apparatus in the inner ear, which monitors acceleration and position relative to gravity.
3) The midbrain is a relay for visual and auditory information and contains much of the reticular activating system (RAS), which is responsible for arousal or wakefulness.

Another term you should be familiar with is **brainstem**. Together, the medulla, pons, and midbrain constitute the brainstem, which contains important processing centers and relays information to or from the cerebellum and cerebrum.

4) The forebrain includes the **diencephalon** and the **telencephalon**.
   a) The diencephalon includes the thalamus and hypothalamus:
      - The thalamus is located near the middle of the brain below the cerebral hemispheres and above the midbrain. It contains relay and processing centers for sensory information.
      - The hypothalamus interacts directly with many parts of the brain. It contains centers for controlling emotions and autonomic functions, and has a major role in hormone production and release. It is the primary link between the nervous and the endocrine systems, and, by controlling the pituitary gland, it is the fundamental control center for the endocrine system (discussed later in this chapter).
   b) All parts of the CNS up to and including the diencephalon form a single symmetrical stalk, but the telencephalon consists of two separate cerebral hemispheres. Generally speaking, the areas of the left and right hemispheres have the same functions. However, the left hemisphere primarily controls the motor functions of the right side of the body, and the right hemisphere controls those of the left side. Also, in most people, the left side of the brain is said to be dominant. It is generally responsible for speech. The right hemisphere is more concerned with visual-spatial reasoning and music.
      - The **cerebral hemispheres** are connected by a thick bundle of axons called the **corpus callosum**. A person with a cut corpus callosum has two independent cerebral cortices and to a certain extent two independent minds![25]
      - The **cerebrum** is the largest region of the human brain and consists of the large, paired cerebral hemispheres. The hemispheres of the cerebrum consist of the **cerebral cortex** (an outer layer of gray matter) plus an inner core of white matter connecting the cortex to the diencephalon.[26] The gray matter is composed of trillions of somas; the

---

[25] Anyone interested in reading about jaw-dropping neurological cases should begin with Oliver Sacks's *The Man Who Mistook His Wife for a Hat*. You will *not* be sorry if you buy this book.

[26] The word cortex means "outside layer"; for example, an orange peel may be called the cortex of the orange; the outside layer of a gland is also known as its cortex.

white matter is composed of myelinated axons. (Most axons in the CNS and PNS are myelinated.) The cerebral hemispheres are responsible for conscious thought processes and intellectual functions. They also play a role in processing somatic sensory and motor information. The cerebral cortex is divided into four pairs of lobes, each of which is devoted to specific functions:

i) The **frontal lobes** initiate all voluntary movement and are involved in complex reasoning skills and problem solving.

ii) The **parietal lobes** are involved in general sensations (such as touch, temperature, pressure, vibration, etc.) and in gustation (taste).

iii) The **temporal lobes** process auditory and olfactory sensation and are involved in short-term memory, language comprehension, and emotion.

iv) The **occipital lobes** process visual sensation.

Figure 10 shows some of the more important cortical areas.

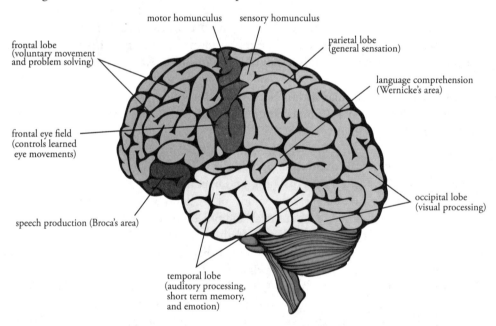

Figure 10   Principal Areas of the Cerebral Cortex

Two last regions of the brain deserve mention:

- The **basal nuclei** (also called the "cerebral nuclei," and previously known as the basal ganglia) are composed of gray matter and are located deep within the cerebral hemispheres. They include several functional subdivisions, but broadly function in voluntary motor control and procedural learning related to habits. The basal nuclei and cerebellum work together to process and coordinate movement initiated by the primary motor cortex; the basal nuclei are inhibitory (preventing excess movement), while the cerebellum is excitatory.
- The **limbic system** is located between the cerebrum and the diencephalon. It includes several substructures (such as the amygdala, the cingulate gyrus, and the hippocampus) and works closely with parts of the cerebrum, diencephalon, and midbrain. The limbic system is important in emotion and memory.

The information above describes the general functions of each region of the brain. Table 3 on the next page summarizes the brain functions and provides a little more specific detail for each region.

3.4

Structure	General Function	Specific Functions
Spinal cord	Simple reflexes	• controls simple stretch and tendon reflexes • controls primitive processes such as walking, urination, and sex organ function
Medulla	Involuntary functions	• controls autonomic processes such as blood pressure, blood flow, heart rate, respiratory rate, swallowing, vomiting • controls reflex reactions such as coughing or sneezing • relays sensory information to the cerebellum and the thalamus
Pons	Relay station and balance	• controls antigravity posture and balance • connects the spinal cord and medulla with upper regions of the brain • relays information to the cerebellum and thalamus
Cerebellum	Movement coordination	• integrating center • coordination of complex movement, balance and posture, muscle tone, spatial equilibrium
Midbrain	Eye movement	• integration of visual and auditory information • visual and auditory reflexes • wakefulness and consciousness • coordinates information on posture and muscle tone
Thalamus	Integrating center and relay station	• relay center for somatic (conscious) sensation • relays information between the spinal cord and the cerebral cortex
Hypothalamus	Homeostasis and behavior	• controls homeostatic functions (such as temperature regulation, fluid balance, appetite) through both neural and hormonal regulation • controls primitive emotions such as anger, rage, and sex drive • controls the pituitary gland
Basal nuclei	Movement	• regulate body movement and muscle tone • coordination of learned movement patterns • general pattern of rhythm movements (such as controlling the cycle of arm and leg movements when walking) • subconscious adjustments of conscious movements
Limbic system	Emotion, memory, and learning	• controls emotional states • links conscious and unconscious portions of the brain • helps with memory storage and retrieval
Cerebral cortex	Perception, skeletal muscle movement, memory, attention, thought, language, and consciousness	• divided into four lobes (frontal, parietal, temporal, and occipital) with specialized subfunctions • conscious thought processes and planning, awareness, and sensation • perception and processing of the special senses (vision, hearing, smell, taste, touch) • intellectual function (intelligence, learning, reading, communication) • abstract thought and reasoning • memory storage and retrieval • initiation and coordination of voluntary movement • complex motor patterns • language (speech production and understanding) • personality
Corpus callosum	Connection	• connects the left and right cerebral hemispheres

Table 3   Summary of Brain Functions

3.4

The motor and sensory regions of the cortex are organized such that a particular small area of cortex controls a particular body part. A larger area is devoted to a body part which requires more motor control or more sensation (Figure 11). For example, more cortex is devoted to the lips than to the entire leg. The body parts represented on the cortex can be sketched. The drawing looks like a distorted person, known as a **homunculus** (little man).

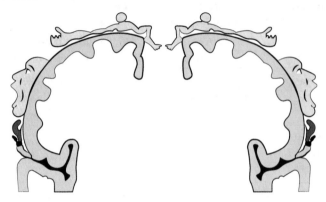

Figure 11 The Sensory Homunculus

PNS Anatomical Organization

All neurons entering and exiting the CNS are carried by 12 pairs of **cranial nerves** and 31 pairs of **spinal nerves**. Cranial nerves convey sensory and motor information to and from the brainstem. Spinal nerves convey sensory and motor information to and from the spinal cord. The different functional divisions of the nervous system have different anatomical organizations (Figure 12).

The **vagus nerve** is an important example of a cranial nerve, and one that you should be familiar with for the MCAT. The effects of this nerve upon the heart and GI tract are to decrease the heart rate and increase GI activity; as such it is part of the *parasympathetic division* of the autonomic nervous system. It is a bundle of axons that end in ganglia on the surface of the heart, stomach, and other visceral organs. The many axons constituting the vagus nerve are preganglionic and come from cell bodies located in the CNS. On the surface of the heart and stomach they synapse with postganglionic neurons. The detailed terminology in this paragraph will make more sense to you as you read through the next couple of sections.

Somatic PNS Anatomy

The somatic system has a simple organization:

- *All* somatic motor neurons innervate skeletal muscle cells, use ACh as their neurotransmitter, and have their cell bodies in the brain stem or the ventral (front) portion of the spinal cord.

- *All* somatic sensory neurons have a long dendrite extending from a sensory receptor toward the soma, which is located just outside the CNS in a **dorsal root ganglion**. The dorsal root ganglion is a bunch of somatic (and autonomic) sensory neuron cell bodies located just dorsal to (to the back of) the spinal cord. There is a pair of dorsal root ganglia for every segment of the spinal cord, and thus the dorsal root ganglia form a chain along the dorsal (back) aspect of the vertebral column. The dorsal root ganglia are protected within the vertebral column but are outside the **meninges** (protective sheath of the brain and cord) and thus outside the CNS. An axon extends from the somatic sensory neuron's soma into the spinal cord. In all somatic sensory neurons, the first synapse is in the CNS; depending on the type of sensory information conveyed, the axon either synapses in the cord, or stretches all the way up to the brain stem before its first synapse!

Autonomic PNS Anatomy

Anatomical organization of autonomic efferents is a bit more complex.[27] The efferents of the sympathetic and parasympathetic systems consist of two neurons: a preganglionic and a postganglionic neuron. The **preganglionic neuron** has its cell body in the brainstem or spinal cord. It sends an axon to an autonomic ganglion, located outside the spinal column. In the ganglion, this axon synapses with a **postganglionic neuron**. The postganglionic neuron sends an axon to an effector (smooth muscle or gland). *All* autonomic preganglionic neurons release acetylcholine as their neurotransmitter. *All* parasympathetic postganglionic neurons also release acetylcholine. Nearly all sympathetic postganglionic neurons release norepinephrine (NE, also known as noradrenaline) as their neurotransmitter.

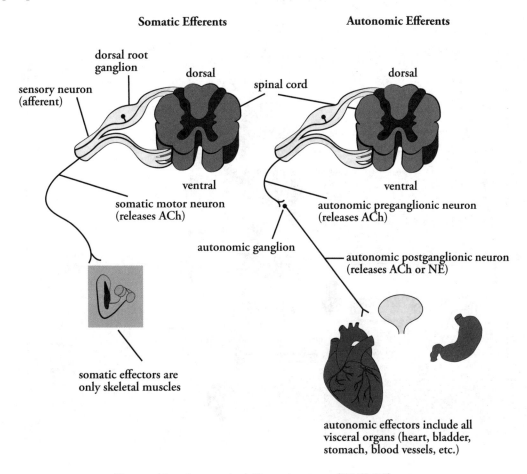

Figure 12   Anatomical Organization of PNS Efferents

---

[27] The anatomy of autonomic sensory neurons (afferents) is poorly defined and will not be on the MCAT.

3.4

All sympathetic preganglionic efferent neurons have their cell bodies in the thoracic (chest) or lumbar (lower back) regions of the spinal cord. Hence the sympathetic system is also referred to as the *thoraco-lumbar system*. The parasympathetic system is known as the *craniosacral system*, because all of its preganglionic neurons have cell bodies in the brainstem (which is in the head or cranium) or in the lowest portion of the spinal cord, the sacral portion. In the sympathetic system, the preganglionic axon is relatively short, and there are only a few ganglia; these sympathetic ganglia are quite large. The sympathetic postganglionic cell sends a long axon to the effector. In contrast, the parasympathetic preganglionic neuron sends a long axon to a small ganglion which is close to the effector. For example, parasympathetic ganglia controlling the intestines are located on the outer wall of the gut. The parasympathetic postganglionic neuron has a very short axon, since the cell body is close to the target.[28] These differences are visualized in Figure 13 and summarized in Table 4.

Autonomic Nervous System

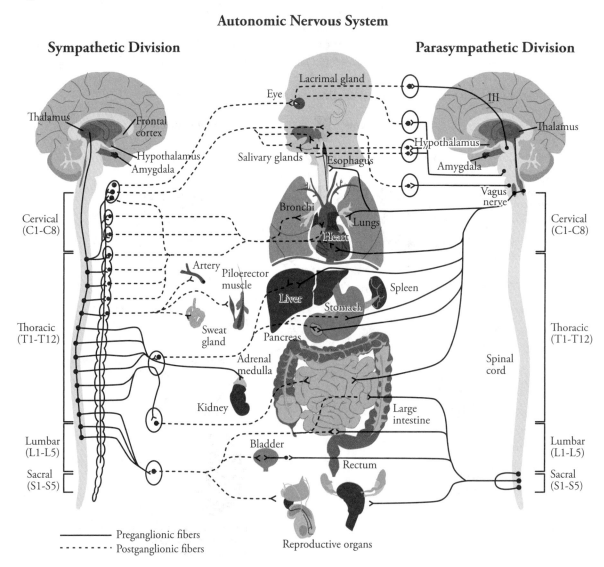

Figure 13   Pre- and Post-Ganglionic Fibers of the Autonomic Nervous System

---

[28] The mnemonic "*para long pre*" will help you in med school.

The autonomic afferent (sensory) neurons are similar to the somatic afferent neurons with one exception: They can synapse in the PNS (at the autonomic ganglia) with autonomic efferent neurons in what is known as a "short reflex." (Recall that the first synapse of somatic afferent neurons is in the CNS.)

	Sympathetic	Parasympathetic
General function	fight or flight, mobilize energy	rest and digest, store energy
Location of preganglionic soma	thoracolumbar = thoracic and lumbar spinal cord	craniosacral = brainstem ("cranial") and sacral spinal cord
Preganglionic axon neurotransmitter = acetylcholine (ACh)	short	long
Ganglia	close to cord, far from target	far from cord, close to target
Postganglionic axon (usual neurotransmitter)	long (norepinephrine [NE])	short (ACh)

Table 4   Sympathetic vs. Parasympathetic

The Adrenal Medulla

The **adrenal gland** is named for its location: "Ad-" connotes "above," and "renal" refers to the kidney. There are two adrenal glands, one above each kidney. The adrenal has an inner portion known as the **medulla** and an outer portion known as the **cortex**. The cortex is an important endocrine gland, secreting **glucocorticoids** (the main one is cortisol), **mineralocorticoids** (the main one is aldosterone), and some sex hormones.

The adrenal medulla, however, is part of the sympathetic nervous system. It is embryologically derived from sympathetic postganglionic neurons and is directly innervated by sympathetic preganglionic neurons. Upon activation of the sympathetic system, the adrenal gland is stimulated to release **epinephrine**, also known as **adrenaline**. Epinephrine is a slightly modified version of *nor*epinephrine, the neurotransmitter released by sympathetic postganglionic neurons. Epinephrine is a hormone because it is released into the bloodstream by a ductless gland. But in many ways it behaves like a neurotransmitter. It elicits its effects very rapidly, and the effects are quite short-lived. Epinephrine release from the adrenal medulla is what causes the sudden flushing and sweating one experiences when severely startled. In general, epinephrine's effects are those listed in Table 2 for the sympathetic system. Stimulation of the heart is an especially important effect.

3.5 SENSATION AND PERCEPTION

Sensation is the process by which we receive information from the world around us. Sensory receptors detect data, both internally (from within the body) and externally (from the environment), and send this information to the central nervous system for processing. Sensation is the act of receiving information, while perception is the act of organizing, assimilating, and interpreting the sensory input into useful and meaningful information.

Types of Sensory Receptors

Sensory receptors are designed to detect one type of stimulus from either the interior of the body or the external environment. Each sensory receptor receives only one kind of information and transmits that information to sensory neurons, which can in turn convey it to the central nervous system. [How does the brain know the difference between stimulation of visual receptors and olfactory receptors?[29]] Sensory receptors that detect stimuli from the outside world are **exteroceptors** and receptors that respond to internal stimuli are **interoceptors**. A more important distinction between sensory receptors is based on the type of stimulus they detect. The types of sensory receptors are listed below.

1) **Mechanoreceptors** respond to mechanical disturbances. For example, **Pacinian corpuscles** are pressure sensors located deep in the skin. The Pacinian corpuscle is shaped like an onion. It is composed of concentric layers of specialized membranes. When the corpuscular membranes are distorted by firm pressure on the skin, the nerve ending becomes depolarized and the signal travels up the dendrite (note that these are graded potential changes—*not* action potentials). Another important mechanoreceptor is the **auditory hair cell**. This is a specialized cell found in the cochlea of the inner ear. It detects vibrations caused by sound waves. **Vestibular hair cells** are located within special organs called semicircular canals, also found in the inner ear. Their role is to detect acceleration and position relative to gravity. An example of an autonomic mechanoreceptor would be a receptor detecting stretch of the intestinal wall.

2) **Chemoreceptors** respond to particular chemicals. For example, **olfactory receptors** detect airborne chemicals and allow us to smell things. Taste buds are **gustatory receptors**. Autonomic chemoreceptors in the walls of the carotid and aortic arteries respond to changes in arterial pH, PCO_2, and PO_2 levels.

3) **Nociceptors** are pain receptors.[30] They are stimulated by tissue injury. Nociceptors are the simplest type of sensory receptor, generally consisting of a free nerve ending that detects chemical signs of tissue damage. (In that sense the nociceptor is a simple chemoreceptor.) Nociceptors may be somatic or autonomic. Autonomic pain receptors do not provide the conscious mind with clear pain information, but they frequently give a sensation of dull, aching pain. They may also create the illusion of pain on the skin, when their nerves cross paths with somatic afferents from the skin. This phenomenon is known as **referred pain**.

4) **Thermoreceptors** are stimulated by changes in temperature. There are autonomic and somatic examples. Peripheral thermoreceptors fall into three categories: cold-sensitive, warm-sensitive, and thermal nociceptors, which detect painfully hot stimuli.

5) **Electromagnetic receptors** are stimulated by electromagnetic waves. In humans, the only examples are the rod and cone cells of the retina of the eye (also termed **photoreceptors**). In other animals, electroreceptors and magnetoreceptors are separate. For example, some fish can detect electric fields with electroreceptors, and magnetoreceptors allow animals to sense the Earth's magnetic field, which can help them navigate during migration.

---

[29] Both signals are received in the brain as action potentials from sensory neurons. The brain distinguishes the sensory stimuli based on which sensory neurons are signaling.

[30] *Noci-* is from the Latin *nocuus*, meaning harmful, as in *noxious*.

Encoding of Sensory Stimuli

All sensory receptors need to encode relevant information regarding the nature of the stimulus being detected. There are four properties that need to be communicated to the CNS:

3.5

1) Stimulus **modality** is the type of stimulus. As mentioned above, the CNS determines the stimulus modality based on which type of receptor is firing.

2) Stimulus **location** is communicated by the receptive field of the sensory receptor sending the signal. Localization of a stimulus can be improved by overlapping receptive fields of neighboring receptors. This works like a Venn diagram, and allows the brain to localize a stimulus activating neighboring receptors to the area in which their receptive fields overlap. Discrimination between two separate stimuli can be improved by lateral inhibition of neighboring receptors.

3) Stimulus **intensity** is coded by the frequency of action potentials. The dynamic range, or range of intensities that can be detected by sensory receptors, can be expanded by range fractionation—including multiple groups of receptors with limited ranges to detect a wider range overall. One example of this phenomenon is human cone cells responding to different but overlapping ranges of wavelengths to detect the full visual spectrum of light.

4) Stimulus **duration** may or may not be coded explicitly. *Tonic receptors* fire action potentials as long as the stimulus continues. However, these receptors are subject to adaptation, and the frequency of action potentials decreases as the stimulus continues at the same level (see below). *Phasic receptors* only fire action potentials when the stimulus begins, and do not explicitly communicate the duration of the stimulus. These receptors are important for communicating changes in stimuli and essentially adapt immediately if a stimulus continues at the same level.

The ability to adapt to a stimulus is an important property of sensory receptors. This allows the brain to tune out unimportant information from the environment. **Adaptation** is a decrease in firing frequency when the intensity of a stimulus remains constant. For example, if you walk into a kitchen where someone is baking bread, the bread odor molecules stimulate your olfactory receptors to a great degree and you smell the bread baking. But if you remain in the kitchen for a few minutes, you stop smelling the bread; the continuous input to the olfactory receptors causes them to stop firing even though the odor molecules are still present. This is what allows us to "get used to" certain environments and situations, for example, cold pool water, loud background noise, etc. The receptors don't stop being *able* to respond; they can be retriggered if the stimulus intensity increases. For example, if you open up the oven door, you will smell the bread again. Likewise, if you are used to the background noise in a restaurant, but someone drops a plate, you'll hear it. In other words: the nervous system is programmed to respond to *changing stimuli* and not so much to constant stimuli, because for the most part, constant stimuli are not a threat whereas changing stimuli might need to be dealt with. (Note that nociceptors *do not adapt* under any circumstance. We can learn to ignore them, but pain is something that the nervous system wants us to *do* something about since it is an indication that something is wrong.)

Proprioceptors

This is a broad category including many different types of receptors. **Proprioception** refers to awareness of self (that is, awareness of body position) and is also known as your **kinesthetic sense**.[31] An important example of a proprioceptor is the **muscle spindle**, a mechanoreceptor. This is a sensory organ specialized to detect muscle stretch. You are already familiar with it because it is the receptor that senses muscle

---

[31] *Proprio-* means *of or pertaining to the self*, as in "proprietary."

stretch in the muscle stretch reflex. Other proprioceptors include **Golgi tendon organs**, which monitor tension in the tendons, and **joint capsule receptors**, which detect pressure, tension, and movement in the joints. By monitoring the activity of the musculoskeletal system, the proprioceptive component of the somatic sensory system allows us to know the positions of our body parts. This is most important during activity, when precise feedback is essential for coordinated motion. [What portion of the CNS would you expect to require input from proprioceptors?[32]]

Gustation and Olfaction

Taste and smell are senses that rely on chemoreceptors in the mouth and nasal passages. **Gustation** is taste, and **olfaction** is smell. Much of what is assumed to be taste is actually smell. (Try eating with a bad head cold.) In fact, taste receptors (known as **taste buds**) can only distinguish five flavors: sweet (glucose), salty (Na^+), bitter (basic), sour (acidic), and umami (amino acids and nucleotides). Each taste bud responds most strongly to one of these five stimuli. The taste bud is composed of a bunch of specialized epithelial cells, shaped roughly like an onion. In its center is a **taste pore**, with **taste hairs** that detect food chemicals. Information about taste is transmitted by cranial nerves to an area of the brain in the temporal lobe not far from where the brain receives olfactory information.

Olfaction is accomplished by olfactory receptors in the roof of the **nasopharynx** (nasal cavity). The receptors detect airborne chemicals that dissolve in the mucus covering the nasal membrane. Humans can distinguish thousands of different smells. Olfactory nerves project directly to the **olfactory bulbs** of the brain. The olfactory bulbs are located in the temporal lobe of the brain near the limbic system, an area important for memory and emotion (which may explain why certain smells can bring back vivid memories and feelings).

Interestingly, the perception of a smell as "good" or "bad" is entirely learned, based on experiences with those smells. There is no smell that is universally noxious to people (though the military has tried to find one in order to develop a "stink" bomb), because different smells can be associated with good or bad experiences based on culture and upbringing.

Pheromones are chemical signals that cause a social response in members of the same species. Though not well understood in humans, pheromones have been studied extensively in insects, particularly those species with complex social structures (such as bees and ants). Pheromones are an important means of communicating information; for example, alarm pheromones will alert the rest of the beehive of danger, food-trail pheromones allow ants to follow a trail to a promising food source, and sex pheromones play an important role in mating between most species. In humans, pheromones are much harder to study.

---

[32] The cerebellum, which is responsible for motor coordination.

Hearing and the Vestibular System

Structure of the Ear

The **auricle** or **pinna** and the external **auditory canal** comprise the **outer ear**. The **middle ear** is divided from the outer ear by the **tympanic membrane** or eardrum. The middle ear consists of the **ossicles**, three small bones called the **malleus** (hammer), the **incus** (anvil), and the **stapes** (stirrup). The stapes attaches to the **oval window**, a membrane that divides the middle and **inner ear**. Structures of the inner ear include the **cochlea**, the **semicircular canals**, the **utricle**, and the **saccule**. The semicircular canals together with the utricle and saccule are important to the sense of balance. The **round window** is a membrane-covered hole in the cochlea near the oval window. It releases excess pressure. The **Eustachian tube** (also known as the **auditory tube**) is a passageway from the back of the throat to the middle ear. It functions to equalize the pressure on both sides of the eardrum and is the cause of the "ear popping" one experiences at high altitudes or underwater.

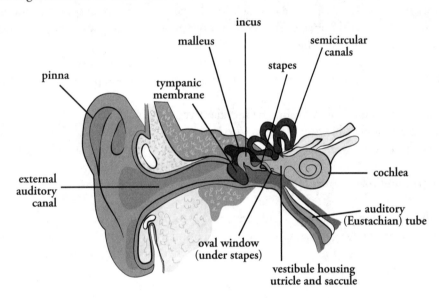

Figure 14 The Ear

Mechanism of Hearing

Sound waves enter the external ear to pass into the auditory canal, causing the eardrum to vibrate. The malleus attached to the eardrum receives the vibrations, which are passed on to the incus and then to the stapes. The bones of the middle ear are arranged in such a way that they amplify sound vibrations passing through the middle ear. The stapes is the innermost of the three middle-ear bones, contacting the oval window. Vibration of the oval window creates pressure waves in the **perilymph** and **endolymph**, the fluids in the cochlea. Note that sound vibrations are first conveyed through air, next through bone, and then through liquid before being sensed. The pressure waves in the endolymph cause vibration of the **basilar membrane**, a thin membrane extending throughout the coiled length of the cochlea. The basilar membrane is covered with the auditory receptor cells known as **hair cells**. These cells have **cilia** (hairs) projecting from their apical (top) surfaces (opposite the basilar membrane). The hairs contact the **tectorial membrane** (tectorial means "roof"), and when the basilar membrane moves, the hairs are dragged across the tectorial membrane and they bend. This displacement opens ion channels in the hair cells, which results in neurotransmitter release. Dendrites from bipolar auditory afferent neurons are stimulated by this neurotransmitter, and thus sound vibrations are converted to nerve impulses. The basilar membrane, hair cells, and tectorial membrane together are known as the **organ of Corti**. The outer ear and middle ear convey sound waves to the cochlea, and the organ of Corti in the cochlea is the primary site at which auditory stimuli are detected.

> **Summary: From Sound to Hearing**
> sound waves → auricle → external auditory canal → tympanic membrane → malleus → incus → stapes → oval window → perilymph → endolymph → basilar membrane → auditory hair cells → tectorial membrane → neurotransmitters stimulate bipolar auditory neurons → brain → perception

Pitch (frequency) of sound is distinguished by which *regions* of the basilar membrane vibrate, stimulating different auditory neurons. The basilar membrane is thick and sturdy near the oval window and gradually becomes thin and floppy near the apex of the cochlea. Low frequency (long wavelength) sounds stimulate hair cells at the apex of the cochlear duct, farthest away from the oval window, while high-pitched sounds stimulate hair cells at the base of the cochlea, near the oval window. **Loudness** of sound is distinguished by the *amplitude* of vibration. Larger vibrations cause more frequent action potentials in auditory neurons.

Locating the source of sound is also an important adaptive function. Having two ears allows for stereophonic (or three-dimensional) hearing. The auditory system can determine the source of a sound based on the difference detected between the two ears. For example, if a horn blasts to your right, your right ear will receive the sound waves slightly sooner and slightly more intensely than your left ear. Sound stimuli are processed in the **auditory cortex**, located in the temporal lobe of the brain.

In humans, audition is highly adaptive. While we are able to hear a wide range of sounds, those sounds with frequencies within the range corresponding to the human voice are heard best, and we are able to differentiate variations among human voices. For example, when answering the phone, you will recognize your mom's voice within a fraction of a second.

- If a sensory neuron leading from the ear to the brain fires an action potential more rapidly, how will the brain perceive this change?[33]
- In some cases of deafness, sound can still be detected by conduction of vibration through the skull to the cochlea. If the auditory nerve is severed, can sound still be detected by conductance through bone?[34]
- If the bones of the middle ear are unable to move, would this impair the detection of sound by conductance through bone?[35]

---

[33] More rapid firing of a cochlear neuron indicates an increase in volume of sound. If the pitch changed, a different set of neurons would fire action potentials.

[34] Conductance through bone allows some hearing by causing the cochlea to vibrate, which stimulates action potentials that pass through the auditory nerve to the brain. However, if the auditory nerve is severed, no hearing of any kind is possible.

[35] The bones of the middle ear serve to conduct vibration from the outer ear to the liquid within the cochlea but are not involved directly in detecting sound. Bone conductance can still stimulate the cochlea and result in hearing if the middle ear is nonfunctional.

Equilibrium and Balance

The vestibular complex is made up of the three **semicircular canals**: the **utricle**, the **saccule**, and the **ampullae**. All are essentially tubes filled with endolypmh, like the cochlea, they contain hair cells that detect motion. However, their function is to detect not sound, but rather rotational acceleration of the head. They are innervated by afferent neurons which send balance information to the pons, cerebellum, and other areas. The vestibular complex monitors both static equilibrium and linear acceleration, which contribute to your sense of balance.

Vision: Structure and Function

The eye is the structure designed to detect visual stimuli. The structures of the eye first form an image on the retina, which detects light and converts the stimuli into action potentials to send to the brain. Light enters the eye by passing through the **cornea**, the clear portion at the front of the eye. Light is bent or **refracted** as it passes through the cornea (which is highly curved and thus acts as a lens), since the refractive index of the cornea is higher than that of air. The cornea is continuous at its borders with the white of the eye, the **sclera**. Beneath the sclera is a layer called the **choroid**. It contains darkly-pigmented cells; this pigmentation absorbs excess light within the eye. Beneath the choroid is the **retina**, the surface upon which light is focused.

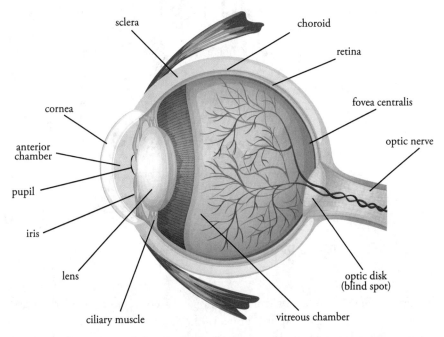

Figure 15 The Eye

Just inside the cornea is the **anterior chamber** (front chamber), which contains a fluid termed **aqueous humor**. At the back of the anterior chamber is a membrane called the **iris** with an opening called the **pupil**. The iris is the colored part of the eye, and muscles in the iris regulate the diameter of the pupil. Just behind the iris is the **posterior chamber**, also containing aqueous humor. In the back part of the posterior chamber is the **lens**. Its role is to fine-tune the angle of incoming light, so that the beams are perfectly focused upon the retina. The curvature of the lens (and thus its refractive power) is varied by the **ciliary muscle**.

Light passes through the **vitreous chamber** en route from the lens to the retina. This chamber contains a thick, jelly-like fluid called **vitreous humor**. The retina is located at the back of the eye. It contains electromagnetic receptor cells (photoreceptors) known as **rods** and **cones** which are responsible for detecting light. The rods and cones synapse with nerve cells called **bipolar cells**. In accordance with the name "bipolar," these cells have only one axon and one dendrite. The bipolar cells in turn synapse with **ganglion cells**, whose axons comprise the **optic nerve**, which travels from each eye toward the occipital lobe of the brain where complex analysis of a visual image occurs. In Figure 16, you may notice that light has to pass through two layers of neurons before it can reach the rods and cones. The neurons are fine enough to not significantly obstruct incoming rays.

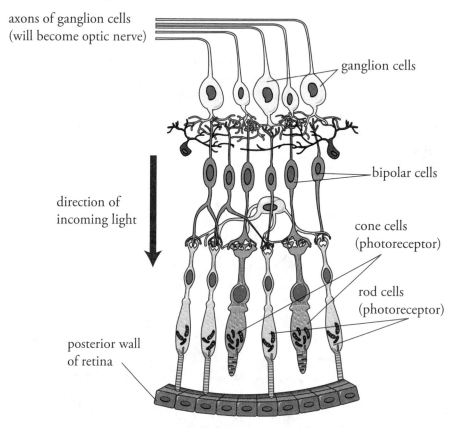

Figure 16 Organization of the Retina

The point on the retina where many axons from ganglion cells converge to form the optic nerve is the **optic disk**. It is also known as the **blind spot** (Figure 17) because it contains no photoreceptors. Another special region of the retina is the **macula**. In the center of the macula is the **fovea centralis** (focal point), which contains only cones and is responsible for extreme visual acuity. When you stare directly at something, you focus its image on the fovea.

A ● ● B

Cover your left eye and focus your right eye on dot A while holding the page about 5 inches away from your face. Move the page forward and back. You will find that at a certain distance, dot B becomes invisible. You are placing dot A on the fovea by focusing on it, and at the correct distance, dot B becomes focused on the blind spot.

Figure 17 Demonstrating the Blind Spot

The Photoreceptors: Rods and Cones

Rods and cones, named because of their shapes, contain special pigment proteins that change their tertiary structure upon absorbing light. Each protein, called an opsin, is bound to one molecule and contains one molecule of **retinal**, which is derived from vitamin A. In the dark, when the rods and cones are resting, retinal has several *trans* double bonds and one *cis* double bond. In this conformation, retinal and its associated opsin keep a sodium channel open. The cell remains depolarized. Upon absorbing a photon of light, retinal is converted to the **all-trans form**. This triggers a series of reactions that ultimately closes the sodium channel, and the cell hyperpolarizes.

Rods and cones synapse on bipolar cells. Because of their depolarization in the dark, both types of photoreceptors release the neurotransmitter **glutamate** onto the bipolar cells, inhibiting them from firing. Upon the absorption of a photon of light and subsequent hyperpolarization, the photoreceptor stops releasing glutamate. Because glutamate has an inhibitory effect on the bipolar cells, when glutamate is no longer present, the bipolar cell can depolarize (removal of inhibition causes excitation in this system). This then causes depolarization of the ganglion cells, and an action potential along the axon of the ganglion cell. All of the axons of the ganglion cells together make up the optic nerve to the brain.

Night vision is accomplished by the rods, which are more sensitive to dim light and motion, and are more concentrated in the periphery of the retina. Cones require abundant light and are responsible for color vision and high-acuity vision, and hence are more concentrated in the fovea.[36] Color vision depends on the presence of three different types of cones. One is specialized to absorb blue light, one absorbs green, and one absorbs red. [What physical difference allows this functional difference?[37]] The brain perceives hues by integrating the relative input of these three basic stimuli.

—

[36] Remember: *Cones—Color—aCuity.*

[37] Each type of cone makes a particular pigment protein which is specialized to change conformation when light of the appropriate frequency strikes it.

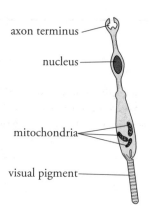

Figure 18   Rod Cell Structure

Defects in Visual Acuity

Normal vision is termed **emmetropia**. Too much or too little curvature of the cornea or lens results in visual defects. Too much curvature causes light to be bent too much and to be focused in front of the retina. The result is **myopia**, or nearsightedness. Myopia can be corrected by a concave (diverging) lens, which will cause the light rays to diverge slightly before they reach the cornea. **Hyperopia**, farsightedness, results from the focusing of light behind the retina. Hyperopia can be corrected by a convex (converging) lens, which causes light rays to converge before reaching the cornea. **Presbyopia** is an inability to **accommodate** (focus). It results from loss of flexibility of the lens, which occurs with aging.

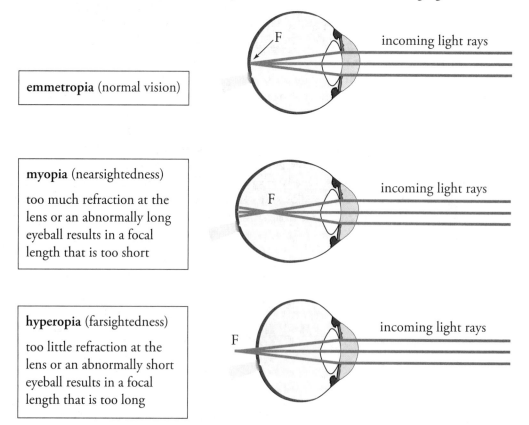

Figure 19   Defects in Visual Acuity ("F" denotes the focal point)

Vision: Information Processing and Perception

For humans, vision is the primary sense; even if other information (such as sound or smell) counters visual information, we are more likely to "believe our eyes." The processing of visual information is extremely complex, and highly reliant on expectations and past experience. Neurons in the **visual cortex** fire in response to very specific information; feature detecting neurons are specific neurons in the brain that fire in response to particular visual features, such as lines, edges, angles, and movement. This information is then passed along to other neurons that begin to assimilate these distinct features into more complex objects, and so on. Therefore, **feature-detection theory** explains why a certain area of the brain is activated when looking at a face, a different area is activated when looking at the letters on this page, etc. In order to process vast amounts of visual information quickly and effectively, our brain employs **parallel processing**, whereby many aspects of a visual stimulus (such as form, motion, color, and depth) are processed simultaneously instead of in a step-by-step or serial fashion. [Note: parallel processing is also employed for other stimuli as well.] The occipital lobe constructs a holistic image by integrating all of the separate elements of an object, in addition to accessing stored information. For example, the brain is simultaneously processing the individual features of an image, while also accessing stored information, to rapidly come to the conclusion that you are not only viewing a face, but you are specifically viewing your mom's face. All of this requires a tremendous amount of resources; in fact, the human brain dedicates approximately 30% of the cortex to processing visual information, while only 8% is devoted to processing touch information, and a mere 3% processes auditory information!

Depth perception describes the ability to see objects in three dimensions despite the fact that images are imposed on the retina in only two dimensions. Depth perception allows us to judge distance, oftentimes with amazing accuracy. Experiments conducted on babies using something called a visual cliff demonstrate that depth perception appears to be largely innate. For these visual cliff experiments, babies were placed on a clear glass surface above a steep drop-off (Figure 20). The glass surface would allow the baby to safely crawl over the seep drop to their mother, but most babies would not venture out over the visual cliff, indicating that their depth perception was developed enough to understand that the drop was dangerous.

Figure 20   Visual Cliff Experiments Show Depth Perception is Innate

Binocular cues and monocular cues are responsible for our ability to perceive depth and distance. **Binocular cues** are depth cues that depend on information received from both eyes and are most important for perceiving depth when objects are close to us in our visual field. **Retinal disparity** is a binocular cue whereby the brain compares the images projected onto the two retinas in order to perceive distance. The greater the difference or disparity between the two images on each retina, the shorter the distance to the observer. For example, suppose you are looking at a tree far in the distance, and hold your thumb about 18 inches in front of your face (feel free to try this!). When you focus on the tree far in the distance (or any object farther away than your thumb), your thumb appears to "double" (you see two sort of see-through versions of your thumb while you focus on the object farther from you). These two versions of your thumb are the two different images from each retina. If you move your thumb farther from your face (while still focusing past it), the two images of your thumb get closer together. If you move your thumb closer to your face, the two images get farther apart. Now focus on your thumb. Your brain is still receiving two disparate representations of your thumb from each retina, but now it converses these two representations into one, and also provides information about how far your thumb is from your face. This is how retinal disparity works. Farther images have less disparity (the images from each retina are more similar, indicating to your brain that the object is farther away), while closer images have more disparity, indicating to your brain that they are closer to your face. **Convergence** is another binocular cue that describes the extent to which the eyes turn inward when looking at an object; the greater the angle of convergence or inward strain, the closer the object. In other words, if you hold your thumb right in front of your nose, your eyes have to turn inward a great deal to focus on your thumb (this is known as going "cross-eyed"), which signals to your brain that the object you are focusing on is quite close.

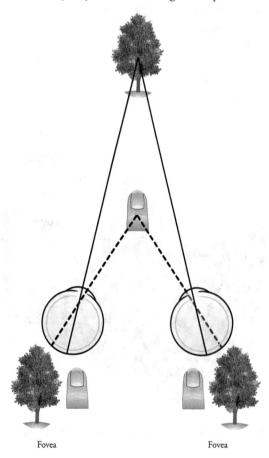

Fovea

Fovea

Figure 21 Retinal Disparity Helps Us to Determine Distance

Monocular Cues are depth cues that depend on information that is available to either eye alone and are important for judging distances of objects that are far from us since the retinal disparity is only slight. Since we cannot rely on binocular cues for objects at farther distances, we rely on any combination of the following monocular cues:

- **Relative Size**: If objects are assumed to be the same size, the one that casts the smaller image on the retina appears more distant. For example, in Figure 22, our brain assumes the elk in the foreground are roughly the same size as those in the background; therefore, since some of the elk are perceived by our retina as smaller, those that are smaller are perceived as farther away than those elk that are perceived by our retina as larger.
- **Interposition**: If one object blocks the view of another, we perceive it as closer. In Figure 22, the horns of the elk in the foreground partially obscure the elk in the immediate background (and the elk in the immediate background is partially obscuring elk in the more distant background and so on); therefore, the elk that are partially blocking the view of other elk are perceived by our brains as closer.
- **Relative Clarity**: We perceive hazy objects as being more distant than sharp, clear objects. In Figure 22, the elk in the far background are fuzzier and less sharp than the elk in the foreground; therefore, we perceive the sharper elk as closer and the fuzzier elk as farther away.
- **Texture Gradient**: Change from a coarse, distinct texture to a fine, indistinct texture indicates increasing distance. In Figure 23, the poppies in the foreground appear as distant flowers, but those in the background begin to sort of blend in together until it looks like a continuous stretch of red. The distant poppies are perceived as closer and the indistinct poppies that all blend into a stretch of red are perceived as farther away.
- **Relative Height**: We perceive objects that are higher in the visual field as farther away. In Figure 23, the red area of poppies higher in the visual field (and on the hill) are perceived as farther away than the poppies at the bottom of the visual field.
- **Relative Motion**: As we move, stable objects appear to move as well. Objects that are near to us appear to move faster than objects that are farther away. This is easily demonstrated whenever you are in a car or train—the farther away something is on the horizon, the slower it moves past you, while nearby objects fly past. This difference in motion cues our brains that the objects moving quickly by are close while those moving by more slowly are farther away.
- **Linear Perspective**: Parallel lines appear to converge as distance increases. The greater the convergence, the greater the perceived distance. This is seen in Figure 24, where the parallel lines of the rail tracks appear to get closer together, which signals out brains that as the lines converge, the distance increases.
- **Light and Shadow**: Closer objects reflect more light than distant objects. The dimmer of two identical objects will seem farther away. In Figure 24, the closer rail tracks are brighter than the more distant tracks, signaling our brains that the brighter tracks are closer while the dimmer tracks are farther away.

3.5

Figure 22

Figure 23

Figure 24

Modality	Receptor	Receptor type	Organ	Stimulus
Vision	• rods and cones	• electromagnetic	• retina	• light
Hearing	• auditory hair cells	• mechanoreceptor	• organ of Corti	• vibration
Olfaction	• olfactory nerve endings	• chemoreceptor	• individual neurons	• airborne chemicals
Taste	• taste cells	• chemoreceptor	• taste bud	• food chemicals
Touch (a few examples)	• Pacinian corpuscules • free nerve endings • temperature receptors	• mechanoreceptor • nociceptor • thermoreceptor	• skin	• pressure • pain • temperature
Interoception (two examples)	• aortic arch baroreceptors • pH receptors	• baroreceptor • chemoreceptor	• aortic arch • aortic arch / medulla oblongata	• blood pressure • pH

Table 5   Summary of Sensory Modalities

3.5

Perception

Absolute Thresholds

We are very sensitive to certain types of stimuli. The minimum stimulus intensity required to activate a sensory receptor 50% of the time (and thus detect the sensation) is called the **absolute threshold**. In other words, for each special sense, the 50% recognition point defines the absolute threshold. (Note that this threshold can vary between individuals and different organisms—the absolute smell threshold for a human and a dog differs greatly.) Absolute thresholds also vary with age. For example, as we age, we gradually lose our ability to detect higher-pitched sounds. [What is the anatomical reason for this?[38]]

Difference Thresholds

Absolute thresholds are important for detecting the presence or absence of stimuli, but the ability to determine the change or difference in stimuli is also vital. The **difference threshold** (also called the *just noticeable difference*, or JND) is the minimum noticeable difference between any two sensory stimuli, 50% of the time. The magnitude of the initial stimulus influences the difference threshold; for example, if you lift a one pound weight and a two pound weight, the difference will be obvious, but if you lift a 100 pound weight and 101 pound weight, you probably won't be able to tell the difference. Indeed, **Weber's law** dictates that two stimuli must differ by a constant *proportion* in order for their difference to be perceptible. Interestingly, the exact proportion varies by stimulus; but for humans, two objects must differ in weight by 2% [in the weight example above, what is the minimum weight needed to detect a difference between it and the 100 pound weight?[39]], two lights must differ in intensity by 8%, and two tones must differ in frequency by 0.3%.

Signal Detection Theory

Detecting sensory stimuli not only depends on the information itself, but also on our psychological state, including alertness, expectation, motivation, and prior experience. **Signal detection theory** attempts to predict how and when someone will detect the presence of a given sensory stimulus (the "signal") amidst all of the other sensory stimuli in the background (considered the "noise"). There are four possible outcomes: a hit (the signal is present and was detected), a miss (the signal was present but not detected), a false alarm (the signal was not present but the person thought it was), and a correct rejection (the signal was not present and the person did not think it was). Signal detection can have important life-or-death consequences—imagine how crucial it is for doctors to be able to detect the signal (perhaps a tumor on a CT scan) from the noise.

Gestalt Psychology

Gestalt is the German word for "form" or "shape," and has come to mean, in English, an organized whole perceived as more than the sum of its individual parts. Therefore, in psychology, gestalt refers to the idea that the whole exceeds the sum of its parts; in other words, when humans perceive an object, rather than seeing lines, angles, colors, and shadows, they perceive the whole—a face or a table or a dog. Importantly, gestalt does not explain *how* the brain is able to perceive in such a way, merely that it does. There are many different gestalt principles to explain perceptual organization; below the most common are covered. (Note that gestalt principles can be applied to any sensory modality, but they are most often described using visual perception examples, as we have here).

---

[38] Loud sounds can mechanically harm the hair cells, causing them to die. When this occurs, the hair cell can no longer send sound signals to the brain. In people, once a hair cell dies, it will never regrow. The hair cells that detect higher frequency sounds are the smallest and the most easily damaged; therefore, as people age and more hair cells are damaged and lost, hearing loss occurs. Since the smallest hair cells are the ones most likely lost, loss of sensitivity to high-pitched sounds is common in older people.

[39] 102 pounds, which is 2% heavier than 100 pounds.

Emergence. Look at the image in Figure 25. This is essentially a series of black irregular shapes on a white background. Those are the individual *parts* of the image. However, the whole that our brain perceives is a dog. You did not recognize the dog by first identifying its parts and constructing the whole ("there is the nose, there is the collar, there is a leg, this must be a dog!"), rather, the dog appears as a whole, all at once—it sort of pops out at you. This is an example of the gestalt principle of emergence. According to this gestalt principle, when attempting to identify an object, we first identify its outline, which then allows us to figure out what the object is. Only after the whole emerges do we start to identify the parts that make up the whole, such as the dog's face, legs, or the chain attached to his collar in Figure 25.

3.5

Figure 25

Figure/Ground. This gestalt principle describes our perceptual tendency to separate the figure or object from everything else (the background) based on a number of possible variables, like size, shadow, contrast, color, etc. According to this principle, everything that is not figure is ground. Consider the image in Figure 26; you have probably seen the very common face/vase optical illusion before. As your attention shifts from the faces to the vase, the ground also shifts from the white part to the black part of the image. In simple images, the figure and ground are usually static, but our brains are also capable of perceiving when an object shifts from figure to ground and then back again. This principle helps explain why it is nearly impossible to perceive both a vase and two faces simultaneously—you brain needs to focus on one or the other and make the rest background.

Figure 26

Multistability. The image in Figure 26 is also a great example of the gestalt principle of multistability or multistable perception, which is the tendency of ambiguous images to pop back and forth unstably between alternative interpretations in our brains. Other examples include the images of two impossible objects in Figure 27. Again, gestalt does not explain *how* images appear multistable, only that they *do*.

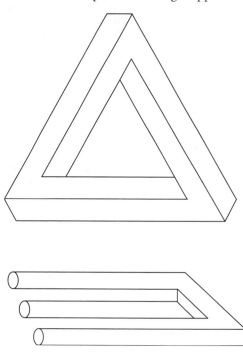

Figure 27

Gestalt Laws of Grouping. There are also several gestalt grouping laws meant to help explain how we tend to perceive things. While there are more than five laws, the five most common are discussed here. The **law of proximity** suggests that things that are near each other seem to be grouped together. Nearby objects tend to be perceived as a unit or group (see A in Figure 28: do you perceive 25 individual dots, or a square composed of dots? The law of proximity predicts that you perceive a square composed of dots). The law of similarity suggests that things that are similar tend to appear grouped together. In other words, we tend to perceive similar items as a unit or group (see B in Figure 28 below: what do you see? According to the law of similarity, you are likely to perceive the columns as important, and will perceive columns composed of circles and squares). The **law of continuity** (also known as the law of good continuation) suggests that points that we perceive the smooth, continuous lines and forms, rather than disjoined one. For example, in Figure 28, the law of continuity predicts that we will perceive the image in C as two overlapping circles, rather than two black semicircular lines and a red football shape in the middle. Even though the lines are different colors, we still tend to perceive the lines as continuous, forming two circles. The gestalt **law of closure** predicts that we will perceive things as complete a logical entity, because our brains will fill in the gaps in the information. For example, what do you see in D in Figure 28? The law of closure predicts that you will perceive a triangle! The **gestalt law of common fate** predicts that objects moving in the same direction or moving in synchrony are perceived as a group or unit. This applies to things like a group of dancers moving in unison or a flock of birds all moving together (like E in Figure 28). The gestalt **law of connectedness** predicts that things that are joined or linked or grouped are perceived as connected. In Figure 28, F shows the same set of circles in the shape of a square as in A, but the box around some of those circles connects them in our brains. The law of connectedness predicts that we are likely to perceive those nine circles are connected and differentiated from the rest.

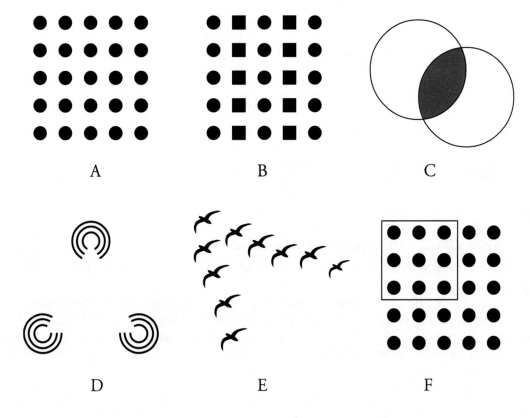

A   B   C

D   E   F

Figure 28

If a lot of these gestalt principles and laws seem similar to you, it is because there is a fair amount of overlap (it doesn't help that they are described as either principles or laws by different sources, called by multiple different names, and similar images can be used as examples for many different concepts!). Therefore, familiarize yourself with the basic principles here and try not to get too wrapped up in differentiating between each individual law or principle—our visual perception is the result of many of these principles or laws working simultaneously!

Perceptual Processing

Bottom-up processing begins with the sensory receptors and works up to the complex integration of information occurring in the brain. Bottom-up processing is also known as data-driven processing; information enters the eyes in one direction (this sensory input is the "bottom"), and is then turned into an identifiable image by the brain (this final image is the "top"). We tend to use more of a bottom-up approach when we have no or little prior experience with a stimulus. **Top-down processing** occurs when the brain applies experience and expectations to interpret sensory information. Instead of focusing on the sensory input (the "bottom"), we can use our prior experience and knowledge to impose our expectations on the stimulus, which tends to occur with stimuli we are more familiar with. Note that the brain in fact uses a combination of the two: information is received in a bottom-up fashion from sensory receptors while the brain is superimposing assumptions in a top-down manner.

3.6   THE ENDOCRINE SYSTEM

The nervous system and endocrine system represent the two major control systems of the body. The nervous system is fast-acting with relatively short-term effects, whereas the endocrine system takes longer to communicate signals but has generally longer lasting effects. These two control systems are interconnected, as neurons can signal the release of hormones from endocrine glands. [What is one such connection in the sympathetic nervous system?[40]] A primary connection between the nervous and endocrine systems is the *hypothalamic-pituitary axis*, which is described in more detail below.

Hormone Types: Transport and Mechanisms of Action

While the nervous system regulates cellular function from instant to instant, the endocrine system regulates physiology (especially metabolism) over a period of hours to days. The nervous system communicates via the extremely rapid action potential. The signal of the endocrine system is the **hormone**, defined as a molecule which is *secreted into the bloodstream* by an endocrine gland, and which has its effects upon *distant* target cells possessing the appropriate receptor. An **endocrine gland** is a *ductless* gland whose secretory products are picked up by capillaries supplying blood to the region. (In contrast, **exocrine glands** secrete their products into the external environment by way of ducts, which empty into the gastrointestinal lumen or the external world.) A **hormone receptor** is a polypeptide that possesses a ligand-specific binding site. Binding of ligand (hormone) to the site causes the receptor to modify target cell activity. *Tissue-specificity of hormone action is determined by whether the cells of a tissue have the appropriate receptor.*

---

[40] The sympathetic nervous system directly innervates the adrenal medulla to stimulate the release of epinephrine.

Some signaling molecules modify the activity of the cell which secreted them; this is an **autocrine** activity (*auto-* means self). For example, a T cell secretes interleukin 2, which binds to receptors on the same T cell to stimulate increased activity.

Hormones can be grouped into one of two classes. *Hydrophilic* hormones, such as **peptides** and **amino-acid derivatives**, must bind to receptors on the cell surface, while *hydrophobic* hormones, such as the **steroid hormones**, bind to receptors in the cellular interior.

Peptide Hormones
Peptide hormones are synthesized in the rough ER and modified in the Golgi. Then they are stored in vesicles until needed, when they are released by exocytosis. In the bloodstream they dissolve in the plasma, since they are hydrophilic. Their hydrophilicity also means they cannot cross biological membranes and thus are required to communicate with the interior of the target cell by way of a ___[41]. To briefly review, the peptide hormone is a first messenger which must bind to a cell-surface receptor. The receptor is a polypeptide with a domain on the inner surface of the plasma membrane that contains the ability to catalytically activate a second messenger. The end result of second messenger activation is that the function of proteins in the cytoplasm is changed. A key feature of second messenger cascades is signal amplification, which allows a few activated receptors to change the activity of many enzymes in the cytoplasm.

Because peptide hormones modify the activity of existing enzymes in the cytoplasm, their effects are exerted rapidly, minutes to hours from the time of secretion. Also, the duration of their effects is brief.

There are two subgroups within the peptide hormone category: polypeptides and amino acid derivatives. An example of a polypeptide hormone is insulin, which has a complex tertiary structure involving disulfide bridges. It is secreted by the β cells of the pancreatic islets of Langerhans in response to elevated blood glucose and binds to a cell-surface receptor with a cytoplasmic domain possessing protein kinase activity. Amino acid derivatives, as their name implies, are derived from single amino acids and contain no peptide bonds. For example, tyrosine is the parent amino acid for the catecholamines (which include epinephrine) and the thyroid hormones. Despite the fact that these two classes are derived from the same precursor molecule, they have different properties. The catecholamines act like peptide hormones, while the thyroid hormones behave more like steroid hormones. Epinephrine is a small cyclic molecule secreted by the adrenal medulla upon activation of the sympathetic nervous system. It binds to cell-surface receptors to trigger a cascade of events that produces the second messenger cyclic adenosine monophosphate (cAMP) and activates protein kinases in the cytoplasm. Thyroid hormones incorporate iodine into their structure. They enter cells, bind to DNA, and activate transcription of genes involved in energy mobilization.

Steroid Hormones
Steroids are hydrophobic molecules synthesized from cholesterol in the smooth endoplasmic reticulum. Due to their hydrophobicity, steroids can freely diffuse through biological membranes. Thus they are not stored but rather diffuse into the bloodstream as soon as they are made. If a steroid hormone is not needed, it will not be made. Steroids' hydrophobicity also means they cannot be dissolved in the plasma. Instead they journey through the bloodstream stuck to proteins in the plasma, such as albumin. [What holds the steroid bound to a plasma protein?[42]] The small, hydrophobic steroid hormone exerts its effects upon target cells by *diffusing through the plasma membrane to bind with a receptor in the cytoplasm*. Once it has bound its ligand, the steroid hormone-receptor complex is transported into the nucleus, where it acts as a sequence-specific regulator of transcription. Because steroid hormones must modify transcription to

---

[41] second messenger cascade

[42] No bond—just hydrophobic interactions

change the *amount* and/or *type* of proteins in the cell, their effects are exerted slowly, over a period of days, and persist for days to weeks.

Steroids regulating sexuality, reproduction, and development are secreted by the testes, ovaries, and placenta. Steroids regulating water balance and other processes are secreted by the adrenal cortex. All other endocrine glands secrete peptide hormones. (Note that although thyroid hormone is derived from an amino acid, its mechanism of action more closely resembles that of the steroid hormones.)

	Peptides	Steroids
Structure	hydrophilic, large (polypeptides) or small (amino acid derivatives)	hydrophobic, small
Site of synthesis	rough ER	smooth ER
Regulation of release	stored in vesicles until a signal for secretion is received	synthesized only when needed and then used immediately, not stored
Transport in bloodstream	free	stuck to protein carrier
Specificity	only target cells have appropriate surface receptors (exception: thyroxine = cytoplasmic)	only target cells have appropriate cytoplasmic receptors
Mechanism of effect	bind to receptors that generate second messengers which result in modification of *enzyme activity*	bind to receptors that alter *gene expression* by regulating DNA transcription
Timing of effect	rapid, short-lived	slow, long-lasting

Table 6 Peptide vs. Steroid Hormones

Organization and Regulation of the Human Endocrine System

The endocrine system has many different roles. Hormones are essential for gamete synthesis, ovulation, pregnancy, growth, sexual development, and overall level of metabolic activity. Despite this diversity of function, endocrine activity is harmoniously orchestrated. Maintenance of order in such a complex system might seem impossible to accomplish in a preplanned manner. Regulation of the endocrine system is not preplanned or rigidly structured, but is instead generally automatic. Hormone levels rise and fall as dictated by physiological needs. The endocrine system is ordered yet dynamic. This flexible, automatic orderliness is attributable to feedback regulation. The amount of a hormone secreted is controlled not by a preformulated plan but rather by changes in the variable the hormone is responsible for controlling. Continuous circulation of blood exposes target cells to regulatory hormones and also exposes endocrine glands to serum concentrations of physiological variables that they regulate. Thus *regulator* and that which is *regulated* are in continuous communication. Concentration of a species X in the aqueous portion of the bloodstream is denoted "serum [X]."

An example of feedback regulation is the interaction between the hormone calcitonin and serum [Ca^{2+}]. The function of calcitonin is to prevent serum [Ca^{2+}] from peaking above normal levels, and the amount of calcitonin secreted is directly proportional to increases in serum [Ca^{2+}] above normal. When serum

[Ca^{2+}] becomes elevated, calcitonin is secreted. Then when serum [Ca^{2+}] levels fall, calcitonin secretion stops. The falling serum [Ca^{2+}] level (*that which is regulated*) feeds back to the cells which secrete calcitonin (*regulators*). The serum [Ca^{2+}] level is a **physiological endpoint** which must be maintained at constant levels. This demonstrates the role of the endocrine system in maintaining **homeostasis**, or physiological consistency.

An advantage of the endocrine system and its feedback regulation is that very complex arrays of variables can be controlled automatically. It's as if the variables controlled themselves. However, some integration (a central control mechanism) is necessary. Superimposed upon the hormonal regulation of physiological endpoints is another layer of regulation: hormones that regulate hormones. Such meta-regulators are known as **tropic hormones**.

3.6

For example, adrenocorticotropic hormone (ACTH) is secreted by the anterior pituitary. The role of ACTH is to stimulate increased activity of the portion of the adrenal gland called the **cortex**, which is responsible for secreting cortisol (among other steroid hormones). ACTH is a tropic hormone because it does not directly affect physiological endpoints, but merely regulates another regulator (cortisol). Cortisol regulates physiological endpoints, including cellular responses to stress and serum [glucose]. Feedback regulation applies to tropic hormones as well as to direct regulators of physiological endpoints; the level of ACTH is influenced by the level of cortisol. When cortisol is needed, ACTH is secreted, and when the serum [cortisol] increases sufficiently, ACTH secretion slows.

You may have noticed that in both of our examples the effect of feedback was *inhibitory*: The result of hormone secretion inhibits further secretion. Inhibitory feedback is called **negative feedback** or **feedback inhibition**. Most feedback in the endocrine system (and if you remember, most biochemical feedback) is negative. There are few examples of positive feedback which we will not discuss here.

There is yet another layer of control. Many of the functions of the endocrine system depend on instructions from the brain. The portion of the brain which controls much of the endocrine system is the **hypothalamus**, located at the center of the brain. The hypothalamus controls the endocrine system by releasing tropic hormones that regulate other tropic hormones, called **releasing and inhibiting factors** or **releasing and inhibiting hormones**.

For example (Figure 29), the hypothalamus secretes corticotropin releasing hormone (CRH, also known as CRF, where "F" stands for factor). The role of CRH is to cause increased secretion of ACTH. Just as ACTH secretion is regulated by feedback inhibition from cortisol, CRH secretion, too, is inhibited by cortisol. You begin to see that regulatory pathways in the endocrine system can get pretty complex.

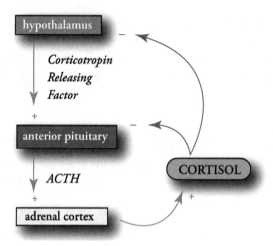

Figure 29   Feedback Regulation of Cortisol Secretion

Understanding that the hypothalamus controls the anterior pituitary and that the anterior pituitary controls most of the endocrine system is important. Damage to the connection between the hypothalamus and the pituitary is fatal, unless daily hormone replacement therapy is given. This endocrine control center is given a special name: **hypothalamic-pituitary control axis** (Figure 30). The hypothalamus exerts its control of the pituitary by secreting its hormones into the bloodstream, just like any other endocrine gland; what's unique is that a special miniature circulatory system is provided for efficient transport of hypothalamic releasing and inhibiting factors to the anterior pituitary. This blood supply is known as the **hypothalamic-pituitary portal system**. You will also hear the term *hypothalamic-hypophysial portal system*. **Hypophysis** is another name for the pituitary gland.

A Note on Portal Systems: As a general rule, blood leaving the heart moves through only one capillary bed before returning to the heart, since the pressure drops substantially in capillaries. A portal system, however, consists of two capillary beds in sequence, allowing for direct communication between nearby structures. The two portal systems you need to understand are: the hypothalamic-pituitary portal system and the hepatic portal system (from the gastrointestinal tract to the liver).

One more bit of background information is necessary before we can delve into specific hormones. The pituitary gland has two halves: front (*anterior*) and back (*posterior*); see Figure 30. The **anterior pituitary** is also called the **adenohypophysis** and the **posterior pituitary** is also known as the **neurohypophysis**. It is important to understand the difference. The anterior pituitary is a normal endocrine gland, and it is controlled by hypothalamic releasing and inhibiting factors (essentially tropic hormones). The posterior pituitary is composed of axons which descend from the hypothalamus. These hypothalamic neurons that send axons down to the posterior pituitary are an example of **neuroendocrine cells**, neurons which secrete hormones into the bloodstream. The hormones of the posterior pituitary are ADH (antidiuretic hormone or vasopressin), which causes the kidney to retain water during times of thirst, and oxytocin, which causes milk let-down for nursing as well as uterine contractions during labor. [Are these hormones made by axon termini in the posterior pituitary or by somas in the hypothalamus?[43]]

---

[43] All hypothalamic and pituitary hormones are peptides, and there is no protein synthesis at axon termini. Hence, ADH and oxytocin must be made in nerve cell bodies in the hypothalamus and transported down the axons to the posterior pituitary.

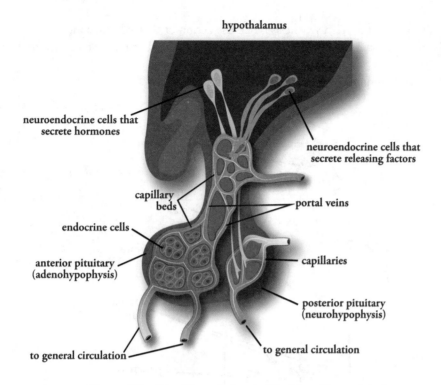

Figure 30 The Hypothalamic-Pituitary Control Axis

Major Glands and Their Hormones

The major hormones and glands of the endocrine system are listed in Table 7. Many of these hormones will be discussed in detail in the MCAT Biology Review. The function of epinephrine has already been presented as part of the sympathetic nervous system response. In general, the hormones are involved in development of the body and in maintenance of constant conditions, homeostasis, in the adult. [Is epinephrine secreted by a duct into the bloodstream?[44]]

Thyroid hormone and **cortisol** have broad effects on metabolism and energy usage. Thyroid hormone is produced from the amino acid tyrosine in the thyroid gland and comes in two forms, with three or four iodine atoms per molecule. The production of thyroid hormone is increased by thyroid stimulating hormone (TSH) from the anterior pituitary, which is regulated by the hypothalamus and the central nervous system in turn. The mechanism of action of thyroid hormone is to bind to a receptor in the cytoplasm of cells that then regulates transcription in the nucleus. The effect of this regulation is to increase the overall metabolic rate and body temperature, and, in children, to stimulate growth. Exposure to cold can increase the production of thyroid hormone. Cortisol is secreted by the adrenal cortex in response to ACTH from the pituitary. In general, the effects of cortisol tend to help the body deal with stress. Cortisol helps to mobilize glycogen and fat stores to provide energy during stress and also increases the consumption of proteins for energy. These effects are essential, since removal of the adrenal cortex can result in the death of animals exposed to even a small stress. Long-term high levels of cortisol tend to have negative effects, however, including suppression of the immune system.

---

[44] No. Endocrine hormones are not secreted through ducts.

- Would an inhibitor of protein synthesis block the action of thyroid hormone?[45]
- Would the production of ATP by mitochondria be stimulated or repressed by thyroid hormone?[46]
- Would thyroid hormone affect isolated mitochondria directly?[47]

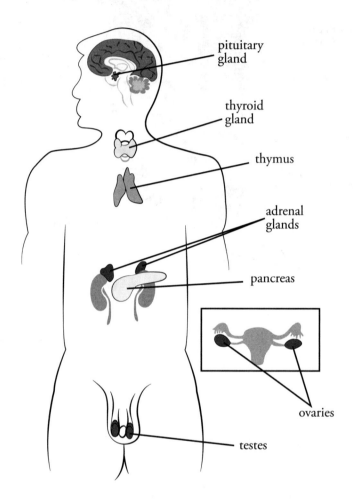

Figure 31   The Major Endocrine Glands

---

[45] Yes. Thyroid hormone binds to a receptor that regulates transcription. The mRNA stimulated by thyroid hormone receptor in the nucleus must be processed and translated before the effects of thyroid hormone can become evident.

[46] Thyroid hormone stimulates the basal metabolic rate throughout the body. More ATP will be consumed, so the mitochondria are stimulated to make more ATP.

[47] No. Thyroid hormone affects mitochondria *indirectly*, through the regulation of nuclear genes.

Gland	Hormone (class)	Target/effect
Hypothalamus	releasing and inhibiting factors (peptides)	anterior pituitary/modify activity
Anterior pituitary	growth hormone (GH) (peptide)	↑ bone & muscle growth, ↑ cell turnover rate
	prolactin (peptide)	mammary gland/milk production
tropic	thyroid stimulating hormone (TSH) (peptide)	thyroid/↑ synthesis & release of TH
	adrenocorticotropic hormone (ACTH) (peptide)	↑ growth & secretory activity of adrenal ctx
gonadotropic	luteinizing hormone (LH) (peptide)	ovary/ovulation, testes/testosterone synth.
	follicle stimulating hormone (FSH) (peptide)	ovary/follicle development, testes/ spermatogenesis
Posterior pituitary	antidiuretic hormone (ADH, vasopressin) (peptide)	kidney/water retention
	oxytocin (peptide)	breast/milk letdown, uterus/contraction
Thyroid	thyroid hormone (TH, thyroxine) (modified amino acid)	child: necessary for physical & mental development; adult: ↑ metabolic rate & temp.
thyroid C cells	calcitonin (peptide)	bone, kidney; lowers serum [Ca^{2+}]
Parathyroids	parathyroid hormone (PTH) (peptide)	bone, kidney, small intestine/raises serum [Ca^{2+}]
Thymus	thymosin (children only) (peptide)	T cell development during childhood
Adrenal medulla	epinephrine (modified amino acid)	sympathetic stress response (rapid)
Adrenal cortex	cortisol ("glucocorticoid") (steroid)	longer-term stress response; ↑ blood [glucose]; ↑ protein catabolism; ↓ inflammation & immunity; many other
	aldosterone ("mineralocorticoid") (steroid)	kidney/↑ Na+ reabsorption to ↑ b.p.
	sex steroids	not normally important, but an adrenal tumor can overproduce these, causing masculinization or feminization
Endocrine pancreas (islets of Langerhans)	insulin (β cells secrete) (peptide) —absent or ineffective in diabetes mellitus	↓ blood [glucose]/↑ glycogen & fat storage
	glucagon (α cells secrete) (peptide)	↑ blood [glucose]/↓ glycogen & fat storage
	somatostatin (SS—δ cells secrete) (peptide)	inhibits many digestive processes
Testes	testosterone (steroid)	male characteristics, spermatogenesis
Ovaries/placenta	estrogen (steroid)	female characteristics, endometrial growth
	progesterone (steroid)	endometrial secretion, pregnancy
Heart	atrial natriuretic factor (ANF) (peptide)	kidney/↑ urination to ↓ blood pressure
Kidney	erythropoietin (peptide)	bone marrow/↑ RBC synthesis

3.6

Table 7 Summary of the Hormones of the Endocrine System

Chapter 3 Summary

- The neuron is the basic structural and functional unit of the nervous system. It has several specialized structures that allow it to transmit action potentials.

- Neurons receive incoming information via dendrites. Signals are summed by the axon hillock, and if the signal is greater than the threshold, an action potential is initiated.

- The action potential is an all-or-none signal that includes depolarization (via voltage-gated sodium channels) and repolarization (via voltage-gated potassium channels); it begins and ends at the cell's resting potential of −70 mV.

- Since action potentials are all-or-none events, intensity is coded by the frequency of the action potential.

- Neurons communicate with other neurons, organs, and glands at synapses. Most synapses are chemical in nature; an action potential causes the release of neurotransmitter into the synaptic cleft, and binding of the neurotransmitter to receptors on the postsynaptic cell triggers a change, either stimulatory or inhibitory, in that cell.

- The central nervous system includes the spinal cord and the brain; specialized areas control specific aspects of human behavior, movement, intelligence, emotion, and reflexes.

- The peripheral nervous system includes the somatic (voluntary) and autonomic (involuntary) subdivisions.

- The sympathetic branch of the autonomic system controls our fight-or-flight response; norepinephrine is the primary neurotransmitter of this system, and it is augmented by epinephrine from the adrenal medulla.

- The parasympathetic branch of the autonomic system controls our resting and digesting state; acetylcholine is the primary neurotransmitter of this system.

- Humans have several types of receptors (mechanoreceptors, chemoreceptors, nociceptors, thermoreceptors, electromagnetic receptors, and proprioceptors) that allow us to detect a variety of stimuli.

- Weber's law dictates that two stimuli must differ by a constant proportion in order for their difference to be perceptible.

- Gestalt psychology asserts that when humans perceive an object, rather than seeing lines, angles, colors, and shadows, they perceive the whole, not just the individual parts.

- The endocrine system controls our overall physiology and homeostasis by hormones that travel through the bloodstream. Hormones are released from endocrine glands, travel to distant target tissues via the blood, bind to receptors on target tissues, and exert effects on target cells.

- Peptide hormones are made from amino acids, bind to receptors on the cell surface, and typically affect target cells via second messenger pathways. Effects tend to be rapid and temporary.

- Steroid hormones are derived from cholesterol, bind to receptors in the cytoplasm or nucleus, and bind to DNA to alter transcription. Effects tend to occur more slowly and are more permanent.

CHAPTER 3 FREESTANDING PRACTICE QUESTIONS

1. A demyelinating disorder, such as multiple sclerosis, would cause all of the following symptoms EXCEPT:

A) a reduction of white matter in the central nervous system.
B) increased saltatory conduction.
C) slower propagation of signals along the axon.
D) a deficiency of sensation.

2. Which area of the brain is responsible for coordinating complex motor functions?

A) Frontal lobe
B) Occipital lobe
C) Reticular activating system
D) Cerebellum

3. What structure in the middle ear generates vibrations that match the sound waves striking it?

A) Basilar membrane
B) Tympanic membrane
C) Cochlea
D) Malleus

4. In the human visual pathway, what cell type comprises the bundle of fibers called the optic nerve?

A) Photoreceptors
B) Bipolar cells
C) Ganglion cells
D) Fovea cells

5. All of the following brain areas are associated with the experience of emotion EXCEPT the:

A) temporal lobes.
B) amygdala.
C) hypothalamus.
D) pons.

6. Acetylcholine is stimulatory to which of the following?

I. Skeletal muscle
II. Postganglionic neurons
III. Cardiac muscle

A) I only
B) I and II only
C) II and III only
D) I, II, and III

7. Cortisol has a direct inhibitory effect on:

A) the posterior pituitary.
B) the hypothalamus.
C) the adrenal cortex.
D) glycogen mobilization.

8. Instead of perceiving a series of lines in the figure below, humans perceive two shapes: a circle and a rectangle. What best accounts for this phenomenon?

A) The principles of Gestalt psychology
B) Bottom-up processing
C) Parallel processing
D) Weber's Law

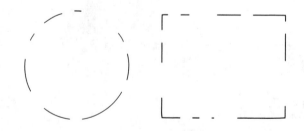

CHAPTER 3 PRACTICE PASSAGE

Long-term potentiation (LTP) involves communication between two neurons and is a major cellular mechanism underlying learning and memory processes. During LTP, a presynaptic neuron releases the neurotransmitter glutamate, which binds to receptors on the postsynaptic neuron. This leads to an influx of sodium, and ultimately calcium, followed by activation of various genes (see Figure 1). The initial receptor activated by glutamate is the AMPA receptor; the NMDA receptor is blocked by extracellular Mg^{2+} that must be displaced by a sufficient change in membrane potential before that channel will fully open.

LTP has been shown to be disrupted in neurodegenerative disorders, such as Alzheimer's disease, leading to memory deficits. In brains of Alzheimer's patients, loss of vital neurons occurs in the hippocampus (a region of the brain involved in memory acquisition). Several mechanisms are hypothesized to lead to this neurodegeneration. One involves calcium-mediated toxicity and occurs due to excessive glutamate-induced neuronal excitation.

Another potential contributing factor to this cell loss is exposure to chronic stress, which results in elevated levels of corticosteroids that can influence neuronal activity in the brain. This has led to the formation of the "Glucocorticoid Hypothesis of Aging." The intact hippocampus has an inhibitory effect on the stress axis (hypothalamic-pituitary-adrenal axis) that is responsible for inducing release of cortisol from the adrenal gland during times of stress. Thus, if the hippocampal region is compromised, it could lead to lack of inhibition of the stress axis and further release of cortisol, causing a feed-forward cycle of excessive release of steroids with each stressful event.

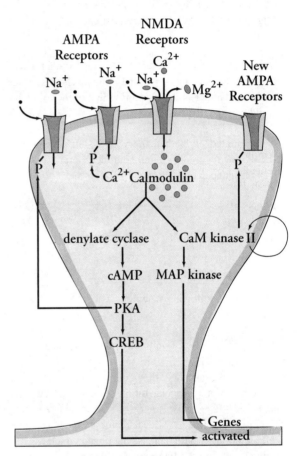

Figure 1 Synaptic Transmission During LTP

1. In which region of the brain is the hippocampus located?

A) Cerebellum
B) Occipital lobe
C) Temporal lobe
D) Hypothalamus

2. One treatment for Alzheimer's disease involves a drug that blocks NMDA receptors. This treatment could lead to all of the following EXCEPT:

A) a suppression of LTP.
B) a suppression of gene expression.
C) a significant decrease in intracellular sodium.
D) a significant decrease in intracellular calcium.

3. A researcher removes the adrenal glands from a rat and then supplements the rat with baseline levels of steroids for the remainder of its lifespan. Which of the following would be expected?

    I.   Blunted sympathetic nervous system response
    II.   Slowing of age-related neurodegeneration
    III.   Enhancement of LTP

A) II only
B) II and III
C) I and II
D) I, II, and III

4. Which of the following statements is LEAST likely to be true?

A) Drugs that increase Cl^- influx into the postsynaptic cell could disrupt LTP.
B) Drugs that increase K^+ efflux from the postsynaptic cell would result in hyperpolarization of the cell and would increase LTP.
C) The insertion of new AMPA receptors in the postsynaptic cell membrane would increase the rate at which Mg^{2+} is displaced from NMDA receptors upon subsequent stimulation by glutamate.
D) The influx of Na^+ upon initial stimulation by glutamate depolarizes the postsynaptic cell in order to displace Mg^{2+}.

5. AMPA receptors are found throughout the central nervous system and are comprised of four different subunits. Not all AMPA receptors have all the subunits. If a knockout mouse was made deficient for the gene for one of the AMPA receptor subunits, what would be the expected outcome?

A) An observed deficit only in LTP and the mouse's ability to learn.
B) Altered function in any region containing an AMPA receptor.
C) No change in LTP function due to the NMDA receptor still being present and functional.
D) Altered function and/or compensatory expression of other AMPA receptor subunits in regions with AMPA receptors that lack the affected subunit.

6. Based on Figure 1, what is a logical function of CREB?

A) Interact with the genomic DNA to enhance transcription
B) Interact with RNA to enhance translation
C) Bind ribosomes to enhance transcription
D) Bind RNA polymerase to enhance replication

7. Symptoms of Alzheimer's disease include all of the following EXCEPT:

A) disorientation.
B) forgetfulness.
C) mood swings.
D) slow, uncoordinated fine movements.

SOLUTIONS TO CHAPTER 3 FREESTANDING PRACTICE QUESTIONS

1. **B**   Myelin is an insulating sheath wrapped around the axons of neurons. White matter in the central nervous system is composed of myelinated axons; thus, a reduction in myelination would result in a decrease in white matter (choice A is a symptom and can be eliminated). Gaps in the myelin sheath (called nodes of Ranvier) allow depolarization of the axon and conduction of neuronal signals along the length of the axon. Myelination speeds the movement of the action potential along the length of the axon (choice C would be a symptom and can be eliminated), in a process called saltatory conduction; a reduction in myelination would decrease (not increase) saltatory conduction (choice B is not a symptom and is the correct answer choice). This would decrease sensation, as sensory information from the peripheral nervous system would be hindered from reaching the central nervous system (choice D is a symptom and can be eliminated).

2. **D**   The cerebellum, located behind the pons and below the cerebrum, receives input from the primary motor cortex in the forebrain, and coordinates complex motor function (choice D is correct). The frontal lobe contains the primary motor cortex, which is responsible for initiating movement, but does not coordinate complex motor functions (choice A is wrong). The occipital lobe is responsible for vision (choice B is wrong) and the reticular activating system is responsible for arousal and wakefulness (choice C is wrong).

3. **B**   The tympanic membrane (also known as the eardrum), located in the middle ear, generates vibrations that match the sound waves striking it (choice B is correct). Vibrations generated in the tympanic membrane pass through three small bones—the malleus (the hammer), the incus (anvil), and the stapes (stirrup); these bones magnify the incoming vibrations by focusing them onto a structure known as the oval window (choice D is wrong). Once the vibrations pass through the oval window, they enter the cochlea, a fluid-filled spiral structure in the inner ear (choice C is wrong). The base of the cochlea is lined with a long, fluid-filled duct known as the basilar membrane (choice A is wrong). Sound waves passing along the basilar membrane cause it to move up and down, stimulating hair cells in the organ of Corti. These hair cells, in turn, connect with the acoustic, or auditory nerve.

4. **C**   The axons of ganglion cells in the retina make up the optic nerve, which carries visual information to the brain (choice C is correct). Photoreceptors are specialized cells in the retina that transduce light energy into nerve cell activity; they synapse with bipolar cells, which synapse with ganglion cells, but neither are part of the optic nerve (choices A and B are wrong). The fovea is the area of highest visual acuity and contains a high concentration of cones, which are a type of photoreceptor, and do not comprise the optic nerve (choice D is wrong).

5. **D**   The pons is located below the midbrain and above the medulla oblongata, and connects the brain stem and the cerebellum. Along with the medulla, the pons controls some autonomic functions and plays a role in equilibrium and posture, but is not associated with the experience of emotion (choice D is correct). The amygdala, located in the temporal lobes, is part of the limbic system, and is responsible for processing information about emotion (choices A and B are associated with emotion and can be eliminated). The hypothalamus links the nervous system to the endocrine system, and also plays a role in emotion (choice C is associated with emotion and can be eliminated).

6. **B**   Item I is true: acetylcholine is the neurotransmitter released by motor neurons onto skeletal muscle to cause contraction (choice C can be eliminated). Item II is true: the preganglionic neurons of both the sympathetic and parasympathetic nervous systems release acetylcholine onto the postganglionic neurons, triggering action potentials (choice A can be eliminated). Item III is false: acetylcholine on cardiac muscle is inhibitory and reduces the heart rate (choice D can be eliminated and choice B is correct).

7. **B**   The hypothalamic-pituitary axis (HPA) regulates the release of cortisol via negative feedback. The hypothalamus releases corticotropin releasing hormone (CRH), which stimulates the anterior pituitary to release adrenocorticotropic hormone (ACTH), which in turn stimulates the adrenal cortex to release cortisol. Cortisol then inhibits the hypothalamus from releasing further CRH and the anterior pituitary from releasing more ACTH, thus having an inhibitory effect on both (choice B is correct). The posterior pituitary releases oxytocin and antidiuretic hormone; cortisol does not inhibit the posterior pituitary (choice A is wrong). Additionally, cortisol does not inhibit the adrenal cortex directly, but rather inhibits the hypothalamus and anterior pituitary from releasing the hormone that stimulate the adrenal cortex; thus cortisol has an indirect inhibitory effect on the adrenal cortex (choice C is wrong). Cortisol stimulates glycogen mobilization (choice D is wrong).

8. **A**   Gestalt psychology proposes that humans tend to see objects in their entirety, and our visual processing systems and brain will superimpose larger organization or structure that makes holistic sense. The "shapes" are technically composed of a series of unconnected lines, but according to gestalt psychologists, humans are more likely to use both top-down and bottom-up processing to perceive them as a complete circle or a complete rectangle (choice A is correct). Bottom-up processing begins with the sensory receptors and works up to the complex integration of information occurring in the brain; while bottom-up processing is a requirement of perceiving the lines in the figure, it does not explain why we see two shapes instead of a bunch of unconnected lines (choice B is wrong). Parallel processing refers to the fact that the brain is capable of processing multiple sensory inputs simultaneously and Weber's Law explains how much two stimuli must differ in order for their difference to be perceptible; neither accounts for the phenomenon described in the question stem (choices C and D are wrong).

SOLUTIONS TO CHAPTER 3 PRACTICE PASSAGE

1. **C** The passage states that the hippocampus is involved in memory acquisition; thus, it is likely to be located in the temporal lobe of the cerebrum (choice C is correct). The cerebellum is involved in balance and coordination, not memory (choice A is wrong), the occipital lobe is responsible for vision (choice B is wrong), and the hypothalamus is involved in maintaining homeostasis and hormonal regulation (choice D is wrong).

2. **C** If NMDA receptor activation is necessary for LTP, then blocking this receptor would likely suppress LTP (choice A could occur and can be eliminated). Based on Figure 1, activation of the NMDA receptor triggers an influx of intracellular calcium and a cascade of events resulting in activation of gene expression; thus, blocking this receptor could lead to both a significant decrease in intracellular calcium and a suppression of gene expression (choices B and D could occur and can be eliminated). Since the NMDA receptor allows an influx of sodium, some reduction in intracellular sodium could be expected; however, this is unlikely to be significant since the AMPA receptor would still be functional and is the main source of Na^+ influx (choice C would not occur and is the correct answer choice).

3. **C** Item I is true: The adrenal glands secrete both steroid hormones (from the adrenal cortex) and epinephrine (from the adrenal medulla). If the researcher only replaces the steroids, then the sympathetic response (which relies on epinephrine) could be blunted (choices A and B can be eliminated). Since both remaining answer choices include Item II, then Item II must be true and we only need to evaluate Item III. Item III is false: Based on Figure 1, corticosteroids do not seem to play an integral role in LTP. In addition, the passage only discusses their possible involvement in neuronal cell death at high concentrations. Keeping baseline levels may not lead to cell death, but would not necessarily enhance LTP (choice D can be eliminated and choice C is correct). Note that Item II is in fact true: Based on information in the passage (the Glucocorticoid Aging Hypothesis), stress levels of corticosteroids could lead to age-related neurodegeneration. Thus, if the levels of these hormones are kept at baseline throughout the life of the animal, it is possible to attenuate age-related neurodegeneration.

4. **B** The passage states that the NMDA receptor is blocked by extracellular Mg^{2+} that must be displaced by a sufficient change in membrane potential. It is fair to assume that this change must be a depolarization, since the initial receptor activated is the AMPA receptor, and according to the figure, that receptor allows an influx of Na^+ (choice D is likely to be true and can be eliminated). Additional AMPA receptors would increase the rate of depolarization and thus the rate of Mg^{2+} displacement. This is in fact the basis for LTP; the first stimulation leads to the effects shown in the figure, including new receptors in the membrane, thus the effect of subsequent stimulation is enhanced (choice C is likely to be true and can be eliminated). Anything that would lead to a hyperpolarization of the cell would not displace Mg^{2+} and would disrupt the calcium influx and all associated events, including LTP. An increase of Cl^- influx would hyperpolarize the cell and disrupt LTP (choice A is likely to be true and can be eliminated), but an increase in K^+ efflux, while it would hyperpolarize the cell, would not increase LTP (choice B is unlikely to be true and is the correct answer choice).

5.   **D**   The question states essentially that AMPA receptors can be varied (have variable subunits) and are found throughout the CNS. Certainly if the gene for one of the subunits was deficient, we would expect some deficit to be present. However, because of the widespread location of these receptors, we would not expect the deficit to be limited to only the region of the brain responsible for LTP (choice A is wrong), nor would we expect the deficit to be found in ANY region with receptors, because some regions may have AMPA receptors that do not have the knocked out subunit (choice B is wrong). According to the diagram, the function of both AMPA and NMDA receptors are required during LTP, so if one of the receptors was compromised, we might expect some alteration in LTP function (choice C is wrong). The most likely outcome is that there would be altered function or potentially compensatory expression of other AMPA receptor subunits in those regions of the CNS that contain an affected AMPA receptor (choice D is correct).

6.   **A**   In the diagram, CREB is located immediately before gene activation, which would suggest it has something to do with transcription (choices B and D are wrong). Ribosomes do not have anything to do with transcription (choice C is wrong and choice A is correct). CREB stands for cAMP Response Element Binding and is a transcription factor; thus, it interacts with DNA to enhance transcription.

7.   **D**   Alzheimer's disease involves the loss of vital neurons throughout the cerebral cortex; symptoms include disorientation (choice A can be eliminated), forgetfulness (choice B can be eliminated), mood swings (choice C can be eliminated), and impairment of other cognitive functions like speaking, writing, thinking, reasoning, and making judgments and decisions. As the disease progresses, it can also lead to changes in personality and behavior, depression, and social withdrawal. However, Alzheimer's disease does not affect the ability to produce fine movement (choice D is correct).

Chapter 4
Interacting with the Environment

Organisms interact with their environment by taking in information (sensation) and deciding what information is important while filtering out the rest (attention), making complex decisions about that information (cognition), sometimes in a split-second, and reacting (behavior). Reacting includes a number of complex events, some conscious and some subconscious, some physical and some emotional. Humans are complex creatures, and emotion and stress play important roles in our interaction with the environment. Also, language is an important means for communicating with the environment for humans, and indeed, language is so important to what it means to be human, that it is difficult to imagine what "thinking" even means without language.

4.1 ATTENTION

Imagine the attention to detail necessary to perform a complicated procedure such as a heart transplant. These details may include the tools being utilized, the various monitors, the incision site, the support staff, the status of the patient, etc. There might also be countless other things that the surgeon could pay attention to…the trim on the walls, the numbers on the clock, the glasses on the face of the nurse…in fact, if the surgeon *did* pay attention to these things, he or she would find it more difficult to complete the surgery successfully. How is it that the surgeon is able to avoid distractions, choosing instead to pay attention to only particular inputs out of the many available in the environment? What limits people in general from paying attention to all things at once? Further, imagine that the surgeon was chewing gum while performing the surgery (not recommended!). This would likely not have an impact on the surgeon's performance; however, if the surgeon were giving a speech while performing the surgery (definitely not recommended!), the surgeon's performance would likely be impaired. All of the above are examples of different aspects of attention. Let's look at two unique components of attention—selective attention and divided attention—and the models that have been used to explain each.

Selective Attention

Selective attention is the process by which one input is attended to and the rest are tuned out. This is necessary because we do not have the capacity to pay attention to everything in our environment. A resource model suggests that we only have a limited capacity to pay attention and so must devote our resources carefully.

One way that selective attention has been studied is using a dichotic listening setup. A person wears headphones and each ear hears a different dialogue. The individual is instructed to listen to information coming into one ear, called the **attended channel**, and to ignore input to the other ear, the **unattended channel**. When people do this, they are able to remember some of the message from the attended ear but lose almost everything from the unattended ear. The same observation has been made with visual stimuli; when people are told to focus on one visual aspect, they may miss other visual details.

Donald Broadbent thought of the brain as a processing system with a limited capacity and sought to map out the steps that went into creating memories from raw sensory data. He developed the **Broadbent Filter Model of Selective Attention** (Figure 1). In this model, inputs from the environment first enter a sensory buffer. One of these inputs is then selected and filtered based on physical characteristics of the input (e.g. sensory modality). This theoretical filter is designed to keep us from becoming overloaded and overwhelmed with information. Other sensory information stays in the sensory buffer briefly, but then quickly decays. At this point in the process, the information is still raw data that has just been filtered—it has not yet been transformed. It is in the next step, when the information enters short-term memory storage, where semantic (meaning-making) processes occur.

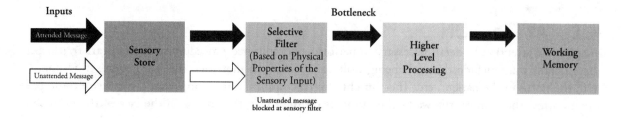

Figure 1   Broadbent Filter Model of Selective Attention

In the dichotic listening task described above, only information from the attended ear is allowed to pass through the filter. If an input in the sensory buffer does not go through the filter, the theory proposes that it remains briefly but then quickly decays and disappears.

To make matters more complicated, it seems that some unattended inputs are still detected. Imagine you are in a conversation with someone at a party in a room full of people. You are not aware of the content of any of the other conversations until suddenly you hear the name of your best friend mentioned in a conversation behind you. This phenomenon is known as the **cocktail party effect**. It happens when information of personal importance from previously unattended channels catches our attention. This observation cannot be well accounted for by the filter model of attention. Later adaptations of the original model have thus suggested that information from the unattended ear is not completely filtered out, but rather dampened, like turning the volume down on a television. Information from the unattended ear can still be processed at some level.

Anne Treisman's Attentuation Model tried to account for the cocktail party effect. Treisman believed that rather than a filter, the mind has an attenuator, which works like a volume knob—it "turns down" the unattended sensory input, rather than eliminating it.

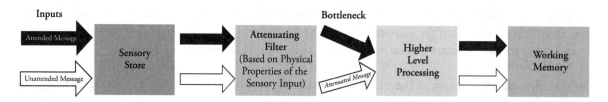

Figure 2   Treisman Attenuation Model of Selective Attention

The cocktail party effect has also been explained through the concept of **selective priming**. This idea suggests that people can be selectively primed to observe something, either by encountering it frequently or by having an expectation. If one is primed to observe something, one is more likely to notice it when it occurs. Over the course of our lifetimes, we have frequently encountered our own names and the names of our friends and are thus primed to hear them. The more something is primed, the more it will be picked up despite distractions. Researchers have also studied priming by providing people with stimuli, sometimes subliminally, and testing whether these stimuli have an impact on later performance.

For example, if asked to read a list of words including the word "lettuce" before embarking on a word completion task, subjects are more likely to complete "LET____" with T-U-C-E to make the word "lettuce" than people who were not initially primed with the list of words. Even if people are not conscious of remembering the stimuli, it can still have an impact on later performance.

Visual attention has often been explained via a **spotlight model**. In this model, the spotlight is a beam that can shine anywhere within an individual's visual field. It is important to note that this beam describes the movement of attention, not the movement of the eyes. Shifts in attention actually precede the corresponding eye movements. The shifting of attention requires us to unlock the beam from its current target, move the focus, and lock onto a new target.

Information from visual perception is processed in the brain by feature detectors that examine the different aspects of an object, such as color, shape, orientation, etc. One problem with visual processing is called the **binding problem**—the problem of how all these different aspects are assembled together and related to a single object, rather than something else in the visual field. Visual attention is the solution to this problem. If our visual attention is on a particular object such as a cup, then the feature detectors' input of shape, color, etc. will all be related to the object being attended to—the cup. It has been found that when people are distracted while viewing two items, they may have issues with binding; for example, the color of one item may be attributed to the other.

Divided Attention

Divided attention concerns when and if we are able to perform multiple tasks simultaneously. It turns out that this depends on the characteristics of the activities one is trying to multitask. The **resource model of attention** says that we have a limited pool of resources on which to draw when performing tasks, both modality-specific resources and general resources. In general, if the resources required to perform multiple tasks simultaneously exceeds the available resources to do so, then the tasks cannot be accomplished at the same time. Three factors are associated with performance on multi-tasking: task similarity, task difficulty, and task practice.

Imagine listening to a talk radio program while trying to write a paper. It is likely that these two activities would be very difficult to pay attention to at the same time. They would interfere with each other because of their task similarity, in this case, the use of the same modality for processing. One activity requires verbal input while the other requires verbal output. However, if instead you were listening to classical music, you might be able to write a paper at the same time because you would be doing two dissimilar tasks; one requires auditory input resources while the other requires verbal output.

Task difficulty also plays a role. If a task is more difficult, it requires more resources in general and would be hard to do simultaneously with another task without passing resource capacity. Imagine driving a car while conversing with your passengers. When driving through familiar neighborhoods in a single lane (an easy task), you may have no trouble carrying on a conversation. However, if you are about to enter a complicated intersection involving a lane change and a quick turn, attention to the conversation may have to stop or you may become silent or miss what was said during that time. Alternatively, while deep in conversation, it is easy to miss a turn!

Finally, practice helps. That is, practice diminishes task resource demand so that we may free up those resources to allow for multitasking. For example, a new driver may have a hard time changing the radio station while driving, while an experienced driver may not find this difficult. This suggests that tasks tend to become automatic with practice, and no longer need mechanisms of control to oversee them [which brain area is responsible for "muscle memory," or the ability to perform motor tasks unconsciously?[1]]. These tasks are well-learned routines that require fewer resources. On the other hand, novel, controlled tasks require flexibility and drain more resources, thus are typically not multitasked.

4.2 COGNITION

Information-Processing Models

With the advent of computers, psychologists were influenced to think about the human mind as if it were a computer processor. Contrary to behaviorism, which is concerned mostly with the link between stimulus and response, **information-processing models** focus on what happens between the ears. These models have a few basic assumptions. They assume that information is taken in from the environment and processed through a series of steps including **attention, perception**, and **storage into memory**. Along the way, information is systematically transformed. Thus, our minds are like mental computer programs or assembly lines that change, store, use, and retrieve information.

Two theories of attention and perception were described above (the Broadbent Filter Model of Selective Attention and the Treisman Attenuation Model of Selective Attention). **Alan Baddeley's model** sought to better define short-term memory, which he renamed **working memory**. In his model, working memory consists of four components—a phonological loop, a visuospatial sketchpad, an episodic buffer, and a central executive. The **phonological loop** allows us to repeat verbal information to help us remember it. This may be what you use to remember a phone number that someone tells you when you have nothing with which to write it down. The **visuospatial sketchpad** serves a similar purpose for visuospatial information through the use of mental images. The **episodic buffer** is theorized to integrate information from the phonological loop and visuospatial sketchpad with a sense of time, and to interface with long-term memory stores. In other words, the episodic buffer is responsible for combining information from a variety of sources into coherent episodes (hence the name, episodic buffer). For example, if a man sees a station wagon much like the one his father used to drive, he is able to make this connection through the interaction between his memory of his father's car and his current visual experience in the episodic buffer. The **central executive** is the overseer of the entire process, and orchestrates the process by shifting and dividing attention.

[1] The cerebellum

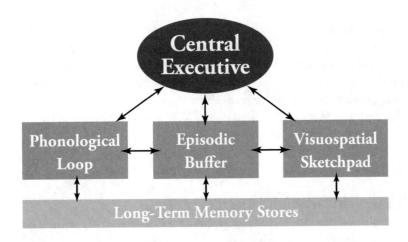

Figure 3   Baddeley Model of Working Memory

Cognitive Development

Piaget's Stages of Cognitive Development

Jean Piaget was one of the first developmental psychologists who studied cognitive development in children; he argued against the prevailing belief that children were much like miniature adults in their thought processes and abilities. He thought that the process of cognitive development involved forming **schemas**, or mental frameworks that shape and are shaped by our experience. As we encounter new experiences, Piaget believed that we either **assimilate** those experiences by conforming them into our existing schemas or we **accommodate** by adjusting our schemas to take into account the new experiences. For example, if a young girl believes that there is a monster under the bed but her parent turns on the light to reveal that there is nothing there, the girl can take two paths. She can assimilate this experience by believing that the monster still exists but runs away from light, or accommodate her schema by agreeing that there must be no monster.

Jean Piaget

Piaget's theory included four developmental stages. They are as follows:

1) **Sensorimotor Stage:** from birth to roughly age 2. Babies and young infants experience the world through their senses and movement, such as looking, touching, mouthing, and grasping. During this time, they learn about **object permanence**—the understanding that things continue to exist when they are out of sight. They also demonstrate stranger anxiety: distress when confronted with an unfamiliar person.

2) **Preoperational Stage:** roughly from ages 2 to 7. During this time, children learn that things can be represented through symbols such as words and images. This accompanies their learning during pretend play and development of language, but they still lack logical reasoning. They also are egocentric, meaning they do not understand that others have different perspectives.

3) **Concrete Operational Stage:** roughly from age 7 to 11. Children learn to think logically about concrete events. This helps them learn the principle of **conservation:** the idea that quantity remains the same despite changes in shape. For example, if water from a wide bowl is poured into a thin cylinder, it still has the same volume despite the difference in height. They also grasp mathematical concepts during this time.

4) **Formal Operational Stage:** roughly from age 12 through adulthood. People learn abstract reasoning (e.g. hypothesizing) and moral reasoning.

Cognitive Changes in Late Adulthood

During early and middle adulthood, most cognitive abilities remain stable or increase. Beyond the age of 60, the following cognitive declines have been noted:

1) The elderly show some memory declines in recall, while their recognition abilities remain relatively intact. **Recall** involves retrieving information from memory without any clues, while **recognition** involves retrieving information from memory with clues. Asking an eyewitness to describe the face of a suspect is a test of recall; asking an eyewitness to identify a suspect out of a lineup is a test of recognition.

2) Time-based tasks can also be challenging for older adults, such as a regimen involving medication taken three times a day.

3) Older adults also have slower information-processing abilities, as evidenced by slower reaction times and speech.

Role of Culture in Cognitive Development

The process of learning is in many ways the process of internalizing information provided by a given culture. Higher mental processes may have their roots in broader social processes. Thus, instead of the individual developing and learning how to utilize developed skills in a social context, consider the possibility that the individual learns social relationships and converts these into mental capabilities. The developing individual and the environment are in a reciprocal relationship in which the social context can shape thinking and behavior. For example: the expression of thoughts is limited by the thinker's language. Furthermore, internalized speech is only developed after a child speaks out loud and receives feedback from others in the environment. As you can imagine, different languages result in different ways of thinking. Multilingual people have even been shown to perform differently on personality testing depending on in which language the test is given.

Influence of Heredity and Environment on Cognitive Development

Heredity and the environment interact during the course of an individual's life to create a developmental trajectory. One way of thinking about this is that genetics provides the biological predispositions, or raw material that an individual has. Sociocultural influences then help mold and channel this potential into the development of particular capabilities. The amount and quality of schooling and the richness of the child's environment can heavily influence performance on tests of cognitive functioning. Thus, neither "nature" (genetics) nor "nurture" (environment) may be sufficient to explain the developmental path of an individual—it may instead be explained by their complex interaction. For an example, consider the case of language. Noam Chomsky convincingly argued that children could not learn the wealth of vocabulary that they quickly acquire simply through environmental influence; genetics and heredity are also involved. At the same time, the quality of reading education in school influences a child's ability to acquire this skill.

Biological Factors that Affect Cognition

Many aspects of cognitive functioning can be traced back to structures in the brain. Sensory information provides the raw material for cognitive processes and is transmitted to the parietal, occipital, and temporal lobes of the brain (discussed in Chapter 3). The frontal lobes play a role in executive functions, including planning, organizing, inhibiting impulses, and flexible thinking. The hippocampus has been shown to be involved in the formation of new memories. Furthermore, emotional arousal is necessary to provide the motivation and alertness necessary to complete tasks and is managed by the amygdala and the rest of the limbic system. The interconnectivity of these various regions underlies our cognitive skills.

Problem Solving and Decision Making

Types of Problem Solving and Problem Solving Approaches

What detours can I take to get out of this traffic jam? How do I change a flat tire? Should I hitchhike with this stranger? A strange morning commute may require us to use various strategies for solving problems. For some problems, we may use a strategy of **trial and error**. For others, we may rely on following an **algorithm**, a step-by-step procedure. For others, we may use mental shortcuts, called **heuristics**. At times, we may use a combination of these strategies. For example, when changing a tire, an algorithm may be followed until it is discovered that a needed wrench is missing. At this point, other tools may be pulled out and experimented with through trial and error, until an appropriate one for the bolts is found. Sometimes we use problem-solving strategies consciously, while at other times this is an unconscious process. For example, we may not be actively thinking about a problem, but may be struck later in the shower with a sudden flash of inspiration, called **insight**.

Barriers to Effective Problem Solving

Think about a time when you struggled with solving a problem to no avail. There are two cognitive tendencies that can lead us astray when looking for solutions: confirmation bias and fixation.

Confirmation bias is a tendency to search only for information that confirms our preconceived thinking, rather than information that might not support it. This can prevent you from approaching a problem from multiple perspectives, because you are more likely to view it from one way—your way. As a result, this bias can lead to faulty decision making; one-sided information may leave you without a complete picture of the situation. For example, suppose you are in charge of staffing the nurses at the hospital ER where you work, and you believe that during college football game nights there are more admissions than on other days. You will tend to take notice of admissions during college football game nights, but be inattentive to admissions during other nights of the month. A tendency to do this over time unjustifiably strengthens your belief, and it could lead to poor staffing decisions.

A second obstacle to problem solving is **fixation**, an inability to see the problem from a fresh perspective. At times, this fixation results from the existence of a **mental set**, a tendency to fixate on solutions that worked in the past though they may not apply to the current situation. For example, a parent trying to control their child's behavior may not realize that time-outs at age 15 are just not as effective as they were at age 5. Another type of fixation is **functional fixedness**, a tendency to perceive the functions of objects as fixed and unchanging. Thus, one may search high and low to find a box-cutter to open a package, when a readily available key would work just as well.

Heuristics, Biases, Intuition, and Emotion

It may not surprise you to know that humans are not always logical in their decision-making. Often, we don't put a great deal of time and effort into a decision because the decision may be trivial, or because it must be made quickly, or because no clear logical path for problem solving is available.

Mental shortcuts, or heuristics, can increase efficiency in decision-making and although they are helpful most of the time, they can also lead to errors in judgment. Who was a more prolific composer, Joseph Haydn or Ludwig van Beethoven? Most of us would assume Beethoven, because his name and possibly even examples of his work come more readily to mind. Haydn was actually Beethoven's teacher, and composed nearly three times more music than Beethoven! When you make a decision about something based on the examples that are most available in your mind, this is known as the availability heuristic. While the availability heuristic relies more on our memory of specific instances, the representativeness heuristic has more to do with our generalizations about people and events. For example, let's say you go to the Post Office three different times and each time a different employee is rude to you. You might conclude, "people who work at the Post Office are rude!" This would be an example of the representativeness heuristic – you have developed a generalization about Postal workers. Another example: what does a taxicab look like? Most Americans would use the adjective "yellow" when describing a taxicab, because a yellow car fits our prototype of what a taxicab looks like. Again, this generalization is the result of the representativeness heuristic. The representativeness and availability heuristics may seem quite similar, but the representativeness heuristic is based more on generalizations (rather than specific examples), whereas the availability heuristic is based on how readily particular examples come to mind.

Another susceptibility is **belief bias**, which is the tendency to judge arguments based on what one believes about their conclusions rather than on whether they use sound logic. In other words, we tend to accept conclusions that fit with our beliefs and tend to reject assertions that do not fit with their beliefs. For example, you probably believe that doctors are good people; therefore, if you read a story about a doctor who potentially murdered his wife, no matter the strength of the evidence, you might be more inclined to believe that the death was an accident. On the other hand, you might easily believe that a drug-dealer killed his wife, despite any compelling evidence. Once these preexisting beliefs are formed, they become resistant to change through a phenomenon known as **belief perseverance**, a tendency to cling to beliefs despite the presence of contrary evidence.

Overconfidence and Belief Perseverance

The use of intuitive heuristics and a tendency to confirm preconceived beliefs combine to lead to **overconfidence**, an overestimation of the accuracy of knowledge and judgments. For example, after hearing that a classmate completed an assignment quickly, along with their belief that a particular class is easy, students can be overconfident in how much time it would take to complete assignments or write papers, estimating that they would take less time than they actually do. People can also be influenced by how information is **framed**. For example, one study found that consumers are more likely to buy meat advertised as 75% lean than that labeled 25% fat. Similarly, rather than informing customers that they will be charged a "fee" for using a credit card, a company may choose to offer those who use cash a "discount" to make the same situation more palatable.

4.3 CONSCIOUSNESS

Consciousness is something that science has not yet been able to pin down and religion has wrestled with. It has been explained through concepts such as the soul by some and thought of as inseparable from the body by others. **Consciousness** is defined as the awareness that we have of ourselves, our internal states, and the environment. It is also important for reflection and exerts control by directing our attention. Thus, consciousness is always needed to complete novel and complex tasks, however we may complete practiced and simple tasks, such as driving a familiar path, with little conscious awareness. We may also be influenced by subconscious cues without them entering our consciousness. These subconscious cues can be a basis for first impressions of others and even for prejudice.

States of Consciousness

Alertness

Alertness and arousal involve the ability to remain attentive to what is going on. It is something that we often take for granted, however, many patients who arrive in an emergency room are not alert for various reasons. These can include head injuries and toxins. The ability to be alert is also impaired in a variety of disorders, including narcolepsy, attention deficit disorder, depression, and chronic fatigue syndrome. Even without these disorders, it is not possible to maintain a heightened state of alertness indefinitely, and alertness varies over a 24-hour cycle. Alertness and arousal are controlled by structures within the brainstem. These structures are known as the **reticular formation** (also known as the reticular activating system, or RAS).

Sleep

Stages of Sleep

Although the purpose of sleep and exact definition of sleep are unclear, the stages of sleep have been empirically determined. The best way to explain the stages of sleep is to put them in context of how they are measured and distinguished. **Polysomnography** (PSG) is a multimodal technique to measure physiological processes during sleep. PSG includes electroencephalogram (EEG—measures of electrical impulses in the brain), electromyogram (EMG—measures of skeletal muscle movements), electrooculogram (EOG—measures of eye movement), and other physiological indicators of sleep. Through experiments using PSG, research has shown there are several distinct stages of sleep.

When a person is awake, but sleepy and relaxed, the individual's EEG changes from when they are alert. In this relaxed state, the EEG shows **alpha waves**, which have low amplitudes and high frequencies (8-12 Hz; Figure 4). These waves are the first indicator that a person is ready to drift off to sleep: the body relaxes; the person feels drowsy and closes his or her eyes.

When sleep begins, the first stage of non-REM (**Rapid Eye Movement**) sleep is entered. This is called **Stage 1 sleep**. During this stage, the EEG is dominated by **theta waves**: waves of low to moderate intensity and intermediate frequency (3-7 Hz; Figure 4). Further, EOG measures slow rolling eye movements and EMG measures moderate activity. The person becomes less responsive to stimuli and has fleeting thoughts.

Stage 2 sleep is denoted by a change to two distinct wave patterns on the EEG. Although a person still experiences theta waves, these waves are intermixed with these two patterns: K-complexes and sleep spindles. A **K-complex** typically has a duration of a half second and is large and slow. These each occur as a single wave amongst the theta waves. **Sleep spindles** are bursts of waves. They have a frequency of 12-14 Hz and are moderately intense. Like K-complexes, these spindles do not last long: only a half to one and a half seconds. During stage 2, there is no eye movement and EMG measures moderate activity. This stage brings increased relaxation in the body that is characteristic of sleep, such as decreased heart rate, respiration, and temperature.

During **Stage 3 and Stage 4 sleep**, a person transitions into slow wave sleep. Stage 3 and Stage 4 are characterized by **delta waves**, which are high amplitude, low frequency waves (0.5-3 Hz) and signify the deepest level of sleep. Initially, delta waves are mixed with higher-frequency waves, but as Stage 3 progresses to Stage 4, delta waves come to dominate. During slow wave sleep, a person continues to show no eye movement and moderate muscle movement. The heart rate and digestion slow, and growth hormones are secreted.

The final stage of sleep is **REM sleep**, which is characterized by bursts of quick eye movements. Also unique to REM sleep, the EEG measures waves that most resemble the beta waves seen in individuals when awake. However, the waves in REM sleep are sawtooth waves with low intensity and variable frequency. These waves are more jagged in appearance than beta waves, which are also low intensity, but high frequency (16-25 Hz). Unlike the conscious state, REM sleep is characterized by low (almost no) skeletal muscle movement: hence the name "**paradoxical sleep**." Although the person physiologically appears to be awake, their muscle movement does not corroborate, as the individual is nearly paralyzed except for sudden bursts or twitches. REM sleep is generally when dreams occur.

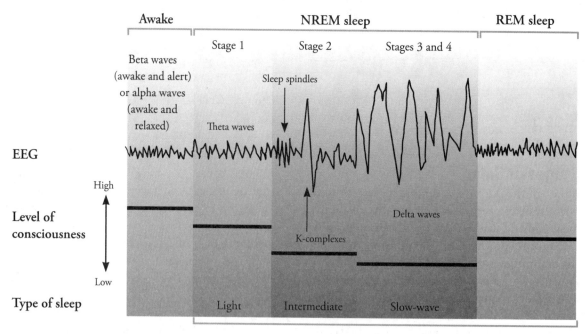

Figure 4   EEG Wave Forms During Wakefulness and Sleep

During normal sleep, an individual passes through the non-REM sleep stages, then enters into REM sleep, then passes back through the non-REM sleep stages. This may happen in sequence (stages 1, 2, 3, 4, then REM), but it is also possible to jump between various stages while sleeping. Regardless, the average sleep cycle is about 90 minutes (for a typical adult), and includes periods of non-REM and REM sleep. We complete multiple sleep cycles per night. Periods of REM sleep are shortest early in the night, and get longer as the night progresses. Deep sleep (stages 3 and 4) periods are longest early in the night and less frequent as the night progresses (Figure 5). The amount of sleep needed for optimal functioning changes throughout one's lifespan. Infants spend a much larger fraction of their sleep in REM than adults do (and need much more sleep – young babies spend about 16 out of every 24 hours sleeping!). Teens need, on average, about 9-10 hours a night of uninterrupted sleep. As we age we require less and less sleep – it is not uncommon for individuals in their 60s and 70s to sleep about 6 hours a night. Without an adequate amount of sleep the body is not able to complete all of the restorative phases needed for muscle repair, memory consolidation, and the release of various hormones, including those that regulate growth and appetite. When we do not get enough sleep, we wake up less prepared to concentrate, focus, and engage in decision-making.).

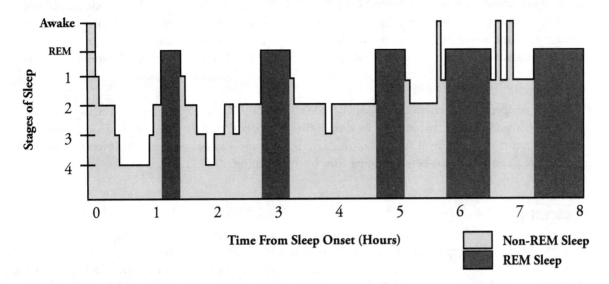

Figure 5 Normal Sleep Stages Throughout the Night

Sleep and Circadian Rhythms

There are several possible explanations for why organisms sleep. Since humans (and most other non-nocturnal animals) are better suited to survival in the daytime when we can best use our vision to navigate and stay out of harm's way, sleep may have served as a survival mechanism to reduce nighttime activity (when our ancestors were more likely to become prey). A second theory is that sleep helps heal the body by restoring tissues, including those in the brain. While we are asleep, the brain is still active, and could be reorganizing connections and consolidating memories into long-term memory storage. A third idea is that sleep plays a role in growth. During sleep, the pituitary gland releases growth hormone, with lower levels of the hormone released as an individual ages.

Circadian rhythms (sometimes referred to as the biological clock) are the biological waxing and waning of alertness over the 24-hour day. Most people feel their most alert during the mid-morning, experience an energy dip in early afternoon (when some people take siestas or grab a second cup of coffee!), and then feel alert again in the early evening; later in the evening, as alertness wanes, sleep becomes more and more enticing. Although this is a general description of the ebb and flow of alertness throughout the day, it varies by individual, and circadian rhythms also vary with age. Newborns can spend two-thirds of a day asleep. Older adults tend to peak in the morning and decline as the day progresses, while adolescents and young adults tend to be more energetic in the mid- to late-evening.

A key factor in how sleep is regulated involves exposure to light, which stimulates a nerve pathway from the retina to the suprachiasmatic nucleus (SCN) in the hypothalamus. The SCN signals other parts of the brain, which regulate body temperature and control the production and release of hormones. The SCN is essentially our internal clock; it helps regulate the pattern of neurophysiological activities that affect the entire body. When exposed to light at the beginning of the day, our body temperature begins to rise and hormones (like cortisol) are released; these signals indicate that it is time to wake up.

Melatonin is a hormone made by the pineal gland. Darkness causes the SCN to signal the pineal gland to start producing and releasing melatonin. As melatonin levels rise, you begin to feel tired. Melatonin levels stay elevated throughout the night; the light of a new day causes melatonin levels to fall. Bright light both regulates the function of the SCN and directly inhibits the release of melatonin. Artificial indoor lighting can also sometimes be bright enough to prevent the release of melatonin (which is why some studies suggest that turning off mobile devices an hour before bedtime can improve your sleep!).

Core body temperature fluctuates between about 96.8 and 100.4° F over 24-hours, and this is also regulated by the hypothalamus. For most of us with normal circadian rhythms, sleep tends to occur when the core temperature is dropping at the end of the day. The average adult experiences their lowest core body temperature about two hours before waking time in the morning.

Dreaming

As mentioned earlier, the REM stage of sleep is when dreams typically occur. This stage is absolutely necessary. Missing REM sleep for one night results in an increase in REM sleep later to make up for it, called **REM rebound**. Some of the dreams during the REM stage can be exciting, including lucid dreams (in which one might be aware that one is dreaming and have some conscious control of the dreams). Most dreams are about daily events, like missing an exam, playing a sport, or talking to a friend. But why is it that we dream? Freud believed that the plotlines of dreams, or **manifest content**, were symbolic versions of underlying **latent content**, unconscious drives and wishes that are difficult to express. Thus, he believed that dreams are a way of understanding our inner conflicts. Other theories for why dreams exist have emerged since Freud. Some studies have found that dreaming can improve learning and problem-solving. It was found that brain regions used by rats to navigate a maze while they were awake were also active while the rats slept, as if the rats were running the maze in their dreams. When they woke, the rats demonstrated improved performance compared to both their previous performance and to the performance of other rats that did not get REM sleep. The same is true for human performance on tasks. You may find that a night of consolidating information you've learned while studying for the MCAT is beneficial to retaining that information. Finally, the **activation-synthesis theory** suggests that dreams are byproducts of brain activation during REM sleep. This theory allows for the possibility that dreams are far from purposeful. Some proponents have suggested that the purpose of dreams is to provide a template of consciousness on which the mind can practice consciousness-development.

Sleep Disorders

While there may be some debate as to the purpose of sleep, it cannot be disputed that sleep is necessary when we consider how debilatating sleep disorders can be. Sleep disorders can be subdivided into dyssomnias and parasomnias.

Dyssomnias are abnormalities in the amount, quality, or timing of sleep, and include insomnia, narcolepsy, and sleep apnea. **Insomnia** is the most common sleep disorder and is characterized by difficulty falling or staying asleep. Insomnia is not the occasional inability to fall asleep due to anxiety or excitement, but rather is a persistent problem that can stem from chronic stress. Common quick treatments are sedatives such as sleeping pills, but these have a risk of dependency and overdose, and become less effective with time. They also create abnormal sleep cycles that include less time in REM and slow-wave stages, which can lead to drowsy carry-over effects. Natural alternatives include relaxation before bedtime, avoiding stimulants and exercise in the evening, and sleeping on a regular schedule. Those with **narcolepsy** experience periodic, overwhelming sleepiness during waking periods that usually last less than 5 minutes. They can occur without warning at dangerous times, such as while driving or walking down stairs. Recent research suggests that the cause of narcolepsy is a dysfunction in the region of the hypothalamus that produces the neurotransmitter hypocretin (also called orexin). Narcolepsy has been treated with stimulants with modest success. **Sleep apnea** is a disorder that causes people to intermittently stop breathing during sleep, which results in awakening after a minute or so without air. This process can repeat hundreds of times a night, and can deprive sufferers of deep sleep. Those with sleep apnea may not even be aware that they have it, although their partners may be, as it can be accompanied by heavy snoring. The incidence of sleep apnea is associated with obesity.

Parasomnias are abnormal behaviors that occur during sleep and include somnambulism and night terrors. **Somnambulism** (or sleepwalking) tends to occur during slow wave sleep (Stage 3), usually during the first third of the night. There may be genetic predispositions for sleepwalking and sleeptalking. **Night terrors** also usually occur during Stage 3 (unlike nightmares, which occur during REM sleep toward morning). A person experiencing a night terror may sit up or walk around, babble, and appear terrified, although none of this is recalled the next morning. Both of these disorders are more likely to appear in children.

Hypnosis and Meditation

Hypnotism has been portrayed in so many different ways in movies and other media that it is important to separate fact from fiction. **Hypnotism** is a social interaction in which a hypnotist has a subject focus attention on what is being said, relax and feel tired, "let go," and accept suggestions easily through the use of vivid imagination. Nearly everyone is hypnotizable to some extent, although some have a stronger capacity. Hypnotized people do NOT acquire superhuman physical abilities—this is a myth. Hypnotism can promote recall of memories by putting someone in a relaxed state, but a patient is also susceptible to constructing **false memories**—that is, using imagination to create inaccurate memories. It cannot help a patient remember events from infancy. Finally, hypnotism cannot force people to do extreme things against their will, such as commit murder. Studies show that the presence of the authoritative hypnotist equally influences hypnotized and non-hypnotized people to commit acts that are of similar danger levels.

This does not imply that hypnotized people are "faking it". In fact, post-hypnotic suggestions have been utilized to help alleviate headaches, asthma, and stress-related skin disorders. In addition, 50% of people can gain some pain relief from hypnosis. Hypnosis works not by preventing sensory input, but by blocking attention to those sensory inputs. People may experience physiological states such as pain or a

4.3

pounding heart, but are not consciously aware of these sensations. Some studies indicate that hypnotism results in changes in brain activity, insinuating that it is an actual altered state of consciousness (although this idea is controversial). There are two theories for how it works. The **Dissociation theory** suggests that hypnotism is an extreme form of divided consciousness. In hypnosis, just as in everyday life, many behaviors occur on autopilot. Have you ever driven somewhere and not recalled anything about the actual drive? Thus, hypnotism may be an extended form of this normal dissociation where the individual is on autopilot and the hypnotist takes over the executive control, which directs action. The **Social Influence theory** suggests that people do and report what's expected of them. They are not consciously faking it, but are like actors who get caught up in their roles and thus behave in ways that fit them.

Meditation refers to a variety of techniques, many of which have been practiced for thousands of years, and which usually involve the training of attention. Meditators may focus intensely on one object of attention, such as their breathing, or they may broaden their attention and be aware of multiple stimuli, such as anything in their auditory field. Meditation has been utilized successfully to manage pain, stress, and anxiety disorders. **Mindfulness-based stress reduction** (MBSR) is a protocol commonly used in the medical setting to help alleviate stress. Meditators have increased alpha and theta waves while they are meditating (and to some extent an increase above baseline after they stop), with more experienced meditators showing greater improvements.

Consciousness Altering Drugs

There are three main categories of psychoactive drugs: depressants, stimulants, and hallucinogenics. All of these drugs work by altering actions at the neuronal synapses, either enhancing, dampening, or mimicking the activity of the brain's natural neurotransmitters.

Depressants include alcohol, barbiturates (tranquilizers), and opiates. They work by depressing, or slowing down, neural activity. When drinking alcohol, people are more likely to be impulsive and may appear hyperactive, but this is due to the slowing of brain activity related to judgment and inhibition in the frontal lobe. In larger doses, alcohol can lead to deterioration in skilled motor performance, decreased reaction time, and slurring of speech [which brain area is impacted when this occurs?[2]]. Excessive drinking can lead to memory blackouts for recent memories (those that have not been consolidated into long-term memory). Alcohol also suppresses REM sleep, which may contribute to the loss of short-term memory and less restful sleep the night of drinking. Thus, a heavy drinker may not remember what happened the night before when they wake up the next morning. While impaired motor control after drinking has caused countless vehicular deaths, an "overdose" of alcohol can also cause death by depressing the respiratory control centers in the medulla to the point that breathing ceases. Alcohol works by stimulating GABA and dopamine systems. GABA is an inhibitory neurotransmitter and is associated with the reduced anxiety, while dopamine leads to the feeling of minor euphoria. Prolonged and excessive alcohol use can actually shrink the brain.

Both alcohol and **barbiturates** depress the sympathetic nervous system ("fight or flight") activity. Barbiturates are often prescribed as sleep aids. They are dangerous in combination with alcohol and prone to

---

[2] The cerebellum, which is responsible for smoothing out motor commands from the primary motor cortex of the frontal lobe. The cerebellum controls precision, timing, coordination, and plays a role in muscle memory. The altered speech demonstrated with inebriation might lead you to believe that Broca's area is impaired; actually, slurred speech is the result of loss of motor control of the lips.

overdose—too much of a depressive effect can actually shut down life-sustaining organs. **Opiates**, which are derivatives of opium (including morphine and heroin), also depress neural functioning. They temporarily reduce pain by mimicking the brain's own pain relievers, neurotransmitters known as endorphins; pain is replaced with a blissful feeling. With prolonged use, the brain may stop producing endorphins, leading to a painful withdrawal from the drug.

Stimulants include caffeine, nicotine, cocaine, and amphetamines ("speed"). They typically work by either increasing the release of neurotransmitter, reducing the reuptake of neurotransmitter, or both. Their overall effect is to speed up body functions, resulting in increased energy, respiratory rate, heart rate, and pupil dilation. People use stimulants to stay awake, enhance physical performance, and boost mood. Cocaine works by causing a "rush," a release of the brain's supply of neurotransmitters including dopamine, serotonin, and norepinephrine. While this creates a brief period of intense pleasure, it is followed by a depressive crash. MDMA, also known as ecstasy, is a stimulant and a mild hallucinogen. It works by triggering the release of dopamine and serotonin, as well as by blocking the reabsorption of serotonin so that it stays in the synapse longer. It causes emotional elevation, but long-term effects include damage to serotonin-producing neurons. The resulting reduction in serotonin levels can cause a depressed mood.

Hallucinogens, also known as psychedelics, distort perceptions in the absence of any sensory input, creating hallucinations. These include LSD and marijuana. After taking LSD, a user may see vivid images and colors. The experience may peak with a feeling of being separated from one's body or experiencing imagined scenes as if they were reality. Emotions related to LSD can vary from euphoria to panic, depending on the person's mood and the context. Marijuana's active ingredient is THC, which affects functioning by stimulating cannabinoid receptors in the brain. It relaxes and disinhibits like alcohol, but also acts as a hallucinogen by amplifying sensory perceptions including colors, sounds, tastes, and smells. Marijuana can also impair motor skills, reaction time, and judgment. Marijuana has been used medically to help with nausea and pain.

Drug Addiction and the Reward Pathway in the Brain

The defining feature of drug addiction is a compulsion to use a drug repeatedly. Users can have psychological and/or physical dependence on drugs. A **psychological dependence** is often associated with the use of a drug in response to painful emotions related to depression, anxiety, or trauma. For example, an individual with social anxiety may feel compelled to drink alcohol excessively in order to lower anxiety at parties. Sometimes this dependence can be stopped by removing the individual from a painful situation. **Physical dependence** is evidenced by withdrawal. Withdrawal is an uncomfortable and often physically painful experience without the use of a drug. This discomfort is alleviated when the user takes the drug, thus reinforcing further drug use. Alcohol withdrawal is especially dangerous—excessive users must be slowly detoxified, as stopping suddenly is life-threatening. Even caffeine addiction can cause withdrawal, with the user experiencing headache, fogginess, and irritability that end when more caffeine is taken.

Addiction is biologically based.[3] Enjoyable behaviors produce activity in dopamine circuits in the brain, most notably in the **nucleus accumbens**, the "pleasure center" of the brain. This dopaminergic pathway is a natural pathway to a feeling of reward and pleasure. Many addictive drugs share the characteristic of stimulating the release of dopamine in the nucleus accumbens.

---

[3] While some have argued that addiction should be viewed as a disease, this view is still controversial due to disagreement over the implications it could have for addicts, such as disempowerment.

4.4 EMOTION

You walk through your front door, set your keys down, and turn on the light just like you always do when, "Surprise!" Balloons fall from the ceiling, friends jump out of their hiding places, and a cake is brought out, "happy birthday!" Without any conscious effort, you scream, cover your mouth with your hands, and explode into a giant grin. You feel a pang as your heart skips a beat and then feel a warm glow as you look around at the smiling faces. The thought pops into your head, "A surprise party! How exciting!"

Emotion is quite an interesting phenomenon. It blurs the arbitrary boundary between what we consider mental and what we consider physical. What is really going on when an emotional state arises?

Three Components of Emotion

Emotion is complex and consists of three components: a physiological (body) component, a behavioral (action) component, and a cognitive (mind) component. The physical aspect of emotion is one of **physiological arousal**, or an excitation of the body's internal state. For example, when being startled at a surprise party, you may feel your heart pounding, your breathing becoming shallow and rapid, and your palms becoming sweaty. These are the sensations that accompany emotion (in this instance, surprise). The behavioral aspect of emotion includes some kind of expressive behavior; for example, spontaneously screaming and bringing your hands over your mouth. The cognitive aspect of emotion involves an appraisal or interpretation of the situation. Initially upon being startled, the thought "dangerous situation" or "fear" may arise, only to be reassessed as "surprise" and "excitement" after recognizing the circumstances as a surprise party. This describes how the situation is interpreted or labeled. Interestingly, many emotions share the same or very similar physiological and behavioral responses; it is the mind that interprets one situation that evokes a quickened heart rate and tears as "joyful" and another with the same responses as "fearful."

Universal Emotions

Darwin assumed that emotions had a strong biological basis. If this is true, then emotions should be experienced and expressed in similar ways across cultures, and in fact, this has been found to be the case. There are six major universal emotions: happiness, sadness, surprise, fear, disgust, and anger. Regardless of culture, most people can readily identify these emotions simply by observing facial expressions. Further supporting the idea that emotions have an innate basis is the finding that children's capacities for emotional expression and recognition appear to develop along similar timelines, regardless of their environment. However, environmental factors like culture do play a role in how emotion is expressed.

| Happiness | Sadness | Surprise | Fear | Disgust | Anger |

Courtesy Wikimedia Commons

Figure 6 Universal Emotions

Adaptive Role of Emotion

The relationship between performance and emotional arousal is a U-shaped correlation: people perform best when they are moderately aroused. This is known as the **Yerkes-Dodson Law**. A student will perform best when neither too complacent nor too overwhelmed, but rather in a "sweet spot" of optimum arousal (though this "sweet spot" can vary greatly from person to person and from task to task).

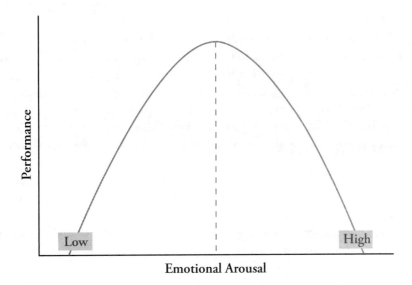

Figure 7 Yerkes-Dodson Law Regarding the Relationship Between Arousal and Performance

In addition to moderating performance, emotion has several other adaptive roles. It enhances survival by serving as a useful guide for quick decisions. A feeling of fear when walking alone down a dark alley while a shadowy figure approaches can be a valuable tool to indicate that the situation may be dangerous. A feeling of anger may enhance survival by encouraging attack on an intruder. Other emotions may have a role in influencing individual behaviors within a social context. For example, embarrassment may encourage social conformity. Additionally, in social contexts, emotions provide a means for nonverbal communication and empathy, allowing for cooperative interactions.

On a more subtle level, emotions are a large influence on our everyday lives. Our choices often require consideration of our emotions. A person with a brain injury to their prefrontal cortex (which plays a role in processing emotion) has trouble imagining their own emotional responses to the possible outcomes of decisions. This can lead to making inappropriate decisions that can cost someone a job, a marriage, or his or her savings. Imagine how difficult it could be to refrain from risky behaviors, such as gambling or spending huge sums of money, without the ability to imagine your emotional response to the possible outcomes.

Theories of Emotion

The most commonsense way to think about emotion is that something happens (a stimulus), then you experience the emotion, and then you have a physiological and behavioral response. For example, you're walking down the street and a scary dog starts chasing you (stimulus), you first experience the emotion (fear), then the physiological response (your heart begins to race) and behavioral response (you run away).

Indeed, this commonsense logic was how emotions were assumed to operate until the late 1800s, when scientists began proposing very different theories. There are three predominant theories that attempt to explain how the components of emotion—the physiological, the behavioral, and the cognitive—are interconnected.

James-Lange Theory

The James-Lange Theory of emotion was proposed in the late 1800s, and basically flips the commonsense notion of how emotion is experienced: instead of first experiencing the emotion and then the physiological reaction, the James-Lange theory proposes that first we experience the physiological response and then we experience the emotion. In other words, if a scary dog begins to chase you, first you experience an increased heart rate and this is followed by the conscious labeling of the experience as "fear." This may seem counterintuitive; it implies you feel afraid because your heart is racing. This theory suggests that the emotional experience (the brain labeling the situation as fear-inducing) is the result of the physiological response.

We frequently experience situations and events (stimuli) that result in various physiological reactions like increased muscle tension, increased heart rate, sweating, and many others, which are caused by the autonomic nervous system. This theory suggests that emotions are a result of these physiological responses, and not their cause. James and Lange suggested that autonomic activity induced by emotional stimuli generate the feeling of emotion, not the other way around.

There is some evidence in support of the James-Lange theory. For example, breathing patterns can also lead to certain emotions; short, shallow breathing creates a feeling of panic, while long, deep breathing creates a feeling of calm. People with cervical spine damage often experience less arousal and reduced emotions, because they no longer perceive physiological arousal from their bodies. However, the theory does not explain all scenarios and makes two assumptions that may be problematic. First, it assumes that each emotion originates from a distinctive physiological state. However, many emotions share very similar if not identical physiological profiles; for example, fear and sexual arousal involve very similar physiological patterns. Second, the theory assumes that we possess the ability to label these physiological states accurately. However, there is some evidence that the same physiological state can be interpreted differently based on context. For example, a physiological state similar to fear can be interpreted as excitement at a surprise party.

Cannon-Bard Theory

Walter Cannon, a critic of the James-Lange theory suggested (1) that in order for the James-Lange theory to adequately describe the process of emotion, there must be different physiological responses corresponding to each different emotion; and (2) that physiological experiences do not appear to differ from each other to the extent that would be essential to discriminate one emotion from another based only on our bodily reactions. Cannon also conducted a series of experiments in the early 1900s on cats whereby he severed the afferent nerves of the sympathetic branch of the autonomic nervous system (thereby preventing the cats from receiving any physiological input from their bodies) and exposed them to emotion-inducing stimuli. Cannon (and his grad student, Philip Bard) found that the cats still experienced emotion, even in the absence of physiological input from their bodies, thus casting significant doubt on the James-Lange theory. Therefore, the Cannon-Bard theory of emotion suggests that after a stimulus, the physiological response and the experience of emotion occur simultaneously and independently of each other. For example, a scary dog comes running after you (stimulus) and you then experience fear (emotion) and an increased heart rate (physiological response) at the same time; the fear does not cause the increased heart rate and the increased heart rate does not cause the fear. The Cannon-Bard theory is able to explain the overlap in physiological states between emotions like fear and sexual arousal, because the cognitive labeling is independent from the physiological, rather than directly caused by it. However, it struggles to explain phenomena in which controlling the physiological response influences the experience of emotion (e.g. deep breathing causes us to feel more calm).

Schachter-Singer Theory

According to the **Schachter-Singer Theory** of emotion, once we experience physiological arousal, we make a conscious cognitive interpretation based on our circumstances, which allows us to identify the emotion that we are experiencing. Thus, like the James-Lange theory, this suggests that each emotional experience begins with an assessment of our physiological reactions. Unlike James-Lange, however, it suggests that the cognitive label is given based on the situation, rather than being a one-to-one correlate of the physiological experience. Therefore, as in the Cannon-Bard theory, physiological states can be similar but cognitively labeled differently (for example, fear and sexual arousal). Therefore, the sight of the scary dog would cause the physiological change of an increased heart rate, which would be interpreted as the result of fearing the dog because of the situation. This would then inform a behavioral response (running away). This theory accounts for several situations, but suffers from the same shortcoming as the Cannon-Bard theory in that it does not explain how physiological responses influence cognitive aspects of emotion.

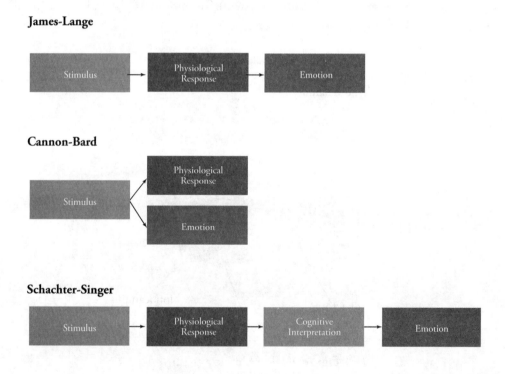

Figure 8   Schematic Comparison of the Theories of Emotion

The Role of Biological Processes in Perceiving Emotion

Someone who openly expresses emotions is sometimes referred to as "wearing his heart on his sleeve." But while romantics tend to believe that emotion is purely a matter of the heart, it turns out that the brain is very much involved in emotional states.

Generation and Experience of Emotions Involve Many Brain Regions

Mapping emotions to brain regions is difficult because thinking of different emotions as based in different parts of the brain has proven to be too simplistic. There is no "surprise center" in the brain. Rather, widespread areas of the brain appear to be associated with specific emotions. And instead of emotional "centers," there appear to be emotional "circuits" that involve many brain structures.

The Role of the Limbic System in Emotion

The limbic[4] system is a collection of brain structures that lies on both sides of the thalamus; together, these structures appear to be primarily responsible for emotional experiences. The main structure involved in emotion in the limbic system is the **amygdala**, an almond-shaped structure deep within the brain. The amygdala serves as the conductor of the orchestra of our emotional experiences. It can communicate with the **hypothalamus**, a brain structure that controls the physiological aspects of emotion, such as sweating and a racing heart. It also communicates with the **prefrontal cortex**, located at the front of the brain, which controls approach and avoidance behaviors—the behavioral aspects of emotion (the prefrontal cortex is not, however, part of the limbic system). The amygdala plays a key role in the identification and expression of fear and aggression.

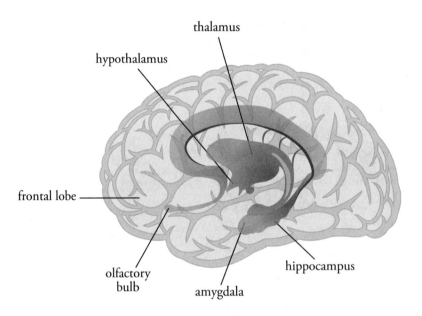

Figure 9   The Limbic System

Emotion and Memory

Emotional experiences can be stored as memories that can be recalled by similar circumstances. The limbic system also includes the **hippocampus**, a brain structure that plays a key role in forming memories.

---

4   In Latin, limbus is the term for "border" or "edge," or, particularly in medical terminology, a border of an anatomical component.

When memories are formed, often the emotions that are associated with these memories are also encoded. Take a second to close your eyes and imagine someone whom you love very much. Notice the emotional state that arises with your memory of that person. Recalling an event can bring about the emotions associated with it. Note that this isn't always a pleasant experience. It has an important role in the suffering of patients who have experienced traumatic events. Similar circumstances to a traumatic event can lead to recall of the memory of the experience, referred to as "flashback." Sometimes this recall isn't even conscious; for example, for someone who was involved in a traumatic car accident, driving past the intersection where the incident occurred might cause increased muscle tension, heart rate, and respiratory rate.

Emotions, Temperament, and Decision Making

The prefrontal cortex is critical for emotional experience, and is also important in temperament and decision making. The prefrontal cortex is associated with a reduction in emotional feelings, especially fear and anxiety. It is the soft voice that calms down the amygdala when it is overly aroused. Methods of emotion regulation and stress relief often activate the prefrontal cortex. The prefrontal cortex also plays a role in **executive functions**—higher order thinking processes such as planning, organizing, inhibiting behavior, and decision making. Damage to this area may lead to inappropriateness, impulsivity, and trouble with initiation. This area is not fully developed in humans until they reach their mid-twenties, explaining the sometimes erratic and emotionally charged behavior of teenagers. The most famous case of damage to the prefrontal cortex occurred to a man in the 1800s named **Phineas Gage**. Gage was a railroad worker who, at age 25, suffered an accident where a railroad tie blasted through his head, entering under his cheekbone and exiting through the top of his skull. After the accident, Gage was described as "no longer himself," prone to impulsivity, unable to stick to plans, and unable to demonstrate empathy. The accident severely damaged his prefrontal cortex, and while the reports about the change to his personality and behavior have been debated, this case led to the discovery of the role of the prefrontal cortex in personality.

Phineas Gage Injury

Emotion and the Autonomic Nervous System

The autonomic nervous system (ANS, Chapter 3) is responsible for controlling the activities of most of the organs and glands, and controls arousal. As mentioned earlier, it answers primarily to the hypothalamus.

The sympathetic nervous system (SNS) provides the body with brief, intense, vigorous responses. It is often referred to as the "fight or flight" system because it prepares an individual for action. It increases heart rate, blood pressure, and blood sugar levels, in preparation for action. It also directs the adrenal glands to release the stress hormones epinephrine and norepinephrine. The parasympathetic nervous system (PNS) provides signals to the internal organs during a calm resting state when no crisis is present. When activated, it leads to changes that allow for recovery and the conservation of energy, including an increase in digestion and the repair of body tissues.

Physiological Markers of Emotion (Signatures of Emotion)

Many physiological states associated with emotion have been discussed. These include heart rate, blood pressure, respiratory rate, sweating, and the release of stress hormones. An increase in these physiological functions is associated with the sympathetic (fight-or-flight) response. In order to measure autonomic function, clinicians can measure heart rate, finger temperature, skin conductance (sweating), and muscle activity. Keep in mind that different patterns tend to exist during different emotional states, but states such as fear and sexual arousal may display very similar patterns.

4.5 STRESS

The Nature of Stress

Stress is a great reminder that often what is considered to be psychological is simultaneously physiological. Under acute conditions of stress, such as while giving a formal presentation, it is common to feel physical symptoms such as increased heart rate and sweating. Prolonged periods of stress can have negative consequences, including immunosuppression, infertility, and hypertension. However, stress is not a simple stimulus-response phenomenon. How a stimulus is perceived plays a large role in how much stress is experienced.

Appraisal

Not everyone responds the same way to events that can trigger a stressful reaction. For example, imagine that a couple is at home in bed when suddenly they hear a creaking sound in another room. One person may assume that the sound is due to the age of the house or the steps of a pet, while the other may attribute the sound to a possible burglar sneaking around the house. Obviously, though the stimulus is the same, one person is going to become much more stressed than the other. What is most important for determining the stressful nature of an event is its **appraisal**, or how it is interpreted by the individual. When stressors are appraised as being challenges, as one may perceive the MCAT exam, they can actually be motivating. On the other hand, when they are perceived as threatening aspects of our identity, well-being, or safety, they may cause severe stress. Additionally, events that are considered negative and uncontrollable produce a greater stress response than those that are perceived as negative but controllable.

Different Types of Stressors

There are three main types of stressors, which differ in terms of their severity: catastrophes, significant life changes, and daily hassles.

1) **Catastrophes** are unpredictable, large-scale events that include natural disasters and wartime events. They are events that almost everyone would appraise as dangerous and stress-inducing. The repercussions of a catastrophic event are often felt for years after the event. In the months following 9/11, many people developed psychological disorders including anxiety, depression, and Post-Traumatic Stress Disorder (PTSD). Health consequences can also follow prolonged periods of stress, as may be common in refugee camps or shelters.
2) **Significant life changes** include events such as moving, leaving home, losing a job, marriage, divorce, death of a loved one, and other such changes. The frequency of these events during young adulthood may explain the high degree of stress during this time. These events can be

risk factors for disease and death, with several concurrent events creating greater risk than single stressful events would.

3) **Daily hassles** are the everyday irritations in life including bills, traffic jams, misplacing belongings, and scheduling activities. These things are fairly universal events, but some people take them lightly, while others may become overwhelmed. These little stressors can accumulate and lead to health problems such as hypertension and immunosuppression.

4.5

Effects of Stress on Psychological Functions

Moderate amounts of stress can actually improve psychological functioning by providing more energy and motivation for cognitive activities (for example, cramming the day before a final exam). However, when stress is not at an optimal level, it can impair psychological functioning by leading to fatigue, decreased ability to concentrate, and irritability. In addition, when stress is accompanied by perceiving a lack of control over the stress-inducing events, over time someone may develop **learned helplessness**, which is a sense of exhaustion and lack of belief in one's ability to manage situations. With severe or prolonged stress, some people may develop PTSD. This disorder is characterized by symptoms of re-experiencing the traumatic event through flashbacks or nightmares, hypervigilance to one's surroundings, and avoidance of situations related to the stressful event.

Stress Outcomes/Response to Stressors

Physiological

Our bodies respond to stress through activating two parallel systems. The first is the sympathetic nervous system, the "fight or flight" response. This system responds to acute stress situations; it releases the stress hormones epinephrine (adrenaline) and norepinephrine (noradrenaline) into the bloodstream from the adrenal glands. This response results in an increased heart and respiratory rate, directs blood flow toward the skeletal muscles rather than the digestive system, releases sugar into the bloodstream, and dulls pain. It is a fast-acting response.

The second is a cognitive system initiated by the hypothalamus, located just above the brainstem. The hypothalamus releases corticotropin-releasing hormone (CRH), a messenger that stimulates the pituitary gland to release adrenocorticotropic hormone (ACTH). ACTH then signals the adrenal glands to release cortisol into the bloodstream. **Cortisol** is a glucocorticoid, a hormone that shifts the body from using sugar (glucose) as an energy source towards using fat as an energy source. This "glucose-sparing" effect keeps blood sugar levels high during stress situations (important because the only energy source the brain can use is glucose), thus ensuring that the brain will have enough fuel to stay active. This chain of events is a slower process than the near-instantaneous fight or flight response, and it is primarily triggered during long-term stress.

While short-term cortisol release can be helpful, prolonged release due to chronic stressors is harmful. Most notably, prolonged cortisol release inhibits the activity of white blood cells and other functions of the immune system. Thus, stress itself does not make us sick but rather increases the vulnerability for illness. It has been shown that stress can exacerbate the course of diseases including AIDS, cancer, and heart disease.

Emotional

Emotional stresses can be correlated with worse medical outcomes. For example, anger can trigger cardiac events such as heart attacks, arrhythmias, and even sudden death in people who already have heart disease. High levels of stress can contribute to the development of anxiety and depressive disorders, which are characterized by negative mood and irritability.

Behavioral

People respond in many different ways to stress, and an individual may respond differently to the same stressor depending on the circumstances. Sometimes we confront stressful situations, while at other times we avoid uncomfortable situations or emotions. Avoidance can be accompanied by habits such as cigarette smoking, consuming alcohol, or eating as a means of temporary physical comfort. In response to high stress situations, some people develop PTSD, which involves three clusters of symptoms: avoidance, hyperarousal, and re-experiencing. Avoidance involves avoiding both circumstances that remind one of the trauma and emotions associated with the trauma. Thus, someone with PTSD may tell a horrific story of personal trauma in a flat tone that is disconnected from the associated emotion. Hyperarousal involves heightened sensitivity (making a person easily startled) and hypervigilance to surroundings due to fear of danger. Re-experiencing symptoms are responses to triggers related to the traumatic event, such as flashbacks and nightmares. Sleep disturbances are common side effects of stress.

Managing Stress

There is an optimal level of stress that is motivating and invigorating. Too little stress can lead to complacency, while too much can be overwhelming and debilitating. However, stress is largely a personal experience based on appraisal of situations. People vary in their ability to modulate their stress levels to remain close to the optimum.

One effective way of coping with stress is aerobic exercise. Exercise has been shown to be a useful adjunct to antidepressant drugs and psychotherapy, and is about as effective as these treatments in reducing depression. In addition to lowering blood pressure, aerobic exercise may help by increasing the production of neurotransmitters that boost mood, including norepinephrine, serotonin, and endorphins.

A second means for managing stress is through the use of biofeedback and relaxation. **Biofeedback** is a means of recording and feeding back information about subtle autonomic responses in an attempt to train the individual to control those involuntary responses. For example, people can be trained to adjust their muscle tension, heartbeats, and respiratory rates. This has been a particularly effective means of treating tension headaches. Many of the same benefits can occur through relaxation training, including meditation, progressive muscle relaxation, visual imagery, and yoga.

A third means of effectively managing stress is through the utilization of social support. Stronger social support has been associated with lower blood pressure, lower stress hormones, and stronger immune system function. The impact of stressful events can be mediated when individuals can express their emotional reactions and recollection of traumatic events through talking about them, writing in journals, or other means best suited to those individuals.

There is an unclear relationship between spirituality and health. Many studies have established that religious activity is associated with longer life expectancy and healthier immune functioning; however, it is unclear whether this is a causal relationship. Those who are more involved religiously also tend to have

4.5

healthier diets and are less likely to smoke or drink. They also tend to have stronger social support systems within the religious community of which they are part. Thus, it is unclear whether other variables explain the improvement in health. Regardless, there may be important aspects inherent in or associated with spirituality and religion that can promote health.

4.6 LANGUAGE

One of the most characteristically *human* ways of interacting with the environment is to communicate using language. Indeed, our ability to learn and use language is often cited as the most defining human characteristic, the thing that distinguishes us from all the other animals. Even today, questions about what exactly language *is*, how it develops, and the role it plays in cognition remain important topics of debate and research.

Debates about these questions echo larger divisions in psychology. Behaviorists who argue that language is just another example of conditioned behavior are *empiricist* in their approach; they believe that the study of psychology should focus on directly observable environmental factors as opposed to abstract mental states. By contrast, nativists, who argue that language is a human ability prewired into the brain, are *rationalist* in their approach; they hold that certain ideas and capabilities cannot come from experience, and so must be innate. Still other researchers take a *materialist* approach to language and cognition, grounding their work in the belief that all discussion of "ideas," linguistic "expression," and the like is a set of convenient metaphors for real physical changes in the brain and actions of the body. Materialists believe that "only grey matter matters," and study thoughts and words by looking at what happens in the brain when people think, speak, write, and listen. In this section, we will define the ways these different schools of thought have explained how people learn language and how language relates to mental processes.

Theories of Language Development

Language acquisition is the term used by psychologists to refer to the way infants learn to understand and speak their native language (usually the language used by their parents). Language aquisition is the process of language learning in school or that of learning a foreign language. These other forms of language acquisition seem to work much differently.

B.F. Skinner's **behaviorist** model of language acquisition holds that infants are trained in language by operant conditioning (see Chapter 5 for more on behaviorism). Skinner argued that language use, though complex, is a form of behavior like any other, and so it is as subject to conditioning as a rat pulling a lever to receive a food pellet. Describing a beautiful sunset or persuading a friend to help you move obviously result in more complicated outcomes than receiving a food pellet after pulling a lever, but all three can be described as physical actions intended to produce effects (e.g., the production of sound using your vocal chords or the movement of your arm). How can learning to speak be analogous to learning other behaviors? Consider an infant babbling nonsense as its father repeats "bottle" while holding a bottle. By random chance the baby will eventually make some noise like "bu-ba," at which point daddy will say "very good!" and smile delightedly before calling in mommy to praise their little genius. This positive reinforcement accomplishes two things: first, it conditions the infant to make the sound in association with the stimulus (the sight of the bottle), and second and more important, it encourages imitative behavior, so that the baby begins more regularly to copy the sounds made by the parent. This imitation is how the second, third, and five hundredth words and phrases are learned progressively faster, as each subsequent "correct" utterance produces some reinforcing behavior like a hug or a piece of candy, whereas nonsense utterances achieve no reinforcement and are abandoned.

Linguist **Noam Chomsky** pointed out several major flaws with the application of behaviorism to language acquisition, and proposed an alternative to Skinner's model. Chomsky suggested that we all possess an innate feature unique to the human mind that allows people to gain mastery of language from limited exposure during the sensitive developmental years in early childhood. This idea was later named "**universal grammar**" (UG). Chomsky's device was theoretical, in that he provided no anatomical evidence for the exact location or structure of this device in the brain. However, research into the function of the device is empirical; linguists study UG by studying actual languages and actual cases of language acquisition. Their goal is to find the basic rules that apply to all or almost all languages and that are presumably innate in the brain, allowing the child to, for example, distinguish nouns, verbs, and adjectives without ever being taught these terms. It is important to note the distinction between language rules being prewired in the brain and language itself being hardwired: many songbirds, for example, are hatched knowing how to sing the territorial songs of their species, but no human is ever born knowing English or Mandarin. Rather, the theory states that humans have an innate ability to make grammatical distinctions and do so naturally when exposed to (not actively taught) language at a young age.

Influence of Language on Cognition

The relationship between language and cognition is still under debate. Some experts argue that language is first and foremost a social phenomenon, and that speech is not developmentally equivalent with thought. In other words, children first learn how to think and how to speak as separate enterprises, and only later is there overlap between the two. The first stage of acquiring language is immersion in "social speech," which is analogous to other social phenomena. This moves gradually into "egocentric speech" or "private speech," wherein children begin talking to themselves, experimenting with language as kind of thinking out loud. The final stage of language acquisition is "inner speech," the point at which a child's understanding of grammar and the relationship between words and objects is sufficiently advanced to allow him to think in words without mouthing them. This is a critical stage in the development of the relationship between language and thought. Prior to this point, speech and thought are separate activities, but at this point, some thought becomes "verbal," able to be expressed in words and clauses.

The "linguistic relativity hypothesis" asserts that not only do language and thought overlap, but cognition and perception are *determined* by the language one speaks. Unlike Chomsky's Universal Grammar, which emphasizes the commonality among all human languages, this hypothesis focuses on important distinctions among families of languages, such as Western European versus East Asian languages. Because of these distinctions, the argument goes, native speakers in these language groups conceptualize the world differently. The famous example is that Inuit peoples conceive of snow differently from English speakers, as evidenced by the fact that they have so many more words for snow. Subsequent research has called this "fact" into question, pointing out, for example, that Inuits do not have a very large number of words for snow compared to speakers of other languages and that skiers who speak different languages also have many different words in each to describe conditions of snow.

Different Brain Areas Control Language and Speech

Broca's area, located in the dominant hemisphere (usually left) of the frontal lobe of the brain, is involved in the complicated process of speech production. Broca's area was discovered when several people who had an injury to this area lost the ability to speak; a disorder now termed **Broca's aphasia**[5]. People with Broca's aphasia (also known as *expressive aphasia*) know what they want to say, but are unable to communicate it. They are typically able to comprehend words and simple sentences but are unable to generate fluent speech. Sometimes they can produce very simple, telegraphic speech ("Take. Car. Store."), or are limited to one or two words that they repeat over and over.

Wernicke's area, located in the posterior section of the temporal lobe in the dominant hemisphere of the brain (the left for most people), is involved in the comprehension of speech and written language. Wernicke's area was also discovered with the help of people with injuries to this area; in these individuals, speech production retains a natural sounding rhythm and syntax, but is completely meaningless. In other words, people with **Wernicke's aphasia** (also known as *receptive aphasia*) do not have a problem producing speech, but are incapable of producing intelligible, meaningful language. For example, someone with Wernicke's aphasia might say something like: "You know how go what moodle winkered and what you can't toodle doodle do so show him little litty round and cake you make more want to." A sentence such as this would be uttered with fluidity, with normal-sounding inflections. So, it would sound as though the person were merely speaking in an unknown language. As you might imagine, it is often difficult to decipher what the person is trying to communicate. People with Wernicke's aphasia usually have great difficulty understanding speech, and they are often unaware of their mistakes. Furthermore, these individuals usually have no body weakness or movement issues because their injury is not near the parts of the brain that control movement.

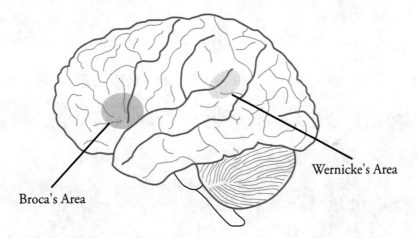

Figure 10 Approximate Location of Broca's Area and Wernicke's Area in the Brain

---

[5] From the Greek word aphatos meaning "speechlessness."

Chapter 4 Summary

- The Broadbent Filter Model of Selective Attention proposes that all sensory input first enters a buffer, then is selectively filtered so that only some of the information is sent on for higher processing. The helps keep our brains from being overloaded with sensory information.

- The cocktail party effect is the phenomenon where you can pick up on relevant information (such as your name) from previously unattended auditory channels.

- Treisman's Attenuation Model proposed that rather than a filter, sensory input is attenuated—turned up or turned down—before moving on to working memory.

- Selective priming describes the process whereby exposure to a stimulus can prime the brain to process subsequent stimuli faster.

- The resource model of attention asserts that there are limited resources for tasks in general. While accomplishing two simple, dissimilar tasks simultaneously might be possible, if one of the tasks is significantly harder or significantly similar, resource capacity will be surpassed.

- Baddeley's Model of Working Memory considered working memory to have four components: a phonological loop (for verbal information), a visuospatial sketchpad (for visual information), an episodic buffer (where information in the working memory interacts with long-term memory), and a central executive (which oversee the process).

- Jean Piaget proposed a four-stage theory for cognitive development, which included: the sensorimotor stage, preoperational stage, concrete operations stage, and formal operations stage.

- Confirmation bias is the tendency to search only for information that will confirm what we already think is true, while fixedness is the inability to see a problem from a fresh perspective. Heuristics helps us make short-cuts in problem solving, but may lead to errors in judgement.

- Consciousness is defined as the awareness that we have of ourselves, our internal states, and the environment.

- Sleep progresses through four stages, each characterized by specific physiological differences.

- Circadian rhythms involve normal fluctuations in behavioral and physiological functions on a typical 24-hour cycle.

- Depressants are drugs, such as alcohol and barbiturates, that slow down activity of the central nervous system, while stimulants, such as nicotine and caffeine, speed up the central and peripheral nervous systems.

- Hallucinogens, like LSD and marijuana, cause distortions in sensory perception.

- Drug use causes increased dopamine activity in the nucleus accumbens, which can lead to drug addiction.

- The three components of emotion are physiological, behavioral, and cognitive.

- The limbic system, including the amygdala and hypothalamus, are involved in processing emotion in the brain.

- The three main types of stressors are: catastrophes (large-scale events affecting many people), significant life changes (high stress personal events like death and divorce), and daily hassles (everyday irritations). The sympathetic nervous system and cortisol help us deal with stress.

- The behaviorist approach to language acquisition contends that infants learn language through operant conditioning.

- Noam Chomsky proposed that humans have a "language acquisition device" that is innate to our ability to learn language.

- Broca's area is involved with speech production while Wernicke's area is involved with speech comprehension.

CHAPTER 4 FREESTANDING PRACTICE QUESTIONS

1. Suppose that a researcher subliminally flashed words for negative and positive emotions (i.e., sad, happy) for a millisecond before showing subjects a neutral picture of people in a room. The words flashed so quickly that they were only perceived as a flash of light, but subjects were more likely to describe the scene in negative or positive terms (corresponding to the word that was flashed before the image), than subjects who did not see a subliminal word beforehand. What phenomenon does this describe?

   A) Primacy effect
   B) Priming
   C) Divided attention
   D) Episodic memory

2. If a two-year-old child repeatedly asks his mother for his favorite toy after it has been lost, what understanding has the child obtained, according to Piaget's theory of cognitive development?

   A) Schemas
   B) Conservation
   C) Object permanence
   D) Formal operations

3. After hearing a telephone number, one only has a few seconds to write it down before the information is lost. What aspect of Baddeley's information processing model accounts for this ability?

   A) Phonological loop
   B) Visuospatial sketchpad
   C) Episodic buffer
   D) Central executive

4. The "candle problem" is a famous experiment whereby the subject is given a wax candle, a small cardboard box containing several thumbtacks, and a book of matches. The subject is asked to affix the candle to a corkboard so that wax will not drip onto the floor below. The only correct way to solve the task is to empty the box of thumbtacks, tack the box onto the corkboard, and light the candle and place it inside the box. Most subjects are unable to figure out the solution to this task, but if the thumbtacks are presented next to the box, not inside of it, they can solve the task easily. Why can't the subjects solve the task in the first scenario?

   A) They are bound by a mental set that does not comprehend how to light a candle in this way.
   B) They are unable to employ trial and error quickly enough to solve the task.
   C) They are overconfident about they own strategies for solving the task.
   D) They are unable to see alternative uses for the box containing the thumbtacks due to functional fixedness.

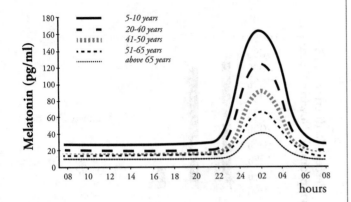

Figure 1 Average Melatonin Production (in ng/mL) over a 24-hour Period by Age Group

5. A normal 15 year old is participating in a sleep study and falls asleep at 10:30. This subject enters her first REM cycle at midnight. According to Figure 1 above, which of the following measures would most likely be recorded at midnight?

    I.   Melatonin levels of 90 ng/mL
    II. Moderate to high EMG activity
    III. EEG measures include theta waves and K-complexes

A) I only
B) III only
C) I and III only
D) I, II, and III

6. Alcohol withdrawal syndrome occurs when an individual with a dependence on alcohol suddenly limits or stops alcohol consumption. Symptoms of withdrawal can be very dangerous, including seizures, uncontrollable shaking of the extremities, and other nervous system issues. What is the most plausible mechanism of action for these physical symptoms?

A) Chronic alcohol consumption causes down-regulation of GABA receptors, leading to a reduction in CNS inhibition, and excito-neurotoxicity.
B) Long-term alcohol abuse stimulates the autonomic nervous system, causing tremors.
C) Cessation of alcohol consumption leads to a reduction in dopamine production in the nucleus accumbens.
D) Alcohol is a hallucinogenic, and withdrawal acts by relaxing, disinhibiting, and amplifying sensory information.

7. A patient recently admitted to the ER is reported to have had a stroke. At present, he is having some trouble communicating with hospital staff. When he addresses the doctor, he seems to have great difficulty forming sentences. His speech is rather monotone and lacks many function words. This patient is most likely experiencing:

A) Somnambulism
B) Wernicke's aphasia
C) Broca's aphasia
D) Receptive aphasia

8. According to the James-Lange Theory:

A) motivation follows action.
B) emotion follows physiologic arousal.
C) physiologic arousal follows emotion.
D) emotions are validated by inner dialogue.

CHAPTER 4 PRACTICE PASSAGE

Guided meditation and deep-breathing exercises have long been used as effective techniques for stress reduction. The mechanism of action for this non-pharmacologic intervention is not entirely known, but scientists believe that the act of focusing ones thoughts and deep belly-breathing both serve to somehow inhibit the stress response activated by the hypothalamic-pituitary-adrenal axis. Practitioners of meditation are capable of reducing their heart and respiration rates seemingly on command.

Irritable Bowel Syndrome (IBS) is a disorder that causes a range of abdominal discomfort and bowel irregularities, but unlike bowel diseases with similar symptoms, there are no physical abnormalities; rather, the disorder appears to be the physical manifestation of psychological triggers. For example, IBS is often comorbid with anxiety disorders or episodes of extreme stress. Acute anxiety and stress are known triggers for IBS symptoms, which usually include severe abdominal cramping, bloating, gassiness, constipation and/or diarrhea (sometimes sufferers experience one or the other more frequently, and a minority of sufferers experience both in an alternating pattern). IBS symptoms usually begin during late teen or early adult years, and a majority of sufferers are women.

The current standard non-pharmacologic treatment for IBS is cognitive behavior therapy (CBT). CBT treats IBS sufferers by treating the emotional and psychological triggers that cause physical symptoms. A trained therapist uses a structured, goal-oriented plan to identify thought patterns and behaviors that trigger IBS symptoms, and provides patients with very specific tools for recognizing these, and implementing techniques to replace these negative thoughts and behaviors with more positive ones.

In an attempt to determine if meditation is as beneficial as CBT for treating IBS, a recent six-month study was conducted on female IBS sufferers. Eligible participants had active IBS symptoms for at least three months during the past year. Participants with and without a diagnosed anxiety disorder were recruited to participate in this study. Subjects were randomly assigned to one of three groups: a CBT group, a guided-meditation group, and a no-treatment group. Approximately 65% of the participants had an anxiety disorder, and these subjects were roughly equally represented in each of the three groups. The results of this study, measured by percent reduction of IBS symptoms after treatment, are summarized in Figure 1.

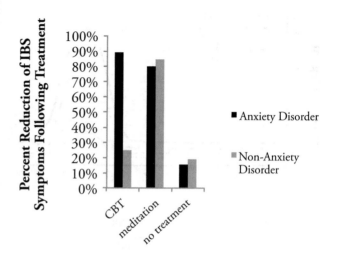

Figure 1   IBS symptom reduction for participants with and without anxiety disorders, by treatment condition

1. Based on the results of this study, what can be most reasonably concluded about the efficacy of CBT for IBS sufferers who do not have an anxiety disorder?

A) CBT is more effective than no treatment and more effective than meditation.
B) CBT and meditation combined provide the most effective treatment possible.
C) CBT is not as effective as meditation.
D) CBT is equally effective for IBS sufferers with and without anxiety disorders.

2. What is the role of the adrenal gland in the stress response?

A) The adrenal gland produces epinephrine and norepinephrine as part of the parasympathetic response to stressful triggers.
B) At the onset of a stressful event, the adrenal gland triggers a cascade of events in the hypothalamus and pituitary, resulting in activation of the sympathetic nervous system's "fight or flight" response.
C) The adrenal medulla produces cortisol, which helps regulate blood pressure and heart rate, in response to stress.
D) The adrenal medulla produces adrenaline in response to acute stressors and the adrenal cortex produces cortisol in response to longer-term, low-grade stressors.

3. The average individual diagnosed with IBS is a 40-50 year old female who is white, educated, married, and middle to upper-middle class. Based on this information, what might you conclude about IBS?

A) IBS is underdiagnosed in less-affluent populations.
B) IBS rarely affects younger men and women.
C) There is a causal relationship between education status and IBS.
D) Getting a divorce could be an effective treatment for married women who develop IBS.

4. Given the description of the study in this passage, which unknown factor might have the most influence on the validity of the results?

A) Sample size
B) Duration of IBS symptoms before entering the study
C) Participants' previous exposure to medication to treat IBS symptoms
D) Length of the treatment protocols

5. Suppose that a recent study, using advanced neuroimaging techniques, found increased activity in the anterior cingulate cortex during meditation. Given the types of physical responses to meditation described in the passage, what functions are likely associated with this area of the brain?

A) Sympathetic functions, including inhibition of the hypothalamus to prevent release of corticotropin releasing hormone (CRH)
B) Somatic functions, including control of the diaphragm
C) Autonomic functions, including heart rate and blood pressure
D) Rational cognitive functions, including decision-making

6. Which of the following represents a stressor that would be considered a "catastrophe?"

    I. A terrorist attack that kills hundreds of people
    II. Divorce
    III. Death of a child

A) I only
B) III only
C) I and III
D) I, II, and III

SOLUTIONS TO CHAPTER 4 FREESTANDING PRACTICE QUESTIONS

1. **B** The scenario in this question stem is describing priming, whereby subjects are provided with some sort of subliminal information (in this instance, the word for a negative or positive emotion) before another stimulus, and their response is impacted by the primed word (choice B is correct). The primacy effect refers to the phenomenon that people are more likely to recall the first information they hear or see, and less likely to recall later information (choice A is wrong). Divided attention refers to the ability to complete multiple tasks at once, and the ability to pay attention to one or both of those tasks; because the images were not flashed simultaneously, nor were the subjects even aware of the subliminal image, this scenario is not demonstrating divided attention (choice C is wrong). Episodic memory refers to the type of memory that would be encoded surrounding an event that is of personal significance; this scenario is not demonstrating episodic memory (choice D is wrong).

2. **C** A two-year-old is likely in the earliest stages of preoperational thought and has thus attained object permanence, the ability to understand that something still exists even if they cannot see it (choice C is correct). Schemas are mental frameworks for organizing concepts; while the child likely has a schema for "toy" that he fits his favorite toy into mentally, this does not describe why the child would ask for the toy after it is lost (choice A is wrong). Conservation (the ability to understand that quantity does not change despite a change in size) is attained during the concrete operational stage (ages 7 to 11), and does not explain the described scenario (choice B is wrong). Formal operational thought occurs around age 12 (choice D is wrong).

3. **A** According to Alan Baddeley's information processing model, the phonological loop is the component of working memory that allows us to remember auditory information for a very brief amount of time before it is either processed or lost; therefore, this is the best explanation for why, after hearing a telephone number, we only have a few seconds to write it down before forgetting it (choice A is correct). The visuospatial sketchpad works similar to the phonological loop, but is specific for visual, not auditory, information (choice B is wrong). The episodic buffer does not store auditory information for short periods of time (the phonological loop does), but rather allows information from the phonological loop and visuospatial sketchpad to interact, incorporates a temporal element to information, and communicates with long-term memory (choice C is wrong). The central executive is the overseer of the entire system, responsible for shifting and dividing attention; while the central executive is responsible for the ability to focus on the important information—the telephone number—it is not the part of the system that explains why this information decays so quickly if it isn't written down (choice D is wrong).

4. **D** Functional fixedness is the inability to perceive of various possibilities for an object. In this scenario, when presented with a box of thumbtacks, the subjects do not see the box as a potential tool for solving the task, because they are fixed on the idea that the box is merely a tool for holding the thumbtacks (choice D is correct). A mental set is the tendency to focus on past solutions to a problem, even if they do not apply to the problem at hand; there is no evidence in the question stem that subjects are bound by a mental set (choice A is wrong). Similarly, there is no mention of a time constraint, trial and error does not best describe what is happening in this scenario (choice B is wrong), and overconfidence also does not explain what is happening here (choice C is wrong).

5.   **A**   Item I is true: according to Figure 1, 90 ng/mL of melatonin would be within the normal range for a 15 year old at approximately midnight (choice B can be eliminated). Item II is false: during REM sleep, the brain stem inhibits movement, therefore EMG activity is very low or absent (choice D can be eliminated). Item III is false: theta waves and K-complexes are present during stage 2 sleep, but absent during REM sleep (choice C can be eliminated and choice A is correct).

6.   **A**   Alcohol is a depressant (choice D is wrong) and inhibits neural activity. GABA receptors in the central nervous system respond to GABA, an inhibitory neurotransmitter. Alcohol acts on GABA receptors, inhibiting neuronal signaling. Chronic alcohol consumption causes a down-regulation of GABA receptors; therefore, once the artificial depressant (alcohol) is removed from the system, the CNS no longer has an inhibitory influence, and excito-neurotoxicity occurs, which can result in seizures and tremors (choice A is correct). Alcohol is a depressant and does not stimulate the autonomic nervous system (choice B is wrong). While alcohol consumption does promote dopamine release in the nucleus accumbens (which stimulates the reward pathway in the brain and helps to explain why alcohol is addictive), and cessation of alcohol consumption would surely lead to a decrease in dopamine, this does not explain the physical symptoms of withdrawal described in the question stem (choice D is wrong).

7.   **C**   Broca's aphasia is characterized by difficulty producing speech; moreover, inflection and function words (such as pronouns or prepositions) may disappear (choice C is correct). Somnambulism is sleepwalking, which is not typically a result of stroke and does not explain the patient's impairments described in the question stem (choice A is wrong). In cases of Wernicke's aphasia, speech is preserved; however, some words are substituted for others or used incorrectly. Utterances may seem confusing or nonsensical (choice B is wrong). Receptive aphasia is another term for Wernicke's aphasia (choice D is wrong; note also that there cannot be two correct answers).

8.   **B**   The James-Lange Theory of Emotion posits that emotion is experienced after the body's physiological response to a stimulus (choice B is correct; choice C is wrong). Motivation is not part of the James-Lange theory (choice A is wrong), and neither is inner dialogue (choice D is wrong).

SOLUTIONS TO CHAPTER 4 PRACTICE PASSAGE

1. **C** According to Figure 1, CBT appears to be far less effective than meditation at reducing IBS symptoms for participants without an anxiety disorder (choice C is correct and choice A is wrong). It is also far less effective for participants without an anxiety disorder than it is for participants with an anxiety disorder (choice D is wrong). CBT and meditation were not tested in combination (choice B can be eliminated).

2. **D** The adrenal glands are endocrine glands above the kidneys; in response to stress, they release hormones. The adrenal medulla (inner portion) produces epinephrine and norepinephrine (choice C is wrong) in response to direct input from the sympathetic nervous system (not the parasympathetic, choice A is wrong). This is the body's response to acute stress. The adrenal cortex (outer portion) produces corticosteroids, including cortisol; the amount of cortisol released increases as a result of long-term stress (choice D is correct). The hypothalamus and pituitary gland release hormones that trigger the release of hormones from the adrenal gland, not the other way around (choice B is wrong).

3. **A** Since the passage states at the end of the second paragraph that "IBS symptoms usually begin during late teen or early adult years," choice B is wrong, and we might conclude that these individuals are not being diagnosed because they are less-affluent, and have perhaps less access to medical care (choice A is correct). In fact, many psychiatric illnesses and disorders are underdiagnosed in less affluent populations. Based solely on the information provided, you cannot conclude that there is a causal relationship between the listed factors and IBS (choice C is wrong), nor can you assume that any of these factors increase one's risk for developing IBS such that eliminating one of the factors (marriage) will cause the IBS to go away (choice D is wrong). Correlation does not imply or prove causation.

4. **A** In statistics, validity refers to the whether results of a given study are able to answer the question being posed by that study. In the case of this study, the question is whether meditation is as effective as the current standard therapy (CBT), at reducing IBS symptoms for participants with and without an anxiety disorder. Based on the description provided in the passage, we do not know all of the specifics about this study, though we do know that the study duration is six months (choice D is wrong). While we do not know the overall duration of IBS symptoms for participants, we do know that participants must have had active IBS for at least three months in the past year (choice B is wrong). Prior exposure to medication to treat IBS symptoms is of unknown importance, but the sample size of this study is definitely not known, and the results cannot prove that meditation is as effective as CBT without an appropriately large sample size (choice A is better than choice C).

5. **C** The first paragraph of the passage describes the physical responses to meditation as reduced heart rate and respiration rate. Thus, it is most likely that the anterior cingulate cortex plays a role in autonomic functions (in this case parasympathetic activity, choice A is wrong and choice C is correct), including the regulation of heart rate, resting respiratory rate, and blood pressure. While practitioners of meditation can reduce their respiratory rate, and while this might involve the somatic nervous system (the diaphragm is a skeletal muscle), this would not account for the reduction in heart rate (choice B is wrong). The anterior cingulate cortex is involved with rational cognitive functions, however this does not help to explain how activity in this area during meditation might inhibit the stress response (choice D is wrong).

6. **A** Item I is true: catastrophes are unpredictable, large-scale events that include natural disasters and wartime. Catastrophes are events that almost everyone would appraise as dangerous and stress-inducing (choice B can be eliminated). Item II is false: divorce is considered a significant life change, not a catastrophe (choice D can be eliminated). Item III is false: while emotionally devastating, the death of a child would be considered a significant life change, not a catastrophe, because it is not a large-scale event affecting many people (choice D can be eliminated, choice A is correct).

Chapter 5
Learning, Memory, and Behavior

Learning is an important way that organisms interact with, are changed by, and change their environment. The basis of learning is that experiences can alter and change behavior, sometimes permanently. While learning occurs in many organisms, humans demonstrate the broadest range of different types of learning.

Human learning is influenced by many factors, including both innate and environmental variables. Learning and memory are intimately related and both play critical roles in human behavior, personality, attitudes, and development over the entire lifetime of an individual.

5.1 TYPES OF LEARNING

We have been learning since the day we were born. At times, it comes more formally, like learning how to add and subtract in school, how to throw a baseball, or studying for the MCAT. Other times, learning occurs more informally, like learning how to walk, how to behave in certain social situations, or how to talk. Any way it happens, learning is an important part of how humans (and other animals) interact with each other and with the world around them.

Nonassociative Learning

Nonassociative learning occurs when an organism is repeatedly exposed to one type of stimulus. Two important types of nonassociative learning are habituation and sensitization. A **habit** is an action that is performed repeatedly until it becomes automatic, and **habituation** follows a very similar process. Essentially, a person learns to "tune out" the stimulus. For example, suppose you live near train tracks and trains pass by your house on a regular basis. When you first moved into the house, the sound of the trains passing by was annoying and loud, and it always made you cover your ears. However, after living in the house for a few months, you become used to the sound and stop covering your ears every time the trains pass. You may even become so accustomed to the sound that it becomes background noise and you don't even notice it anymore.

Dishabituation occurs when the previously habituated stimulus is removed. More specifically, after a person has been habituated to a given stimulus, and the stimulus is removed, this leads to dishabituation; the person is no longer accustomed to the stimulus. If the stimulus is then presented again, the person will react to it as if it was a new stimulus, and is likely to respond even more strongly to it than before. In the train example above, dishabituation could occur when you go away on vacation for a few weeks to a quiet beach resort. The train noise is no longer present, so you become dishabituated to that constant noise. Then, when you return to your home and the noisy train tracks, the first time you hear the train after you return, you notice it again. The noise may cause you to cover your ears again or react even more strongly because you have become dishabituated to the sound of the trains passing.

Sensitization is, in many ways, the opposite of habituation. During sensitization, there is an increase in the responsiveness due to either a repeated application of a stimulus or a particularly aversive or noxious stimulus. Instead of being able to "tune out" or ignore the stimulus and avoid reacting at all (as in habituation), the stimulus actually produces a more exaggerated response. For example, suppose that instead of trains passing by outside your house, you attend a rock concert and sit near the stage. The feedback noise from the amplifier may at first be merely irritating, but as the aversive noise continues, instead of getting used to it, it actually becomes much more painful and you have to cover your ears and perhaps even eventually move. Sensitization may also cause you to respond more vigorously to other similar stimuli. For example, supposed that as you leave the rock concert, an ambulance passes. The siren noise, which usually doesn't bother you, seems particularly loud and abrasive after being sensitized to the noise of the rock concert. Sensitization is usually temporary and may not result in any type of long-term behavior change (you may or may not avoid rock concerts in the future and you are unlikely to respond so strongly to an ambulance siren when you hear one next week).

Desensitization occurs when a stimulus that previously evoked an exaggerated response (something that we were sensitized to), no longer evokes an exaggerated response. Going back to the example of leaving a rock concert and being more sensitized to noise: at first the sound of the siren is very abrasive, but by the next morning loud noises no longer bother you—you have become desensitized.

Associative Learning

Associative learning describes a process of learning in which one event, object, or action is directly connected with another. There are two general categories of associative learning: classical conditioning and operant conditioning.

Classical Conditioning

Classical (or respondent) **conditioning** is a process in which two stimuli are paired in such a way that the response to one of the stimuli changes. The archetypal example of this is Pavlov's dogs. **Ivan Pavlov**, who first named and described the process of classical conditioning, did so by training his dogs to salivate at the sound of a ringing bell. Dogs naturally salivate at the sight and smell of food; it is a biological response that prepares the dogs for food consumption. The stimulus (food) naturally produces this response (salivating), however, dogs do not intrinsically react to the sound of a bell in any particular way. Pavlov's famous experiment paired the sound of a bell (an auditory stimulus) with the presentation of food to the dogs, and after a while, the dogs began to salivate to the sound of a bell even in the absence of food. The process of pairing the two initially unrelated stimuli changed the dogs' response to the sound of the bell over time; they became conditioned to salivate when they heard it. The dogs effectively learned that the sound of the bell was meant to announce food.

This example demonstrates a few key concepts about classical conditioning. This type of learning relies on specific stimuli and responses.

- A **neutral stimulus** is a stimulus that initially does not elicit any intrinsic response. For Pavlov's dogs, this was the sound of the bell prior to the experiment.
- An **unconditioned stimulus** (US) is a stimulus that elicits an **unconditioned response** (UR). Think of this response like a reflex. It is not a learned reaction, but a biological one: in this case, the presentation of food is the unconditioned stimulus and the salivation is the unconditioned response.
- A **conditioned stimulus** (CS) is an originally neutral stimulus (bell) that is paired with an unconditioned stimulus (food) until it can produce the conditioned response (salivation) without the unconditioned stimulus (food).
- Finally then, the **conditioned response** (CR) is the learned response to the conditioned stimulus. It is the same as the unconditioned response, but now it occurs without the unconditioned stimulus. For the dogs, salivating at the sound of the bell is the conditioned response.

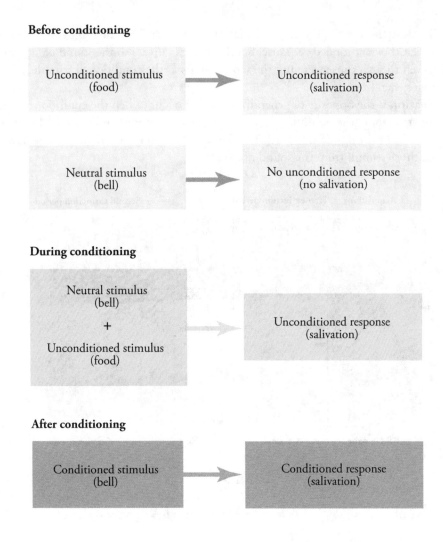

Before conditioning

Unconditioned stimulus
(food) → Unconditioned response
(salivation)

Neutral stimulus
(bell) → No unconditioned response
(no salivation)

During conditioning

Neutral stimulus
(bell)

+

Unconditioned stimulus
(food) → Unconditioned response
(salivation)

After conditioning

Conditioned stimulus
(bell) → Conditioned response
(salivation)

Figure 1   Conditioning in Pavlov's Dogs

Acquisition, extinction, spontaneous recovery, generalization, and discrimination are the processes by which classically conditioned responses are developed and maintained.

1) **Acquisition** refers to the process of learning the conditioned response. This is the time during the experiment when the bell and food are always paired.

2) **Extinction**, in classical conditioning, occurs when the conditioned and unconditioned stimuli are no longer paired, so the conditioned response eventually stops occurring. After the dogs have been conditioned to salivate at the sound of bell, if the sound is presented to the dogs over and over without being paired with the food, then after some period of time the dogs will eventually stop salivating at the sound of the bell.

3) **Spontaneous recovery** is when an extinct conditioned response occurs again when the conditioned stimulus is presented after some period of time. For example, if the behavior of salivating to the sound of the bell becomes extinct in a dog, and it is then presented to the dog again after some amount of lapsed time and the dog salivates, the conditioned response was spontaneously recovered.

4) **Generalization** refers to the process by which stimuli other than the original conditioned stimulus elicit the conditioned response. So, if the dogs salivate to the sound of a chime or a doorbell, even though those were not the same sounds as the conditioned stimulus, the behavior has been generalized.

5) **Discrimination** is the opposite of generalization, and occurs when the conditioned stimulus is differentiated from other stimuli; thus, the conditioned response only occurs for conditioned stimuli. If the dogs do not salivate at the sound of a buzzer or a horn, they have differentiated those stimuli from the sound of a bell.

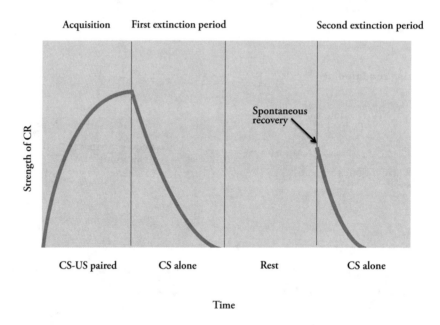

Figure 2   Curve of Acquisition, Extinction, and Spontaneous Recovery in Classical Conditioning

Organisms seem predisposed to learn associations that are adaptive in nature. One powerful and very long-lasting association in most animals (including humans) is **taste-aversion** caused by nausea and/or vomiting. An organism that eats a specific food and becomes ill a few hours later will generally develop a strong aversion to that food. Most organisms develop the aversion specifically to the smell or taste of the food (occurs in most mammals), but it is also possible to develop an aversion to the sight of the food (occurs in birds). The function of this quickly-learned response is to prevent an organism from consuming something that might be toxic or poisonous in the future. This response happens to be one that does not need a long acquisition phase (it is typically acquired after one exposure) and has a very long extinction phase; in fact for most organisms, it never extinguishes.

Operant Conditioning

The other category of associative learning is **operant** (or instrumental) **conditioning.** Whereas classical conditioning connects unconditioned and neutral stimuli to create conditioned responses, operant conditioning uses reinforcement (pleasurable consequences) and punishment (unpleasant consequences) to mold behavior. However, just as with classical conditioning, timing is everything. In classical conditioning, it was important for the neutral stimulus to be paired with the unconditioned stimulus (that is, for them to occur together or very close together in time), in order for the neutral stimulus to become conditioned. In operant conditioning, it is just as important for the reinforcement or the punishment to occur around the same time as the behavior in order for learning to occur.

One of the most famous people to conduct research in the area of operant conditioning was **B.F. Skinner**. Skinner worked with animals and designed an operant conditioning chamber (later called a "Skinner box") that he used in a series of experiments to shape animal behavior. For example, in one series of experiments, a hungry rat would be placed inside a Skinner box that contained a lever. If the rat pressed the lever, a food pellet would drop into the box. Often the rat would first touch the lever by mistake, but after discovering that food would appear in response to pushing the lever, the rat would continue to do so until it was sated. In another series of experiments, the Skinner box would be wired to deliver a painful electric shock until a lever was pushed. In this example, the rat would run around trying to avoid the shock at first, until accidentally hitting the lever and causing the shock to stop. On repeated trials, the rat would quickly push the lever to end the painful shock.

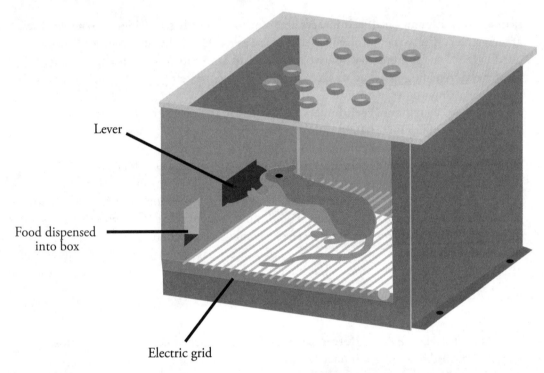

Lever

Food dispensed
into box

Electric grid

Figure 3 Example of a "Skinner Box"

These examples demonstrate a few key concepts about operant conditioning.

1) **Reinforcement** is anything that will increase the likelihood that a preceding behavior will be repeated; the behavior is supported by a reinforcement. There are two major types of reinforcement: positive and negative.
   - **Positive reinforcement** is some sort of desirable stimulus that occurs immediately following a behavior. In the above experiments, the food pellet was a positive reinforcer for the hungry rat because it causes the rat to repeat the desired behavior (push the lever).
   - **Negative reinforcement** is some sort of undesirable stimulus that is *removed* immediately following a behavior. In the above experiments, the electric shock is a negative reinforcer for the rat because it causes the rat to repeat the desired behavior (again, push the lever) to remove the undesirable stimulus (the painful shock).

Anything that *increases* a desired behavior is a reinforcer; both positive and negative reinforcements increase the desired behavior, but the process by which they do so is different. Positive reinforcement does it by adding a positive stimulus (something desirable) and negative reinforcement does it by removing a negative one (something undesirable). Positive reinforcement *adds* and negative reinforcement *subtracts* (this will be important when contrasted with punishment later). While several brain structures are involved in operant conditioning, the amygdala is understood to be particularly important in negative conditioning, while the hippocampus is believed to be particularly important in positive conditioning.

Another key distinction for reinforcement is between primary and secondary or unconditioned and conditioned reinforcers.

1) **Primary** (or unconditioned) **reinforcers** are somehow innately satisfying or desirable. These are reinforcers that we do not need to learn to see as reinforcers because they are integral to our survival. Food is a primary positive reinforcer for all organisms because it is required for survival. Avoiding pain and danger are primary negative reinforcers for the same reason; avoidance is important for survival.

2) **Secondary** (or conditioned) **reinforcers** are those that are learned to be reinforcers. These are neutral stimuli that are paired with primary reinforcers to make them conditioned. For example, suppose that every time a child reads a book, she receives a stamp. After accruing ten stamps, she can exchange these for a small pizza. The pizza, being food, is the primary reinforcer, and the stamps are secondary reinforcer. The child learns to find the stamps desirable because they help her get something she wants—pizza. Secondary reinforcers can also be paired with other secondary reinforcers. For example, suppose that after collecting ten stamps, instead of receiving a pizza, the child receives a coupon that is good for one small pizza. In this example, both the stamps and the coupon are secondary reinforcers. Almost any stimulus can become a secondary reinforcer, but it must be paired with a primary reinforcer in order to produce learned behavior.

Operant conditioning relies on a **reinforcement schedule**. This schedule can be **continuous**, in which every occurrence of the behavior is reinforced, or it can be **intermittent**, in which occurrences are sometimes reinforced and sometimes not. Continuous reinforcement will result in rapid behavior **acquisition** (or rapid learning), but will also result in rapid **extinction** when the reinforcement ceases. Intermittent reinforcement typically results in slower acquisition of behavior, but great persistence (or resistance to extinction) of that behavior over time. Therefore, it is possible to initially condition a behavior using a continuous reinforcement schedule, and then **maintain** that behavior using an intermittent reinforcement schedule. For instance, a dog can be trained to sit in response to a hand motion in a continuous reinforcement schedule where a treat is given every time the dog sits; once the dog has sufficiently mastered this behavior, you can switch to an intermittent reinforcement schedule, where the dog receives a treat only occasionally when it sits in response to the hand motion.

There are four important intermittent reinforcement schedules: fixed-ratio, variable-ratio, fixed-interval, and variable-interval. Ratio schedules are based on the number of instances of a desired behavior, and interval schedules are based on time.

1) A **fixed-ratio schedule** provides the reinforcement after a set number of instances of the behavior. Returning to the example of a hungry rat in a Skinner box, if the rat receives a food pellet every 10 times it pushes the lever, after it has been conditioned, the rat will demonstrate a high rate of response (in other words, it will push the lever rapidly, many times to get the food).

2) A **variable-ratio schedule** provides the reinforcement after an unpredictable number of occurrences. A classic example of reinforcement provided on a variable-ratio schedule is gambling; the reinforcement may be unpredictable, but the behavior will be repeated with the hope of a reinforcement. Both fixed-ratio schedules and variable-ratio schedules produce high response rates; the chances that a behavior will produce the desired outcome (a treat or a jackpot or some other reinforcement) increases with the number responses (times the behavior is performed).

3) A **fixed-interval schedule** provides the reinforcement after a set period of time that is constant. The behavior will increase as the reinforcement interval comes to an end. For example, if an employee is reinforced by attention from the boss, the employee might work hard all the time, thinking the boss will walk by at any second and notice the hard work (and provide the positive reinforcement, attention). Once the employee learns that the boss only walks by at the top of the hour every hour, the employee may become an ineffective worker throughout the day, but be more effective as the top of the hour approaches.

4) A **variable-interval schedule** provides the reinforcement after an inconsistent amount of time. This schedule produces a slow, steady behavior response rate, because the amount of time it will take to get the reinforcement is unknown. In the employee-boss example, if the boss walks by at unpredictable times each day, the employee does not know when they might receive the desired reinforcement (attention). Thus, the employee will work in a steady, efficient manner throughout the day, but not very quickly. The employee knows it doesn't matter how quickly he works at any given time, because the potential reinforcement is tied to an unpredictable time schedule.

Figure 4 demonstrates behavior response patterns to each of the four reinforcement schedules.

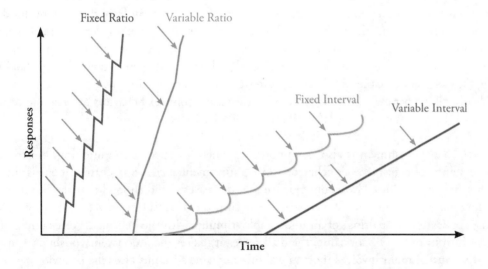

Figure 4   Behavior Response Patterns to Each of the Four Reinforcement Schedules.

	Definition	Response Rate	Extinction Rate	Notable Behavior Patterns
Continuous	Reinforcer given after every single response	SLOW	FAST	**Best way to teach new behavior,** but has the fastest rate of extinction
Fixed Ratio	Reinforcer given after set number of responses	FAST	MEDIUM	Post-reinforcement pause may be an analogue to procrastination
Fixed Interval	Reinforcer given after set amount of time	MEDIUM	MEDIUM	Long pause in responding following reinforcement, followed by accelerating rate
Variable Ratio	Reinforcer given after variable number of responses	FAST	SLOW	**Slowest rate of extinction** (behavior persists longest despite lack of reinforcer)
Variable Interval	Reinforcer given after variable amount of time	FAST	SLOW	Tends to produce a low to moderate steady rate of responding

Note: these same schedules can also be used for punishments

Table 1 Reinforcement Schedules: Response and Extinction Rates

Reinforcement and reinforcement schedules explain how behaviors can be learned, but not every behavior is learned by simply providing a reinforcement. For example, think about how a baby learns to walk. Do babies spontaneously walk one day and then receive some sort of reinforcement from their parents for doing so? Of course not. Instead, parents **shape** the desired behavior by reinforcing the smaller intermediate behaviors necessary to achieve the final desired behavior, walking. Thus, parents will reinforce their child's attempts to pull herself up, so she will try again. Once she's mastered pulling herself up and standing while holding onto something, they will reinforce the child's attempts to stand while not holding anything. And so on until the child is able to walk on her own. Shaping is a way to learn more complex behaviors by breaking them down and reinforcing the "pieces of the puzzle" until the whole behavior is strung together.

Like reinforcement, punishment is also an important element of operant conditioning, but the effect is the opposite: reinforcement *increases* behavior while punishment *decreases* it. **Punishment** is the process by which a behavior is followed by a consequence that decreases the likelihood that the behavior will be repeated. Like reinforcement, punishment can be both positive AND negative. **Positive punishment** involves the application, or pairing, of an undesirable stimulus with the behavior. For example, if cadets speak out of turn in military boot camp, the drill sergeant makes them do twenty pushups. On the contrary, **negative punishment** involves the removal of a desirable stimulus after the behavior has occurred. For example, if a child breaks a window while throwing a baseball in the house, they lose TV privileges for a week. Positive punishment *adds* and negative punishment *subtracts*. Commonly, reinforcement and punishment are used in conjunction when shaping behaviors; however, it is uncommon for punishment to have as much of a lasting effect as reinforcement. Once the punishment has been removed, then it is no longer effective. Furthermore, punishment only instructs what *not* to do, whereas reinforcement instructs what *to* do. Reinforcement is therefore a better alternative to encourage behavior change and learning. Additionally, the processes described for classical conditioning (acquisition, extinction, spontaneous recovery, generalization, and discrimination) occur in operant conditioning, as well.

Note that the term "negative reinforcement" is often used incorrectly; colloquially, people use the term when they mean punishment.

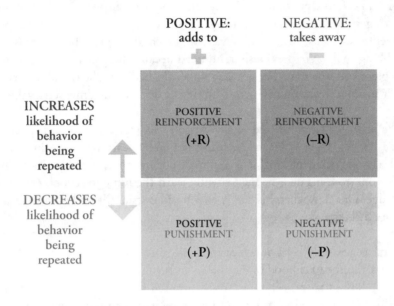

Figure 5   Schematic of Positive and Negative Reinforcements and Punishments

In conclusion, let's examine two specific types of operant learning: escape and avoidance. In **escape,** an individual learns how to get away from an aversive stimulus by engaging in a particular behavior. This helps reinforce the behavior so they will be willing to engage in it again. For example, a child does not want to eat her vegetables (aversive stimulus) so she throws a temper tantrum. If the parents respond by not making the child eat the vegetables, then she will learn that behaving in that specific way will help her escape that particular aversive stimulus. On the other hand, **avoidance** occurs when a person performs a behavior to ensure an aversive stimulus is not presented. For example, a child notices Mom cooking vegetables for dinner and fakes an illness so Mom will send him to bed with ginger ale and crackers. The child has effectively avoided confronting the aversive stimulus (the offensive vegetables) altogether. As long as either of these techniques work (meaning the parents do not force the child to eat the vegetables), the child is reinforced to perform the escape and/or avoidance behaviors.

Cognitive Processes that Affect Associative Learning

Classical and operant conditioning fall under the behaviorist tradition of psychology, which is most strongly associated with Skinner. In **behaviorism,** all psychological phenomena are explained by describing the observable antecedents of behaviors and its consequences. Behaviorism is not concerned with the unobservable events occurring within the mind. This perspective views the brain as a "black box" which does not need to be incorporated into the discussion. While Skinner and other behaviorists contributed a great deal to science, this extreme form of behaviorism has lost favor. As a reaction to behaviorism, **cognitive psychology** emerged. In cognitive psychology, researchers began to focus on the brain, cognitions (thoughts), and their effects on how people navigate the world. Cognitive psychologists do not see learning as simply due to stimulus pairing and reinforcement. Although its importance is acknowledged, cognitive psychologists do not believe that all learning can be explained in this way. For example, say a child learns that he can slide on his belly to reach a toy he wants under the bed. And, he learns that a grabbing tool can be used to pick up his toys from the ground. What will the child do when his toy is under the bed out of reach? He may figure out that he can combine the two behaviors: sliding on his belly and using the grabbing tool to get the toy. **Insight learning** is the term used to describe when previously learned behaviors are suddenly combined in unique ways. For the child, the two behaviors (sliding on the belly and using the grabbing tool) were previously reinforced because he got the toy he wanted each time. A new situation was presented (the toy is out of reach under the bed), and he was able to combine previously reinforced behavior in a novel way on his own to attain the desired outcome (retrieval of the toy).

This also works the other way around: previously unseen behavior can manifest quickly when required. The learning that is present here is **latent learning**. In latent learning, something is learned but not expressed as an observable behavior until it is required. For instance, if a child in middle school always receives a ride to school from his dad, he may latently learn the route to school, even if he never demonstrates that knowledge. One day, when his dad is on a business trip, the child is able to navigate to school along the same route by bike.

Finally, conditioning is not only behavioral learning. For instance, in operant conditioning certain behaviors are reinforced and the likelihood of that behavior being repeated increases as a result. Cognitively, the reinforcement establishes an expectation for a future reinforcer, so the process is not exclusively behavioral. There is thinking involved in this kind of learning. Expectations may also present themselves in stimulus generalization. If you were rewarded in one class for raising your hand before speaking, then you would expect that to be reinforced in another class, as well.

	Classical Conditioning	**Operant Conditioning**
Defined	Organisms learn associations between stimuli that they don't control	Organisms learn associations between behaviors and resulting consequences
Response	Involuntary, automatic	Voluntary
Acquisition	Associating two stimuli	Associating response with consequence (reinforcement or punishment)
Extinction	Conditioned response decreases as the conditioned stimulus is continually presented alone	Response decreases without reinforcement
Spontaneous recovery	Reappearance, after a rest period, of a response	Reappearance, after a rest period, of a response
Generalization	Response to a stimulus similar (but not identical) to the conditioned stimulus	Response to a similar stimulus is also reinforced
Discrimination	Ability to distinguish between conditioned stimulus and other stimuli	Learning that certain responses, not others, will be reinforced

Table 2   Comparison of Classical Conditioning and Operant Conditioning

Biological Factors that Affect Nonassociative and Associative Learning

Learning is a change in behavior as a result of experience. While many extrinsic factors can influence learning, learning is also limited by biological constraints of organisms. For example, chimpanzees can learn to communicate using basic sign language, but they cannot learn to speak, in part because they are constrained by a lack of specialized vocal chords that would enable them to do so. It was long believed that learning could occur using any two stimuli or any response and any reinforcer. But again, biology serves as an important constraint. Associative learning is most easily achieved using stimuli that are somehow relevant to survival. Furthermore, not all reinforcers are equally effective. As previously discussed, a dramatic example of this is illustrated by food aversions. If an organism consumes something that tastes strongly of vanilla and becomes nauseous a few hours later (even if the nausea was not caused by the vanilla food), that organism will develop a strong aversion to both the taste and the smell of vanilla, even if the nausea occurred hours after consuming the food. This aversion defies many of the principles of associative learning previously discussed because it occurs after one instance, it can occur after a significant time delay of hours, and it is often an aversion that can last for a very long time, sometimes indefinitely. In studies, researchers tried to condition organisms to associate the feeling of nausea with other things, such as a sound or a light, but were unable to do so. Therefore, food aversions demonstrate another important facet of learning: learning occurs more quickly if it is biologically relevant.

The process of learning results in physical changes to the central nervous system (see Chapter 3). Different areas of the brain are involved with learning different types of things. For example, the cerebellum is involved with learning how to complete motor tasks and the amygdala is involved with learning fear responses (brain lesion studies have helped scientists determine this).

Learning and memory are two processes that work together in shaping behavior, and it is impossible to discuss how learning is processed in the brain without discussing memory. Certain synaptic connections develop in the brain when a memory is formed. **Short-term memory** lasts for seconds to hours, and can potentially be converted into **long-term memory** through a process called **consolidation**. Newly acquired information (such as the knowledge that a reward follows a certain behavior) is temporarily stored in short-term memory and can be transferred into long-term memory under the right conditions.

Long-term Potentiation

When something is learned, the synapses between neurons are strengthened and the process of long-term potentiation begins. **Long-term potentiation** occurs when, following brief periods of stimulation, an increase in the synaptic strength between two neurons leads to stronger electrochemical responses to a given stimuli. When long-term potentiation occurs, the neurons involved in the circuit develop an increased sensitivity (the sending neuron needs less prompting to fire its impulse and release its neurotransmitter, and/or the receiving neurons have more receptors for the neurotransmitter), which results in increased potential for neural firing after a connection has been stimulated. This increased potential can last for hours or even weeks. Synaptic strength is thought to be the process by which memories are consolidated for long-term memory (so learning can occur). At a given synapse, long-term potentiation involves both presynaptic and postsynaptic neurons. For example, dopamine is one of the neurotransmitters involved in pleasurable or rewarding actions. In operant conditioning, reinforcement activates the limbic circuits that involve memory, learning, and emotions. Since reinforcement of a good behavior is pleasurable, the circuits are strengthened as dopamine floods the system making it more likely the behavior will be repeated.

After long-term potentiation has occurred, passing an electrical current through the brain doesn't disrupt the memory associations between the neurons involved, although other memories will be wiped out. For example, when a person receives a blow to the head resulting in a concussion, he or she loses memory for events shortly preceding the concussion. This is due to the fact that long-term potentiation has not had a chance to occur (and leave traces of memory connections), while old memories, which were already potentiated, remain.

Long-term memory storage involves more permanent changes to the brain, including structural and functional connections between neurons. For example, long-term memory storage includes new synaptic connections between neurons, permanent changes in pre- and postsynaptic membranes, and a permanent increase or decrease in neurotransmitter synthesis. Furthermore, visual imaging studies suggest that there is greater branching of dendrites in regions of the brain thought to be involved with memory storage. Other studies suggest that protein synthesis somehow influences memory formation; drugs that prevent protein synthesis appear to block long-term memory formation.

Not all behaviors are learned of course. The neural processes described above occur when animals or people learn new behaviors, or change their behaviors based on experience (that is, environmental feedback). As our learned behaviors change, our synapses change, too. On the other hand, some behaviors are **innate**. These are the things we know how to do instinctively (or our body just does without us consciously thinking about it), not because someone taught us to do them (for example, breathing or pulling away from a hot stove). Further, innate behaviors are always the same between members of the species, even for the ones performing them for the first time.

Observational Learning

More advanced organisms, particularly humans, do not learn only through direct experience. **Observational learning,** also known as **social learning** or **vicarious learning**, is learning through watching and imitating others.

Modeling

Modeling is one of the most basic mechanisms behind observational learning. In modeling, an observer sees the behavior being performed by another person. Later, with the model in mind, the observer **imitates** the behavior she or he observed. You likely participated in this behavior as a child (or even now). Think back to when you were little and you played with your friends; perhaps you played house or pretended to be a superhero. Typically, you would play your role ("mom" or "Superman") according to the model you have seen: your mother or Superman on TV. As an adult, your appearance may be based on models in society; you dress, talk, and walk like your friends. Modeling is not limited to humans either; think about how lions learn to hunt in the wild. A lioness will take her cubs with her to hunt and her cubs watch her during the process and hunt based on what they observe.

Typically, the likelihood of imitating a modeled behavior is based on how successful someone finds that behavior to be, or the type of reinforcement that the model received for his behavior. However, individuals may choose to imitate behaviors even if they do not observe the consequences of the model's behavior. For instance, **Albert Bandura** (considered a pioneer in the field of observational learning) conducted a series of experiments using a Bobo doll (a large inflatable toy with a heavy base that will spring back up after being punched). Bandura showed children videos of adults either behaving aggressively towards the Bobo doll (punching, kicking, and shouting at the doll) or ignoring the doll all together. Even when children did not see the consequences of the adult's behavior, they tended to imitate the behavior they saw. Later studies conducted by others support that humans are prone to imitation and modeling, and we are particularly likely to imitate those that we perceive as similar to ourselves, as successful, or as admirable in some way. Therefore modeling, and social learning in general, is a very powerful influence on individuals' behaviors.

Biological Processes that Affect Observational Learning

Mirror neurons have been identified in various parts of the human brain, including the premotor cortex, supplementary motor area, primary somatosensory cortex, and the inferior parietal cortex. In monkeys, mirror neurons fire when the monkey performs a task, as well as when the monkey observes another monkey performing the task. Humans also possess mirror neurons, and while there is still some debate about the exact function of these neurons, there are several hypotheses. Some believe that mirror neurons are activated by connecting the sight and action of a movement (that is, they are programmed to mirror). Some postulate that mirror neurons help us understand the actions of others and help us learn through imitation. It has also been proposed that mirror neurons in humans are responsible for **vicarious emotions**, such as empathy, and that a problem in the mirror neuron system might underlie disorders such as autism. However, this has yet to be proven, and there is clearly still much research needed to determine the exact function or functions of mirror neurons. Despite that, many believe that they are somehow involved in observational learning in animals, including humans.

Applications of Observational Learning to Explain Individual Behavior

As social organisms, observational learning connects humans. We learn from and behave like each other, but this mimicking is not perfect. There are individual differences between people and animals. Personality differences and psychological disorders can affect observational learning. For example, much of the research on observational learning has focused on violence and how observing violence increases violence in society, but not everyone who observes violence is violent. Cognition plays a role in how we use what we learn.

5.2 ATTITUDE AND BEHAVIOR

Attitudes are an important part of what makes us human and what makes us unique. Our attitudes about people, places, and things are shaped by experience, but can be highly mutable. Attitude and behavior are intimately related, and it is important to understand how both develop and change over time.

Elaboration Likelihood Model

Persuasion is one method of attitude and behavior change. When you change your beliefs about something there are a few factors that likely come into play. For example, say you are listening to two speeches about the importance of increasing the ban on smoking in public spaces. The first orator is attractive, but his argument is not well-formulated. The second orator's speech has better, more logical arguments, but he is not as attractive. Whose argument will persuade you more? The **elaboration likelihood model** explains when people will be influenced by the content of the speech (or the logic of the arguments), and when people will be influenced by other, more superficial characteristics like the appearance of the orator or the length of the speech.

Since persuasion can be such a powerful means for influencing what people think and do, much research has gone into studying the various elements of a message that might have an impact on its persuasiveness. The three key elements are message characteristics, source characteristics, and target characteristics.

1) The **message characteristics** are the features of the message itself, such as the logic and number of key points in the argument. Message characteristics also include more superficial things, such as the length of the speech or article, and its grammatical complexity.
2) The **source characteristics** of the person or venue delivering the message, such as expertise, knowledge, and trustworthiness, are also of importance. People are much more likely to be persuaded by a major study described in the *New England Journal of Medicine* than in the pages of the local supermarket tabloid.
3) Finally, the **target characteristics** of the person receiving the message, such as self-esteem, intelligence, mood, and other such personal characteristics, have an important influence on whether a message will be perceived as persuasive. For instance, some studies have suggested that those with higher intelligence are less easily persuaded by one-sided messages.

The two **cognitive routes** that persuasion follows under this model are the central route and the peripheral route. Under the **central route,** people are persuaded by the *content* of the argument. They ruminate over the key features of the argument and allow those features to influence their decision to change their point of view. The **peripheral route** functions when people focus on superficial or secondary characteristics of the speech or the orator. Under these circumstances, people are persuaded by the attractiveness of the orator, the length of the speech, whether the orator is considered an expert in his field, and other features. The elaboration likelihood model then argues that people will choose the central route only when they are both motivated to listen to the logic of the argument (they are interested in the topic), and they are not distracted, thus focusing their attention on the argument. If those conditions are not met, individuals will choose the peripheral route, and, if persuaded at all, will be persuaded by more superficial factors. Messages processed via the central route are more likely to have longer-lasting persuasive outcomes than messages processed via the peripheral route.

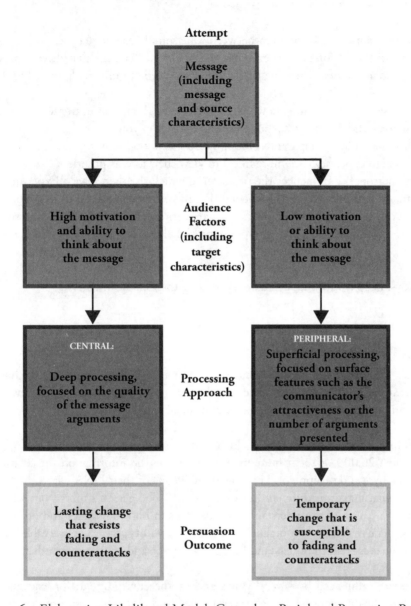

Figure 6   Elaboration Likelihood Model: Central vs. Peripheral Processing Routes

Social Cognitive Theory

The social cognitive perspective incorporates elements of cognition, learning, and social influence. **Social Cognitive Theory** is a theory of behavior change that emphasizes the interactions between people and their environment. However, unlike behaviorism (where the environment controls us), cognition (how we process our environment) is also important in determining our behavior. Social cognitive theory focuses on how we interpret and respond to external events, and how our past experiences, memories, and expectations influence our behavior. According to social cognitive theory, **social factors**, observational learning, and environmental factors can also influence a person's attitude change. The opinions and attitudes of your friends, family members, and other peer groups often have a major influence on your beliefs. Social cognition will be discussed in greater depth in Chapter 7.

Reciprocal determinism is the interaction between a person's behaviors (conscious actions), personal factors (individual motivational forces or cognitions; personality differences that drive a person to act), and environment (situational factors). There are three different ways that individuals and environments interact.

1) People choose their environments which in turn shape them. For example, the college that you chose to attend had some sort of a unique impact on you.
2) Personality shapes how people interpret and respond to their environment. For example, people prone to depression are more likely to view their jobs as pointless.
3) A person's personality influences the situation to which she then reacts. Experiments have demonstrated that how you treat someone else influences how they will treat you. For example, if you call customer service because you are furious about something, you are more likely to receive a defensive or aggressive response on the phone.

In these three ways, people both shape and are shaped by their environments.

Behavioral Genetics

Genetics plays an important role in the behavior of humans and other animals. **Behavioral genetics** attempts to determine the role of inheritance in behavioral traits; the interaction between heredity and experience determines an individual's personality and social behavior.

Almost every cell in the body contains DNA [which cells in humans do not contain DNA?[1]], and this DNA contains genes, some 20,000 or so in humans. Genes encode the information for creating proteins, the building blocks of physical development. Humans share 99.9% of their DNA with other species, therefore, to help determine what makes us different (for example, why one person suffers from schizophrenia while his brother does not), it is vital to understand the variations in both our genes and our environment. The **genotype** is the genetic makeup of an organism, while the **phenotype** is the observable characteristics and traits. Behavioral genetics seeks to understand how the genotype and environment affect the phenotype.

Most phenotypes are influenced by several genes and by the environment; for example, tallness in humans is the result of the interaction between several genes, and is also the result of proper nutrition at key developmental stages. If someone is born with genes for tallness, but is malnourished as a child, they will not grow nearly as tall as their genotype might indicate. Therefore, in order to determine the influence of genes vs. the environment (the old "nature versus nurture" argument!), behavioral genetics uses two types of studies in humans: twin studies and adoption studies.

Twin studies compare traits in monozygotic (identical) and dizygotic (fraternal) twins. Monozygotic (MZ) twins have essentially identical genotypes[2] and an almost identical environment, starting from the womb[3]. Dizygotic (DZ) twins share roughly 50% of their DNA (they are genetically no more similar than ordinary siblings), and an arguably similar environment, starting in the womb. The classic twin

---

[1] Mature red blood cells do not contain DNA.

[2] Though MZ twins have the same genes, they don't always have the same number of copies of a gene; this may help to explain why one develops a disease while the other does not. Furthermore, X inactivation in female somatic cells is not identical between MZ female twins, therefore female MZ twins are actually not *quite* as identical as male MZ twins!

[3] About 70% of MZ twins share a placenta in the womb, and in some instances, one twin will receive more blood flow, resulting in differential nutrition and growth between the two. Additionally, approximately 30% of MZ twins develop separate placentas and therefore may have slightly different prenatal conditions, as well.

study attempts to assess the variance of a phenotype (behavior, psychological disorder) in a large group in order to estimate genetic effects (heritability) and environmental effects (both from shared environment or experiences and unshared/unique environment or experiences). If identical twins share the phenotype more than fraternal twins (which is the case for most traits), genes likely play an important role. For example, if one MZ twin develops Alzheimer's disease, the other MZ twin has a 60% chance of developing it as well. Alternatively, if one DZ twin develops the disease, the other only has a 30% chance of developing it. By comparing hundreds of twin pairs, researchers can then understand more about the roles of genetic effects, shared environment, and unique environment in shaping behavior.

Adoption studies present another unique way to study the effect of genetics and environment on phenotype. Adoption creates two groups: genetic relatives and environmental relatives. Adopted individuals can be compared with both groups to determine if they are more similar to their genetic relatives or their environmental relatives. The advantage of adoption studies over twin studies is that they can help to elucidate the impact of both heredity and environment on phenotype. Twin studies can only examine the impact of genetics because the environment is so similar for each twin. Interestingly, hundreds of studies have shown that people who grow up together do not much resemble each other's personality. Adopted children have personalities more similar to their biological parents than their adopted parents; traits such as agreeableness, extraversion, introversion, etc. tend to pass from parents to biological offspring. However adopted children are more similar to their adoptive families in terms of attitudes, values, manners, faith, and politics.

Interestingly, there have been a few examples of identical twins separated at birth and raised independently by different adopted families. Psychologists have noted that these individuals, despite being raised in completely different environments with no contact with each other while growing up, are remarkably similar in terms of the tastes, physical abilities, personality, interests, attitudes, and fears.

Using twin and adoption studies, behavioral geneticists can mathematically estimate heritability for many phenotypes. Heritability does not pertain to an individual, but rather to how two individuals differ. For example, the estimated heritability of intelligence (the variation of intelligence scores attributable to genetic factors) is roughly 50%. This does not mean that your genes are responsible for 50% of your intelligence, rather, it means that heredity is responsible for 50% of the variation in intelligence between you and someone else. In fact, it means that genetic differences account for 50% of the variation in intelligence *among all people.*

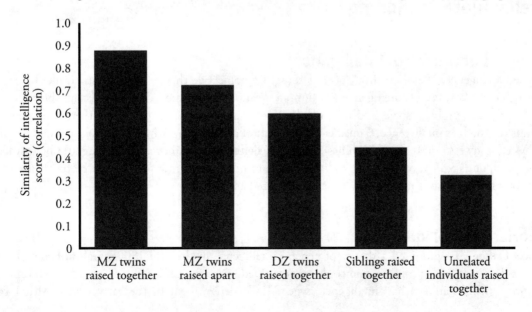

Figure 7 The Heritability of Intelligence, Estimated Using Twin Studies and Adoption Studies

In animals, the interaction between genotype and phenotype is easier to study because genes and environment can be more tightly controlled. Researchers can use **transgenesis** (the introduction of an exogenous[4] or outside gene) or knockout genes to alter genotype while controlling for environment. Transgenic animal models are useful for helping researchers understand what happens when a certain gene is present. For example, transgenic mice that have had human cancer genes introduced can help researchers study how and when cancer develops, and how cancer responds to various treatment in the mouse model (before trying the treatment on humans). Knock-out animal models are useful for helping researchers understand what happens when a gene is absent. For example, knockout mice that are missing a specific gene known to protect against cancer can also help researchers understand how and why cancer develops, and how it responds to treatment.

One of the most important adaptive aspects of all life—from single-celled organisms to human begins—is the capacity for adaptation. Genes and environment work together; not only do genes code for proteins, but they also respond to the environment. Genes might be turned on in one environment and turned off in another. For example, in response to an ongoing stressor, one gene might begin producing more of a neurotransmitter involved in overeating, which then leads to obesity. The gene itself was not hard-wired to produce obesity, but an interaction between the gene and the environment resulted in obesity.

Genes and environment interact. Consider the example of **temperament** (emotional excitability): infants who are considered "difficult" have a temperament that is more irritable and unpredictable, while infants who are considered "easy" have a more placid, quiet, and easygoing temperament. While heredity might predispose infants towards these temperament differences, an easy baby will be treated differently than a difficult baby, and studies have shown that temperament persists through childhood and beyond. Do difficult babies grow up to be aggressive, pugnacious teenagers because their temperament is genetically wired, or because their parents reacted to their irritability and unpredictability in infancy with frustration and unsupportive caregiving? It is difficult to say, but it is important to understand that both heredity and environment play an important role in many complex human traits, such as personality (of which temperament is one aspect), intelligence, motivation, etc.

Intellectual Functioning

Multiple Definitions of Intelligence

What is intelligence? We often think of it as something objective that can be measured like height and weight, but the concept of intelligence is a human creation. A common definition is the ability to learn from experience, problem-solve, and use knowledge to adapt to new situations. But there is no neurological trait that defines intelligence. Consider the concept of athleticism. Athleticism can be broadly defined as physical prowess. However, it becomes difficult to define details since athleticism could be defined by one's speed, one's agility, one's ability to lift weights, or one's visual-motor skills. Based on the criteria, a golfer or a football player may or may not be considered an athlete.

Theories of Intelligence

Francis Galton first proposed a theory of general intelligence in the mid 1800s. Galton believed intelligence had a strong biological basis and could be quantified by testing certain cognitive tasks. Galton's book, *Hereditary Genius*, argues that intelligence is genetically determined. In the early 1900s, **Alfred Binet**

---

[4] In Greek, "exo" means "outside" and "gignomi" means "to come to be."

administered intelligence tests to schoolchildren in France, with the goal of developing a measure to determine which children were in need of special education. The intelligence test created by Binet (and his collaborator, Theodore Simon) was later revised by a psychologist at Stanford Universory and renamed the Stanford-Binet Intelligence Scale, which is better known as the Intelligence Quotient (or IQ) test. Also in the early 1900s, **Charles Spearman** first coined the term general intelligence (also referred to as "g"); Spearman, like Binet, believed that intelligence could be strictly quantified through cognitive tests, and those who possessed high general intelligence would do well on lots of different measures of cognitive ability.

In the mid-twentieth century, psychologist **Raymond Cattell** proposed two types of intelligence: fluid intelligence (Gf), which is the ability to "think on your feet" and solve novel problems, and crystallized intelligence (Gc), which is the ability to recall and apply already-learned information (which is the majority of what you are expected to do in school—learn and memorize information, then apply it on test day). In the 1980s, **Howard Gardner** put forth a theory on multiple intelligences, which breaks intelligence down into eight different modalities: logical, linguistic, spatial, musical, kinesthetic, naturalist, intrapersonal and interpersonal intelligences. This theory is a nice counter to the idea that intelligence is a single general ability that can be conveniently measured and quantified with an IQ test. While Gardner was not the first to consider the importance social intelligence (**Edward Thorndike** first proposed the idea of social intelligence in the 1920s, defined as the ability to manage and understand people), the theory of multiple intelligences did renew interest in the concept of social intelligence. This renewed interest led to the idea of emotional intelligence in the 1990s. Emotional intelligence involves being well attuned to one's own emotions, being able to accurately intuit the emotions of others, and using this information as a guide for thinking and acting. Studies suggest that both emotional intelligence and social intelligence are correlated with good leadership skills, good interpersonal skills, positive outcomes in classroom situations, and better functioning in the world.

Influence of Heredity and Environment on Intelligence

Is it natural ability, or is it the environment and experiences that lead to one's intellectual abilities? As you might expect, it's a little bit of both. Studies of twins, family members, and adopted children indicate that there is significant heritability of intelligence. Scores on intelligence tests taken by identical twins correlate highly, while those of adopted children more closely resemble scores of their birth parents than of their adoptive parents. However, although genes are a predisposing factor, life experiences affect one's performance on intelligence tests. Malnutrition, sensory deprivation, social isolation, and trauma can affect normal brain development in childhood. On the other hand, early intervention and schooling can increase intelligence scores.

Also remember that intelligence is a social construct. The way it is measured is determined by cultural context. In many Western cultures, intelligence is often thought of as superior performance on academic and cognitive tasks. Some of these tasks emphasize speed, because it is valued in those societies. However, other cultures may emphasize emotional and spiritual knowledge, or social skills.

Variations in Intellectual Ability

Some differences have been found in how various groups perform on intelligence test scores. These differences have often been attributed to biases within the tests themselves or related to outside confounding factors. For example, controversial but well-established findings are that racial groups differ in their average scores on intelligence tests, and that high-scoring people are more likely to attain high levels of education and income. However, these differences are potentially due to environmental factors, such as the availability of quality schooling.

Intellectual abilities at the upper and lower extremes have profound social and functional implications. At the lower extreme are individuals whose intelligence scores fall below 70. On intelligence tests, a score of 70 is two standard deviations below the average score of 100. Individuals who not only have a score below 70, but also have difficulty adapting to everyday demands of life are classified as having an **intellectual disability**. Sometimes, intellectual disability is the product of a physical cause, such as Down's syndrome or an acquired brain injury. Students with mild intellectual disabilities are educated in the least restrictive environments in which they can learn, and they are integrated into regular classrooms with accommodations if possible. At the upper extreme, high intelligence scores (130+) often serve as criteria in selection for gifted education.

Experience and Behavior

While it is true that our genes play an important role in our behavior, our individual experiences and our social experiences also shape our behavior in important ways. As social animals, we learn ways of thinking and behavior from our families and peer groups. An individual's development, then, is determined by a complex interplay of biology, psychology, society, and culture. Biological influences include the inherited genome, prenatal development, sex-related genes, hormones, and physiology. Psychological influences include gene-environment interactions, prior experiences, responses evoked in others by our own traits (such as our temperament or gender), and beliefs, feelings, and expectations. Social and cultural influences include families, peers, friends, cultural ideals, cultural mores, and cultural norms.

5.3   HUMAN DEVELOPMENT

Developmental psychology is the study of how humans develop physically, cognitively, and socially, throughout their lifetime. As previously discussed, genetics and environment play an important role in human development.

Prenatal Development

At conception, the female and male gametes (ovum and sperm, respectively) fuse to form a zygote—a single cell with the entire genetic complement necessary[5] for developing into a human being (Note: see Princeton Review's *MCAT Biology Review* for a more detailed description of embryological development). During the prenatal stage (from conception to birth), genetic and environmental factors have an impact on development. The placenta transfers nutrients and oxygen to the developing fetus, and transports waste and carbon dioxide away from the fetus. The placenta acts as a barrier, protecting the fetus from most harmful substances, but some substances can still cross this barrier. Alcohol, for example, easily crosses the placental barrier and has been shown to have a negative impact on neurological development.

---

[5] 46 total chromosomes in a normal zygote—23 from the ovum and 23 from the sperm

Infancy

Newborns have some automatic behaviors, called **reflexes**, which are useful for survival. These reflexes are considered primitive because they originate in the central nervous system and are exhibited by all normal infants.

1) Moro (startle) reflex—in response to a loud sound or sudden movement, an infant will startle; the baby throws back its head and extends its arms and legs, cries, then pulls the arms and legs back in. This reflex is present at birth and lasts for about six months.
2) Rooting reflex—in response to touching or stroking one of the baby's cheeks, the baby will turn its head in the direction of the stroke and open its mouth to "root" for a nipple.
3) Sucking reflex—linked with the rooting reflex, in response to anything touching the roof of the baby's mouth, it will begin to suck.
4) Babinski reflex—in response to the sole of the foot being stroked, the baby's big toe moves upward or toward the top surface of the foot and the other toes fan out.
5) Tonic neck reflex—in response to its head being turned to one side, the baby will stretch out its arm on the same side and the opposite arm bends up at the elbow. This reflex lasts about six to seven months.
6) Palmar grasp reflex—in response to stroking the baby's palm, the baby's hand will grasp. This reflex lasts a few months.
7) Walking/stepping reflex—in response to the soles of a baby's feet touching a flat surface, they will attempt to "walk" by placing one foot in front of the other. This reflex disappears at around six weeks and reappears at around 8-12 months when a baby learns to walk.

In is difficult to determine what babies think, but some research indicates that infants do have certain preferences. For example, humans are born with a preference for sights and sounds that facilitate social responsiveness. Newborns turn their heads toward human voices, for example. When shown the two images in Figure 8, newborns prefer (gaze longer at) the first, because it more similar to a human face. Other experiments determine that babies can distinguish their mother's voice and smell. It appears that from the very beginning of life, humans use their senses to learn about the world around them.

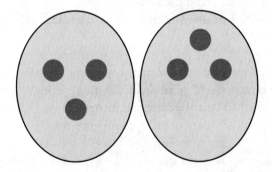

Figure 8   Two Images Shown to Newborns to Test Human Preference for Faces

Motor Development

5.3

Humans undergo a fairly predictable course of motor development, beginning with these rudimentary reflexes and progressing through the learning of specialized movements to assist with daily living and recreational activities (see Figure 9).

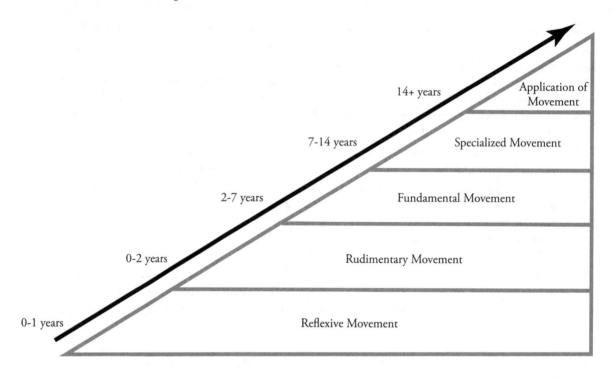

Figure 9   Motor Development Throughout a Lifetime

Reflexive movements are primitive, involuntary movements that serve to "prime" the neuromuscular system and form the basis for the more sophisticated movement to come. For example, the palmar grasp reflex primes the nervous system for the more controlled grasping learned at later stages. Reflexes, and learning to inhibit reflexes, occurs during the first year of a child's life and overlaps with the stage in which rudimentary movements are learned.

Rudimentary movements serve as the first voluntary movement performed by a child. They occur in very predictable stages from birth to age 2, and include rolling, sitting, crawling, standing, and walking. These form the foundation on which the fundamental movements are built and is primarily dictated by genetics (that is, these movements are more or less "pre-programmed").

The **fundamental movement** stage occurs from age 2 to age 7; during this time the child is learning to manipulate his or her body through actions such as running, jumping, throwing, catching. This stage is highly influenced by environment, much more so than the rudimentary movement stage that precedes it. Children are typically in school at this stage, and physical activity and games are necessary for proper motor development. Movements initially start out uncoordinated and poorly controlled, but as the child advances in age, movements become more refined, coordinated, and efficient.

During the stage of **specialized movement**, children learn to combine the fundamental movements and apply them to specific tasks. This stage can be subdivided into two shorter stages: a transitional stage and an application stage. The **transitional substage** is where the combination of movements occur; for example, grasping, throwing, and jumping are combined to shoot a basket in basketball. The **application substage** is defined more by conscious decisions to apply these skills to specific types of activity; for example, one child might choose to play basketball, whereas another might use the same set of skills and abilities to play baseball. Additionally, the application of strategy to movement is now possible, with the child say, choosing to delay shooting the basketball until she has a clear shot at the basket.

Ultimately, children progress to a **lifelong application stage**, typically beginning in adolescence and progressing through adulthood. During this time movements are continually refined and applied to normal daily activities as well as recreational and competitive activities.

Early Brain Development

During prenatal development, the brain actually produces more neurons than needed. At birth, humans have the highest number of neurons at any point in their life, and these are pruned throughout the ensuing lifetime. However, the immature brain does not have many **neural networks**, or codified routes for information processing (the types that are generated in response to learning and experience throughout a lifetime). During infancy and early childhood development, these neurons form neural networks, and networks are reinforced by learning and behavior. From ages 3 to 6, the most rapid growth occurs in the frontal lobes, corresponding to an increase in rational planning and attention. The association areas, linked with thinking, memory, and language, are the last cortical areas to develop. (For more information on cognitive development, see Jean Piaget in Chapter 4.)

Maturation is the sequence of biological growth processes in human development. Maturation, while largely genetic, is still influenced by environment. For example, while humans are programmed to learn how to speak, first using one-word utterances, then developing progressively more complex speech, severe deprivation can significantly delay this process, while an incredibly nurturing environment might speed it up. The developing brain allows for motor development; as the nervous system and muscles mature, more and more complex physical skills develop. The sequence of motor development is almost entirely universal. Babies learn to roll over, then sit, then crawl, then stand, then walk (see rudimentary movements above). The development of the cerebellum is a necessary precursor to walking, and most humans learn to walk around age one.

The average age of earliest conscious memory is roughly 3.5 years. Before this age, we are unable to remember much, if anything; this is referred to as **infantile amnesia**. Even though humans are unable to recall memories from this period, babies and young children are still capable of learning and memory. In one famous experiment, a researcher tied a string to an infant's foot and attached the other end of the string to a mobile. When the baby kicked its foot, the mobile moved. Babies demonstrated learning—they associated kicking with mobile movement—because they kicked more when attached to the mobile, both on the day of the experiment and the day after. Interestingly, if the babies were attached to a different mobile, they did not kick more, however when attached to the same mobile a month later, they remembered the association and began kicking again.

5.3

Social Development and Attachment

Humans are social organisms. From approximately 8-12 months of age, young children display **stranger anxiety** (crying and clinging to caregiver). Around this time, infants have developed schemas for familiar faces, and when new faces do not fit an already developed schema, the infant becomes distressed. Infant-parent attachment bonds are an important survival impulse. Stranger anxiety seems to peek around 13 months for children and then gradually declines. For many years it was assumed that infants attached to their parents because they provided nourishment, but an accidental experiment actually countered this assumption.

In the 1950s, two psychologists (**Harry Harlow** and **Margaret Harlow**) bred monkeys for experiments. To control for environment and to reduce the incidence of disease, infant monkeys were separated from their mothers at birth (maternal deprivation) and provided with a baby blanket. When the blankets were removed for laundering the baby monkeys became very distressed because they had formed an intense attachment to the object. This physical attachment seemed to contradict the idea that attachment was formed based on nourishment, so the Harlows designed a series of experiments to further investigate. In one experiment, the Harlows fashioned two artificial mothers—one nourishing (a wire frame with a wooden head and a bottle) and the other cloth (wire frame with a wooden head and a cloth blanket wrapped around it). They found that the baby monkeys preferred the cloth mother, clinging to her and spending the majority of their time with her, and visiting the other mother only to feed. Harlow concluded that "contact comfort" was an essential element of infant/mother bonding, as well as to psychological development. Keep in mind, however, that even though these baby monkeys were provided with a surrogate wire mother, this mother was still largely inadequate. Therefore, when the monkeys from these experiments matured, they demonstrated social deficits when reintroduced to other monkeys. Harlow's monkeys demonstrated aggressive behavior as adults, were unable to socially integrate with other monkeys, and did not mate. If female monkeys were artificially inseminated, they would neglect, abuse, or even kill their offspring.

Mary Ainsworth conducted a series of experiments called the "strange situation experiments," where mothers would leave their infants in an unfamiliar environment (usually a laboratory playroom) to see how the infants would react. These studies suggested that attachment styles vary among infants. **Securely attached** infants in the presence of their mother (or primary caregiver) will play and explore; when the mother leaves the room, the infant is distressed, and when the mother returns, the infant will seek contact with her and is easily consoled. **Insecurely attached** infants in the presence of their mother (or primary caregiver) are less likely to explore their surroundings and may even cling to their mother; when the mother leaves they will either cry loudly and remain upset or will demonstrate indifference to her departure and return. Observations indicate that securely attached infants have sensitive and responsive mothers (or primary caregivers) who are quick to attend to their child's needs in a consistent fashion. Insecurely attached infants have mothers (or primary caregivers) who are insensitive and unresponsive, attending to their child's needs inconsistently or sometimes even ignoring their children. In the Harlow's monkeys experiments described above, the cloth mother would be considered rather insensitive and unresponsive; when these monkeys were put in situations without their artificial mothers they became terrified[6].

Psychologists believe that early interactions with parents and caregivers lay the foundation for future adult relationships. Securely attached infants grow up to demonstrate better social skills, a greater capacity for effective intimate relationships, and are better able to promote secure attachments in their children. Alternatively, children who are neglected or abused are *more likely* to neglect or abuse their own children.

---

6   Note: this type of extreme deprivation experiment would no longer be considered ethical or humane today; research animals in captivity are treated much better.

Note that more likely does not imply a destiny; most abused children do not grow up to abuse their own children. Humans display a large degree of resiliency, and most insecurely attached or abused children grow into normal adults.

Parenting styles vary but tend to fall largely into three categories: authoritarian, permissive, and authoritative.

- **Authoritarian** parenting involves attempting to control children with strict rules that are expected to be followed unconditionally. Authoritarian parents will often utilize punishment instead of discipline, and will not explain the reasoning behind their rules. Typically, authoritarian parents are very demanding, but not very responsive to their children, and do not provide much warmth or nurturing. Children raised by authoritarian parents may display more aggressive behavior towards others, or may act shy and fearful around others, have lower self-esteem, and have difficulty in social situations.

- **Permissive** parents, on the other hand, allow their children to lead the show. With few rules and demands, these parents rarely discipline their children. Permissive parents are very responsive and loving toward their children, but are rather lenient; if rules exist, they are enforced inconsistently. Children raised by permissive parents tend to lack self-discipline, may be self-involved and demanding, and may demonstrate poor social skills.

- **Authoritative** parents listen to their children, encourage independence, place limits on behavior and consistently follow through with consequences when behavior is not met, express warmth and nurturing, and allow children to express their opinions and to discuss options. Authoritative parents have expectations for their children, and when children break the rules they are disciplined in a fair and consistent manner. Authoritative parenting is the "best" parenting style, as it tends to produce children that are happier, have good emotional control and regulation, develop good social skills, and are confident in their abilities.

Please remember that parenting style and a child's disposition is merely correlated; while it is possible that parenting style causes these outcomes in children, there are other possible explanations, as well [what are some potential alternative explanations for these results?[7]].

Adolescence

Despite the fact that infancy is crucial for development, development continues throughout our lifetime. **Adolescence**[8] is the transitional stage between childhood and adulthood; this period roughly begins at puberty and ends with achievement of independent adult status. Therefore, adolescence generally encompasses the teenage years. Adolescence involves many important physical, psychological, and social changes. The onset of puberty (typically around age 10 or 11 in girls, and age 11 or 12 in boys) involves surging estrogens and androgens (sex hormones) that cause a cascade of physical changes. In girls, increased estrogen causes the development of secondary sex characteristics (increased body and pubic hair, increased fat distribution, breast development) as well as the initiation of the menstrual cycle. In boys, increased testosterone (the primary androgen) also causes the development of secondary sex characteristics (increased body and pubic hair, increased muscle mass, voice deepening, enlargement of the penis and testes), and the onset of ejaculation.

---

[7]   It is possible that certain children have a genetic disposition to be easygoing, confident, and socially adjusted, so the authoritative parent has an "easy time" raising this easy child, and their resultant behavior is attributed to the parent when, in actuality, there was something innate about the child that caused the parent to respond to him in that way.

[8]   From the Latin word *adolescere*, which means "to grow up."

While the sequence of events in puberty is fairly predictable, the onset of these events is less so, which can be distressing. For example, early puberty for a girl means that she will begin developing breasts and menstruating before her peers, which can be psychologically upsetting.

During adolescence, the brain undergoes three major changes: cell proliferation (in certain areas, particularly the prefrontal lobes and limbic system), synaptic pruning (of unused or unnecessary connections), and myelination (which strengthens connections between various regions). The prefrontal cortex—responsible for abstract thought, planning, anticipating consequences, and personality—continues to develop during this period[9]. The limbic system—involved in emotion—develops more rapidly than the prefrontal cortex during adolescence, which may explain behavior that appears to be emotionally rather than rationally driven. Though it may seem contradictory, adolescents are actually improving their self-control, judgment, and long-term planning abilities during this time.

Adulthood and Later Life

While the transition to "adulthood" is not marked by any definitive biological event (indeed, the term is essentially defined by society), attainment of "adulthood" is marked by a feeling of comfortable independence. Interestingly, while childhood and adolescence is marked by clear developmental milestones and attainment of physical abilities, adulthood is less clearly defined. For example, if you met a 4-year old and a 14-year old, you would probably be able to reasonably guess at some of the things they were and were not capable of, and the differences between them would be drastic. If, on the other hand, you met a 40-year old and 50-year old, it may be much harder to pinpoint the difference, if there was much of one at all.

5.4   MEMORY

Encoding

Process of Encoding Information

As you may recall from Information Processing models, information first enters a sensory register before encoding occurs. **Encoding** is the process of transferring sensory information into our memory system.

Working memory—where information is maintained temporarily as part of a particular mental activity (learning, solving a problem)—is thought to include a phonological loop, visuospatial sketchpad, central executive, and episodic buffer (Chapter 4). Working memory is quite limited, and this model helps to explain the **serial position effect**. This effect occurs when someone attempts to memorize a series, such as a list of words. In an immediate recall condition (shortly after the information is first presented), the individual is more likely to recall the first and last items on the list. These phenomena are called the **primacy**

---

[9] In fact the frontal lobes are not completely developed until roughly age 26!

effect and the **recency effect**. It is hypothesized that first items are more easily recalled because they have had the most time to be encoded and transferred to long-term memory. Last items may be more easily recalled because they may still be in the phonological loop, and thus may be readily available. When the individual is asked to recall the list at a later point, the individual tends to remember only the first items well. This may be because that was the only information that was transferred to long-term memory, whereas recent information from the phonological loop would quickly decay and be lost.

Processes That Aid in Encoding Memories

A **mnemonic** is any technique for improving retention and retrieval of information from memory. One simple process that aids memory is use of the phonological loop through **rehearsal**. If someone were to give you a phone number and you didn't have any way to record the information, you might repeat the digits over and over in your head until you were able to write them down. In some cases, such as the re-cital of the Pledge of Allegiance, repeated rehearsal can lead to encoding into long-term memory.

Chunking is a strategy in which information to be remembered is organized into discrete groups of data. For example, with phone numbers, one might memorize the area code, the first three digits, and the last four digits as discrete chunks. Thus, the number of "things" being remembered is decreased—in the case of a phone number, there are now three "things" to memorize instead of 10 individual digits. This is an important strategy because the limit of working memory is generally understood to be about seven digits. Even the process of remembering that a group of letters makes a particular word involves chunking.

When memorizing information, people make use of **hierarchies** for organization. For example, imagine that a child is learning about the different animals in the zoo. It would be useful to have a category of "birds" to include ostriches, penguins, etc. and a category of "big cats" to remember lions, tigers, and so on. As the child learns more, these hierarchies are reorganized to match incoming information. When words are organized into groups, recall significantly improves. For example, it would be easier to remember the list "chair, table, desk, lamp, recliner, sofa" if you realized that all of these words were pieces of furniture.

There is some evidence that the **depth of processing** is important for encoding memories. Information that is thought about at a deeper level is better remembered. For example, it is easier to remember the general plot of a book than the exact words, meaning that semantic information (meaning) is more easily remembered than grammatical information (form) when the goal is to learn a concept. On the other hand, rhyme can be useful in aiding phonological processing. Another useful mnemonic device is to use short words or phrases that represent longer strings of information. For example, ROYGBIV is an **acronym** that is helpful in memorizing the colors of the rainbow (red, orange, yellow, green, blue, indigo, violet).

The **dual coding hypothesis** indicates that it is easier to remember words with associated images than either words or images alone. By encoding both a visual mental representation and an associated word, there are more connections made to the memory and an opportunity to process the information at a deeper level. For this reason, imagery is a useful mnemonic device. One aid for memory is to use the **method of loci**. This involves imagining moving through a familiar place, such as your home, and in each place, leaving a visual representation of a topic to be remembered. For recall, then, the images of the places could be called upon to bring into awareness the associated topics.

It is also easier to remember things that are personally relevant, known as the **self-reference effect**. We have excellent recall for information that we can personally relate to because it interacts with our own views or because it can be linked to existing memories. A useful tool for memory is to try to make new information personally relevant by relating it to existing knowledge.

Memory Storage

Types of Memory Storage

Different stores of memory include sensory memory, short-term memory, and long-term memory. **Sensory memory,** the initial recording of sensory information in the memory system, is a very brief snapshot that quickly decays. Two types of sensory memory are iconic memory and echoic memory. **Iconic memory** is brief photographic memory for visual information, which decays in a few tenths of a second. **Echoic memory** is memory for sound, which lasts for about 3–4 seconds. This is why sometimes in a conversation, you might ask what someone said if you had trouble hearing him or her, only to hear and make sense of the words yourself a second later. Information from sensory memory decays rapidly if it is not passed through Broadbent's filter into short-term memory. **Short-term memory** is also limited in duration and in capacity. Recall capacity for an adult is typically around seven items, plus or minus two. This is why phone numbers with seven digits (excluding area code) are conveniently remembered. As discussed earlier, although chunking increases the amount of information remembered by putting more information into each chunk, it is still subject to this limit of about seven chunks. Information in short-term memory is retained only for about 20 seconds, unless it is actively processed so that it can be transferred into long-term memory. **Long-term memory** is information that is retained sometimes indefinitely; it is believed to have an infinite capacity.

It is important to draw a distinction between short-term memory and working memory. Short-term memory, which is strongly correlated with the hippocampus, is where new information sought to be remembered resides temporarily and is then encoded to long-term memory or forgotten. Thus, if you meet a new person, you will store the person's name in short-term memory and, perhaps through rehearsal, encode the name in long-term memory. Working memory, which is strongly correlated with the prefrontal cortex, is a storage bin to hold memories (short-term or long-term) that are needed at a particular moment in order to process information or solve a problem. For example, if you need to mentally determine the area of a triangle, you will bring the formula and your knowledge of multiplication into your working memory while you process the result.

Implicit or **procedural memory** refers to conditioned associations and knowledge of how to do something, while **explicit** or **declarative memory** involves being able to "declare" or voice what is known. For example, one could read a book on how to develop a great shot in basketball from cover to cover and be able to explain in great detail the necessary steps. However, this book knowledge would not likely translate into being able to execute the shot on the court without practice. Explaining the concept involves explicit or declarative memory, while not having practiced it indicates a lack of implicit or procedural memory. Semantic and episodic memory are two subdivisions of explicit memory. **Semantic memory** is memory for factual information, such as the capital of England. **Episodic memory** is autobiographical memory for information of personal importance, such as the situation surrounding a first kiss. Typically, semantic memory deteriorates before episodic memory does.

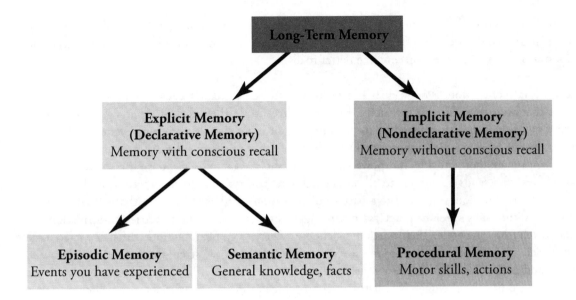

Figure 10   Types of Long-Term Memory

The distinction between explicit and implicit memory is supported by neurological evidence. Brain structures involved in memory include the hippocampus, cerebellum, and amygdala. The hippocampus is necessary for the encoding of new explicit memories. The cerebellum is involved in learning skills and conditioned associations (implicit memory). The amygdala is involved in associating emotion with memories, particularly negative memories; for example, a fear response to a dentist's drill involves fear conditioning. The roles of the hippocampus, cerebellum, and amygdala are shown by studies on patients who have the capacity for either implicit or explicit memory (but not both). For example, amnesic patients with hippocampal damage may not have declarative memory for a skill they have recently learned (due to amnesia), and yet may be able to demonstrate the skill, indicating that implicit memory exists. Interestingly, the implicit memories that infants make are retained indefinitely, but the explicit memories that infants make are largely not retained beyond about age four—a phenomenon known as infantile amnesia. It is only later, after the hippocampus has fully developed, that explicit memories are retained long-term.

Semantic Networks and Spreading Activation

If our long-term memories contained isolated pockets of information without any organization, they might be more difficult to access. A person might have numerous memories for directions, people's faces, the definitions of tens of thousands of words, and other such content; with that much information, it could be nearly impossible to find anything. Just as hierarchies are a useful tool for processing information during the encoding process, it is believed that information is stored in long-term memory as an organized network. In this network exist individual ideas called **nodes**, which can be thought of like cities on a map. Connecting these nodes are **associations**, which are like roads connecting the cities. Not all roads are created equal; some are superhighways and some are dirt roads. For example, for a person living in a city, there may be a stronger association between the nodes "bird" and "pigeon" than between "bird" and "penguin." According to this model, the strength of an association in the network is related to how frequently and how deeply the connection is made. Processing material in different ways leads to the establishment of multiple connections. In this model, searching through memory is the process of starting at one node and traveling the connected roads until one arrives at the idea one is looking for. Retrieval of information improves if there are more and stronger connections to an idea. Because all memories are, in essence, neural connections, the road analogy provides a useful visual aid in understanding access to memories; strong neural connections are like better roads.

Like any neural connection, a node does not become activated until it receives input signals from its neighbors that are strong enough to reach a **response threshold**. The effect of input signals is cumulative: the response threshold is reached by the **summation** of input signals from multiple nodes. Stronger memories involve more neural connections in the form of more numerous dendrites, the stimulation of which can summate more quickly and powerfully to threshold. Once the response threshold is reached, the node "fires" and sends a stimulus to all of its neighbors, contributing to their activation. In this way, the activation of a few nodes can lead to a pattern of activation within the network that spreads onward. This process is known as **spreading activation**. It suggests that when trying to retrieve information, we start the search from one node. Then, we do not "choose" where to go next, but rather that activated node spreads its activation to other nodes around it to an extent related to the strength of association between that node and each other. This pattern continues, with well-established links carrying activation more efficiently than more obscure ones. The network approach helps explain why hints may be helpful. They serve to activate nodes that are closely connected to the node being sought after, which may therefore contribute to that node's activation. It also explains the relevance of contextual cues. If you are reading this book while jumping up and down on a trampoline, you are more likely to later recall this information if you are once again on the trampoline. This is because you would have developed some associations between the learned information and the cues in the environment when learning the information.

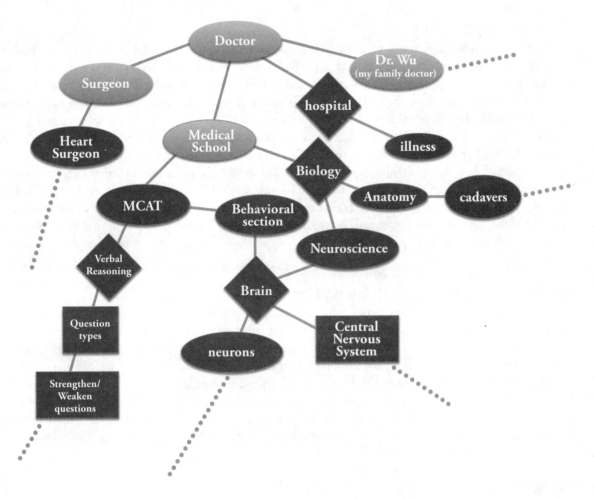

Figure 11   Example of Spreading Activation Theory

Retrieval

Recall, Recognition, and Relearning

Retrieval is the process of finding information stored in memory. When most people think of retrieval, they think of **recall**, the ability to retrieve information. **Free recall** involves retrieving the item "out of thin air," while **cued recall** involves retrieving the information when provided with a cue. For example, a test of free recall would be to ask a student to name all of the capital cities of the world. A test of cued recall would be to provide the student with a list of countries and then ask him or her to name all of the capital cities of the world. Another type of retrieval is **recognition,** which involves identifying specific information from a set of information that is presented. One recognition task would be a multiple-choice question. Finally, **relearning** involves the process of learning material that was originally learned. Once we have learned and forgotten something, we are able to relearn it more quickly than when it was originally learned, which suggests that the information was in the memory system to be retrieved.

Retrieval Cues

Retrieval cues provide reminders of information. Within the network model of memory, we have already discussed how hints may activate a closely related node, making it easier to retrieve the node being searched for. Prior activation of these nodes and associations is called **priming**. Often, this process occurs without our awareness. For example, if you are shown several red items and then asked to name a fruit, you will be more likely to name a red fruit. The best retrieval cues are often contextual cues that had associations formed at the time that the memory was encoding, such as tastes, smells, and sights. Almost everyone has had the experience of not recognizing someone familiar because of seeing the person in another context. For example, running into your coffee shop barista at a concert might make it harder to recognize her or him. Or a man may associate happiness with beagles because he had one as a child. When looking in a shelter to adopt a dog decades later, he may find himself emotionally drawn to select a beagle. Although he may not consciously be thinking of his childhood dog, his memories predispose him to connect a beagle with feeling happy.

The Role of Emotion in Retrieving Memories

In addition to words, events, and sensory input serving as retrieval cues, emotion can also serve as a retrieval cue. What we learn in one state is most easily recalled when we are once again in that emotional state, a phenomenon known as **mood-dependent memory**. Thus, when someone is depressed, events in the past that were sad are more likely to emerge to the forefront of his or her mind. This plays a role in maintaining the cycle of depression. When we are happy, we tend to remember past times that were also happy. In addition, emotion can bias the recall of memories. If someone is angry at a friend, the person is more likely to feel that the friendship has always been rotten, whereas in a moment when the friendship feels joyful, the person is more likely to perceive the relationship as having always been a joyful one.

Forgetting

Remembering information is achieved through the process of paying attention, encoding, retaining information (storage), and finally retrieval. Failure along any step of this process can cause forgetting. A failure to pay attention or encode means that the information never got into the memory system. A failure to store information is decay. A failure in retrieval could result from a lack of retrieval cues or interference.

Aging and Memory

Older adults vary in their memory abilities. Decline in memory is influenced by how active the person is: increased activity (both physical and mental) is a protective factor against neuronal atrophy. Memory loss may parallel the age-related loss of neurons. As we age, memory decline tends to follow some common trends, with certain types of memory being affected earlier. As you might expect, older adults have accumulated many experiences and so have a rich network of nodes and associations. Information that is meaningful and connects well to that existing web of information, and information that is skill-based, show less decline with age. However, there is greater decline for information that is less meaningful and less richly connected.

Due to having a more extensive memory network, retrieval can also become trickier with time. Older adults show minimal decline in recognition, but greater decline in free recall. One type of recall is **prospective memory**, remembering to do things in the future. Prospective memory is stronger when there are cues in the environment. As an example, an older adult may be asked to remember to take a particular medication three times a day. However, unless there is a reminder cue such as a readily visible pillbox or an alarm, it may be difficult to remember that there is a task that needs to be completed. Thus, the person fails to "remember to remember." Difficulty with prospective memory without cues also makes it difficult to complete time-based tasks, since one must remember to look at a clock or keep track of a schedule.

Memory Dysfunctions

Remember that memory has a neurological basis, with the hippocampus playing a role in the encoding of new explicit memories, the cerebellum playing a role in encoding implicit memories, and the amygdala helping to tie emotion to memories. Once information is in long-term memory, it is stored in various areas spread throughout the brain. Damage to parts of the brain by strokes, brain tumors, alcoholism, traumatic brain injuries, and other events can cause memory impairment. Patients with damage to the hippocampus could develop **anterograde amnesia**, an inability to encode new memories, or **retrograde amnesia**, an inability to recall information that was previously encoded (or both types of amnesia). In addition, neurological damage involving neurotransmitters can also cause memory dysfunction. One theory about the cause of Alzheimer's disease, for example, involves an inability to manufacture enough of the neurotransmitter acetylcholine, which results in, among other things, neuronal death in the hippocampus.

Decay

Memory decay results in a failure to retain stored information. Even if information is successfully encoded into memory, it can decay from our memory storage and be forgotten. However, decay does not happen in a linear fashion. Rather, the "forgetting curve" indicates that the longer the **retention interval**, or the time since the information was learned, the more information will be forgotten, with the most forgetting occurring rapidly in the first few days before leveling off. It is unclear why memories fade or erode with the passage of time. It is possible that the brain cells involved in the memory may die off, or perhaps that the associations among memories need to be refreshed in order not to weaken.

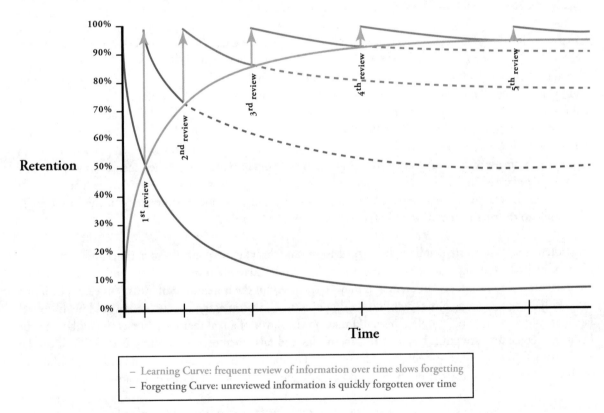

– Learning Curve: frequent review of information over time slows forgetting
– Forgetting Curve: unreviewed information is quickly forgotten over time

Figure 12 Forgetting Curve

Interference

Interference can result in a failure to retrieve information that is in storage. The passage of time may create more opportunity for newer learning to interfere with older learning, which is especially common if the learned information is similar. **Proactive interference** happens when information previously learned interferes with the ability to recall information learned later. For example, remembering where you had parked your car in a parking garage will be more difficult once you have parked in that parking garage for months in different locations. **Retroactive interference** happens when newly learned information interferes with the recall of information learned previously. For example, someone who has moved frequently may find that learning new addresses and directions interferes with his or her ability to remember old addresses and directions. Of course, old and new information do not always interfere. Sometimes, old information facilitates the learning of new information through **positive transfer**. For example, knowing how to play American football may make it easier for someone to learn how to play rugby.

Memory Construction and Source Monitoring

Our memories are far from being snapshots of actual experience. We already know that when memories are encoded, they pass through a "lens"; the mood and selective attention of the observer influence how they are encoded. Memory is once again altered when passing through the "lens" of retrieval. When we remember something, we do not pull from a mental photo album, but rather, we draw a picture, *constructing* the recalled memory from information that is stored. This process is not foolproof.

Sometimes the information that we retrieve is based more on a **schema** than on reality. A schema is a mental blueprint containing common aspects of some part of the world. For example, if asked to describe what your 4th grade classroom looked like, you might "remember" a chalkboard, chalk, desks, posters encouraging reading, and books, based on your schema for such a classroom, even though the actual room may not have had posters. In this way, when we construct a memory, we tend to "fill in the blanks" by adding details that may not have been present at the time. We may also unknowingly alter details. For example, in eyewitness testimony, leading questions often cause witnesses to misestimate or misremember. When participants in an experiment were asked how fast cars were going when they *smashed* into each other, instead of just *hit* each other, they indicated higher speeds. Individuals in the first group also reported seeing broken glass and car parts, when there actually were none. After people are exposed to subtle misinformation, they are usually susceptible to the **misinformation effect**, a tendency to misremember.

Individuals may also misremember when asked to repeatedly imagine nonexistent actions and events. Simply repeatedly imagining that one did something can create **false memories** for an event. False memories are inaccurate recollections of an event and may be the result of the implanting of ideas. For example, if one repeatedly imagined being lost as a child in a shopping mall, this imagined occurrence would begin to feel familiar, and as it felt more familiar, it would take on the flavor of a real memory. In fact, it can be very difficult for people to distinguish between real memories and false memories by feeling, because both can be accompanied by emotional reactions and the sense of familiarity. For this reason, an individual's confidence in the validity of a memory has not been found to be a good indication of how valid it actually is.

When recalling information people are also susceptible to forgetting one particular fact—the information's source. This is an error in **source monitoring**. For example, you may find yourself angry with an individual in your life for doing something hurtful, only to later realize that the action occurred in a dream. Or you may recognize someone, but have no idea where you have seen the person before.

Changes in Synaptic Connections Underlie Memory and Learning

Neuroscientists have had a difficult time in their search for a physical basis for memory. There has been no central location found for memories, and there seem to be no such thing as special memory neurons. The process of forming memories involves electrical impulses sent through brain circuits. Somehow, these impulses leave permanent neural traces that are physical representations of information. More and more evidence indicates that what is important for memory and for learning is the synapses—those sites where nerve cells communicate with each other through neurotransmitters.

Neural Plasticity

It was once believed that after the brain develops in childhood, it remains fixed. However, scientists are finding that the brain is not a static organ. **Neural plasticity** refers to the malleability of the brain's pathways and synapses based on behavior, the environment, and neural processes. In fact, the brain undergoes changes throughout life. As you will see, changes in memory and learning are reflected physiologically by changes in the associations between neurons. Connections in the brain are constantly being removed and recreated. In fact, if someone sustains a brain injury, neurons will reorganize in an attempt to compensate for or work around the impaired connections. As an example, shortly after someone becomes blind, neurons that were devoted to vision take on different roles, potentially improving other sensory perception. Furthermore, while it was previously thought that neurons of the central nervous system were irreplaceable, **neurogenesis**, the birth of new neurons, has been found to occur to a small extent in the hippocampus and cerebellum.

Memory and Learning

"What fires together, wires together." In other words, nearby neurons that fire impulses simultaneously form associations with each other. These associations can create neural nets, or patterns of activation, that represent information that is learned or stored in memory. Therefore, if any part of the neural net is activated, a memory may be recalled. This provides a neurological basis for the usefulness of retrieval cues discussed earlier. The process of learning and memory through the lifetime does not involve the enlarging of the brain or the gaining of neurons, but rather involves increased interconnectivity of the brain through increasing the synapses between existing neurons. As neurons fire together, more associations are formed. The strength of these associations is further based on the frequency with which simultaneous firing occurs, and other aspects such as the presence of emotion (which strengthens associations).

Chapter 5 Summary

- Nonassociative learning occurs when an organism is repeatedly exposed to a stimulus and includes habituation and sensitization.

- Associative learning occurs when an organism learns that an event, object, or action is connected with another; the two major types are classical conditioning and operant conditioning.

- Classical conditioning pairs a neutral stimulus with an unconditioned stimulus to generate a conditioned stimulus and conditioned response (for example, Pavlov's dogs). In acquisition the response is learned, in extinction the response is "lost," and in spontaneous recovery an extinct response occurs again when the stimulus is presented after some period of time.

- Taste-aversion is a very strong and long-lasting association between a specific taste or smell and illness; taste-aversion challenges some of the tenets of classical conditioning because it is learned quickly (after one time) and is very slow to extinguish.

- Operant conditioning uses reinforcement and punishment to mold behavior and eventually cause associative learning; B. F. Skinner and his work with rats and pigeons in a "Skinner box" is a famous example of operant conditioning.

- Reinforcement increases the likelihood that a preceding behavior will be repeated; positive reinforcement is a positive stimulus that occurs immediately following a behavior whereas negative reinforcement is a negative stimulus that is removed immediately following a behavior.

- A fixed-ratio schedule provides the reinforcement after a set number of instances of the behavior while a variable-ratio schedule provides the reinforcement after an unpredictable number of occurrences.

- A fixed-interval schedule provides the reinforcement after a set period of time that is constant while a variable-interval schedule provides the reinforcement after an inconsistent amount of time.

- Punishment is a consequence that follows a behavior and decreases the likelihood that the behavior will be repeated; positive punishment pairs a negative stimulus with the behavior while negative punishment removes a reinforcing stimulus after the behavior has occurred.

- Insight learning occurs when previously learned behaviors are suddenly combined in unique ways.

- Latent learning occurs when previously unseen behavior can manifest quickly when required.

- Long-term potentiation occurs when, following brief periods of stimulation, a persistent increase in the synaptic strength between two neurons leads to stronger electrochemical responses to a given stimuli.

- Observational learning is a social process; in modeling, an observer sees the behavior and later imitates it; Albert Bandura's Bobo doll experiment is a famous example of modeling.

- Mirror neurons have been identified in various parts of the human brain, and are believed to fire when observing another performing a task.

- The elaboration likelihood model of persuasion is a theory that attitudes are formed by dual processes; the central processing route (which includes high motivation and deep processing of the message) or by the peripheral processing route (which includes low motivation and superficial processing of the messenger).

- Behavioral genetics attempts to determine the role of inheritance in behavioral traits; the interaction between heredity and experience determines an individual's personality and social behavior.

- Twin studies and adoption studies are used to help elucidate the roles of genetic effects, shared environment, and unique environment in shaping behavior.

- Newborns have many automatic behaviors, called reflexes (such as the moro reflex, rooting reflex, and suckling reflex), which are useful for survival.

- Important information about attachment was discovered through studies conducted by Mary Ainsworth, and the impact of deprivation through studies conducted by Harry and Margaret Harlow.

- A mnemonic is any technique for improving retention and retrieval of information from memory.

- Short-term memory is also limited in duration and in capacity; recall capacity for an adult is typically around seven items, plus or minus two.

- Long-term memory is information that is retained sometimes indefinitely; it is believed to have an infinite capacity. Long-term memory consists of implicit (procedural) memory and explicit (declarative) memory; explicit memory includes episodic and semantic memory.

- The spreading activation theory of memory posits that during recall, nodes (concepts) are activated, which are connected to other nodes, and so on.

- Anterograde amnesia is an inability to encode new memories, while retrograde amnesia is an inability to recall information that was previously encoded.

- Decay results in a failure to retain stored information; decay does not occur linearly, but is a process of the amount of time since the information was learned.

- Proactive interference happens when information previously learned interferes with the ability to recall information learned later; retroactive interference happens when newly learned information interferes with the recall of information learned previously.

CHAPTER 5 FREESTANDING PRACTICE QUESTIONS

1. Retroactive interference occurs when:

A) old information interferes with learning new material.
B) new material interferes with recalling old material.
C) new information decays over time.
D) old information decays over time.

2. Which of the following types of memory does not affect behavior consciously and can be measured only indirectly?

A) Nondeclarative memory
B) Declarative memory
C) Episodic memory
D) Explicit memory

3. A five-year-old boy has formed a habit of writing on his parents' living room walls. Based on operant conditioning principles, which of the following types of punishment would be least effective in stopping this behavior?

A) Giving the child a time out immediately after he writes on the wall, every time the child writes on the wall.
B) Providing the child with a cookie at the end of each day that he abstains from writing on the walls.
C) Spanking the child (an intense punishment) every time that the child writes on the wall.
D) Punishing the child occasionally, when the parents happen to notice writing on the wall.

4. Jay joins a social media website to lose weight, and he receives points based on the intensity of his daily exercise and praise from fellow website users for each workout he logs on the website. This increases his exercise frequency and intensity. Eventually he stops logging onto the website, but continues to exercise with increased frequency. This is an example of:

A) vicarious reinforcement.
B) operant conditioning.
C) innate behavior.
D) classical conditioning.

5. A student cramming for finals memorizes the steps in solving a physics problem early in the afternoon and then studies for his other subjects for several hours before his physics exam. When he arrives at the exam he can no longer remember how to solve the physics equation. This is an example of:

A) retroactive interference.
B) proactive interference.
C) retrieval cues.
D) long term potentiation.

6. A researcher studying several patients gives each of them the same maze to solve. Although each works independently on it for 30 minutes—with varying degrees of success—none of them recalls seeing the maze when presented with it the next day. Nonetheless, their overall speed and success in solving it has improved significantly. These patients are likely experiencing impairment in:

   I. procedural memory
  II. episodic memory
 III. echoic memory

A) I only
B) II only
C) I and II
D) II and III

CHAPTER 5 PRACTICE PASSAGE

Elizabeth Loftus is widely known as one of the leading experts in the field of false memories, especially regarding childhood sexual abuse. However, this particular topic is deeply controversial, with many experts divided over whether these memories are truly false, or if they are instead repressed to protect the individual from reliving further trauma. Loftus is most famous for her theory of the *misinformation effect*, which refers to the phenomenon in which exposure to incorrect information between the encoding of a memory and its later recall causes impairment to the memory. That is to say, if you witnessed a hit-and-run car accident, and heard a radio commercial for Ford before giving your testimony to the police, you might incorrectly recall that the offending vehicle was a Ford, even if it was not. Loftus' research has been used in many cases of eyewitness testimony in high-profile court cases to demonstrate the malleability of the human memory.

To test this theory, researchers in New York City set up a "crime" for participants to "witness" (unbeknownst to them). 175 local female college students were recruited to participate in a study about memory, and were directed to complete some computer tasks involving word and picture recall in a room overlooking an alley. While completing the computer tasks, participants witnessed a young woman being "mugged" by a young man in the alley outside the lab—both individuals were confederates of the researchers. After reporting the "crime" to the researchers, participants were escorted out of the lab and told that this crime would be reported to the local police, and that they might be called back in to give a testimony. For half of the participants, a research confederate acting as a custodial worker was present as they were being escorted out. For the other half, no decoys were present. Participants were randomly assigned to either the decoy or control group. Participants who did not report the "crime" to the researchers were excluded from the study (25 women were excluded).

One week later, participants were called back to the lab to give their testimony to a police officer—another confederate. Participants were told that the police had several leads on who the mugger might be, and were asked to pick out the suspect from five different photo options. Included in the photo set were photos of the mugger, the custodial worker, and three neutral faces chosen to be similar to the two experimental faces. After recalling the event to the police officer and choosing a face, participants were debriefed (they were told that the mugging was fake) and awarded course credit for their participation. The results of this study are summarized in Table 1.

Table 1 Number of positive identifications in photo line-up

	Photo				
	"Mugger"	"Custodial Worker"	Neutral Photo #1	Neutral Photo #2	Neutral Photo #3
Decoy Group (n = 75)	18	37	7	5	8
Control Group (n = 75)	23	13	12	14	13

1. What conclusions can be drawn from the data presented in Table 1?

A) The misinformation effect is present in the decoy group.
B) The control group had a better memory than the decoy group.
C) There are no significant differences between the decoy and the control group.
D) No conclusions can be drawn from these data.

2. What part of the brain is most associated with the formation of long-term memories?

A) Pre-frontal cortex
B) Amygdala
C) Hippocampus
D) Thalamus

3. The inability to form new memories is called:

A) retrograde amnesia.
B) anterograde amnesia.
C) source amnesia
D) infantile amnesia.

4. Suppose that after selecting someone from the photo line-up, all of the subjects in the control group watched a ten-minute film presentation in which a "police officer" provided additional evidence about why the custodial worker (whom the control subjects never met) was suspected to be the culprit responsible for the mugging. Half of the control subjects had a "very handsome" police officer presenting the information, and the other half had an "unattractive" police officer presenting the same information. 85% of the control subjects who watched the video with the handsome police officer either changed their answer to the custodial worker (or if they had initially selected the custodial worker, confirmed that selection). 45% of the control subjects who watched the video with the unattractive police officer either changed their answer to the custodial worker (or if they had initially selected the custodial worker, confirmed that selection). The elaboration likelihood model suggests that the discrepancy in the two groups is based on:

A) the peripheral route of information processing.
B) target characteristics.
C) message characteristics.
D) the central route of information processing.

5. What type of memory is used in a multiple-choice test, such as this one?

A) Recall
B) Recognition
C) Repressed
D) Déjà vu

6. What are the three main stages of memory, according to the information processing perspective?

A) Encoding, storage, and retrieval.
B) Recognition, detection, and regurgitation.
C) Consolidation, reconsolidation, and recovery.
D) Identification, encrypting, and reclamation.

7. What part of the brain is responsible for procedural memories for skills?

A) Hypothalamus
B) Parietal lobe
C) Occipital lobe
D) Basal ganglia

SOLUTIONS TO CHAPTER 5 FREESTANDING PRACTICE QUESTIONS

1. **B**   Retroactive interference is a type of memory interference in which new information interferes with our ability to recall older material (choice B is correct). Proactive interference occurs when old information interferes with learning new material (choice A is wrong). Answer choices C and D refer to memory decay which occurs regardless of intereference (choices C and D are wrong).

2. **A**   Nondeclarative memory, or implicit memory, is a form of memory that is not conscious. It is the autopilot of memory (so it does not affect behavior consciously) and may be difficult to verbalize, making it measurable only indirectly (choice A is correct). Declarative memory, also referred to as explicit memory, is a long-term recollection that can be consciously or intentionally called upon (choices B and D are wrong). Episodic memory is a type of declarative memory that is responsible for the recall of autobiographical events (choice C is wrong).

3. **D**   Operant conditioning employs consequences to modify behavior. Reinforcement is more effective at modifying behavior than punishment is, but for both, the timing/schedule and intensity of the reinforcement or punishment is important. In general, delivering punishment consistently for every occurrence of the behavior produces more effective suppression of the behavior than does delivering punishment intermittently or inconsistently. Punishing the child only when the negative behavior happens to be noticed would not qualify as consistent and would thus not be very effective (choice D is correct). Immediacy, or delivering the punishment immediately after the act, will increase the effectiveness of the punishment, as will consistency (choice A would be more effective than D, and is therefore wrong). Positive reinforcement is generally more effective than punishment for increasing the frequency of a desired behavior (not writing on the walls) and diminishes the child's motivation to engage in the undesired response (choice B is more effective than D, and is therefore wrong). Finally, while severe punishment can have undesirable side effects, in general, the more intense the punishment, the more effective the punishment is in producing major, rapid, and long lasting suppression (choice C is more effective than D, and is therefore wrong).

4. **B**   Operant conditioning is accomplished when someone receives a reward after performing a task; after the person has performed the task and received the reward enough times, they will perform the task without the reward (choice B is correct). Vicarious reinforcement involves watching another person receive a reward for his or her behavior; there is no mention of Jay being motived by other people getting rewarded (choice A is wrong). An innate behavior is one that does not need to be conditioned, and therefore not what is being described in the question stem (choice C is wrong). Classical conditioning is accomplished by pairing two stimuli, one that is neutral with another that is unconditioned. Over time, the neutral stimulus becomes the conditioned stimulus. Since the question is not describing the pairing of two stimuli, nor is a stimulus presented before the behavior, classical conditioning does not explain the behavior described in the question stem (choice D is wrong).

5. **A** Retroactive interference occurs when new information interferes with the storage of information learned beforehand (choice A is correct). Proactive interference occurs when information that is learned first interferes with the ability to recall later information; the opposite is described in this question (choice B is wrong). Retrieval cues are used to retrieve stored memories; there is no mention of retrieval cues in this question (choice C is wrong). Long term potentiation is part of long term memory storage; while a failure to remember information is partially a result of a failure to convert information via long-term potentiation, it does not explain the interference of information learned after memorizing the step to a physics problem (choice D is wrong).

6. **B** Item I is false: the subjects have no recall of the maze, meaning that their *declarative* memory (long-term, concerning specific facts, details, situations, and context) is not functioning properly; *procedural* memory, which concerns development of specific skills for how to do something, is biologically distinct from declarative memory, and must be functioning if they display improvement on the maze (choices A and C can be eliminated). Note that both remaining answer choices include Item II, so Item II must be true: episodic memory, (part of declarative memory) includes memory of events that have been experienced personally. Amnesic patients with hippocampal damage may not have declarative memory for a skill they have recently learned (due to amnesia), and yet may be able to demonstrate the skill, indicating that implicit (procedural) memory exists, much like the patients described in the question stem. Item III is false: echoic memory, part of the short-term sensory memory system, is brief memory for sound. The question stem does not provide any information about the patients' ability to process or remember sound information (choice D can be eliminated and choice B is correct).

SOLUTIONS TO CHAPTER 5 PRACTICE PASSAGE

1. **A** Based on the data presented in Table 1, one can reasonably conclude that the misinformation effect is present in the decoy group. As noted in the table, the overwhelming majority of participants positively identified the custodial worker as the mugger, most likely because his face was presented to the participants before the memory of the mugging could be fully encoded (choice A is correct). Although the control group chose the mugger at a higher rate than did the decoy group, this is not enough information to reasonably conclude that the control group has a better memory (choice B is wrong). Based on the data in Table 1, there are significant differences between the decoy group and the control group. The decoy group overwhelmingly chose the custodial worker as the suspect over the other photo choices, whereas the control group chose the actual mugger at a slightly higher rate (choice C is wrong). Based on these findings, some conclusions can indeed be drawn from these data (choice D is wrong).

2. **C** The hippocampus is the part of the brain most commonly associated with long-term memory, as it plays a major part in constructing, integrating, and then storing information from short-term into long-term memory (choice C is correct). The pre-frontal cortex stores information on an extremely temporary basis (anywhere from several seconds to several minutes), and thus is more commonly associated with short-term memory than with long-term memory (choice A is wrong). The amygdala has been implicated in encoding and storing memories that include intense emotional themes, but it works in concert with the hippocampus and other limbic area brain systems, and thus is not alone responsible for long-term memory (choice B is wrong). The thalamus is responsible for sensory and motor action, and is not typically associated with memory (choice D is wrong).

3. **B** Anterograde amnesia is defined as the inability to form new memories (choice B is correct). Retrograde amnesia is defined as the inability to retrieve information from one's own past (choice A is wrong). Source amnesia is defined as the attribution of an event one has experienced, heard about, or imagined to the wrong source (choice C is wrong). Infantile amnesia is used to explain why individuals are typically unable to remember anything from before the age of 3; the human brain pathways are not yet fully developed enough to form memories at this age (choice D is wrong).

4. **A** The elaboration likelihood model of persuasion is a theory that attitudes are formed by dual processes, via the central processing route (which includes deep processing of the message itself) or by the peripheral processing route (which includes superficial processing focused on specifics of the messenger). Since the controls with the handsome police officer were far more likely to be persuaded that the photo of the custodial worker was the mugger, this suggests that both groups are focusing on characteristics of the person delivering the message (attractiveness). In the peripheral processing route, people are more likely to be persuaded by attractive messengers (choice A is correct). The central processing route involves focusing on the information of the message; in this scenario, the message was the same for both groups, so the central processing route does not explain the difference in outcome (choice D is wrong). Target characteristics describe the characteristics of the person receiving the message (motivation, interest); there is no information provided in the stem that would indicate that the characteristics of the two groups were responsible for the different outcome (choice B is wrong). Similarly, the message characteristics include specific features of the message itself (like length, logic, and evidence). Since the message was the same for the two groups, message characteristics do not explain the difference in outcomes (choice C is wrong).

5. **B** To the delight of many exhausted college students, multiple-choice tests rely most heavily on recognition memory; that is, test-takers do not have to generate the correct response, but rather have to recognize the correct response from several options (choice B is correct). On the flip side, a test that involved short-answer or essay questions would rely on recall memory, which requires individuals to retrieve previously learned information and repeat it in some context (choice A is wrong). Repressed memories are a phenomenon that is hotly debated in the legal and psychological fields, and would likely not come into play during a multiple-choice test (choice C is wrong). Déjà vu is the phenomenon in which cues from the current situation subconsciously trigger retrieval of an earlier experience, creating that "I've been here before" feeling. This phenomenon is not typically associated with testing (choice D is wrong).

6. **A** The three main stages of memory are encoding (receiving, processing, and combining information), storage (the creation of a permanent record of the encoded information), and retrieval (the recovery of the stored information in response to a particular cue or activity; choice A is correct). The other terms, while sometimes associated with the study of memory, are not part of the formal stages of memory (choices B, C, and D are wrong).

7. **D** The basal ganglia are the part of the brain most commonly associated with procedural memory for skills. They do this by receiving input from the cortex and storing it, but they do not send that information back to the cortex for conscious awareness. This is why one does not typically recall consciously reminding oneself how to pedal a bicycle after having learned as a child (choice D is correct). The hypothalamus is not implicated in memory, but is instead responsible for many of the autonomic functions that keep us alive, such as body temperature, hunger, thirst, sleep, et cetera (choice A is wrong). The parietal lobe is responsible for integrating sensory information, and in particular helps with determining spatial sense and navigation (choice B is wrong). The occipital lobe is the visual processing center of the brain, and it is not associated with memory (choice C is wrong).

Chapter 6
Personality, Motivation, Attitudes, and Psychological Disorders

Many different qualities make up an individual; our personalities are a big part of who we are (some might say *all* of who we are!). Each of us has a personality shaped over time by both internal and external factors. Likewise, everyone is driven or motivated by different things, and we each have opinions or attitudes about things: these are also important aspects of who we are as individuals.

Psychological disorders affect all three of these qualities: personality, motivation, and attitude. The study and treatment of psychological disorders is an important field of psychology. Not only do the disorders help us understand how our minds and bodies function properly (by understanding what happens when something goes awry), but they also constitute a huge area of clinical practice.

6.1 PERSONALITY

Theories of Personality

Personality, while very hard to precisely define, is essentially the individual pattern of thinking, feeling, and behavior associated with each person. Personalities are nuanced and complex. Various theories and perspectives on personality have evolved to help explain this fundamental aspect of individuality, including the psychoanalytic perspective, the humanistic perspective, the behaviorist perspective, the social cognitive perspective, the trait perspective, and the biological perspective. Therapies to treat personality disorders are based on the first four perspectives (psychoanalytic therapy, humanistic, or person-based therapy, and cognitive behavioral therapy).

Psychoanalytic Perspective

According to **psychoanalytic theory**, personality (made up of patterns of thoughts, feelings, and behaviors) is shaped by a person's unconscious thoughts, feelings, and memories. These unconscious elements are derived from past experiences, particularly interactions with primary early caregivers. What a person is conscious of is quite limited, like the tip of an iceberg compared with his or her vast unconscious stores of experiences, memories, needs, and motivations below the surface. According to psychoanalytic theory, the existence of the unconscious is inferred from behaviors such as dreams, slips of the tongue, posthypnotic suggestions, and free associations.

Within classical psychoanalytic theory as developed by **Sigmund Freud**, two instinctual drives motivate human behavior. The **libido**, or life instinct, drives behaviors focused on survival, growth, creativity, pain avoidance, and pleasure. Note that the libido is commonly defined as "sex drive," but the libido includes more than just sexual energy. The **death instinct** drives aggressive behaviors fueled by an unconscious wish to die or to hurt oneself or others.

Sigmund Freud

Psychic energy is distributed among three personality components that function together: id, ego, and superego.

1) The largely unconscious **id** is the source of energy and instincts. Ruled by the **pleasure principle**, the id seeks to reduce tension, avoid pain, and gain pleasure. It does not use logical or moral reasoning, and it does not distinguish mental images from external objects. According to Freud, young children function almost entirely from the id.
2) The **ego**, ruled by the **reality principle**, uses logical thinking and planning to control consciousness and the id. The ego tries to find realistic ways to satisfy the id's desire for pleasure.
3) The **superego** inhibits the id and influences the ego to follow moralistic and idealistic goals rather than just realistic goals; the superego strives for a "higher purpose." Based on societal values as learned from one's parents, the superego makes judgments of right and wrong and strives for perfection. The superego seeks to gain psychological rewards such as feelings of pride and self-love, and to avoid psychological punishment such as feelings of guilt and inferiority.

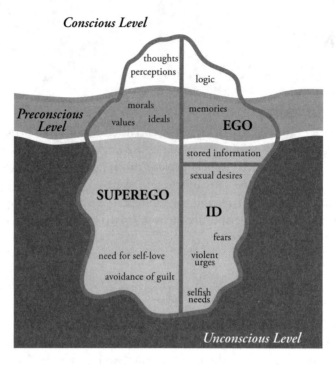

Figure 1   Freud's Iceberg Analogy to the Human Mind and Personality

According to Freud, anxiety is a feeling of dread or tension, a warning of potential danger, that occurs when a person begins to become aware of repressed feelings, memories, desires, or experiences. To cope with this anxiety and protect the ego, all people develop **ego defense mechanisms** that unconsciously deny or distort reality. Ego defense mechanisms are therefore normal, and become unhealthy only when taken to extremes. Several (but not all) common ego defense mechanisms are described in Table 1.

Defense Mechanism	Description
Repression	Lack of recall of an emotionally painful memory
Denial	Forceful refusal to acknowledge an emotionally painful memory
Reaction Formation	Expressing the opposite of what one really feels, when it would feel too dangerous to express the real feeling (such as acting hateful toward someone to whom one is sexually attracted)
Projection	Attributing one's own unacceptable thoughts or feelings to another person ("I'm not angry, you are!")
Displacement	Redirecting aggressive or sexual impulses from a forbidden action or object onto a less dangerous one (as when a person goes home and kicks the dog instead of expressing anger at a boss)
Rationalization	Explaining and intellectually justifying one's impulsive behavior
Regression	Reverting to an earlier, less sophisticated behavior (as when a child reverts to bedwetting after a trauma)
Sublimation	Channeling aggressive or sexual energy into positive, constructive activities, such as producing art

Table 1   Some Common Ego Defense Mechanisms

According to psychoanalytic theory, at each developmental stage throughout the lifespan, certain needs and tasks must be satisfied. When these needs and tasks are not met, a person harbors unresolved unconscious conflicts that lead to psychological dysfunction. There are two different theories of developmental stages that you should be familiar with, Freud's psychosexual stages and Erik Erikson's psychosocial stages.

Freud suggested that sexual energy is present from infancy, and that each person matures through **five psychosexual stages** (the oral, anal, phallic, latent, and genital stages), each corresponding to which part of the body is the focus of sensual pleasure. In the **oral stage**, the child seeks sensual pleasure through oral activities such as sucking and chewing. In the **anal stage**, the child seeks sensual pleasure through control of elimination. In the **phallic stage**, the child seeks sensual pleasure through the genitals. At this stage, the child is both sexually attracted to the opposite-sex parent and hostile toward the same-sex parent, who is seen as a rival. This is known as the **Oedipus complex** in a boy, and as the **Electra complex** in a girl. Girls are also said to experience **penis envy** during the phallic stage (as they discover that they do not have penises). During the **latency stage**, sexual interests subside and are replaced by interests in other areas such as school, friends, and sports. The **genital stage** begins in adolescence, when sexual themes resurface and a person's life/sexual energy fuels activities such as friendships, art, sports, and careers.

According to Freud, adult personality is largely determined during the first three psychosexual stages. If parents either frustrate or overindulge the child's expression of sensual pleasure at a certain stage so that the child does not resolve that stage's developmental conflicts, the child becomes **psychologically fixated** at that stage, and will, as an adult, continue to seek sensual pleasure through behaviors related to that stage. For example, if a child represses his or her unconscious incestuous desires for the opposite-sex parent in the phallic stage, as an adult he or she may not fully accept his or her sexuality and sexual feelings.

Carl Jung, Karen Horney, Alfred Adler, and Erik Erikson were followers of Freud who developed their own versions of psychoanalytic theory. Compared with Freud, they all had more optimistic views of humanity and saw personality as being more changeable throughout the lifespan, rather than as determined only by early childhood experiences. Unlike Freud, they also saw people as motivated and influenced by a growth instinct, by a striving for superiority, or by social factors, rather than primarily by sensual urges.

In particular, **Erik Erikson** extended Freud's theory of developmental stages in two ways. Erikson added social and interpersonal factors, to supplement Freud's focus on unconscious conflicts within a person. And Erikson delineated eight developmental stages and conflicts in adolescence and adulthood, to supplement Freud's focus on early childhood.

Erik Erikson

1) In Erikson's first stage, the infant's task is to resolve the crisis of **trust versus mistrust**. If an infant's physical and emotional needs are not met, as an adult he or she may mistrust the world and interpersonal relationships.
2) In the second stage, the toddler must resolve the crisis of **autonomy versus shame and doubt**. If a toddler's need to explore, make mistakes, and test limits are not met, as an adult he or she may be dependent rather than autonomous.
3) In the third stage, the preschool-age child must resolve the crisis of **initiative versus guilt**. If a young child's need to make decisions is not met at this stage, as an adult he or she may feel guilty taking initiative and instead allow others to choose.
4) In Erikson's fourth stage, the school-age child must resolve the crisis of **industry versus inferiority**. If a child's needs to understand the world, develop a gender-role identity, succeed in school, and set and attain personal goals are not met at this stage, as an adult he or she may feel inadequate.

5) The fifth stage occurs in adolescence, and involves resolving the crisis of **identity versus role confusion**. If an adolescent does not test limits and clarify his or her identity, goals, and life meaning, he or she may develop role confusion.

6) The young adult faces the sixth stage: to resolve the crisis of **intimacy versus isolation**. If a person does not form intimate relationships at this stage, he or she may become alienated and isolated.

7) In the seventh stage, which occurs in middle age, a person must resolve the crisis of **generativity versus stagnation**. If a person does not at this stage feel productive by helping the next generation and resolving differences between actual accomplishments and earlier dreams, he or she may become stuck in psychological stagnation.

8) Finally, in later life, a person must resolve the crisis of **integrity versus despair**, Erikson's eighth and final stage. If a person looks back with regrets and a lack of personal worth at this stage, he or she may feel hopeless, guilty, resentful, and self-rejecting.

The needs and tasks for Freud's and Erikson's stages are compared in Table 2.

Psychosexual Stages (Freud)	Age	Psychosocial Stages (Erikson)
Oral • Sensual pleasure in mouth area	Birth to 1 year	Infancy • Trust vs. mistrust • Physical & emotional needs met
Anal • Sensual pleasure in controlling elimination	1–3 years	Early childhood • Autonomy vs. shame and doubt • Explore, make mistakes, test limits
Phallic • Sensual pleasure in genital area • Incestuous desire for the opposite-sex parent	3–6 years	Preschool age • Initiative vs. guilt • Make decisions
Latency • Sexual interests subside • Pursue school, friends, sports	6–12 years	School age • Industry vs. inferiority • Gender-role identity, school success, attain personal goals, understand the world
Genital • Sensual pleasure in genital area • Life/sexual energy fuels friendships, art, sports, careers	12–18 years	Adolescence • Identity vs. role confusion • Identity, goals, life meaning, limit-testing
	18–35 years	Young adulthood • Intimacy vs. isolation • Form intimate relationships
	35–60 years	Middle age • Generativity vs. stagnation • Help next generation and resolve the difference between dreams and accomplishments
	60+ years	Later life • Integrity vs. despair • Look back with no regrets and feel personal worth

Table 2 Freud's and Erikson's Developmental Stages

Psychoanalytic therapy uses various methods to help a patient become aware of his or her unconscious motives and to gain insight into the emotional issues and conflicts that are presenting difficulties. Therefore, one of the goals of therapy is to help the patient become more able to choose behaviors consciously. Another goal of therapy is to strengthen the ego, so that choices can be based on reality rather than on instincts (id) or guilt (superego). Psychoanalytic therapy is sometimes referred to as "talk therapy" because therapy sessions usually focus on patients talking about their lives. The therapist will look for patterns or significant events that may play a role in the client's current difficulties. Psychoanalysts believe that childhood events and unconscious feelings, thoughts, and motivations play a role in mental illness and maladaptive behaviors. Psychoanalytic therapy may also use other techniques such as free association, role-play, and dream interpretation.

Humanistic Perspective

In contrast to classical psychoanalytic theory, which tends to focus on conflicts and psychopathology, the **humanistic theory** focuses on healthy personality development. According to this theory, humans are seen as inherently good and as having free will, rather than having their behavior determined by their early relationships. In humanistic theory, the most basic motive of all people is the **actualizing tendency**, which is an innate drive to maintain and enhance the organism. Like a child learning to walk, a person will grow toward **self-actualization**, or realizing his or her human potential, as long as no obstacle intervenes.

According to humanistic theory, as developed by **Carl Rogers**, when a child receives disapproval from a caregiver for certain behavior, he or she senses that the caregiver's positive regard is conditional. In order to win the caregiver's approval and still see both self and caregiver as good, the child introjects the caregiver's values, taking them on as part of his or her own self-concept. The **self-concept** is made up of the child's conscious, subjective perceptions and beliefs about him- or herself. The child's true values remain but are unconscious, as the child pursues experiences consistent with the introjected values rather than the true values. The discrepancy between conscious introjected values and unconscious true values is the root of psychopathology. This discrepancy between the conscious and unconscious leads to tension, not knowing oneself, and a feeling that something is wrong.

Carl Rogers

People choose behavior consistent with their self-concepts. If they encounter experiences in life that contradict their self-concepts, they feel uncomfortable **incongruence**. By paying attention to his or her emotional reactions to experiences, a person in an incongruent state can learn what his or her true values are, and then become healthy again by modifying the introjected values and self-concept and growing toward fulfillment and completeness of self. However, people usually find it easier to deny or distort such experiences than to modify their self-concepts.

The goal of **humanistic therapy** (also called **person-centered therapy**) is to provide an environment that will help clients trust and accept themselves and their emotional reactions, so they can learn and grow from their experiences. According to Rogers, the essential elements of such an environment are the therapist's trust in the client, and the therapist communicating genuineness (congruence), unconditional positive regard, and empathic understanding to the client. Using the term "client" rather than "patient" is meant to suggest the inherent health of the person and place the person on an equal level with the therapist.

Behaviorist Perspective

According to the **behaviorist perspective**, personality is a result of learned behavior patterns based on a person's environment. Behaviorism is **deterministic**, proposing that people begin as blank slates, and that environmental reinforcement and punishment completely determine an individual's subsequent behavior and personalities. This process begins in childhood and continues throughout the lifespan.

According to behaviorism, learning (and thus the development of personality) occurs through two forms of conditioning, classical conditioning or operant conditioning. In classical conditioning, a person acquires a certain response to a stimulus after that stimulus is repeatedly paired with a second, different stimulus that already produces the desired response. Classical conditioning is also called associational learning (see Chapter 5). In operant conditioning, behaviors are influenced by the consequences that follow them. An operant is a person's action or behavior that operates on the environment and produces consequences. Consequences are either reinforcements (which make it more likely that the operant will be repeated) or punishments (which make it less likely that the operant will be repeated). Both reinforcements and punishments can be positive or negative. In this context, the terms "positive" and "negative" are used to describe whether the consequence involves the presence or the absence of a particular stimulus. A positive reinforcement is the presence of a rewarding stimulus, and a negative reinforcement is the absence of an aversive stimulus. A positive punishment is the presence of an aversive stimulus, and a negative punishment is the absence of a rewarding stimulus (see Chapter 5 for more details on conditioning).

	Reinforcement	Punishment
Positive	Presence of rewarding stimulus	Presence of aversive stimulus
Negative	Absence of aversive stimulus	Absence of rewarding stimulus

Table 3   Postitive and Negative Reinforcment and Punishment

Behavioral therapy, then, uses conditioning to shape a client's behaviors in the desired direction. Using the ABC model, the therapist first performs a functional assessment to determine the antecedents (A) and consequences (C) of the behavior (B). Therapy then proceeds by changing antecedents and consequences, using the least aversive means possible. Common applications of behavioral therapy include relaxation training and systematic desensitization to help clients manage fear and anxiety. In systematic desensitization, the client is helped to relax while repeatedly being exposed to or imagining the situation that provokes anxiety. This technique allows the client to experience the problematic situation without experiencing any adverse consequences.

Social Cognitive Perspective

According to the **social cognitive perspective**, personality is formed by a reciprocal interaction among behavioral, cognitive, and environmental factors. The behavioral component includes patterns of behavior learned through classical and operant conditioning, as well as **observational learning**. Observational, or **vicarious**, learning occurs when a person watches another person's behavior and its consequences, thereby learning rules, strategies, and expected outcomes in different situations. For example, studies found that children who watched aggressive and violent behavior in a video subsequently behaved with more aggression and violence toward a doll[1]. People are more likely to imitate models whom they like or admire, or who seem similar to themselves.

---

[1]   The infamous "Bobo doll" experiments conducted by Albert Bandura in the early 1960s, see Chapter 5.

The cognitive component of personality includes the mental processes involved in observational or vicarious learning, as well as conscious cognitive processes such as self-efficacy beliefs (beliefs about one's own abilities). The environmental component includes situational influences, such as opportunities, rewards, and punishments.

Behavioral therapy is usually combined with a cognitive approach and called **cognitive behavioral therapy** (CBT). From the cognitive perspective, a person's feelings and behaviors are seen as reactions not to actual events, but to the person's thoughts about those events. Each person thus lives by self-created, subjective beliefs about him- or herself, other people, and the world, and these beliefs color the person's interpretations of events. Many of these beliefs are formed during childhood, and they are often unconscious. From the cognitive perspective, the roots of psychopathology are irrational or dysfunctional thoughts and beliefs. The goal of cognitive psychotherapy is to help the client become aware of these and substitute rational or accurate beliefs and thoughts, which will lead to more functional feelings and behaviors.

Therapy	Assumed Problem	Therapy Goals	General Method
Psychoanalytic (also known as psychodynamic or talk therapy)	Unconscious forces and childhood experiences	Reduce anxiety through self-insight	Analysis and interpretation
Humanistic (also known as client-centered or person-centered)	Barriers to self-understanding and self-acceptance	Personal growth through self-insight	Active listening and unconditional positive regard
Cognitive Behavioral (CBT)	Maladaptive behavior and/or negative, self-defeating thoughts	Extinction and relearning of undesired thoughts/behaviors and healthier thinking and self-talk	Reconditioning, desensitization, reversal of self-blame

Table 4   Comparison of the Major Therapy Types

Trait Perspective

A **personality trait** is a generally stable predisposition toward a certain behavior. Trait theories of personality focus on identifying, describing, measuring, and comparing individual differences and similarities with respect to such traits.

Trait theorists distinguish between surface and source traits. **Surface traits** are evident from a person's behavior. For example, a person might be described as talkative or exuberant. There are as many surface traits as there are adjectives for describing human behavior. Conversely, **source traits** are the factors underlying human personality and behavior; source traits are are fewer and more abstract (see Table 5). Each trait is not binary but rather a continuum ranging between two or more extremes, such as extroversion and introversion.

Raymond Cattell used factor analysis with hundreds of surface traits to identify which traits were related to each other. By this process, he identified 16 surface traits, the primary factors in Table 5 on the following page. Further factor analysis reduced 15 of these into five **global factors** (source traits): extroversion, anxiety, receptivity, accommodation, and self-control (some primary factors are associated with more than one global factor). The 16th surface trait, problem-solving, did not sort into any of the five global factors, and was therefore left out. Similar sets of five source traits were independently identified by other researchers. Of these various studies, the **Five-Factor Model** described by McCrae and Costa is widely accepted. The five factors in their model are extroversion, neuroticism, openness to experience, agreeableness, and conscientiousness. The personality traits identified by Cattell and by McCrae and Costa are compared in Table 5.

16 Personality Factors (Cattell)		Big Five Personality Traits (McCrae & Costa)	
5 Global Factors	**16 Primary Factors**	**Source Traits**	**Surface Trait Examples**
Extroversion	1. Reserved / Warm 2. Serious / Lively 3. Shy / Bold 4. Private / Forthright 5. Self-reliant / Group-oriented	Extroversion	Reserved / Affectionate Loner / Joiner Quiet / Talkative Internal stimuli / External stimuli
Anxiety	6. Emotionally stable / Reactive 7. Trusting / Vigilant 8. Assured / Apprehensive 9. Relaxed / Tense	Neuroticism	Calm / Worrying Even-tempered / Emotional Secure / Sensitive Confident / Nervous Emotionally stable / Unstable
Receptivity	1. Reserved / Warm 10. Unsentimental / Sensitive 11. Practical / Abstracted 12. Traditional / Open to change	Openness to experience	Down-to-earth / Imaginative Uncreative / Original Prefer routine / Prefer variety Cautious / Curious Consistent / Inventive
Accommodation	3. Bold / Shy 7. Vigilant / Trusting 12. Traditional / Open to change 13. Dominant / Deferential	Agreeableness	Antagonistic / Acquiescent Ruthless / Softhearted Suspicious / Trusting Cold / Friendly Unkind / Compassionate Antagonistic / Cooperative Not pleasing / Pleasing others
Self-Control	2. Lively / Serious 11. Abstracted / Practical 14. Expedient / Rule-conscious 15. Tolerates disorder / Perfectionist	Conscientiousness	Lazy / Hardworking Aimless / Ambitious Quitting / Persevering Easy-going / Efficient Careless / Organized
	16. Problem-Solving		

Table 5 Cattell and McCrae & Costa Personality Traits

Personality traits are thought to help predict a person's performance and enjoyment in certain careers. Assessments of personality traits are often used for career counseling, and by human resources departments as an aid to hiring and promotion decisions. Trait-based personality assessments are also used to help people understand and accept themselves and others. Each personality type is seen as having its own strengths and weaknesses. No type is identified as pathological, and weaknesses are viewed as characteristics to be aware of and manage, rather than to change. Trait theories are generally not concerned with explaining why a person has particular traits, although some have proposed that certain traits are biologically based.

Biological Perspective

From the biological perspective, much of what we call personality is at least partly due to innate biological differences among people. Support for this view is found in the heritability of basic personality traits, as well as in correlations between personality traits and certain aspects of brain structure and function.

Hans Eysenck proposed that a person's level of extroversion is based on individual differences in the reticular formation (which mediates arousal and consciousness). In this view, introverts are more easily aroused and therefore require and tolerate less external stimulation, whereas extroverts are less easily aroused and are therefore comfortable in more stimulating environments. Eysenck also proposed that a person's level of neuroticism is based on individual differences in the limbic system (which helps mediate emotion and memory). Correlations have been found between extroversion and the volume of brain structures involved with processing rewards, and between neuroticism and the volume of brain regions involved with processing negative emotions and punishment. In addition, twin studies and adoption studies (discussed in Chapter 5) have found strong evidence for the heritability of extroversion and neuroticism.

Jeffrey Alan Gray proposed that personality is governed by interactions among three brain systems that respond to rewarding and punishing stimuli. In this view, fearfulness and avoidance are linked to the "fight-or-flight" sympathetic nervous system, worry and anxiety are linked to the behavioral inhibition system, and optimism and impulsivity are linked to the behavioral approach system. **C. Robert Cloninger** also linked personality to brain systems involved with reward, motivation, and punishment. Cloninger proposed that personality is linked to the level of activity of certain neurotransmitters in three interacting systems. In this view, low dopamine activity correlates with higher impulsivity and novelty seeking, low norepinephrine activity correlates with higher approval seeking and reward dependence, and low serotonin activity correlates with risk avoidance. Correlations have been found between novelty seeking and grey matter volume in the cingulate cortex, between reward dependence and grey matter volume in the caudate nucleus, and between harm avoidance and grey matter volume in the orbitofrontal, occipital, and parietal cortices.

Situational Approach to Explaining Behavior

The **person-situation controversy** (also known and the **trait versus state controversy**) considers the degree to which a person's reaction in a given situation is due to their personality (trait) or is due to the situation itself (state). **Traits** are considered to be internal, stable, and enduring aspects of personality that should be consistent across most situations. **States** are situational; they are unstable, temporary, and variable aspects of personality that are influenced by the external environment. For example, extroversion is a trait, stress is a state. The primary question is whether personality is consistent over time and across situations and contexts. A fair amount of research suggests that while people's personality *traits* are fairly stable, their *behavior* in specific situations can be variable. In other words, people do not act with predictable consistency, even if their personality traits are predictably consistent. In unfamiliar situations, people tend to modify their behavior based on **social cues** (verbal or nonverbal hints that guide social interactions); therefore specific traits may remain hidden. For example, a person who is normally quite extroverted may seem quiet and reserved in an unfamiliar formal situation. In familiar situations, people may "act more like themselves" (the same extroverted person may be considerably more talkative in a familiar situation with friends). Averaging behavior over many situations is the best way to reveal distinct personality traits.

6.2   MOTIVATION

Out of all the behaviors that are possible, what motivates us (and all animals) to act in particular ways in particular moments? This process can be as simple as being motivated to take a drink of water due to a feeling of thirst or as complex as being motivated to undertake a difficult studying regimen and training program in order to become a physician due to a desire to help others.

Factors that Influence Motivation

Instincts

There are several factors that are understood to influence motivation. The first is **instinct**: behaviors that are unlearned and present in fixed patterns throughout a species. An example is imprinting in chicks, who learn to follow objects or organisms that are present when they hatch. In humans, instincts in babies include sucking behaviors, naturally holding the breath under water, and demonstrating fear when approaching drops in elevation. Instincts represent the contribution of genes, which predispose species to particular behaviors.

Drives / Negative Feedback Systems

Physiological drives can also push organisms to act in certain ways, as is the case when we are thirsty. A **drive** is an urge originating from a physiological discomfort such as hunger, thirst, or sleepiness. Drives can be useful for alerting an organism that it is no longer in a state of homeostasis, an internal state of equilibrium. They suggest that something is lacking: food, water, or sleep, for example. Drives often work through negative feedback systems, which are abundant in human physiology. The process of **negative feedback** works by maintaining stability or homeostasis; a system produces a product or end result, which feeds back to stop the system and maintain the product or end result within tightly controlled boundaries. Biological examples of negative feedback include regulation of blood pressure, blood glucose levels, and body temperature. These biological systems can have an important impact on behavior. For example, if blood glucose drops because you haven't eaten in hours, you will feel hungry and have a strong drive to eat. If your temperature begins to drop, you will feel cold and have strong drive to seek warmth.

Arousal

However, instincts and drives cannot explain some of the artistic accomplishments of humans or the exploratory behavior of infants and animals. Even a toddler whose needs have all seemingly been met will wander around the room, putting objects in his or her mouth. This suggests that some behaviors are motivated by a desire to achieve an optimum level of arousal. A toddler who is not stimulated enough may seek stimulation by exploring the surroundings. An adult who is feeling bored will do the same. On the other hand, feeling overstimulated can lead to feelings of stress, which may lead one to seek ways to relax or sleep. Different people may have different optimal levels of arousal.

Needs

While including basic biological needs (physiological drives), this category also includes higher-level needs than those previously discussed. Instincts, drives, and arousal do not explain why a student may aspire to become a physician. In addition to drives, one may experience various needs, including a need for safety, a need for belonging and love, and a need for achievement.

Theories that Explain How Motivation Affects Human Behavior

Drive Reduction Theory

Since drives are physiological states of discomfort, it follows that we are motivated to reduce these drives through behaviors such as eating and drinking. Drive-reduction theory suggests that a physiological need creates an aroused state that drives the organism to reduce that need be engaging in some behavior. If your blood glucose drops, you feel hungry (or light-headed), and have a drive to eat. The greater the physiological need, the greater the physiological drive, an aroused, motivated state.

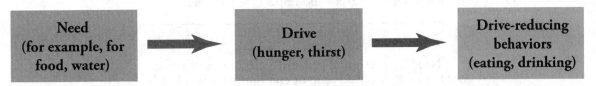

Figure 2   Drive-Reduction Theory

Incentive Theory

While drives are internal physiological needs, **incentives** are external stimuli, objects, and events in the environment that either help induce or discourage certain behaviors. Incentives can be positive and drive us to do something, or they can be negative and repel us from doing something. For example, if you were offered a new job accompanied by a large increase in salary, the salary might serve as a positive incentive. If the job also involved an increase in work hours, the increased workload might serve as a negative incentive. In general, behaviors are most strongly motivated when there are physiological needs, strong positive incentives, and a lack of negative incentives. For example, if you were walking down the street and were very hungry, smelled delicious pizza, and found out it was being given away for free, you'd have a strong motivation to eat it.

Maslow's Hierarchy of Needs

Abraham Maslow sought to explain human behavior by creating a hierarchy of needs (Figure 3). At the base of this pyramid are physiological needs, or the basic elements necessary to sustain human life. If these needs are met, we will seek safety; if the need for safety is met, we will seek love, and so on. His pyramid suggests that not all needs are created equally, some needs take priority over others. For example, an individual who is struggling every day to work and put food on the table will place a higher value on meeting physiological needs than on fulfilling a cognitive need for belongingness by joining a community organization that hopes to increase awareness of global warming. Maslow's hierarchy is somewhat arbitrary—it comes from a Western emphasis on individuality, and some individuals have shown the ability to reorganize these motives (for example, hunger strikes or eating disorders). Nevertheless, it has been generally accepted that we are only motivated to satisfy higher-level needs once certain lower-level needs have been met. The inclusion of higher-level needs, such as self-actualization and the need for recognition and respect from others also explains behaviors that the previous theories do not.

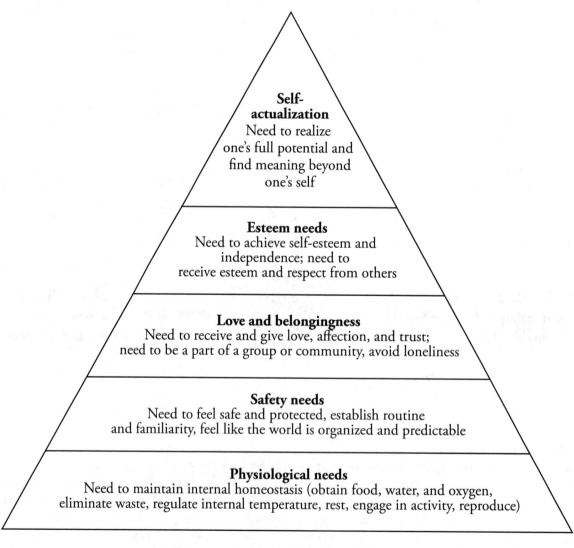

Figure 3 Maslow's Hierarchy of Needs

Application of Theories of Motivation to Understand Behaviors

Biological Factors that Regulate Motivation

As drive reduction theory suggests, biological factors can play a large part in motivation. For many physiological processes, it is theorized that our bodies have a "set point" or a "sweet spot" at which things are in homeostasis. Our bodies also have mechanisms for detecting deviations from the set point and stimulating us to react either internally or behaviorally to regain the set point. Responses to body temperature variations, fluid intake, weight variations, and sexual stimulation are regulated to a large extent by biological processes.

Regulating body temperature is important to survival because it affects protein function, cellular membranes, and the like. Even small elevations in blood temperature can result in heat stroke. The hypothalamus is the primary control center for detecting changes in temperature and receives input from skin receptors. When the hypothalamus determines that the body is cold, it causes vasoconstriction and shivering. When the hypothalamus determines that the body is hot, it causes vasodilation and sweating. Behaviorally, we respond to heat by stretching out to maximize surface area and shedding layers of clothing, as on a hot summer day; we respond to cold by curling inward, snuggling up, and adding layers of clothing, as on a cold winter day.

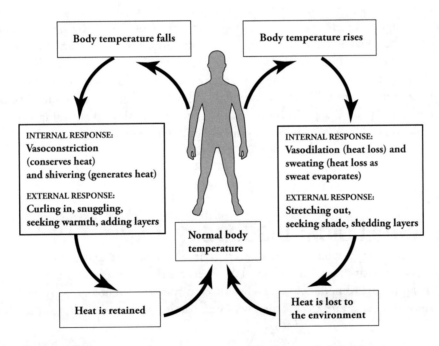

Figure 4   Physiological and Behavioral Processes Regulating Body Temperature

Monitoring fluid levels includes the intake of fluids as well as excretion. The intake of fluids is stimulated by specialized osmoreceptors in the brain that detect dehydration. These receptors communicate with the pituitary gland to stimulate the release of antidiuretic hormone (ADH), which in turn communicates with the kidneys to reduce urine production by reclaiming water. When blood volume is low, including when one has sustained an injury and is losing a significant amount of blood, hunger for sodium is stimulated to increase the concentration of salt in the blood, and thirst to replace the lost fluid. Excess fluid is managed internally through urination and sweating.

Hunger helps regulate the intake of nutrients into the body. Like body temperature, it is controlled by the hypothalamus, which receives information from the stomach, intestines, and liver, as well as through the monitoring of blood glucose levels. The lateral hypothalamus brings on hunger, while the ventromedial hypothalamus depresses hunger. Ghrelin, released by the stomach and pancreas, heightens the sensation of hunger, while leptin, a hormone released by white adipose tissue (fat) reduces hunger.

In addition to directing the development of male and female sexual anatomy, sex hormones are responsible for the activation of sexual behavior. While estrogen and testosterone control sexual drive to a minimal extent in the short-term, long-term behavior can be guided by sex hormones. For example, the spike in feelings of sexual attraction during puberty is correlated with an increase in sex hormones.

Sociocultural Factors that Regulate Motivation

As the presence of both eating disorders and hot dog eating contests suggests, we are more than beings driven simply by biological drives. When considering some of the higher levels of Maslow's hierarchy, sociocultural factors likely play a large role in motivation. In addition, lower levels of Maslow's hierarchy are also influenced by sociocultural factors. For example, how a culture views body weight has an impact on the motivation of its members to reach some desired weight. In many cultures, such as that of the United States, where a thinner image is idolized on television, people may change their eating habits in order to obtain that desired figure. In other cultures, being overweight is idolized as a sign of success and well being, so their members may strive to gain weight. Culture also influences taste preferences, the desire for fatty foods, and the amount of exercise that people get. In addition, appetite is also related to mood. When feeling depressed, we may crave sweet or starchy foods to help boost the neurotransmitter serotonin, which has a calming effect. We may crave food simply for sensory stimulation when bored or may develop food aversions based on experiences of food poisoning. Needless to say, hunger and other drives are far from simple innate biological drives, they are also influenced by experience.

6.3 PSYCHOLOGICAL DISORDERS

It is estimated that in America, roughly one in every four adults (ages 18 and over) meets the diagnostic criteria for a psychological disorder. Psychological disorders are therefore an important part of our culture and comprise a significant component of our health care system. Psychological disorders, particularly when they go untreated, also affect our economy, by impacting our social welfare and criminal justice systems.

Understanding Psychological Disorders

Although psychological disorders affect about a quarter of the population, serious psychological disorders are less common, affecting roughly one in 17 people, or 6% of the US population. A **psychological disorder** is a set of behavioral and/or psychological symptoms that are not in keeping with cultural norms, and that are severe enough to cause significant personal distress and/or significant impairment to social, occupational, or personal functioning. Sometimes cultural norms can be ruled out as a source of behavior; for example, when what appears to be a delusion or even a hallucination can be better understood in terms of religious or spiritual practice, that belief or experience would not count as a symptom of a psychological disorder. When cultural norms cannot explain behavior, the core components of diagnosis for a psychological disorder are *symptom quantity and severity*, and *impact on functioning*. A psychological disorder is *diagnosable* based on specific symptoms and symptom thresholds, and *treatable* (or at least *manageable*) with various types of medication and/or therapy.

Biopsychosocial Approach to Mental Health

Today, psychopathology recognizes the role of both nature (genetic predisposition) and nurture (environmental factors) in the occurrence and manifestation of psychological disorders. Culture also plays a role in the prevalence of various psychological disorders. For example, while not exclusive to Western cultures, eating disorders appear to be far more common in wealthier countries that espouse a thin ideal (like the United States) than they are in other parts of the world. It is also possible, for a given psychological disorder, that the underlying genetic and physiological dynamics are similar, but that the manifestation of the disorder for a particular person is influenced by cultural or social factors. Figure 5 presents the separate and overlapping influences that have been shown to correlate with psychological disorders.

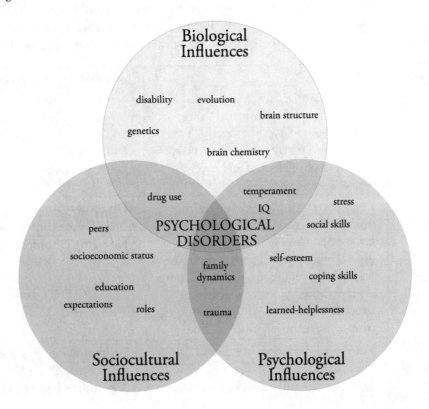

Figure 5   Biopsychosocial Model of Psychological Disorders

Classifying Psychological Disorders

It is important to understand the classification of psychological disorders in order to understand the symptoms and prevalence of each. Without classification, it would also be impossible to know what the biological and genetic risk factors are, which treatments work the best, and so on. The universal authority on the classification and diagnosis of psychological disorders is the **Diagnostical and Statistical Manual of Mental Disorders**, fifth edition (**DSM-5**), published in May 2013. Each new edition of the DSM reflects changes in research and clinical perspectives. For example, in the 19 years since the publication of the fourth edition (the DSM-IV), research findings and clinical experience prompted the publishers of the DSM-5 to combine the four separate autism disorders into one—Autism Spectrum Disorder—and to change the symptom categories from three to two areas. While the change caused some controversy in the autism community, it is thought to have yielded a clearer, more reliable, and more accurate means of diagnosis (overall the DSM-5 seeks to accomplish this by including more "Spectrum" and "Related" disorders). Accurate diagnosis is critical; most insurance companies require a diagnosis based on DSM criteria before they will cover the cost of therapy.

Although there is substantial overlap in the list of symptoms and the various symptom thresholds between the DSM-5 and the DSM-IV, the DSM-5 represents both a streamlining and a reorganization of most of the major disorders, through changes to their names or their categories or both. For the purposes of the MCAT, familiarize yourself with the categories of disorders presented below in Table 6. Note that this list is neither all-inclusive (for a given category, not all disorders are listed) nor exhaustive (some categories are not included), but instead presents the psychological disorders that are most likely to be tested.

Broad Category	Description	Specific Psychological Disorders
Anxiety Disorders	Anxiety disorders are characterized by excessive fear (of specific real things or more generally) and/or anxiety (of real or imagined *future* things or events) with both physiological and psychological symptoms.	• Separation Anxiety Disorder • Specific Phobia(s) • Social Anxiety Disorder • Panic Disorder • Generalized Anxiety Disorder
Obsessive-Compulsive and Related Disorders	Disorders in this category are distinct from Anxiety Disorders in that they involve a pattern of obsessive thoughts or urges that are coupled with maladaptive behavioral compulsions; the compulsions are experienced as a necessary/urgent response to the obsessive thoughts/urges, creating rigid, anxiety-filled routines.	• Obsessive-Compulsive Disorder • Body Dysmorphic Disorder • Hoarding Disorder
Trauma- and Stressor-Related Disorders	Traumas and stressors are central to the definition of these disorders, which involve unhealthy or pathological responses to one or more harmful or life-threatening events, including witnessing such an event. Subsequent symptoms include patterns of anxiety, depression, depersonalization, nightmares, insomnia, and/or a heightened startle response.	• Posttraumatic Stress Disorder • Acute Stress Disorder • Adjustment Disorders

Broad Category	Description	Specific Psychological Disorders
Somatic Symptom Disorders	Somatic Symptom Disorders are characterized by symptoms that cannot be explained by a medical condition or substance use, and are not attributable to another psychological disorder, but that nonetheless cause emotional distress.	• Somatic Symptom Disorder • Illness Anxiety Disorder • Conversion Disorder • Factitious Disorder (imposed on self or another)
Bipolar and Related Disorders	Separate now from Mood Disorders, Bipolar and Related Disorders involve mood swings or cycles (called episodes) ranging from manic to depressive, in which manic episodes tend to be followed by depressive episodes and vice versa.	• Bipolar I Disorder • Bipolar II Disorder • Cyclothymic Disorder
Depressive Disorders	Depressive Disorders are characterized by a disturbance in mood or affect. Specific symptoms include difficulties in sleep, concentration, and/or appetite; fatigue; and inability to experience pleasure (anhedonia).	• Major Depressive Disorder • Persistent Depressive Disorder (dysthymia) • Premenstrual Dysphoric Disorder
Schizophrenia Spectrum and Other Psychotic Disorders	Psychotic disorders are characterized by a general "loss of contact with reality" which can include "positive" symptoms such as delusions and hallucinations and/or "negative" symptoms such as flattened affect (e.g., monotone vocal expression).	• Delusional Disorder • Brief Psychotic Disorder • Schizophreniform Disorder • Schizophrenia • Schizoaffective Disorder
Dissociative Disorders	Dissociative Disorders are characterized by disruptions in memory, awareness, identity, or perception. Many dissociative orders are thought to be caused by psychological trauma.	• Dissociative Identity Disorder • Dissociative Amnesia • Depersonalization/Derealization Disorder
Personality Disorders	Personality Disorders are characterized by enduring maladaptive patterns of behavior and cognition that depart from social norms, present across a variety of contexts, and cause significant dysfunction and distress. These patterns permeate the broader personality of the person and typically solidify during late adolescence or early adulthood.	Cluster A: • Paranoid Personality Disorder • Schizoid Personality Disorder • Schizotypal Personality Disorder Cluster B: • Antisocial Personality Disorder • Borderline Personality Disorder • Histrionic Personality Disorder • Narcissistic Personality Disorder Cluster C: • Avoidant Personality Disorder • Dependent Personality Disorder • Obsessive-compulsive Personality Disorder

6.3

Broad Category	Description	Specific Psychological Disorders
Feeding and Eating Disorders	Feeding and Eating Disorders are characterized by disruptive emotional and behavioral patterns around feeding and/or eating that negatively impact physical and mental health.	• Anorexia Nervosa • Bulimia Nervosa • Binge-Eating Disorder
Neurocognitive Disorders	Neurocognitive Disorders are characterized by cognitive abnormalities or general decline in memory, problem solving, and/or perception.	• Major and Mild Neurocognitive Disorders (MMND) • MMND Due to Alzheimer's Disease • MMND Due to Parkinson's Disease • Major or Mild Vascular Neurocognitive Disorder
Sleep-Wake Disorders	Sleep-Wake Disorders are characterized by excessive or deficient sleep patterns, abnormalities in circadian rhythm, and/or interruptions to normal sleep.	• Insomnia Disorder • Hypersomnolence Disorder • Narcolepsy • Breathing-Related Sleep Disorders (including various Apneas) • Parasomnias (such as somnambulism, or sleep-walking)
Substance-Related and Addictive Disorders	Substance-Related and Addictive Disorders are characterized by psychological and/or physiological dependence on, or addiction to, one or more substances and behaviors. Symptoms often include tolerance and withdrawal and are generally related to maladaptation of, or damage to, the brain's reward system.	• Substance-Related Disorders • Alcohol-Related Disorders • Tobacco-Related Disorders • Gambling Disorder

Table 6 Categories of Psychological Disorders

Types of Psychological Disorders

The nine categories of psychological disorders discussed in this section correspond to the nine categories of disorders listed by the AAMC that you should be familiar with for the MCAT: Anxiety Disorders, Obsessive-Compulsive and Related Disorders, Trauma- and Stressor-Related Disorders, Somatic Symptom and Related Disorders, Bipolar and Related Disorders, Depressive Disorders, Schizophrenia Spectrum and Other Psychotic Disorders, Dissociative Disorders, and Personality Disorders.

1. Anxiety Disorders

Anxiety is an emotional state of unpleasant physical and mental arousal—a preparation to fight or flee. In a person with an anxiety disorder, the anxiety is intense, frequent, irrational (out of proportion), and uncontrollable; it causes significant distress or impairment of normal functioning (at-work productivity, success in intimate relationships, and so on). Four types of anxiety disorders are discussed here: panic disorder, generalized anxiety disorder, specific phobia, and social phobia (now called "Social Anxiety Disorder").

Symptoms mimicking an anxiety disorder can also be caused by general medical conditions, alcohol, certain drugs, or medication use or withdrawal. If a person has a medical condition or uses substances that are likely to be causing the symptoms, the diagnosis is "anxiety disorder due to a general medical condition" or "substance-induced anxiety disorder." This approach to specifying non-psychological causes applies to the other sections of the DSM-5 as well.

Panic Disorder. A person with **panic disorder** has suffered at least one **panic attack** and is worried about having more of them. The panic attacks can be triggered by certain situations, but they are more often uncued or "spontaneous," occurring unexpectedly and with sometimes unpredictable frequency.

During a **panic attack**, a person commonly experiences intense dread, along with shortness of breath, chest pain, a choking sensation, and cardiac symptoms such as a rapid heartbeat or palpitations. There may also be trembling, sweating, lightheadedness, or chills. Many fear they are dying of a heart attack or stroke during a panic attack. One danger of panic attacks is that they can mask other illnesses, such as heart attacks and mood disorders. Although panic attacks are brief (often less than 30 minutes in duration), they can be excruciating, and people with panic disorder live in fear of having more panic attacks. Panic disorder can be debilitating if left untreated, but people with this disorder do respond well to treatment.

Generalized Anxiety Disorder. A person with **generalized anxiety disorder** (GAD) feels tense or anxious much of the time about many issues, but does not experience panic attacks. The source of this underlying, chronic nervousness can seem like a moving target, shifting from one situation to another, or there may be no identifiable source. The distress and impairment associated with GAD is not often severe; it may include restlessness, tiring easily, poor concentration, irritability, muscle tension, and insomnia or restless sleep.

Specific Phobia and Social Phobia. There are several types of **phobias**. In specific and social phobias, the sufferer feels a strong fear that he or she recognizes as unreasonable. He or she nevertheless almost always experiences either general anxiety or a full panic attack when confronted with the feared object or situation. People with phobias often go to great lengths to avoid the triggers they fear, and this avoidance itself is part of the symptom profile.

Specific phobia is a persistent, strong, and unreasonable fear of a certain object or situation. Specific phobias are classified into four types (plus "other") depending on the types of triggers they involve (see Table 7).

Type of Specific Phobia	Example of Triggers
Situational	Flying, elevators, bridges, crowds (in Agoraphobia)
Natural Environment	Thunderstorms, heights, water, lightning
Blood-Injection-Injury	Injections, blood, surgical procedures
Animal	Spiders, snakes, dogs

Table 7   Types of Specific Phobias

Social Anxiety Disorder, or Social Phobia, is an unreasonable, paralyzing fear of feeling embarrassed or humiliated while one is seen or watched by others, even while performing routine activities such as eating in public or using a public restroom (though there is a separate specifier for public speaking). Here too a prominent symptom is avoidance, in the form of social isolation.

2. Obsessive-Compulsive and Related Disorders

Separated now from Anxiety Disorders (largely for the purpose of clinical utility, again with the goal of streamlining diagnosis), these disorders feature at least one pronounced repetitive behavior that exceeds cultural norms and rituals such as grooming practices or maintaining a healthy body weight. Unsuccessful attempts to decrease or otherwise manage these behaviors are also central to diagnosis. Without therapeutic intervention, these conditions tend to increase over time in terms of severity or level of self-harm or both.

Obsessive-Compulsive Disorder. A person with **obsessive-compulsive disorder (OCD)** has obsessions, compulsions, or both. **Obsessions** are repeated, intrusive, uncontrollable thoughts or impulses that cause distress or anxiety. The person knows the thoughts are irrational, and despite attempts to disregard or suppress them, typically resorts to responding to them through a compulsive behavior. **Compulsions** are repeated physical or mental behaviors (e.g. counting) that are performed in response to an obsession or in accordance with a set of strict rules, in order to reduce distress or prevent something dreaded from occurring. The person realizes that the compulsive behavior is not reasonable, being either unrelated to the dreaded event, or related but clearly excessive. Nevertheless, if the person does not perform the behavior, he or she feels intense anxiety and a conviction that the terrible event will happen. Some common obsessions and compulsions are listed in Table 8.

Obsessions	Compulsions
• Irrational fear of contamination by dirt, germs, or toxins • Pathological doubt that a task was done, or fear of having inadvertently harmed someone or violated a law • Fear of harming someone violently or sexually, or otherwise behaving in an unacceptable way	• Washing self (often hands) or surroundings repeatedly, sometimes with a lengthy ritual • Checking repeatedly that a task was done, sometimes with a lengthy ritual • Counting to a certain number before certain tasks, or performing a behavior a certain number of times (such as folding a shirt) • Arranging objects or performing actions with perfect symmetry or precision

Table 8   Common Obsessions and Compulsions

3. Trauma- and Stressor-Related Disorders

Like the disorders in the previous section, these were also separated in the DSM-5 from what used to be a much broader category for Anxiety Disorders, as anxiety often figures prominently in these disorders as well. This revision was intended to facilitate the diagnosis of specific anxiety-like disorders on the basis of their **etiology** (the cause or set of causes or causal conditions for a particular disease) and to focus research and clinical practice on a more focused and tailored set of treatment options.

Posttraumatic Stress Disorder and Acute Stress Disorder. **Posttraumatic stress disorder (PTSD)** can arise when a person feels intense fear, horror, or helplessness while experiencing, witnessing, or otherwise confronting an extremely traumatic event that involves actual or threatened death or serious injury to the self or others. It is estimated that most people (more than half) will experience at least one traumatic event in their lifetime, but only a small sub-set of those will develop PTSD. Approximately 8% of men and 20% of women develop PTSD after a trauma. Rates of PTSD are higher in males of Latino heritage and males who have served in active combat, for whom the estimated prevalence reaches 20%.

The traumatic event is often *relived* (not just remembered) through dreams and flashbacks in which the person feels as though the event is currently happening, and which can include multi-sensory re-processing, such as the intrusion of smells and sounds from the original event context. Some experience mental or physiological distress (e.g. elevated heart rate or blood pressure) when reminded of the event, however indirectly. A person with PTSD tries to avoid people, places, feelings, thoughts, or conversations that are reminders of the event, or even avoids people and feelings in general. The person is also chronically physiologically hyperaroused, with symptoms such as an increased startle response, insomnia, angry outbursts, poor concentration, and extreme vigilance (called **hypervigilance**).

For a diagnosis of PTSD, these symptoms must have been present for more than a month. **Acute stress disorder** is similar to PTSD, but its symptoms are present for less than a month and for as little as three days. Finally, there is a less severe and shorter-term version of the condition, an **adjustment disorder**, in which the causes include a stressor as opposed to a trauma and the symptoms last less than six months once the stressor has been eliminated. The diagnosis also applies in cases where the subsequent distress appears in some way to be disproportionate to the cause. In all three conditions, and particularly in the latter, it is significant that individuals from low-SES communities or who are otherwise disadvantaged encounter more stressors in their everyday lives and are thus at increased risk for a disorder in this category.

4. Somatic Symptom and Related Disorders

A Somatic Symptom Disorder is a psychological disorder characterized primarily by distress and decreased functioning due to persistent physical symptoms and concerns, which may mimic physical (somatic) disease but generally are not rooted in any detectable pathophysiology. Further, the somatic symptoms do not improve with medical treatment. This symptom/behavior pattern is commonly referred to as "hypochondriasis," but as the differences between these disorders should make clear, that terms lacks precision.

Though they are often treated with skepticism, even by physicians (a large majority of these diagnoses occur in the primary care setting), people with somatic symptom disorders genuinely experience their symptoms and/or believe that there is something physically wrong with them. The DSM-5 accounts for this complexity with streamlined presentation of four sub-types: somatic symptom disorder, illness anxiety disorder, conversion disorder, and factitious disorder.

Somatic Symptom Disorder. For someone with **somatic symptom disorder**, the central complaint is one or more somatic symptoms—such as chronic pain or headaches or fatigue—and diagnosis also requires evidence of diminished functioning stemming from excessive preoccupation with and/or anxiety about the symptoms. Whether the symptoms in any way coincide with a related medical problem or illness, the distress and/or disruption of daily life caused by the symptoms warrants at least consideration of diagnosis.

Illness Anxiety Disorder. One reason "hypochondriasis" can be considered imprecise is that it refers to concern about both illness and (somatic) symptoms. **Illness anxiety disorder** differs from somatic symptom disorder in so far as the somatic aspect of the illness is not as central or can even be nonexistent. In illness anxiety disorder, the distress is predominantly psychological, with people experiencing persistent preoccupation with both their health condition and health-related behaviors, including seeking treatment.

Conversion Disorder. A person with **conversion disorder** experiences a change in sensory or motor function—such as weakness, tremors, seizures, or difficulty talking or eating—that has no discernible physical or physiological cause and that seems to be significantly affected by psychological factors. The symptoms of conversion disorder typically begin or worsen after an emotional conflict or other stressor. As the terminology suggests, the emotion or anxiety is "converted" into a physical symptom. The change in function is severe enough to warrant medical attention, or to cause significant distress or impairment in work, social, or personal functioning. Diagnosis of conversion order is possible, for example, when a person suddenly experience blindness but his or her blink reflex remains intact.

Factitious Disorder. This disorder is colloquially referred to as "Munchhausen Syndrome" (when imposed on one's self) or "Munchausen by Proxy" (when imposed on someone else). In **factitious disorder imposed on self**, a person has not just fabricated an illness but has gone the further step of either falsifying evidence or symptoms of the illness or inflicting harm to him- or herself to induce injury or illness. Though the person presents the illness to others and thus attracts interpersonal and/or medical attention, diagnosis requires evidence that the person behaves this way even without obvious benefit. When someone creates and/or inflicts physical or psychological symptoms in someone else, often a child—and then presents the other person as ill or injured—the perpetrator of the deception is diagnosed with **factitious disorder imposed on another**.

5. Bipolar and Related Disorders

Bipolar Disorders. Most people with a **bipolar disorder** (formerly called manic depression) experience cyclic mood episodes at one or both extremes or "poles": depression and mania. It is thus useful to examine the diagnostic criteria for the various episodes and mood states before discussing these disorders (as well as Depressive Disorders, in the next section).

	Manic Episode	Hypomanic Episode	Major Depressive Episode	Dysthymic syndrome*
Duration	At least one week, nearly every day	At least four consecutive days	At least two weeks	At least two years
Mood	Elevated, expansive, or irritable mood	Elevated, expansive, or irritable mood	Depressed; diminished interest or pleasure in almost all activities	Depressed; general feeling of sadness; feelings of hopelessness
Self-image	Inflated, grandiose	Inflated, grandiose	Feelings of worthlessness or excessive guilt	Low self-esteem
Appetite/ weight	May show diminished appetite or interest in food	May show diminished appetite or interest in food	Increase or decrease in body weight by 5% or more in a month	Poor appetite or overeating
Sleep need	Decreased	Decreased	Insomnia or hypersomnia	Insomnia or hypersomnia
Cognition	Flight of ideas or racing thoughts; distractibility	Flight of ideas or racing thoughts; distractibility	Diminished ability to think or concentrate; recurrent thoughts of death or suicide	Poor concentration
Speech	Rapid, pressured	Rapid, pressured	May manifest muted or flat affect in speech	Self-deprecation and expressed sense of futility are common
Energy/ behavior	Increased energy and goal-directed activity and/ or psychomotor agitation	Increased energy and goal-directed activity and/ or psychomotor agitation	Fatigue or loss of energy; psychomotor agitation or retardation	Low energy or fatigue
Judgment	Lack of consequential thinking	Lack of consequential thinking	May include suicide attempt or a specific plan for committing suicide	Difficulty making decisions
Impairment to functioning	Severe, marked impairment; may require hospitalization (to prevent harm to self or others); may include psychotic features	Unequivocal, observable change that is not typical of the individual; not severe enough to cause marked impairment or to necessitate hospitalization	Clinically significant distress or marked impairment in one or more areas of functioning	Clinically significant distress or marked impairment in one or more areas of functioning

*The DMS-5 diagnostic profile of Persistent Depressive Disorder (Dysthymia) includes description of symptoms of Dysthymia as a chronic mood state or syndrome, but not as a discrete episode type

Table 9   Diagnostic Criteria for Bipolar and Related Disorders and Depressive Disorders

In a **manic episode**, for at least one week, a person has experienced an abnormal euphoric, unrestrained, or irritable mood, and a marked increase in either goal-directed activity (with increased energy and productivity at work, for example) or in psychomotor agitation, stemming from a felt need or urge to be engaged in goal-directed activity but not having the focus or other means to engage in any (thus the "surplus" energy causes agitation and irritability). In the latter category, someone experiencing a manic episode may feel compelled, for example, to spend hours shopping online or looking for an activity to absorb the energy. These symptoms are severe enough to cause psychotic features, hospitalization, or impairment of work, social, or personal function. Sometimes, a manic episode can be caused by antidepressants, light, or electroconvulsive therapy for depression.

Bipolar I disorder is diagnosed only if there has been a spontaneous manic episode not triggered by treatment for depression or caused by another medical condition or medication. It may include a swing to a full depressive episode, or only to partial or moderate depression (dysthymic symptoms), or no depression at all (although this is rare). In a **mixed episode**, a person has met the symptoms for both major depressive and manic episodes nearly every day for at least a week, and the symptoms are severe enough to cause psychotic features, hospitalization, or impaired work, social, or personal functioning. In the simplest terms, the only requirement for a diagnosis of **bipolar I disorder** is that the person has experienced at least one manic or mixed episode.

In a person with **bipolar II disorder**, the manic phases are less extreme. A person with bipolar II disorder has experienced cyclic moods, including at least one major depressive episode and one hypomanic episode, but has not met the criteria for a manic or mixed episode. In a **hypomanic episode**, for at least four days, a person has experienced an abnormally euphoric or irritable mood, with at least three of the symptoms for a manic episode, but at a less severe level. With hypomania, the impairment or distress is less serious, and there is no psychosis or hospitalization. In a **major depressive episode**, a person has felt worse than usual for most of the day, nearly every day, for at least two weeks. The individual also has at least five of the following emotional, behavioral, cognitive, and physical symptoms: depressed mood or decreased interest in activities, significant increase or decrease in weight or appetite, excessive or insufficient sleep, agitated or slowed psychomotor activity, fatigue or loss of energy, feelings of low self-worth or excessive guilt, impaired concentration or decision-making, and thoughts of death or suicide. The diagnosis of bipolar II disorder requires both types of episodes.

Cyclothymic Disorder. **Cyclothymic disorder** is similar to bipolar disorder but the moods are less extreme, with symptoms not meeting the criteria for either a manic or a major depressive episode. A person with cyclothymic disorder has experienced cyclic moods, including multiple hypomanic episodes, as well as episodes of depressed mood that are milder than a major depressive episode, for at least two years. These mood swings have never been absent for more than two months.

Figure 6 compares the various mood states or episodes for depressive disorders and bipolar and related disorders. Persistent depressive disorder is thus a milder (though often more persistent form) of major depressive disorder, whereas bipolar disorder I, bipolar disorder II, and cyclothymia generally involve cycling through either manic or hypomanic episodes, and dysthymic or depressed episodes.

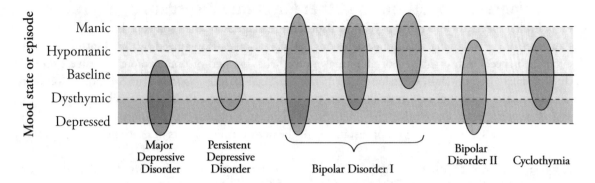

Figure 6 Depressive Disorders and Bipolar (and Related) Disorders Based on Diagnostic Criteria for Mood State or Episode.

6. Depressive Disorders

A **depressive disorder** is more than acute moodiness; it is a persistent pattern of abnormal and often painful mood symptoms severe enough to cause significant personal distress and/or impairment to social, occupational, or personal functioning. While **affect** is a person's observable emotion in the moment, **mood** is a person's sustained internal emotion that colors his or her view of life. Three depressive disorders are discussed in this section: major depressive disorder, persistent depressive disorder (dysthymia), and premenstrual dysphoric disorder (this last condition is new in DSM-5).

Major Depressive Disorder. A person with **major depressive disorder** (MDD) has suffered one or more major depressive episodes (as discussed in the previous section). Ten percent of people with major depressive disorder attempt suicide and many more contemplate it or devise a suicide plan. These symptoms do not indicate major depression if they occur within two months of bereavement, as they may be part of a normal grieving reaction. In seasonal affective disorder (or what DSM-5 refers to as MDD "with seasonal pattern"), episodes of depression occur during certain seasons, usually fall and winter.

Persistent Depressive Disorder (Dysthymia). **Persistent depressive disorder** (PDD), also called **dysthymic disorder** or **dysthymia**, is a less intense, but typically more chronic form of depression. A person with PDD has experienced milder symptoms of depression most days for at least two years, with symptoms never absent for more than two months, but without a major depressive episode. Onset is typically adolescence or early adulthood, and the persistence of the condition often leaves people feeling like they've "always felt this way" or as if they are a "depressed person" to their core.

Premenstrual Dysphoric Disorder. In **premenstrual dysphoric disorder**, which is only diagnosed in women, many of the symptoms of a major depressive episode are present, with the caveat that they intensify in the final week before the onset of menses and then improve and in many cases disappear in the week after menstruation has ended. There are a few symptoms that distinguish the illness from the other two depressive disorders discussed here: feeling keyed up or on edge, specific food cravings, a sense of being overwhelmed or out of control, as well as the physical symptoms of the body's preparation for menstruation: tenderness or swelling in the breasts, joint or muscle pain, and bloating.

7. Schizophrenia Spectrum and Other Psychotic Disorders

Schizophrenia spectrum and other psychotic disorders are diagnosed when someone has been experiencing one or more of the following symptoms: delusions, hallucinations, disorganized thinking (as manifested in disorganized speech), disorganized or abnormal motor behavior, and/or one or more **negative symptoms**, such as decreased emotional expression (presentation of "flat" affect), *avolition* (lack of motivation or purpose), *alogia* (decreased or absent speech). Negative symptoms are generally those in which there is a decrease or lack of a typical behavior or other characteristic. The general profile of the disorders in this section is that they involve some sort of splitting off or distancing of the person from aspects of his or her everyday reality.

Many people incorrectly use the term schizophrenia to mean "multiple personality disorder" (that condition is actually called dissociative identity disorder; see below). Although schizophrenia literally means "split mind," it refers to a split in mental functions, or a split from reality; it does not indicate a split in identity. Four disorders are discussed in this section, each centered on a specific symptom profile.

Delusional Disorder. A **delusion** is a false belief that is not due to culture, and is not relinquished despite evidence that it is false. For example, a person might believe that he or she is a certain movie star. Delusions are different from strongly held beliefs, both in intensity and plausibility. For someone with **delusional disorder**, one or more delusions have been present for at least a month, and counterevidence is generally denied or distorted to keep the delusion intact. Common delusions include erotomania (the belief that someone is in love with you), grandiosity (the belief that you have a special talent or insight), and persecution (the belief that you are being followed, drugged, harassed, and so on).

Brief Psychotic Disorder. When any of the **positive symptoms** (delusions, hallucinations, disorganized speech, or disorganized behavior) are present for at least one day—but the symptoms last less than one month—and there are no negative symptoms, a person can be diagnosed with **brief psychotic disorder**. The definitive feature of the disorder, beyond its symptom profile, is full remission of all symptoms within one month of onset. On the schizophrenia spectrum, brief psychotic disorder represents schizophrenia of the shortest duration.

A **hallucination** is a false sensory perception that occurs while a person is conscious (not during sleep or delirium). It is important to distinguish between true hallucinations, which occur in the absence of related sensory stimuli, and illusions, which are misperceptions of actual sensory stimuli (which may occur in low light). The most common hallucinations are auditory and visual.

Schizophreniform Disorder. Also on the schizophrenia spectrum, **schizophreniform disorder** occupies a middle position: the person experiences at least one positive symptom, but can also experience one or more negative symptoms, and does so for at least a month but not longer than six months. Remission can often occur faster with effective drug treatment.

Schizophrenia. At the end of the spectrum, **schizophrenia** is diagnosed when someone has been experiencing positive and sometimes negative symptoms for longer than six months. Here the impact on functioning is greatest, with impairment in work, relationships, and/or self-care. Though the symptoms may subside at times to a prodromal level (just below the diagnostic threshold), there is no complete remission without medication. On the schizophrenia spectrum, schizophrenia proper thus represents the chronic version of the disorder.

Schizoaffective Disorder. **Schizoaffective disorder** combines mood and psychotic symptoms: in this disorder, both the symptoms of schizophrenia and a major depressive, manic, or mixed episode are experienced for at least one month. What separates this disorder from, for example, major depressive disorder "with psychotic features," is that the person experiences delusions and/or hallucinations at times *in the absence of mood symptoms* as well as, at different times, *during a major mood episode*; schizoaffective disorder thus resembles a (chronic) psychotic disorder with an overlapping bipolar or depressive disorder in which the mood symptoms fully remit for at least two weeks at a time.

Symptoms mimicking a schizophrenia spectrum or other psychotic disorder can also be caused by a general medical condition, or by alcohol, drug, or medication use or withdrawal. If the person has a medical condition or uses substances that could be causing the symptoms, the diagnosis is psychotic disorder due to a general medical condition or substance-induced psychotic disorder. Symptoms of psychosis can also occur with mood or developmental disorders. All of these disorders are ruled out before making a diagnosis of one of the disorders in this section.

8. Dissociative Disorders

During a dissociative experience, some of a person's thoughts, feelings, perceptions, memories, or behaviors are separated from conscious awareness and control, in a way that is not explainable as mere forgetfulness. This separation sometimes occurs as a defense against a traumatic situation that was too overwhelming to hold in awareness. In a **dissociative disorder**, the disruptions in awareness, memory, and identity are extreme and/or frequent, and they cause distress or impair the person's functioning. Dissociative disorders can be triggered by severe stress or psychological conflicts, and they usually begin and end suddenly.

Dissociative Identity Disorder. A person with **dissociative identity disorder** alternates among two or more distinct personality states (or identities), only one of which interacts with other people at a given time. The condition may be experienced as a "possession" by another personality or identity, as it involves amnesia—loss of awareness or memory—for one or more of the personality states. These distinct identities may vary widely in age, gender, and personality traits, and they may or may not be aware of each other. This disorder was previously known as multiple personality disorder (and many people incorrectly call it schizophrenia).

Dissociative Amnesia. A person with **dissociative amnesia** has had at least one episode of forgetting some important personal information, creating gaps in memory that are usually related to severe stress or trauma. The person may wander aimlessly during the episode or experience it as a kind of journey, in what is called a **dissociative fugue.** Most often, the amnesia is localized, meaning that everything that happened during a particular time period is forgotten, but it can also be selective (only some events during a particular time period are forgotten), generalized (the person's whole lifetime is forgotten), continuous (everything since a certain time is forgotten), or systematized (only particular categories of information are forgotten, such as everything relating to the person's family). The disorder usually begins and ends suddenly, with full recovery of memory, though it may also linger with some information only gradually, if ever, fully coming back to consciousness. Unfortunately, when remission means recovery of disturbing memories, amnesia may give way to suicidal ideation or behavior, or to PTSD or another condition.

Depersonalization/Derealization Disorder. A person with **depersonalization disorder** has a recurring or persistent feeling of being cut off or detached from his or her body or mental processes, as if observing themselves from the outside, in something like an out-of-body experience. In a **derealization disorder**, on the other hand, a person experiences a feeling that people or objects in the external world are unreal. In both cases, the person knows that the feeling is not accurate—his or her "reality testing" remains intact—and the depersonalization and/or derealization, plus awareness of this incongruity, causes distress or impairs functioning. The disorder usually first occurs in late adolescence, with almost all cases having a first onset before the person is 25 years old. Onset and remission can be sudden or gradual, with stress or novel situations often playing an exacerbating role.

9. Personality Disorders

Personality traits are stable patterns of thought, feeling, and behavior that influence how a person experiences, thinks about, and interacts with the people and events in his or her life. A **personality disorder** is an enduring, rigid set of personality traits that deviates from cultural norms, impairs functioning, and causes distress either to the person with the disorder or to those in his or her life. The symptom profile is therefore more or less a list of the prominent traits that characterize each "disordered" personality. However, because many personality disorders are **egosyntonic**—generally in harmony with a person's ego or self-image—it is usually the consequences of the personality disorder, not its symptom structure, that causes a person to seek treatment.

The degree of distress or impairment is important. Because personality traits are not simply binary— "normal" versus "pathological"—but instead represent a continuum (for example, from independent to nonconforming to antisocial), the same constellations of traits that are found in personality disorders can also be present to a lesser degree in normal people. A difficult or rigid personality becomes a personality disorder when the pattern causes significant distress or impairment, it has been present since adolescence or young adulthood, it affects nearly all personal and social situations, and it creates dysfunction in two or more of the following areas: affect, cognition, impulse control, and interpersonal functioning.

In the DSM-5, the personality disorders have been organized, or "clustered," into three categories. **Cluster A** includes the paranoid, schizoid, and schizotypal personality disorders associated with irrational, withdrawn, cold, or suspicious behaviors. **Cluster B** includes the antisocial, borderline, histrionic, and narcissistic personality disorders associated with emotional, dramatic, and attention-seeking behaviors, and intense interpersonal conflict. **Cluster C** includes the avoidant, dependent, and obsessive-compulsive personality disorders, associated with tense, anxious, over-controlled behaviors.

Category	Personality Disorder	Traits
Cluster A	Paranoid Schizoid Schizotypal	Irrational, Withdrawn, Cold, Suspicious
Cluster B	Antisocial Borderline Histrionic Narcissistic	Emotional, Dramatic, Attention-Seeking, Intense
Cluster C	Avoidant Dependent Obsessive-Compulsive	Tense, Anxious, Over-controlled

Table 10   Personality Disorders

Paranoid Personality Disorder. A person with **paranoid personality disorder** mistrusts and misinterprets others' motives and actions without sufficient cause, suspecting them of deceiving, harming, betraying, or attacking him or her. The person tends to be guarded, tense, and self-sufficient, generally in counter-productive/maladaptive ways.

Schizoid Personality Disorder. A person with **schizoid personality disorder** is a loner with little interest or involvement in close relationships, even those with family members. The person seems unaffected emotionally by interactions with other people, appearing instead detached or cold.

Schizotypal Personality Disorder. A person with **schizotypal personality disorder** has several traits that cause problems interpersonally, including limited or inappropriate affect; magical or paranoid thinking; and odd beliefs, speech, behavior, appearance, and perceptions. The person tends to have no confidantes other than close relatives. Many cases eventually develop schizophrenia (the disorder is cross-listed in the DSM-5 in the section on Schizophrenia Spectrum and Other Psychotic Disorders).

Antisocial Personality Disorder. A person with **antisocial personality disorder** has a history of serious behavior problems beginning as a young teen, including significant aggression against people or animals; deliberate property destruction; lying or theft; and serious rule violation. In addition, since age 15, the person has a history of repeatedly disregarding the rights of others in various ways, through illegal activities, dishonesty, impulsiveness, physical fights, disregard for safety, financial irresponsibility, and lack of remorse. This disorder is cross-listed in the DSM-5 in the section on Disruptive, Impulse-Control, and Conduct Disorders. It is more frequently encountered in men and specifically in incarcerated men.

Borderline Personality Disorder. A person with **borderline personality disorder** suffers from enduring or recurrent instability in his or her impulse control, mood, and image of self and others. Impulsive and reckless behavior, together with extreme mood swings, reactivity, and anger, can lead to unstable relationships and to damage both of the person with the disorder and of others in his or her life. Feeling empty, with an unstable sense of self, the person is terrified of abandonment by others, whom the person may first idealize and then devalue or demonize. Self-harming and suicidal behaviors may also occur. There is some evidence that this disorder is a generalized and more severe form of a Bipolar Disorder and/or that is linked to childhood sexual abuse. It is more frequently encountered in women.

Histrionic Personality Disorder. A person with **histrionic personality disorder** strongly desires to be the center of attention, and often seeks to attract attention through personal appearance and seductive behavior. The person's expressions of emotion are dramatic, yet the emotions themselves are often shallow and shifting, and the person may believe that his or her relationships are more intimate than they are. The person may also be suggestible, and vague in his or her speech.

Narcissistic Personality Disorder. A person with **narcissistic personality disorder** feels grandiosely self-important, with fantasies of beauty, brilliance, and power. The person feels a desperate need for admiration in a variety of contexts, and feels envy both toward and from others. Lacking empathy for others, the person may exploit others, and feel entitled, arrogant, and haughty.

Avoidant Personality Disorder. A person with **avoidant personality disorder** feels inadequate, inferior, and undesirable and is preoccupied with fears of criticism and conflict. The person feels ashamed, and avoids interpersonal contact and new activities, unless he or she is certain of being liked. The person is also restrained and inhibited in relationships.

Dependent Personality Disorder. A person with **dependent personality disorder** feels a need to be taken care of by others and an unrealistic fear of being unable to take care of him- or herself. The person also has trouble assuming responsibility and making decisions, preferring to gain approval by making others responsible and seeking others' advice and reassurance regarding decisions. In relationships, he or she is clinging, submissive, and afraid to express disagreement. Others often take advantage of the person because he or she is willing to do or tolerate almost anything, even abuse, in order to gain support and nurturing, and to avoid abandonment. He or she urgently seeks another relationship if one is lost.

Obsessive-Compulsive Personality Disorder. A person with **obsessive-compulsive personality disorder** (OCPD) may not have any true obsessions or compulsions, but may instead accumulate money or worthless objects. The person is perfectionistic, rigid, and stubborn, with a need for control interpersonally and mentally. The person resists others' authority, and will not cooperate with or delegate to others unless things are done his or her way. Often workaholic and moralistic beyond the level of the surrounding culture or religion, the person also may be depressed and have trouble expressing affection. A preoccupation with orderliness and list-making across a variety of situations can interfere with effectiveness and efficiency. OCPD is cross-listed in the DSM-5 in the section on Obsessive-Compulsive and Related Disorders.

Biological Bases of Nervous System Disorders

Schizophrenia

Recall that schizophrenia is a disorder characterized by positive symptoms, such as delusions and hallucinations, as well as negative ones, such as flat affect, disorganized speech, and avolition. Although schizophrenia presents as a thought disorder, it is important to remember that psychological characteristics have a physical or neurological basis; the division between these two is largely a conceptual one (based on an outdated **mind-body dualism** framework). Schizophrenia is a neurological disorder with a strong genetic basis. Studies have found that in identical twin pairs, if one twin has schizophrenia, the other has about a 50% chance of also having it; if the second twin does not have schizophrenia, he or she is likely to have a lesser form of it (e.g., schizophreniform disorder). The onset of schizophrenia happens around adolescence. The **stress-diathesis theory** suggests that while genetic inheritance provides a biological predisposition for schizophrenia, stressors elicit the onset of the disease.

There are numerous brain changes that have been noted in people with schizophrenia. One idea formed from observations is the **dopamine hypothesis**, which suggests that the pathway for the neurotransmitter dopamine is hyperactive in people with schizophrenia. This is due both to an overabundance of dopamine and to hypersensitive dopamine receptors. This finding, along with evidence of hyperactivation of the temporal lobes in people with this condition, may explain the presence of the positive signs of schizophrenia (like auditory hallucinations). Dopamine antagonist medications have been found to be helpful as antipsychotics.

Additionally, *hypo*activation of the frontal lobes may be responsible for the negative signs of schizophrenia, creating a kind of pseudodepression, flat affect, and impaired speech. Individuals with schizophrenia have also been found to have smaller brains due to atrophy: schizophrenic individuals display increased ventricles (cavities in the brain), and enlarged sulci and fissures (less folding).

Depression

Depression also appears to have a strong genetic basis—there is increased risk of developing depression when a first-degree family member has it. Depression has been linked to diminished functioning in pathways in the brain that involve the neurotransmitters dopamine, serotonin, and norepinephrine. Antidepressants thus target and try to stimulate these pathways. Depression can often accompany other neurological diseases, such as Parkinson's and traumatic brain injury, due to damage to similar or overlapping areas of the brain.

Alzheimer's Disease

Dementia (the general term for what is called a neurocognitive disorder in DSM-5) is a term for a severe loss of cognitive ability beyond what would be expected from normal aging. Alzheimer's disease ("major or minor neurocognitive disorder due to Alzheimer's disease") is the most prevalent form of dementia, affecting a large number of people who reach their 80s and especially their 90s (over 50% for this latter group, according to some estimates). It is a disease that is characterized behaviorally by **anterograde amnesia**, the inability to form new memories, as well as step-wise **retrograde amnesia**, with more recent memories degrading first, such that the last memories to fade are typically the oldest. Alzheimer's patients may thus be able to recall events from decades earlier but forget people and events that were encountered recently. Their visual memory will be impaired as well, such that they may get lost and confused with regard to orientation. Needless to say, living with Alzheimer's disease can be very confusing, frustrating, and emotionally painful both for the patient and for family members and friends.

Alzheimer's disease is a cortical disease, meaning that it affects the cortex, the outermost tissue of the brain. It is caused by the formation of **neuritic plaques**, hard formations of beta-amyloid protein and **neurofibrillary tangles** (clumps of tau protein). It is unclear why these plaques and tangles form, though there is some evidence of at least partial genetic susceptibility. Some theories suggest that when these plaques build up, they reach a critical mass and then begin to cause cell death by "gunking up" neuronal connections, preventing nutrients and waste from travelling to and from some neurons. Currently, there is no cure for Alzheimer's, and treatments are directed at slowing the progress of the illness rather than reversing it.

Finally, there is some evidence of abnormalities in the activity of the neurotransmitter acetylcholine in the hippocampus. It should be no surprise that the hippocampus could be involved, because this is the area of the brain that plays a major role in the formation of new memories. As mentioned above, the disease tends to progress in a predictable pattern: as it progresses, the patient loses increasingly older memories, as well as language function and spatial coordination. Eventually, patients are not able to perform daily functions without assistance.

Parkinson's Disease

Parkinson's disease ("major or mild neurocognitive disorder due to Parkinson's disease" in the DSM-5) is a movement disorder caused by the death of cells that generate dopamine in the **basal ganglia** and **substantia nigra**, two subcortical structures in the brain. Among the symptoms are a resting tremor (shaking), slowed movement, rigidity of movements and facial expressions, and a shuffling gait. As the disease progresses, language is typically spared. However, depression and visual-spatial problems may arise. It is estimated that 50% to 80% of Parkinson's patients eventually experience dementia as their disease progresses. In order to treat Parkinson's, patients are given L-dopa treatments. L-dopa is a precursor to dopamine and is used because it is able to pass the blood–brain barrier, entering the brain's blood supply (dopamine is not able to cross the blood-brain barrier).

Stem Cell-based Therapy to Regenerate Neurons in the CNS

Cell death is a characteristic of most CNS disorders and neurodegenerative diseases. It has been theorized that neural stem cells, which have the capacity to differentiate into any of the cell types in the nervous system, hold the key to curing damage to the central nervous system caused by trauma or illness. Experiments have demonstrated that neural stem cells can migrate and replace dying neurons in the CNS. These studies hold promise for an eventual cure for diseases such as Parkinson's disease, Alzheimer's disease, multiple sclerosis, and Huntington's disease.

6.4 ATTITUDES

When psychologists refer to a person's **attitude**, they are referring to a person's feelings and beliefs about other people or events around them, and their tendency to react behaviorally based on those underlying evaluations. Attitudes are useful in that they provide a quick way to size things up and make decisions. However, they can also lead us astray when they lead to inaccurate snap judgments or when they remain fixed beliefs in the face of disconfirming evidence.

Components of Attitudes

Attitudes are considered to have three main components (the ABCs): affect (emotion), behavior tendencies, and cognition (thought).

The Link Between Attitudes and Behavior

Processes by Which Attitudes Influence Behavior

To what extent do our attitudes affect our behaviors? As is the case with most answers in psychology, it depends. At times, behavior does not accurately reflect attitudes. Consider the following common experiences:

- an individual believes in a healthy lifestyle, but is unable to sustain a healthy diet,
- a man believes in not judging others, but finds himself avoiding eye contact and the seat next to a dirty homeless man on the bus,
- a juror believes in a guilty verdict but finds himself conforming to the opinions of other jurors to vote "not guilty."

These scenarios suggest that the relationship between who we believe we are and what we do is complex. Social psychologists have found that there are some situations in which attitudes better predict behavior. Those are as follows:

1) *When social influences are reduced.* Compared to attitudes, which are more internal, external behavior is much more susceptible to social influences. People are much more likely to be honest in a secret ballot process than if they must overtly express their opinions. This is in large part due to fear of criticism and the powerful influence of factors such as conformity and groupthink (which will be discussed later).

2) *When general patterns of behavior, rather than specific behaviors, are observed.* Our attitudes are better at predicting overall decision-making rather than specific behaviors. For example, one who believes in a healthy lifestyle will tend to make healthier decisions than someone who does not, yet this attitude does not necessarily prevent someone from occasionally reaching for a slice of cheesecake. This is known as the **principle of aggregation**; an attitude affects a person's aggregate or average behavior, but not necessarily each isolated act.

3) *When specific, rather than general, attitudes are considered.* Belief in a healthy lifestyle can be a poor predictor of a specific behavior, such as eating properly. It would be wiser to compare the specific attitude that the individual has toward eating properly, because it will be a better predictor of this particular behavior. Thus, it is most accurate to consider specific attitudes closely related to the specific behavior of interest.

4) *When attitudes are made more powerful through self-reflection.* People are more likely to behave in accordance with their attitudes if they are given some time to prepare themselves to do so. When people act automatically, they may be impulsive and act in ways that do not match expressed beliefs. However, when given more time to deliberate over actions, they are more likely to act in ways that match. In addition, when people are made more self-conscious, often through the use of mirrors in experiments, they are more likely to behave morally. Self-awareness reminds us of the beliefs that we have attached to our identities.

Processes by Which Behavior Influences Attitudes

What is perhaps more interesting is the notion that behavior sometimes precedes and affects our attitudes. This recalls the James-Lange theory of emotion (Chapter 4), which proposed that behaviors may precede and influence emotions. It has been found that just the act of smiling can somewhat boost mood, and that the act of running away may contribute to a sensation of fear.

There are several situations in which behaviors are likely to influence attitudes.

1) *Role-playing.* The most notable influence of behavior on attitudes is **role-playing**. Like a role in a play, a social role is a script for how to act. The most powerful demonstration of the power of roles is Zimbardo's **prison study** at Stanford. In this experiment, **Philip Zimbardo** randomly divided Stanford students into prisoners and guards in a mock prison. What happened over the course of the study was astonishing. After an initial lighthearted period, the guards and prisoners began really acting out their characters to the point that the guards were actively humiliating and degrading the prisoners. Some prisoners actively rebelled while others broke down or became apathetic. Participants in the study reported feeling a sense of confusion about reality and fantasy as they became caught up in their roles. The study, which was intended to be two weeks long, had to be discontinued after six days. The study demonstrates a powerful lesson about the influence that social roles can have. Consider how social roles such as "soldier" and "slave" may have affected how people have acted over the course of history. In wartime, soldiers' beliefs about the enemy become dramatically altered over time, with feelings of ambivalence giving way to perceiving the enemy as "evil." Actions, such as singing the national anthem and saluting the flag, tend to increase patriotic beliefs. How does your own role of "student" affect your behavior? The same influences can stem from positive roles. Zimbardo is currently researching positive roles, like that of "hero." Someone who is identified with the role of citizen, parent, or spiritual teacher may be influenced toward wholesome actions in order to better play out that role.

2) *Public Declarations.* In order to please others, people may feel a pressure to adapt what they say. What's interesting is that saying something publicly—a **public declaration**—can become believing it in the absence of bribery, coercion, or some other blatant external motive. Since the individual may not be aware of the social pressure that might have influenced the statement, he or she may justify it by concluding that the statement is a personal belief. As we continue to express ourselves, we become more and more entrenched in believing what we say, a habit that is even stronger for statements made publicly. Consider a politician who voices an opinion on the issue of abortion that mirrors the belief of the majority of her supporters, although she is somewhat ambivalent on the issue herself. As she continues to express their opinion, she will find herself becoming more polarized toward that opinion and her feelings of ambivalence will start to subside. Because her statements were made publicly, think how hard it would be for the politician to shift positions if she had a change of heart through her own development. Thus, she will be more likely to maintain a belief that is consistent with the actions she has taken. An emphasis on "political correctness" has developed from the idea that saying can become believing. The use of a term such as "gay" in a derogatory manner can lead to the development of beliefs that justify use of the term; therefore, many people feel terms of that sort should not be used.

3) *Justification of Effort.* Just as people may modify their attitudes to match their language, they may also modify them to match their behaviors. This is often referred to as **justification of effort**. For example, consider a student who works hard to study for the MCAT and earns a fantastic score, only to feel a calling toward becoming an actor rather than going to medical school at the end of the process. In order to justify the effort already put into the process, the student will feel a pressure to go to medical school. Salespeople, political activists, and others trying to influence behavior often take advantage of what is known as the **foot-in-the-door** phenomenon. The strategy involves enticing people to take small actions, such as signing a free petition or joining a mailing list, at first. Upon obtaining this level of involvement, the stakes are raised to accepting bumper stickers or lawn signs. Then, further involvement is encouraged when donations or volunteer time is requested. While people may have agreed to the earlier steps because they required minimal commitment, they will find themselves feeling internal pressure to consent to larger requests to justify their acceptance of the smaller requests. Over time, their attitudes will reflect those of someone who has taken a strong stance on the issue, in order to justify all the steps that they have taken. Another interesting example of justification of effort is the finding that doing favors for someone increases feelings of liking for that person. The internal dialogue is something like: "I must really like this person; otherwise, why would I be doing so many favors for him?"

Cognitive Dissonance Theory

When considering how behaviors can shape attitudes, self-justification plays an important part. In role-playing, public declarations, and justification of effort scenarios, individuals justify their actions (including language) through beliefs. The theory that seeks to explain why self-justification is such a powerful influence on attitude modification is cognitive dissonance theory.

Cognitive dissonance theory explains that we feel tension ("dissonance") whenever we hold two thoughts or beliefs ("cognitions") that are incompatible, or when attitudes and behaviors don't match. When this occurs, we may feel like hypocrites or feel confused as to where we stand. The theory explains that in order to reduce this unpleasant feeling of tension, we make our views of the world match how we feel or what we've done.

Cognitive dissonance theory can explain people's reactions to situations in which there is insufficient justification for actions that were taken. Without sufficient justification for an action, people are likely to experience dissonance, and thus adjust their beliefs to match what they have done. For example, consider two parents trying to motivate their respective children to study and earn good grades. To motivate this, one parent institutes a reward system in which the child gets $100 for every A. The second parent rewards their child with $5 for every A. In the first situation, the child may feel coerced into earning good grades. Thus, although he or she may study hard for the reward and earn a lot of money, the child will be less likely to have an internal belief that the grades themselves are important. The behavior of studying hard is easily justified by the reward. In the second situation, the child may work to receive A's but have insufficient external justification for having done so, because the reward is insufficient. In cases of insufficient justification, cognitive dissonance theory indicates that there will be some tension that needs to be resolved. The child has earned some A's (behavior) but does not have a supporting attitude available to explain the behavior. Thus, the child is likely to adopt the attitude that grades are important to him or her. Consider how cognitive dissonance theory can similarly be used to explain why mild punishment of appropriate severity is more effective at creating internal attitude change than unjustifiably harsh punishment.

Cognitive dissonance can also be used to explain the way people react after they make decisions. Imagine that a woman is trying to decide between two men who have expressed their romantic interest in her. One is exciting and passionate, but utterly undependable and irresponsible. The other is somewhat subdued, but very considerate and dependable. After making her decision, no matter which way she decides, she is sure to experience some dissonant thoughts about the man she rejected. If she chooses the exciting man, she may miss the dependability and consideration of the subdued man; if she chooses the subdued man, she may lament the lack of excitement and passion. According to cognitive dissonance theory, she will tend to change her attitudes to accentuate the positive qualities of her choice and the negative qualities of the alternative. Thus, if she chooses the exciting man, she may internalize beliefs that excitement and passion are important to a relationship and that dependability is overrated. If she chooses the subdued man, she may instead espouse the belief that it is consideration and dependability that are the centerpieces of a relationship and that passion and excitement are fleeting. The important point is that her endorsement of either of these beliefs will come after she makes her decision, in order to alleviate the tension of losing what she turned down.

Chapter 6 Summary

- Personality is defined as the individual pattern of thinking, feeling, and behavior associated with each person.

- Sigmund Freud pioneered psychoanalytic theory, which proposes that personality is the result of an individual's unconscious thoughts, feelings, and memories.

- The id is ruled by the pleasure principle and is unconscious, the ego is ruled by the reality principle and uses logical thinking and planning to control consciousness and the id, and the superego inhibits the id and influences the ego to follow moralistic rather than realistic goals.

- According to Freud, people develop through five psychosexual stages: the oral stage, the anal stage, the phallic stage, the latent stage, and the genital stage; failure to resolve developmental conflicts within each stage leads to fixation.

- Erik Erikson added social and interpersonal factors to supplement Freud's theory; Erikson's developmental stages involved the resolution of the following crises: trust vs. mistrust, autonomy vs. shame, initiative vs. guilt, industry vs. inferiority, identity vs. role confusion, intimacy vs. isolation, generativity vs. stagnation, and integrity vs. despair.

- Psychoanalytic therapy (or "talk therapy") looks at how the unconscious mind influences thoughts and behaviors with the goal of helping the patient learn to control these.

- Carl Rogers pioneered the humanistic perspective in psychology, and believed that incongruence between behavior and self-concept causes psychopathology.

- Humanistic (or "person-centered") therapy involves a relationship between client (not patient) and therapist; the therapist communicates genuineness, unconditional positive regard, and empathy.

- Behaviorists believe that personality is determined by conditioning; environmental reinforcements and punishments determine an individual's personalities and behaviors.

- Behavioral therapy and cognitive behavior therapy employ the tenets of conditioning to modify thoughts and behaviors.

- The social cognitive perspective suggests that personality is formed by a reciprocal interaction among behavioral, cognitive, and environmental factors.

- The Five-Factor Model describes five major personality traits: extroversion, neuroticism, openness to experience, agreeableness, and conscientiousness.

- Motivation is influenced by drives, instincts, feedback, arousal, and needs.

- The drive-reduction theory suggests that individuals engage in certain behavior in an attempt to alleviate physiological states of discomfort.

- Maslow's Hierarchy of Needs explains that individuals will seek to fulfill physiological needs before looking to fulfill higher level needs.

- Mental illness is influenced by a multitude of factors, including biological influences, psychological influences, and sociocultural influences.

- Attitude is defined as an individual's feelings and beliefs about other people or events; attitudes influence behavior.

- The principle of aggregation states that attitudes predict general overall behavior well, but do not always accurately predict specific behaviors.

- Philip Zimbardo discovered that role-playing has a powerful influence on attitudes and behavior.

- Cognitive dissonance theory suggests that individuals will attempt to reduce tension (dissonance) between beliefs (cognitions) that are incompatible.

CHAPTER 6 FREESTANDING PRACTICE QUESTIONS

1. A victim of suspected assault is unable to remember the attack. Follow-up tests demonstrate that the victim has no conscious memory of being attacked, and cannot remember anything about the day leading up to the attack. According to Freud, which of the following ego defense mechanisms is the victim most likely employing?

   A) Rationalization
   B) Regression
   C) Repression
   D) Denial

2. A patient is brought into the hospital. After completing a clinical interview and direct observation, the staff psychologist diagnoses the patient with schizophrenia, catatonic type. Which of the following is most likely true about this patient's clinical presentation?

   I.   Terrifying persecutory hallucinations were dominant
   II. Negative symptoms were dominant
   III. Negative and positive symptoms were equally manifest

   A) I only
   B) II only
   C) III only
   D) I and III

3. Conversion disorder is characterized by:

   A) a constant fear of being ill.
   B) panic attacks and severe anxiety.
   C) frequent vague complaints about a physical symptom.
   D) functional impairment of a limb or sensory ability with no apparent physical cause.

4. Suppose that an individual who proclaims to be staunchly opposed to consuming animal products (a vegan) falls in love with someone who regularly eats meat. According to cognitive dissonance theory, the vegan might do all of the following EXCEPT:

   A) downplay the role of veganism in his or her life.
   B) continue to remain outspoken about his or her views against consuming animal products and remain in the relationship with the person who regularly eats meat.
   C) justify breaking off his or her relationship with the meat-eater due to incompatibility.
   D) attempt to convince his partner to eat less meat by showing her information about the personal and environmental benefits of veganism.

5. A high school girl goes missing, and when she is found in a town 100 miles away a week later, she has assumed a new personality and has no apparent recollection of her life at home. Which category of disorder is she most likely suffering from?

A) Somatoform disorder
B) Delusional disorder
C) Personality disorder
D) Dissociative disorder

6. Lauren, a California native, moved to New York three years ago. Since then, during the winter months, Lauren finds it harder to wake up in the morning, avoids her friends, and has the tendency to overeat. Her psychiatrist prescribed 30 to 90 minutes of light exposure daily to relieve the symptoms. What disorder does the psychiatrist believe Lauren has?

A) Catatonic schizophrenia
B) Seasonal affective disorder
C) Major depressive disorder
D) Bipolar affective disorder

7. Parkinson's disease involves:

  I. overstimulation of dopamine-producing neurons in the peripheral nervous system.
  II. cell death in the basal ganglia and substantia nigra.
  III. neurofibrillary tangles and neuritic plaques in the brain.

A) I only
B) II only
C) I and II
D) II and III

8. Suppose that a study demonstrates that kindergarteners who are asked to pretend that they are first-graders are less disruptive in class and more likely to follow directions than their peers (who are not told to pretend anything). These results demonstrate the influence of:

A) role-playing.
B) the foot-in-the-door phenomenon.
C) a justification of effort.
D) public declarations.

CHAPTER 6 PRACTICE PASSAGE

In the late 1800s, psychiatrist William Gull described one of his patients as suffering from a "perversion of the will" that resulted in "simple starvation." Today, Gull's patient would likely be diagnosed with *anorexia nervosa* (AN), which is characterized by a dramatic distortion of perceived body image and dangerously low weight achieved through food restriction, excessive exercise, or other extreme means (abuse of diet pills, laxatives, etc.). According to multiple studies, AN has the highest mortality rate of all mental illnesses. This finding is likely due to the severe health consequences associated with AN, including cardiovascular stress, gastrointestinal dysfunction, and malnutrition.

Several theories have been advanced to explain the etiology or risk factors of AN and other eating disorders. Some researchers posit that AN is primarily a sociocultural phenomenon rooted in Western culture's espousal of a thin body ideal. According to these theorists, the disorder initially progresses through three stages: exposure to the thin ideal, internalization of the thin ideal, and perceived discrepancy between oneself and the thin ideal. In an effort to conform to the thin ideal, individuals who have AN employ extreme behaviors to reduce their weight. Other researchers point to intrapersonal personality traits or family dynamics as the primary sources of AN pathology. Finally, some theorists prefer to view AN from an addiction's perspective.

In an effort to determine best treatment practices for AN and other eating disorders, some studies have compared treatment results of various clinical interventions. For example, Britain's National Institute for Clinical Excellence (NICE) conducted a comprehensive review of both inpatient and outpatient interventions for all of the AN treatment centers in the United Kingdom, collecting data on psychoanalytic therapy, behavioral therapy (BT), cognitive behavioral therapy (CBT), and family-based treatment (FBT). Published in 2004, the NICE study concluded that no particular treatment approach was significantly superior to any other particular approach in terms of treatment outcome. In another study conducted in 2010, researchers examined treatment outcome differences between FBT and ego-oriented individual therapy (EOIT) with adolescent patients. Selection criteria required a diagnosis of AN between twelve and eighteen months prior to therapy, as well as therapy duration between twelve and twenty sessions. The FBT group contained fifty-two subjects, while the EOIT group contained fifty subjects. Figure 1 displays the results of this study.

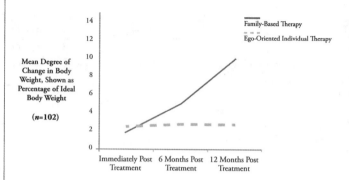

Figure 1   Treatment Outcome Results for FBT and EOIT

Material used in this particular passage was adapted from the following sources:

Risk Factors for Eating Disorders, R. H. Striegel-Moore and C.M. Bulik, in *American Psychologist*. © 2007 by the American Psychological Association.

Eating Disorders: Core interventions in the treatment and management of anorexia nervosa, bulimia nervosa, and related eating disorders. © 2004 by the British Psychological Society and the Royal College of Psychiatrists.

Randomized clinical trial comparing family-based treatment with adolescent-focused individual therapy for adolescents with anorexia nervosa. J. Lock, D. Le Grange, W. S. Agras, A. Moye, S. W. Bryson, and B. Jo, in the *Archives of General Psychiatry.* © 2010 by the American Medical Association.

1. Most AN sufferers demonstrate largely consistent eating patterns marked by some sporadic binging; AN sufferers generally stick to a very specific restrictive diet, eating only "safe foods" a majority of the time, but binging occasionally on other foods. Despite this irregularity in behavior, AN sufferers' attitudes about food remain consistent. What concept best describes this behavior, in terms of AN sufferers maintaining a specific attitude about food, but demonstrating slightly inconsistent eating behavior?

A) The reality principle
B) The principle of aggregation
C) The self-actualizing tendency
D) Vicarious learning

2. Heather was recently diagnosed with anorexia nervosa, and she has experienced continued weight loss and severe stomach pain. According to Learning Theory, for Heather, her physical symptoms would be considered:

   I. positive reinforcement.
   II. extinction.
   III. punishment.

A) I only
B) III only
C) I and III only
D) I, II, and III

3. An empirical basis for the addiction model of AN would most likely come from research that:

A) discovers that a majority of those diagnosed with AN have at least one parent who is alcohol dependent.
B) identifies high comorbidity of AN and tobacco dependence.
C) proves that there is an inverse relationship between dopamine production in the brain and the activity of the satiety center controlled by the hypothalamus in individuals with AN.
D) shows that those with AN have a higher mortality rate than individuals dependent on methamphetamines.

4. Which of the following scenarios best reflects how a psychoanalytic therapist would treat a patient with AN?

A) The therapist would make sure to establish a relationship with the client based on rapport and mutual trust, and would always provide unconditional positive regard to the client.
B) The therapist would help the patient gain awareness of his or her unconscious motives for his or her behavior, and help the patient to transition from self-loathing and guilt to reality.
C) The therapist would attempt to recondition negative behaviors.
D) The therapist would help the patient pinpoint negative thoughts and feelings, and help the patient learn positive self-talk and healthier behaviors.

5. Noreen, who was diagnosed with AN, now participates in family therapy. Based on the chart in Figure 1, what should the therapist expect?

A) Noreen will gain approximately 10% of her ideal body weight by the end of 12 months.
B) Noreen will gain approximately five pounds by the end of six months.
C) Noreen's weight will double halfway through the treatment.
D) Noreen will gain ten pounds by the end of treatment.

6. Which of the following conclusions can be inferred from the results displayed in Figure 1?

A) Family-based therapy is superior to ego-oriented individual therapy in reducing the negative thought processes associated with AN.
B) The distortions in self-image characteristic of those with AN derive from an underdeveloped ego.
C) Attachment theory is relevant to treating AN.
D) AN typically derives from poor parenting.

SOLUTIONS TO CHAPTER 6 FREESTANDING PRACTICE QUESTIONS

1. **C** Repression is employed to keep painful thoughts out of conscious awareness; because the victim is unable to recall the attack and has no conscious memory of the of the attack, the victim is most likely repressing their memories (choice C is correct). Rationalization is an ego defense mechanism whereby unacceptable behaviors or feelings are explained in a rational or logical manner; there is no evidence in the question stem that the victim is rationalizing (choice A is wrong). Regression involves the use of coping mechanisms that are characteristic of an earlier point in psychological development, such as reverting to bed-wetting after a traumatic experience; there is not enough information in the question stem to assume that the victim is employing regression (choice B is wrong). Denial is the act of voluntarily withholding an idea or feeling from conscious awareness. This is, perhaps, most easily confused with repression which involves *involuntarily* withholding an idea or feeling from conscious awareness; because the question stem states that follow up tests demonstrate "no conscious memory," the victim is probably not employing denial (choice D is wrong).

2. **B** Item I is false: the diagnosis of schizophrenia, catatonic type is only given when negative symptoms, such as flat affect and rigidity, are the dominant symptoms. Hallucinations, on the other hand, are considered "positive" symptoms. Thus, if hallucinations were dominant, there would be no designation of catatonic type (choices A and D can be eliminated). Item II is true: the designation of catatonic type requires the predominance of negative symptoms (choice C can be eliminated and choice B is correct). Item III is in fact false: a fairly even distribution of both positive and negative symptoms would not indicate a designation of catatonic type, as described above.

3. **D** Conversion disorder is a somatoform disorder in which a person displays blindness, deafness, or other symptoms of sensory or motor failure without a physical cause (choice D is correct). A constant fear of illness refers to hypochondriasis, not conversion disorder (choice A is wrong). Panic attacks and severe anxiety are symptoms of anxiety disorders, while conversion disorder is a type of somatoform disorder (choice B is wrong). Frequent vague complaints about physical symptoms are characteristic of somatization disorder, not conversion disorder (choice C is wrong).

4. **B** According to cognitive dissonance theory, human behavior can be explained by the idea that people have a bias to seek consonance between their thoughts and beliefs (cognitions). According to this theory, people will engage in "dissonance reduction" when two of their cognitions are incompatible (in this case, avid veganism and falling in love with a meat-eater). Cognitive dissonance theory predicts that people will attempt to lower dissonance in three ways: by lowering the importance of one of the discordant factors, by adding consonant elements, or by changing one of the dissonant factors. Therefore, the individual is most likely to: downplay the role of veganism in his or her life (lowering the importance of one of the discordant factors; choice A is something the individual is likely to do and can be eliminated), justify breaking off the relationship with the meat-eater (changing one of the dissonant factors; choice C is something the individual is likely to do and can be eliminated), or attempt to convince his or her partner to eat less meat (adding consonant elements; choice D is something the individual is likely to do and can be eliminated). Therefore, according to cognitive dissonance theory, the vegan is *least* likely to do nothing at all—remain in the relationship and remain committed to veganism (choice B unlikely and is the correct answer choice).

5. **D** The girl is most likely suffering from dissociative fugue (a type of dissociative disorder), which causes her to experience personal amnesia. Sufferers of dissociative fugue tend to wander or travel and often establish new identities based on who they believe they are, (choice D is correct). Somatoform disorders involve physical illness or injury (choice A is wrong). Delusional disorder is a psychotic illness that is characterized by non-bizarre delusions, with no accompanying hallucinations, mood disturbances, or flattening of affect; furthermore, amnesia is not a symptom of a delusional disorder (choice B is wrong). A personality disorder is characterized by a set of personality traits that deviates from cultural norms, impairs functioning, and causes distress; there are three major clusters of personality disorders, none of which accurately explain the girl described in the question stem (choice C is wrong). Although it is possible that the girl is faking it and seeking attention, a possible symptom of histrionic personality disorder, the question stem would need to provide concrete information to draw this conclusion, which it does not.

6. **B** Lauren demonstrates symptoms of depression in the winter, when the days are shortest (least amount of daylight). Seasonal affective disorder involves depressive episodes in a seasonal pattern, usually during the fall and winter months when there is less sunlight exposure (choice B is correct). Catatonic schizophrenia is a mental illness in which the patient loses touch with reality and behaves in extremes, either by behaving hyperactively or by demonstrating physical immobility (choice A is wrong). Major depressive disorder is characterized by feelings of worthlessness, lack of pleasure, lethargy, and sleep or appetitive irregularities, which last for two or more weeks (choice C is wrong). Bipolar affective disorder is characterized by cycles of abnormal, persistent high mood (manic episodes) and low mood (depressive episodes; choice D is wrong).

7. **B** Item I is false: Parkinson's disease is the result of the death of dopamine-producing neurons in the brain; furthermore, while there are *some* dopamine-producing neurons in the peripheral nervous system, the primary neurotransmitter responsible for muscle movement is acetylcholine, not dopamine (choices A and C can be eliminated). Note that both remaining answer choices include Item II so it must be true: Parkinson's is primarily caused by cellular death of neurons in the basal ganglia and substantia nigra of the brain; these neurons are dopamine-producing and inhibitory, connecting with the motor cortices in the brain and help to smooth out movement and inhibit excessive movement. Death of neurons in these areas results in the characteristic shaking, rigidity, and slowness of movement initiation. Item III is false: neurofibrillary tangles and neuritic plaques in the brain are characteristic of Alzheimer's disease, not Parkinson's disease (choice D can be eliminated and choice B is correct).

8. **A** If kindergarteners are asked to play the role of an older student (by pretending to be first graders) and their behavior changed accordingly (they acted more like older students by being less disruptive and following directions), this effect demonstrates the influence of role-playing (choice A is correct). The foot-in-the-door phenomenon is a tactic whereby first an individual is asked to do something small/easy, and then a subsequent request is a littler bigger/harder, and so on. The question stem does not mention subsequent requests of the kindergartners, nor does the foot-in-the-door phenomenon explain their change in behavior (choice B is wrong). A justification of effort occurs when the amount of effort necessary to complete a task is higher than the reward and people then over-inflate the significance or the value of the reward to better match the effort invested; this scenario does not discuss effort or reward (choice C is wrong). Public declarations include making statements about attitudes in a public way, such that the attitude is more likely to become entrenched because of the public declaration to others; this is not described in the question stem (choice D is wrong).

SOLUTIONS TO CHAPTER 6 PRACTICE PASSAGE

1. **B**   The principle of aggregation explains how attitudes are better at predicting general patterns of behavior, but cannot always account for specific behaviors. The principle of aggregation best explains the periodically inconsistent behavior of binging, despite the fact that the attitude of AN sufferers toward food remains consistent (choice B is correct). According to Freud, the ego is ruled by the reality principle, which employs logical thinking to control consciousness and the id; while the reality principle may be involved in the choices AN sufferers make about eating, it does not explain the inconsistent behavior in light of a consistent attitude (choice A is wrong). The self-actualizing tendency is an innate drive toward recognizing someone's full potential; it does not explain the scenario described in the question stem (choice C is wrong). Vicarious learning involves an individual learning by observing another individual; this does not explain the scenario described in the question stem (choice D is wrong).

2. **C**   Item I is true: according to Learning Theory, positive reinforcement is an operant conditioning term that refers to a favorable consequence that reinforces a particular behavior. In Heather's case, the physical symptom of weight loss is considered a reward of her eating behavior (because she has AN and weight loss is desirable for her) and is thus a positive reinforcement (choice B can be eliminated). Item II is false: extinction is the process by which the behavior in question ceases due to the absence of a favorable consequence; since the question stem makes no mention of Heather ceasing her behavior, extinction does not explain her physical symptoms (choice D can be eliminated). Item III is true: punishment refers to a negative consequence experienced as a result of the behavior; Heather's stomach pain is a punishment for her eating behaviors (choice A can be eliminated and choice C is correct).

3. **C**   The hypothalamus is the brain structure associated with appetite regulation, while dopamine is the neurotransmitter associated with the pleasure pathways of the brain. Many illicit and addictive substances manipulate the dopamine system in some fashion, either by stimulating the release of dopamine or by inhibiting its absorption. If AN is a form of addiction, there would likely be an inverse relationship between the brain region that communicates satiety and the pleasure center of the brain; in other words, when the satiety center is not active (an individual with AN is not sated or full), dopamine is produced. This would indicate that the pleasure center of the brain is triggered when an individual with AN starves him- or herself, thus establishing a biochemical basis for the addiction model (choice C is correct). It is important to recognize that the context in which the passage mentions an addictions model suggests that AN is itself a type of addiction. It does not refer to mere correlations with addiction, such as family members with addictions (choice A is wrong) or comorbidity with other addictions (choice B is wrong). Finally, the possibility that AN is more lethal than substance abuse does not logically yield the conclusion that AN is also an addiction (choice D is wrong).

4. **B** Psychoanalytic therapy focuses on helping the patient gain awareness of his or her unconscious motives, and then make choices that are based on reality rather than on instincts (id) or guilt (superego; choice B is correct). Humanistic therapy is more concerned with establishing a relationship between the therapist and the "client" based on mutual trust and unconditional positive regard (choice A is wrong). Behavioral therapy might involve reconditioning of negative behaviors (choice C is wrong) and cognitive behavior therapy best describes targeting negative thoughts/feelings and learning positive self-talk and healthier behaviors (choice D is wrong).

5. **A** The vertical axis of the chart in Figure 1 reflects the percentage of ideal body weight. Therefore, Figure 1 demonstrates that those in family-based therapy will gain 10% of their ideal body weight by the end of 12 months (choice A is correct). The vertical axis of Figure 1 does not represent pounds gained (choices B and D are wrong). Additionally, although the percentage of ideal body weight doubles six months post-treatment, weight gained during treatment is not depicted in Figure 1. Further, the six-month marker shows a doubling of *percentage* of ideal body weight rather than a doubling of total baseline weight (choice C is wrong).

6. **C** The chart in Figure 1 suggests that family-based therapy is superior to ego-oriented individual therapy in helping those with AN to gain weight post-treatment; but, it does not suggest that family-based therapy is superior to individual therapy at reducing the negative thought processes associated with AN (choice A is wrong). However, it does imply that family relationships play a key role in AN pathology, which is consistent with attachment theory (choice C is correct). Attachment theory maintains that parent-child relationships strongly influence the child's attitudes about the self and the world. Nevertheless, a relevance of attachment and relationships to successful treatment of the disorder does not automatically imply that the disorder was caused by poor parenting. It may simply mean that familial relationships can help the patient to develop more positive self-images or become more aware of unhealthy behavior (choice D is wrong). Although psychodynamic theory may view distorted body image as a function of poor reality testing, which is the domain of the ego, this focus would not be supported (or contradicted) by the relative superiority of family-based therapy to individual therapy (choice B is wrong).

Chapter 7
Self-Identity and
Group Identity

Development of identity can be viewed from a psychological or a sociological perspective. In order to fully understand identity, the self, and the collective, it is important to look at these concepts from multiple perspectives. Understanding the individual as part of a group is central to understanding human nature, as we are inherently social creatures who cannot exist in a vacuum.

7.1 SELF-CONCEPT AND IDENTITY FORMATION

Self-concept or **self-identity** is broadly defined as the sum of an individual's knowledge and understanding of his- or herself. Differing from **self-consciousness**, which is awareness of one's self, self-concept includes physical, psychological, and social attributes, which can be influenced by the individual's attitudes, habits, beliefs, and ideas. For example, if you asked yourself the question "Who am I?" your responses would form the basis of your self-concept. Self-concept is how an individual defines him- or herself based on beliefs that person has about him- or herself, known as **self-schemas**. For example, an individual might hold the following self-concepts: female, African-American, student, smart, funny, future doctor.

Different Types of Identities

These qualities can be further divided into those that form personal identity and those that form social identity. **Personal identity** consists of one's own sense of personal attributes (in the example above, smart and funny constitute attributes of personal identity). **Social identity** consists of social definitions of who you are; these can include race, religion, gender, occupation, and such (in the example above, female, African-American, student, and future doctor constitute attributes of social identity). Thus, the "self" is a personal and social construction of beliefs.

As a quick way to remember different aspects of one's identity, consider the ADRESSING framework: each letter stands for a different characteristic. These characteristics are age, disability status, religion, ethnicity/race, sexual orientation, socioeconomic status, indigenous background, national origin, and gender. Note that gender is a socially constructed concept while sex is biologically determined. Each of these categories contains a dominant group as well as groups that are less dominant in society. For example, here is the breakdown (generally) in American society:

Cultural Characteristics	Power	Less Power
Age	Adults	Children, adolescents, elders
Disability status	Temporarily able-bodied	Persons with disabilities
Religion	Christians	Jews, Muslims, other non-Christians
Ethnicity/race	Euro-American	People of color
Sexual orientation	Heterosexuals	Gay men, lesbians, bisexuals
Socioeconomic class	Owning and middle classes (those with access to higher education)	Poor and working classes
Indigenous background	Non-native	Native
National origin	U.S. born	Immigrants and refugees
Gender	Male	Female, transgender, intersex

Table 1   ADRESSING Framework

Old information that is consistent with one's self-concept is easy to remember, and new information coming in that is consistent with one's self-schemas is easily incorporated. This tendency to better remember information relevant to ourselves is known as the **self-reference effect**. Inconsistent information is more difficult. For example, if someone considers herself to be intelligent but receives an extremely low score on an exam, this would oppose her self-concept. Therefore, this person may choose to externalize the new information from her self-concept by attributing it to a lack of sleep or an unfair test. It is often easier to externalize information that opposes a self-concept by attributing it to an outside factor than it is to internalize the information and adjust one's self-concept.

When people have positive self-concepts (I am intelligent), they tend to act positively and have more optimistic perceptions of the world. When people have negative self-concepts (I am stupid), they tend to feel that they have somehow fallen short, and they are usually dissatisfied and unhappy.

Carl Rogers, founder of the humanistic psychology perspective, pioneered a unique approach to understanding personality and human relationships (see Chapter 6 for more on Carl Rogers). According to Rogers, personality is composed of the ideal self and the real self. The **ideal self** is constructed out of your life experiences, societal expectations, and the things you admire about role models. The ideal self is the person *you ought to be*, while the real self is the person *you actually are*. When the ideal self and the real self are similar, the result is a positive self-concept. However, Rogers suggests that the ideal self is usually an impossible standard to meet, and that when the real self falls short of the ideal self, the result is **incongruity**.

The Role of Self-Esteem, Self-Efficacy, and Locus of Control in Self-Concept and Self-Identity

In addition to how the "self" is defined, there are three powerful influences on an individual's development of self-concept. These are self-efficacy, locus of control, and self-esteem.

1) **Self-efficacy** is a belief in one's own competence and effectiveness. It's how capable we believe we are of doing things. It turns out that this is no small factor; studies have shown that simply believing in our own abilities actually improves performance. Self-efficacy can vary from task to task; an individual may have high self-efficacy for a math task and low self-efficacy for juggling.

2) **Locus of control** can be internal or external. Those with an **internal locus of control** believe they are able to influence outcomes through their own efforts and actions. Those with an **external locus of control** perceive outcomes as controlled by outside forces. Someone with an internal locus may attribute a strong grade to his or her own intelligence and hard work. The same score may lead someone with an external locus to assume that the test was especially easy or that he or she got lucky. In an extreme situation, in which people are exposed to situations in which they have no control, they may learn not to act because they believe it will not affect the outcome anyway. Even once this situation passes and they find themselves once again in arenas in which they can exert some control, this lack of action may persist. This phenomenon is known as **learned helplessness**. It has been shown that believing more in an internal locus of control can be empowering and lead to proactivity. An external locus of control and learned helplessness are characteristics of many depressed and oppressed people, and they often result in passivity.

3) **Self-esteem** is one's overall self-evaluation of one's self-worth. This may be based on different factors for different individuals, depending on which parts of a person's identity he or she has determined to be the most important. For some, self-esteem may rest on intelligence. How would you value yourself if you had low vs. high intelligence? For others, it may rest on athletic ability, beauty, or moral character. Self-esteem is related to self-efficacy; self-efficacy can improve self-esteem if one has it for an activity that one values. However, if the activity is not one that is valued, it may not help self-esteem. For example, a person may have high self-efficacy as a soldier, but still struggle with low self-esteem if this is not her desired occupation. Low self-esteem increases the risk of anxiety, depression, drug use, and suicide. However, inflated self-esteem is also present in gang members, terrorists, and bullies, and may be used to conceal inner insecurities. Unrealistic self-esteem to either extreme can be painful.

Stages of Identity Development

Identity formation or individuation is the development of a distinct individual personality. Identity changes throughout different life stages, but includes the characteristics an individual considers his or her own, which distinguish the individual from others. Erik Erikson's theory of psychosocial development (see Chapter 6) includes a series of crises and conflicts experienced throughout a person's lifetime that help to define and shape identity. According to Erikson, the particular stage relevant to identity formation takes place during adolescence (roughly ages 12–20): the "Identity versus Role Confusion" stage. In this stage, adolescents try to figure out who they are and form basic identities that they will build on throughout the rest of their lives. Other psychological theories concur with Erikson's that adolescence is an important time for establishing identity. Some theories posit that in order to establish identity, an individual has to explore various possibilities and then make commitments to an occupation, religion, sexual orientation, and political values. Gender, moral, psychosexual, and social development are all important elements of identity development. For a review of psychosexual development, see the discussion of Freud in Chapter 6. Interactions with individuals, as well as socialization into broader cultural groups also affect the development of identity.

Influence of Social Factors on Identity Formation

Influence of Individuals

Charles Cooley, an American sociologist, posited the idea of the **looking-glass self**, which is the idea that a person's sense of self develops from interpersonal interactions with others in society and the perceptions of others. According to this idea, people shape their self-concepts based on their understanding of how others perceive them. The looking-glass self begins at an early age and continues throughout life; we never stop modifying it unless all social interactions cease. **George Herbert Mead**, another American sociologist, developed the idea of **social behaviorism**: the mind and self emerge through the process of communicating with others. The idea that the mind and self emerge through the social process of communication or use of symbols was the beginning of the **symbolic interactionism** school of sociology. Mead believed that there is a specific path to development of the self. During the preparatory stage, children merely imitate others, as they have no concept of how others see things. In the play stage, children take on the roles of others through playing (as when playing house and taking on the role of "mom"). During the game stage, children learn to consider multiple roles simultaneously, and can understand the responsibilities of multiple roles. Finally, the child develops an understanding of the **generalized other**, the common behavioral expectations of general society. Mead also characterized the "me" and the "I." The "me" is how the individual believes the generalized other perceives it. The "me" could also be defined as the social self. The "I" is the response to the "me"; in other words, the "I" is the response of the individual to the attitudes of others. The "I" is the self as subject; the "me" is the self as object.

Influence of Culture and Socialization on Identity Formation

Socialization is the process through which people learn to be proficient and functional members of society; it is a lifelong sociological process where people learn the attitudes, values, and beliefs that are reinforced by a particular culture. For older adults, this process often involves teaching the younger generation their way of life; for young children, it predominantly involves incorporating information from their surrounding culture as they form their personalities (the patterns for how they think and feel). It is socialization that allows a culture to pass on its values from one generation to the next.

Clearly, this is a process that occurs through socializing (interacting with others in society). The necessity for social organisms to have early social contact has been demonstrated through deprivation studies. For example, Harlow's monkeys (Chapter 5) were extremely socially deprived from infancy, and were therefore unable to re-integrate successfully with other monkeys. Disturbingly, there are some examples of extreme deprivation in humans, as well. Termed **feral children**, these children are individuals who were not raised with human contact or care, and a large part of our understanding about the importance of socialization is derived from what has been learned about their experiences and the terrible consequences of growing up without proper human care and contact.

Norms

Every society has spoken or unspoken rules and expectations for the behavior of its members, called **norms**; social behaviors that follow these expectations and meet the ideal social standard, then, are described as **normative behavior**. They are reinforced in everyday social interactions by **sanctions**—rewards and punishments for behaviors that are in accord with or against norms. For example, in some nations, it is considered the norm to offer your food to others when eating in a public place. To offer food to a stranger on a bus in the United States, though, would likely result in a sanction such as a disapproving or uncomfortable look.

Norms can be classified in multiple ways, and one way is by formality. **Formal norms** are generally written down; laws are examples of formal norms. They are precisely defined, publicly presented, and often accompanied by strict penalties for those who violate them. **Informal norms** are generally understood but are less precise and often carry no specific punishments. One example is greeting an interviewer with a handshake (a norm in the United States). Not to do so does not carry a fine, but it may affect the interviewer's perception of the job candidate.

Another way of classifying norms is based on their importance. **Mores** ("more-ays") are norms that are highly important for the benefit of society and so are often strictly enforced. For example, animal abuse and treason are actions that break mores in the United States and carry harsh penalties. **Folkways** are norms that are less important but shape everyday behavior (for example, styles of dress, ways of greeting). Although there is a strong relationship between mores and formal norms, and folkways and informal norms, it is not complete. Society may have a formal norm such as walking within a crosswalk when crossing the street; however, the lack of strong enforcement for this formal norm suggests that it is not that important and is more a folkway than a more.

In contrast, those behaviors that customs forbid are described as **taboo**. In the case of a taboo, the endorsement of the norm is so strong that its violation is considered forbidden and oftentimes punishable through formal or non-formal methods. Taboo behaviors, in general, result in disgust toward the violator. There is often a moral or religious component to the taboo, and violation of the norm poses the threat of divine penalties. For example, according to religious laws, Muslims denounce the consumption of pork; thus, in Muslim countries, eating such products would be considered taboo. More widespread examples of taboo behaviors include cannibalism, incest, and murder. Furthermore, forms of prejudice and discrimination might be viewed as taboo, depending on the perspective. Modern research suggests that taboo behavior is a social construct that varies around the world; the idea of taboo changes in response to changes in social structure and there is no universal taboo.

Anomie

The normative effects of social values contribute to social cohesion and social norms are involved in maintaining order. In some cases, societies lack this cohesion and order. This is referred to as **anomie**, a concept that describes the social condition in which individuals are not provided with firm guidelines in relation to norms and values and there is minimal moral guidance or social ethic. For this reason, anomie is often thought of as a state of *normlessness*. The concept was developed through the work of the famous sociologist Émile Durkheim (section 8.1). In researching patterns of suicide in the context of nineteenth-century Europe, Durkheim used the term anomie as an explanation for the differences in suicide rates between Catholics and Protestants. His research suggested that suicide rates were lower in cultures that valued communal ties, as this provided a form of support during times of emotional distress. Anomie, then, is characteristic of societies in which social cohesion is less pronounced; for example, anomie may be more likely to occur in societies where individualism and autonomous decision-making predominate, even at the expense of the greater social order. Anomie suggests the disintegration of social bonds between individuals and their communities, which causes the fragmentation of social identities in exchange for an emphasis on personal success. Discrepancies between personal and social values are thought to contribute to moral deregulations.

Deviance

Complex social processes regulate social behaviors through positioning social norms as the correct method of action. However, there are cases where individuals do not conform to the expectations implicit in social structures. In contrast to normative behavior, **non-normative behavior** is viewed as incorrect because it challenges shared values and institutions, thus threatening social structure and cohesion. These behaviors are seen as abnormal and thus discouraged. Actions that violate the dominant social norms, whether formal or informal, are described as forms of **deviance**. In some cases, deviant behavior is seen as criminal, in which case it violates public policies; thus, studies of deviance are popular among criminologists.

The construction of deviance has important social functions. For example, the process of creating deviant labels affirms and reinforces social norms and values through the dichotomous presentation of the acceptable (normative) behavior and unacceptable (non-normative) behavior. The difference between normal and deviant behavior is maintained through the punishment of transgressions through both formal and informal methods, such as means of criminal justice (for example, court hearings) and unofficial social processes (for example, public condemnation causing humiliation and shame).

However, the concept is problematic because deviance, similar to taboo, is a social construct. There are no behaviors in which deviance is inherent; instead, deviance is situational and contextual. For example, in most circumstances, murder is considered an illegal deviant behavior. However, this non-normative behavior is considered acceptable in certain contexts, such as warfare and self-defense when governments permit it. Furthermore, because social norms are subject to change, examples of deviance are also subject to change, both across time and cultures. For example, in the United States it is considered acceptable for interviewers and interviewees to shake hands, regardless of gender differences; in fact, it is considered a form of respect. However, in some Eastern cultures, this non-verbal form of communication would be offensive because of the different perspectives on relationships between men and women. Thus, it is important to consider differences in cross-cultural communication and the cultural meanings of behaviors in determining their appropriateness.

It is common that deviance is studied through the lens of crime; however, there are additional institutions in societies responsible for controlling deviance. In fact, deviance is an important concept in the context of health care. The purpose of the medical institution is to maintain health and control illness, which involves more than biological concerns. For example, according to the functionalist perspective, individuals experiencing illness are considered deviant because their condition violates conforming behavior and threatens social cohesion through limiting the individual's social contributions.

Functionalism, conflict theory, and symbolic interactionism all provide different descriptions of deviant behavior, according to their premises (section 8.1). In addition to these three perspectives, the following are specific theories often used in the discussion of deviance.

1) Edwin Sutherland's **differential association**: This perspective argues that deviance is a learned behavior resulting from interactions between individuals and their communities (for example, the communication of ideas). The process of learning deviance involves learning the techniques of deviant behaviors as well as the motives and values that rationalize these behaviors, and it is no different than other learning processes in its mechanism. The principal source of exposure is an individual's closest personal groups, whether formal groups, such as professional business associates, or informal groups, such as urban gangs. These groups determine the specific behaviors learned (for example, corporate, organized crime such as fraud, insider trading, or tax evasion versus gang-related offenses such as vandalism or violence). In either case, when an individual participates in communities that condone deviant behaviors, it becomes easier for the individual to learn these behaviors and thus become deviant themselves. The extent of learning is dependent on certain features, such as the frequency and intensity of the interactions. In social situations, it is inevitable that individuals will encounter others with both favorable and unfavorable views of deviance. Sutherland posits that individuals become deviant when their contacts with favorable attitudes toward deviance outweigh their contacts with unfavorable attitudes.

A criticism of differential association is the idea that individuals are reduced to their environments; instead of considering people as independent, rational actors with personal motivations, this perspective suggests that deviant behavior is learned from one's environment without choice. It fails to consider individual characteristics and experiences and how these considerations affect a person's reaction to deviant influences in their current surroundings.

2) Howard Becker's **labeling theory**: This perspective suggests that deviance is the result of society's response to a person rather than something inherent in the person's actions; behaviors become deviant through social processes (it assumes the act itself is not deviant for intrinsic moral reasons). This approach is one of the most important theories in understanding deviance from a social perspective. The use of negative labels can have serious consequences, both for our perception of the deviant person and the person's self-perception. For example, individuals might internalize labels and redefine their concept of the self, which can lead to **self-fulfilling prophecies** (section 7.2). Because of the societal preoccupation with labels, the individual might begin to exhibit more deviant behaviors to fulfill the expectations associated with specific ascribed labels (a form of conforming behavior). Furthermore, because deviance is a social construct, there is no absolute set of characteristics that are viewed as deviant; instead, deviance is contextual. In fact, across the same social context, there are often double standards: the same behavior might be viewed as acceptable in one group and unacceptable in another (for example, the virgin woman versus the virgin man).

Because this perspective views deviance as a social construct, it is often used in interactionist arguments. However, the use of social labels also concerns conflict theorists. Those with the most power in societies, such as politicians, are able to impose the most severe labels while those with the least power in societies, such as criminals, are those whom labels are most often directed toward. In general, it is often the dominant groups (majorities) labeling the subordinate groups (minorities); for example, men labeling women as "less capable" in professional contexts or the upper class labeling the lower class as "less motivated" to achieve economic success. In fact, social structures often contribute to this through allowing the dominant groups the power to enforce the boundaries of normal behavior and thus define the difference between non-deviant and deviant behaviors, perhaps institutionalizing these differences through legal policies. These groups are often referred to as **agents of social control** because of their ability to attach stigmas to certain behaviors (for example, a doctor can define obsessive-compulsive behavior as a mental illness, a form of deviance). The creation of stigmatic roles, in turn, reinforces the power structures and hierarchies inherent in most societies and serves to limit deviant behavior. Furthermore, there is also a functional component to labels, as labeling satisfies the social need to control behaviors and maintain order.

A criticism of the labeling theory is the idea that deviance is assumed to be an automatic process: individuals are seen to be influenced through the use of labels, which ignores their abilities to resist social expectations.

3) Robert Merton's **structural strain theory**: This perspective purports that deviance is the result of experienced strain, either individual or structural. Modern societies have shared perceptions of the ideal life (social goals). These societies also have accepted means of achieving these established goals. In expanding upon Durkheim's research, Merton specified that anomie is the state in which there is a mismatch between the common social goals and the structural or institutionalized means of obtaining these goals. In this state, individuals experience social strain; because existing social structures are inadequate, there is pressure to use deviant methods to prevent failure. When the social goals and means are balanced, deviance is not expected.

For example, economic success is a common goal for most individuals and societies and the legitimate means for obtaining this goal include continued education and professional positions that compensate well. However, in the United States, it is known that there is not equal access to resources among social groups (see section 8.4 for more details on social inequalities). For example, individuals born into lower class families have less financial resources available to obtain an education. Because the means are not serving these individuals in accomplishing the goal of economic success, the result is structural strain, which in turn leads to deviance. Merton's perspective, then, suggests that lower class individuals are more expected to use deviant methods of reaching economic success (for example, stealing, selling drugs).

A criticism of the structural strain theory is the fact that some deviant behaviors, and in particular criminal behaviors, persist in excess that are non-utilitarian. Merton's perspective is applicable to fraud and theft, for example, in the cases where the economic structure is not serving individuals as best as possible (for example, the means of earning is not the best option for the goal of obtaining financial assets). However, it is less applicable to deviant behaviors that are malicious and violent in nature, such as forms of sexual assault. Furthermore, this perspective is more applicable to material, rather than social, goals.

Collective Behavior

In addition to normative or conforming behaviors and non-normative or deviant behaviors, there is a third form of social behavior that is described through the separate and distinct concept of **collective behavior**, in which social norms for the situation are absent or unclear. This concept describes the actions of people operating as a collective group; however, it is important to distinguish collective behavior from group behavior. In general, collective behavior is more short-lived and less conventional values influence the group's behavior and guidelines for membership. Examples of collective behavior, as opposed to those of group behavior, do not reflect the existing social structure but are instead spontaneous situations in which individuals engage in actions that are otherwise unacceptable and violate social norms. Research on collective behavior has suggested that there are characteristics of the behavior that cannot be compared to the independent effect of numerous individual actions. Instead, in collective behavior, there is a loss of the individual and independent moral judgment in exchange for a sense of the group. This can be destructive (for example, mobs and riots) or harmless (for example fads, like the yellow LiveStrong wristbands), depending on the diverse episode. It is important to understand collective behavior to limit its negative consequences—in particular, those negative consequences which are the result of human response rather than unpreventable circumstances. For example, an understanding of collective behavior could help establish effective and safe crowd management and design planning to accommodate for potential issues.

The classification of collective behavior is a point of contention. However, **Herbert Blumer**, a sociologist whose ideas were foundational in the understanding of collective behavior, identified four main forms of collective behavior:

1) **Crowds:** The **crowd** is a defined as a group that shares a purpose. The crowd is the most agreed-upon example of collective behavior and is the most common in modern life (for example, orchestras, theaters, and other performances). In general, crowds are thought to be emotional; often, in the context of the crowds, there is a non-permanent loss of rational thought and the crowd influences individual behaviors, sometimes referred to as **herd behavior**. However, not all crowd behavior is irrational. For example, although the thought of stampedes suggests chaos, in the face of threats, such as during bombings or fires, it is not irrational for individuals to run, rather than walk, to the nearest exit as a response to fear. Crowds can be classified based on their specific intention: acting crowds gather for a specific cause or goal (for example, protesters or revolutionaries), casual crowds emerge spontaneously and include people who are not really interacting (for example, people waiting

in line for something), conventional crowds gather for a planned event (for example, football fans or religious congregants), and expressive crowds aggregate to express an emotion (for example, funeral attenders or rock-concert goers). Crowds can be further classified based on the closeness of the individuals (for example, compact or diffuse crowds) and the emotions caused (for example, fear in the panic, happiness in the craze, and anger in the hostile outburst). The idea of panic is a common theme in examples of collective behavior; **panic** is a situation in which fear escalates to the point that it dominates thinking and thus affects entire groups (for example, during disaster situations). A **mob** is a specific example of a crowd in which emotion is heighted and behavior is directed toward a specific and violent cause. Historical examples of mobs include lynching.

2) **Publics**: A **public** is defined as a group of individuals discussing a single issue, which conflicts with the common usage of the term. This form of collective behavior begins as the discussion begins and ceases as the discussion ceases and there can exist various publics to reflect various discussions. People in publics share ideas.

3) **Masses**: A **mass** is defined as a group whose formation is prompted through the efforts of mass media; masses consist of a relatively large number of people who may not be in close proximity but nevertheless share common interests (section 7.1).

4) **Social movements**: A **social movement** is defined as collective behavior with the intention of promoting change. There are two main categories of social movements: **active movements**, which attempt to foster social change (for example, revolutions), and **expressive movements**, which attempt to foster individual change (for example, support groups). There are numerous forms of social movements identified in sociological tradition: global or local (range), old or new (origin), peaceful or violent (method), et cetera. In contrast to other forms of collective behavior, social movements can become established and permanent social institutions.

There are additional aspects of collective behavior to be familiar with. A **fad**, also known as a **craze**, is an example of a collective behavior in which something (1) experiences a rapid and dramatic incline in reputation, (2) remains popular among a large population for a brief period, and (3) experiences a rapid and dramatic decline in reputation. The enthusiasm for the particular thing is driven through methods such as peer pressure and social media and through actors such as peers and famous celebrities. Fads include examples of clothing, food, language, and other novel ideas that often fade not long after catching on. Internet phenomena are an excellent example of fads; recent viral videos that have lost momentum include dances such as Gangnam Style and the Harlem Shake. It is important to note that fads are separate from **trends**, which are longer-lived and often lead to permanent social changes; for example, the hippie movement created visible trends, such as peace signs, but is also prompted widespread social change.

Another aspect of collective behavior is the concept of **mass hysteria**, which is a diagnostic label that refers to the collective delusion of some threat that spreads through emotions (for example, fear) and escalates until it spirals out of control (for example, panic). Mass hysteria is the result of public reactions to stressful situations; common examples include medical problems and supernatural occurrences, such as periodic interest in crop circles. In these situations, the collective behavior is often irrational as a result of emotional excesses and thus mass hysteria has been described as a form of groupthink (section 7.2). For example, in the context of medical problems, there might be a spontaneous spread of related diseases. Those affected might manifest similar medical symptoms, such as fatigue, headaches, or nausea. It is curious that these popular signs are also connected to high levels of stress. In most cases, the illness cannot be linked to an external source, such as an infectious agent.

It is thus important to distinguish this form of collective behavior from the concepts of **outbreaks**, **epidemics**, and **pandemics**. These cases involve an unexpected increase in the incidence of an infectious disease in a given region, with outbreaks being the most limited and pandemics being the most widespread. For example, the Bubonic plague is a well-known historical epidemic; in modern times, the extent of the dangerous H1N1 influenza virus reached pandemic proportions, spreading across the world. In contrast, famous examples of mass hysteria include larger movements without clear medical explanation, such as the Salem Witch Trials. This series of trials and prosecutions began as the result of a group of adolescent girls experiencing "fits" that were thought to exceed the power of the more common epileptic fits. This caused a **moral panic**—a specific form of panic as a result of a perceived threat to social order—which lead to numerous executions. A second famous example is the broadcast of *The War of the Worlds*, during which communication issues led to some listeners missing portions of the broadcast, causing tension and panic.

Riots are a third example of collective behavior. Riots are a form of crowd behavior (see page 240); however, there is no specific end. Most riots occur as the result of general dissatisfaction with social conditions, with examples including food and bread, police, prison, race, religion, sports, student, and urban riots. In general, collective behavior is often thought to be irrational. However, some research argues that riots are not irrational as there are examples where the source of dissatisfaction is less political and more fundamental; for example, some riots begin as a response to a lack of basic needs (for example, hunger riots). The most famous historical examples include reactions to government oppression, poor living conditions, racial or religious conflicts, and other serious social issues. In these cases, riots can have serious measurable consequences for economics and politics; these effects are often complex. For example, the Arab Spring was a revolution that included riots. It first began in Tunisia but spread across the Arab world, causing civil uprisings that contributed to the eventual fall of governments. The power of riots has lead to increased public attention and participation, due in part to mass media coverage, and certain representations, which were once intended to conceal identities and offer protection (such as facemasks and scarves), have grown to be iconic.

In general, riots are chaotic and disorganized due to a sudden onset, often described as states of civil disorder, civil distress, or civil unrest. There is an increase in criminal behaviors, such as vandalism and violence. The target of this destruction can include both private and public properties, depending on the source of the grievance, but often include institutions such as government or religious buildings. Because of the state of distress common in riots, crowd control is an important consideration. Police measures tend to be non-lethal in nature (for example, arrest or tear gas), but police intervention does lead to occasional injuries and deaths.

Further examples of collective behavior include fashions, rumors, and social movements.

Agents of Socialization

There are many different social forces that influence our lives and the development of culture over time. Six of these "agents of socialization" are family, school, peers, the workplace, religion/government, and mass media/technology.

1) *Family*

   The lifelong process of socialization begins shortly after birth and is generally driven first by family members. Family members attend to a baby's physical needs but also to social development. First relationships heavily influence how an individual will interact in future relationships. Family members teach children the customs, beliefs, and traditions of their cultures through both instruction and modeling. They also influence the situations to which children are exposed, especially in the early years of life.

2) *School*

Like family, schools explicitly teach children the norms and values of their culture. Schools can also affect children's self-identities by accentuating those intellectual, physical, and social strengths that society endorses. For example, schools may differ in how they value logic and linear thinking versus creativity, and can influence children toward one or the other. Finally, schools can reinforce divisive aspects of society, because the quality and availability of schooling is influenced by socioeconomic status.

3) *Peer Groups*

As children grow older, the family typically becomes less important in social development and peer groups become more significant. Fashion, style of speech, gender role identity, sexual activity, drug/alcohol use, and other behaviors are affected by peers and by the influence of hierarchies such as popularity.

4) *Workplace*

People typically spend a good portion of their time at work. The workplace influences behavior through written codes and rules as well as through informal norms. There is pressure to fit in at the workplace that often alters behavior; occupation can also be a large part of one's identity.

5) *Religion/Government*

Both government and organized religion influence the course of cultural change by creating "rites of passage." In religion, this might include traditional milestones and celebrations such as coming of age and marriage. Government sets legal ages for drinking, voting, joining the military, and so on. Laws both influence and are influenced by the societies they apply to. For example, in the United States, stricter laws apply to crack than to cocaine, and this affects society's perceptions of these drugs and of drug addicts.

6) *Mass Media/Technology*

The mass media and technology have extended themselves to influence almost everyone on the planet, through television, movies, the Internet, cell phones, and other communications. The impact of television on culture through displays of sex, violence, and impossible-to-achieve ideals has been much debated. It has also affected culture in ways that most people agree are positive, such as educational programming and introductions to other cultures and lifestyles. The Internet can similarly help shrink the world and increase social influences through tools such as online social networking and blogs.

Cultural Assimilation

Assimilation and amalgamation are two possible outcomes of interactions between multiple cultures in the same space. **Assimilation** is the process in which an individual forsakes aspects of his or her own cultural tradition to adopt those of a different culture. Generally, this individual is a member of a minority group who is attempting to conform to the culture of the dominant group.

$$A + B + C \rightarrow A$$

In the diagram above, A is the dominant group that minority groups B and C work to imitate and become absorbed by. In order to assimilate, members of the minority group may make great personal sacrifices, such as changing their spoken languages, their religions, how they dress, and their personal values. In the United States, minority groups attempting to assimilate not only must learn English if it is not their native language, but must adopt the values of a capitalist society with a heavy emphasis on the individual and independence—a tough transition for those from collectivist cultures. In addition, assimilation does not guarantee that one will not be discriminated against.

Amalgamation occurs when majority and minority groups combine to form a new group.

$$A + B + C \rightarrow D$$

In this case, a unique cultural group is formed that is distinct from any of the initial groups.

Multiculturalism

Multiculturalism or **pluralism** is a perspective that endorses equal standing for all cultural traditions. It promotes the idea of cultures coming together in a true melting pot, rather than in a hierarchy. The United States, despite common description as a melting pot, includes elements of hierarchy. For example, English is the dominant language, and national holidays tend to reflect Eurocentricism.

$$A + B + C \rightarrow A + B + C$$

In true multiculturalism, each culture is able to maintain its practices. It is especially apparent in cities such as New York where there exist pockets of separate cultures (Chinatown, Little Italy, Koreatown). As a practice, multiculturalism is under debate. Supporters say it increases diversity and helps empower minority groups. Opponents say it encourages segregation over unity by maintaining physical and social isolation and hinders cohesiveness of a society.

Subcultures

Bike enthusiasts, bartenders, and medical personnel are examples of groups that can be called subcultures. A **subculture** is a segment of society that shares a distinct pattern of traditions and values that differs from that of the larger society. As the name suggests, a subculture can be thought of as a culture existing within a larger, dominant culture. Members of a subculture do participate in many activities of the larger culture, but also have unique behaviors and activities that are specific to their subculture. This often includes having unique slang, such as that used by medical personnel (for example, *cabbage* for "coronary artery bypass graft"). Sometimes, subcultures are the result of countercultural backlash, an opposition of views widely accepted within a society. Hippies in the late 1960s and early 1970s would be considered a counterculture, because they opposed certain aspects of the dominant culture, such as middle class values and the Vietnam War.

Moral Development

Moral development is an important aspect of socialization and identity formation. Lawrence Kohlberg, an American psychologist, expanded upon Jean Piaget's theory (Chapter 4) of moral development in children. **Kohlberg's stages of moral development** include six identifiable developmental stages of moral reasoning, which form the basis of ethical behavior. Kohlberg's stages are grouped into three levels with two stages each (see Table 2). According to Kohlberg, stages cannot be skipped. Each stage provides a new and necessary moral perspective, and the understanding from each stage is retained and integrated at later stages. Interestingly, most adults attain but do not surpass the fourth stage, in which morality is dictated by outside forces (laws, rules, social obligations). Few people attain a post-conventional level of moral reasoning. In fact, though Kohlberg insisted that stage 6 exists, he found it difficult to identify people who operated at that level.

Level 1	Pre-conventional level of moral reasoning: morality judged by direct consequences to the self (no internalization of "right" and "wrong") Typical of children	Stage 1: Obedience and punishment orientation	Individuals focus on the direct consequences to themselves of their actions ("How can I avoid punishment?")
		Stage 2: Self-interest orientation	Individuals focus on the behavior that will be in their best interest, with limited interest in the needs of others ("What's in it for me?")
Level 2	Conventional level of moral reasoning: morality judged by comparing actions to society's views and expectations (acceptance of conventional definitions of "right" and "wrong") Typical of adolescents and adults	Stage 3: Interpersonal accord and conformity	Individuals focus on the approval and disapproval of others, and try to be "good" by living up to expectations ("What will make others like me?")
		Stage 4: Authority and social-order maintaining orientation	Beyond a need for individual approval, individuals feel a duty to uphold laws, rules, and social conventions ("What am I supposed to do?")
Level 3	Post-conventional level of moral reasoning: morality judged by internal ethical guidelines; rules viewed as useful but malleable guidelines Many people never reach this abstract level of moral reasoning	Stage 5: Social contract orientation	Individuals see laws as social contracts to be changed when they do not promote general welfare ("The greatest good for the greatest number of people")
		Stage 6: Universal ethical principles	Morality is based on abstract reasoning using universal ethical principles; laws are only valid if they are grounded in justice

Table 2 Kohlberg's Stages of Moral Development

7.2 POSITIVE AND NEGATIVE ELEMENTS OF SOCIAL INTERACTION

Attribution

Attribution theory is rooted in social psychology and attempts to explain how individuals view behavior, both our own behavior and the behavior of others. Given a set of circumstances, individuals attribute behavior to internal causes (**dispositional attribution**) or external causes (**situational attribution**). Driving tends to be a situation that generates plenty of salient examples. Imagine you are driving and someone cuts you off. You might think, "Wow, that driver is a real jerk." This would be a dispositional attribution, because the driver's behavior is attributed to an internal cause (he is a jerk). On the other hand, you could alternatively think, "Wow, that driver must be in a hurry because of an emergency; maybe he just found out his mom is in the hospital." This would be a situational attribution (there is an emergency). How often do you think that someone who cut you off might have had a good reason to do so? People tend to assign dispositional attributions to others (they are just jerks), but give themselves the benefit of situational attributions. For example, the last time you cut someone off while driving, did you feel like you had a good reason to? Did you then think to yourself, "Wow, I am a real jerk"?

What determines whether we attribute behavior to internal or external causes? There are three factors that influence this decision: consistency, distinctiveness, and consensus. To consider these, imagine a simple situation: you are walking past your friend, who looks angry and walks past you without saying hello.

1) **Consistency:** is anger consistent with how your friend typically acts? If it is, then you might explain it with internal causes (dispositional). If not, you might think there are external factors that explain it (situational).

2) **Distinctiveness:** is your friend angry toward everyone or just toward you? If your friend is angry toward everyone, the cause likely has to do with your friend (dispositional). If your friend is just angry toward you, it may be situational; perhaps you did something irritating.

3) **Consensus:** is your friend the only one angry or is everyone angry? If your friend is the only one angry, then it is more likely that the anger has something to do with your friend (dispositional). If everyone is angry, then it might be situational (the team lost the playoffs).

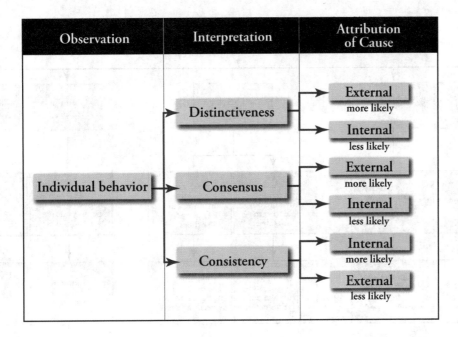

Figure 1   Attributing Behavior to External or Internal Causes

Attributional Biases

Despite the apparent logic in our methods of identifying whether someone's behavior is due to internal or external causes, we are frequently off in our analysis of others. We often make the **fundamental attribution error**, which is that we tend to underestimate the impact of the situation and overestimate the impact of a person's character or personality. Another way of saying this is that we tend to assume that people *are* how they act. Thus, we are more likely to think that the driver who cuts us off is a jerk in general, rather than assuming the driver acted that way because he has to rush to the hospital to be with his ailing mother. Remember, when we attribute our own actions to something, we tend to attribute to external rather than internal causes. So if I cut someone off, it is because I had a good reason to. This tendency to blame our actions on the situation and blame the actions of others on their personalities is also called the **actor-observer bias**.

People tend to give themselves much more credit than they give others. We are wired to perceive ourselves favorably. The **self-serving bias** is the tendency to attribute successes to ourselves and our failures to others or the external environment. If we perform well academically, it is because we are smart and worked hard. If we perform poorly academically, it was because the test was unfair or the teacher graded too hard.

Similarly, we have a tendency to be optimistic and want to believe that the world is a good place. We want to believe that life can be predictable and that actions influence outcomes. The **optimism bias** is the belief that bad things happen to other people, but not to us. This goes hand-in-hand with the fact that we want to believe that life is fair, which also impacts how we think about others. The **just world phenomenon**, is a tendency to believe that the world is fair and people get what they deserve. When bad things happen to others, it is the result of their actions or their failure to act, not because sometimes bad things happen to good people. Similarly, when good things happen to us, it is because we deserved it.

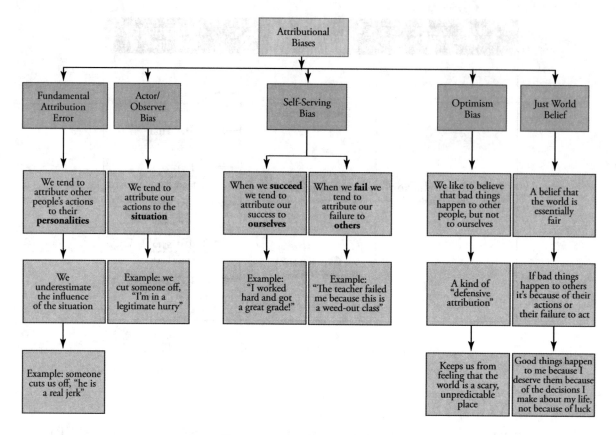

Figure 2 Attributional Biases

Another type of error that occurs when we make assumptions about others is the halo effect (or halo error). The **halo effect** is a tendency to believe that people have inherently good or bad natures, rather than looking at individual characteristics. Our overall impression of a person is influenced by how we feel or think about his or her character. For example, your overall impression of your neighbor might be "he is nice," therefore, you make other assumptions about him ("he must be a good dad"). The **physical attractiveness stereotype** is a specific type of halo effect; people tend to rate attractive individuals more favorably for personality traits and characteristics than they do those who are less attractive.

Culture Affects Attributions

There are cultural differences that influence how attributions are made. Western cultures tend to endorse an individualistic attitude: "You can do anything you put your mind to!" This influences people toward more internal attributions for success and failure. Unemployment is sometimes explained as laziness or stupidity. In Eastern Asian cultures, external attribution is more predominant. Thus, the system as a whole is scrutinized more than the individual. If an insider trading scandal occurs, this attitude would emphasize controlling the financial organization, rather than finding and prosecuting the guilty individuals.

Self-Perceptions Shape Our Perceptions of Others

Social perception involves the understanding of others in our social world; it is the initial information we process about other people in order to try to understand their mindsets and intentions. **Social cognition** is the ability of the brain to store and process information regarding social perception. Social perception is the process responsible for our judgments and impressions about other people, and allows us to recognize how others impact us, and predict how they might behave in given situations. We rely upon our social perception and cognition in order to interpret a range of socially relevant information, such as verbal and non-verbal communication, tone, facial expressions, and an understanding of the social relationships and social goals present in situations. Using social perception, we try to figure out what others are thinking. Sometimes our tendencies lead us to mistakes in social perception. A **false consensus** occurs when we assume that everyone else agrees with what we do (even though they may not). A **projection bias** happens when we assume others have the same beliefs we do. Since people have a tendency to look for similarities between themselves and others, they often assume them even when this is unfounded.

Stereotypes, Prejudice, and Discrimination

Many people may not know the differences between the terms stereotype, prejudice, discrimination, and racism but from a sociological perspective, it is important to know their meanings. **Stereotypes** are over-simplified ideas about groups of people, based on characteristics (race, gender, sexual orientation, religion, disability). Stereotypes can be positive ("X group is successful because they are hard workers") or negative ("Y group is poor because they are lazy").

Prejudice refers to the thoughts, attitudes, and feelings someone holds about a group that are not based on actual experience. As the name implies, prejudice is a prejudgment or biased thinking about a group and its members. The group that one is biased against can be one defined by race, age, gender, religion, or any other characteristic. Some forms of prejudice are blatant or overt, such as the prejudice used to justify the actions taken by Hitler and his regime against the Jews and other groups during World War II. Other forms are more subtle, such as the finding that employers in a study considered more resumes for employment for candidates with "white-sounding names" than "black-sounding names." In this situation, an employer may not even be aware of his or her prejudice. In fact, prejudice has been found at a subconscious level when studying individuals' reactions in relation to pleasant and unpleasant words. For example, when primed with a black face rather than a white face, people are more likely to predict the subject is carrying a gun rather than another object such as a tool or wallet.

While prejudice involves thinking a certain way, **discrimination** involves acting a certain way toward a group. People can discriminate against any number of characteristics and unfortunately, American history is rife with examples of discrimination, and traditions, policies, ideas, practices, and laws that are discriminatory still exist in many institutions. Attempts to limit discrimination, such as **affirmative action** (policies that take factors like race or sex into consideration to benefit underrepresented groups in admissions or job hiring decisions) have been used to benefit those believed to be current or past victims of discrimination. However, these attempts have been controversial, and some have deemed these practices to be "discriminating against the majority," or **reverse discrimination**.

Prejudices and actions that discriminate based on race, or hold that one race is inferior to another, are called **racism**. While the exact definitions of "race," "ethnicity," and "racism" have been subject to much debate over the years, racism tends to be seen when the dominant or majority group (usually white) holds a prejudice or engages in discrimination, whether intentional or not, against non-dominant or minority groups (usually not white). Sometimes racism is used to describe discrimination on an ethnic or cultural basis, independent of whether these differences are described as racial. The confusion largely stems from confusion about the definitions of the terms "race" and "ethnicity."

Institutional discrimination refers to unjust and discriminatory practices employed by large organizations that have been codified into operating procedures, processes, or institutional objectives. An example of institutional discrimination was the "don't ask, don't tell" policy of the U.S. military, which frowned upon openly gay men and women serving in the armed forces. In general, members of minority groups are much more likely to encounter institutional discrimination than members of majorities.

A society's definitions for what groups carry more power, prestige, and class can account for prejudice toward those on the lower rungs of that society. In general, any unequal status sets the stage for prejudice. These symbols of status are all relative, so in order to be of a higher status, one needs other people to be of a lower status. Thus, some people at the "top" are motivated to try to justify and maintain these differences, sometimes using prejudice as a tool. For example, very wealthy individuals may justify their wealth by insinuating that poorer members of society are lazy, and they seek to maintain this gap by voting against welfare programs for this group. Social institutions can also be designed to maintain these differences. For example, in the U.S., good, well-funded schools are in wealthier neighborhoods and below-average, poorly-funded schools are in poorer neighborhoods.

In the United States, wealth is an important source of power and class, with the wealthiest shaping the laws and agenda of the society. Prestige is often based on occupation. Doctors get more respect than janitors, not just in their occupations but also as people. Higher prestige positions are usually taken by members of the dominant groups in societies, as can be seen by the disparate number of men compared to women in many of these prestigious roles.

Emotion and Cognition in Prejudice

Prejudice is an attitude. Remember that attitudes have three components (the ABCs): affect (feelings), behavioral inclinations/tendencies, and cognition (beliefs). Therefore, emotion and cognition both play roles in contributing to prejudice. In addition, there are several social sources of prejudice. Let's consider each of these contributing factors.

Emotion can play a role in feeding prejudices. At the core of prejudice is often fear or frustration. When someone is faced with something intimidating or unknown, especially if it is presumed to be blocking that person from some goal (frustration), hostility can be a natural reaction. There is a tendency to want to direct that hostility at someone, and history shows that displaced aggression often falls on marginalized people. **Scapegoats** are the unfortunate people at whom displaced aggression is directed. Many Germans blamed the Jews for the economic struggles that preceded the genocide of World War II. In the United States, fear and hostility were redirected onto women claimed to be "witches" in the 1600s. In subtler forms, scapegoats for an economic collapse can be those who are impoverished and on welfare.

This is not to say that one has to be some kind of "monster" to experience feelings of prejudice. Although in some of the above examples, drastic actions were taken, the underlying emotions can also influence those who do not take action. For example, when seated next to someone who is clearly very different from them on a bus, even people who do not see themselves as prejudiced may be uncomfortable. When a person sees an unfamiliar person of another race, emotion processing centers in the brain become more active automatically. It is only through active self-monitoring and reflection that people are able to inhibit prejudiced responses despite the presence of prejudiced feelings. Some may feel guilty for having the feelings at all, though they are not unusual. These self-inhibition abilities weaken with age, so many older adults find it hard to inhibit the prejudiced thoughts that they may have suppressed during their younger years.

There are also some aspects of normal thinking and information processing that contribute to prejudice. Our brains seek to categorize and organize data based on similarities, as a shortcut. We create conceptual categories such as "white" just as we do categories like "furniture" and "toys." These conceptualizations can lead to stereotypes. Stereotypes, both positive and negative, stem from our mental shortcuts that simplify our conceptualizations of the world.

Our brains also hone in on differences. Even babies are more interested in new objects presented in their field of vision than they are in things they've seen before. Thus, people who are seen as distinctive draw more attention and are often likely to be seen as representative of groups. For example, all black people may be incorrectly considered good athletes based on examples of distinctive black athletes like Michael Jordan. There is an **illusory correlation**, created between a group of people and a characteristic based on unique cases.

Attributional biases (described above), particularly the optimism bias and just-world belief, also suggest that we are more likely to believe that the world is fair and predictable, things happen for a reason, and people get what they deserve. Thus, the sick or disadvantaged often face prejudice because others believe that they have done something wrong that led them to be in their position. Thus, someone with HIV may face prejudice, including the assumption that he or she contracted the disease through irresponsible behavior, despite how the disease was actually transmitted.

Self-Fulfilling Prophecy and Stereotype Threat

These stereotypes can lead to behaviors that affirm the original stereotypes in what is known as a **self-fulfilling prophecy**. For example, if a college guy believes that the girls in a certain sorority are snobby and prudish, he may avoid engaging in conversations with the girls from that sorority at parties. Because he does not engage them in conversation, his opinion of them as snobby and prudish will probably be reinforced. People may also be affected by stereotypes they know others have of a group to which they belong. **Stereotype threat** refers to a self-fulfilling fear that one will be evaluated based on a negative stereotype. For example, the idea that males are better at math than females is a negative stereotype. In studies where females are asked to complete a math test, if the female is first told that males do better than females on the math test, the female's performance on the test is lower than if she was not first presented with this information. Similarly, if the female is being tested on math concepts with males present, she will perform more poorly than if there are no males present. This phenomenon helps to explain the dearth of women in math and engineering fields.

Ethnocentrism Versus Cultural Relativism

On a broader level, when different cultures interact, there is often a tendency to judge people from another culture by the standards of one's own culture, a phenomenon known as **ethnocentrism**. It is an example of favoritism for one's in-group over out-groups (see Groups below). For example, the tension that exists between those who live in the city and those who live in rural areas is often due to judgments about each other's ways of life. City dwellers may look down on those in rural areas based on their standards of occupation and wealth. Those in the country may look down on city dwellers based on standards of morality, practicality, and quality of life. An alternative to ethnocentrism is **cultural relativism**: judging another culture based on its own standards. This can be very difficult to do, especially when the values of another culture clash with the values of one's own. For example, in India, child labor is common and is often seen as a way in which children can help their families. This may be a difficult viewpoint to accept for someone from a culture in which childhood is equated with a carefree time of play, and child labor is seen as abusive. However, practicing cultural relativism would involve judging this practice in the context of that culture's values.

Groups

A **group** is a collection of any number of people (as few as two) who regularly interact and identify with each other, sharing similar norms, values, and expectations. A team of neurologists may be considered a group, while the entire hospital staff may not be considered a group, if there is little interaction between departments. The concept of social groups is complex, and groups come in numerous varieties. There are sociologists who might view societies as large groups in the context of cohesive social identities. Within a social structure, groups are often the setting for social interaction and influence. Groups help clearly define social roles and statuses.

Groups can be further divided into primary groups and secondary groups. **Primary groups** play a more important role in an individual's life; these groups are usually smaller and include those with whom the individual engages with in person, in long-term, emotional ways. A **secondary group** is larger and more impersonal, and may interact for specific reasons for shorter periods of time. Primary groups serve **expressive functions** (meeting emotional needs) and secondary groups serve **instrumental functions** (meeting pragmatic needs). A family would be an example of a primary group (regardless of how family is defined), whereas the MCAT study group would be an example of a secondary group.

In-groups and out-groups are subcategories of primary and secondary groups. A group that an individual belongs to and believes to be an integral part of who she is is an **in-group**. A group that an individual does not belong to is her **out-group**. Social identity theory asserts that when we categorize other people, we identify with some of them, who we consider our in-groups, and see differences with others, who we consider our out-groups. We tend to have favorable impressions of our in-groups because they bolster our social identities and self-esteem. People tend to have positive stereotypes about their own in-groups ("we are hard-working"). It feels good to have a sense of belonging, and feel positive about the groups you belong to. On the other hand, we may have more negative impressions of members of out-groups. Different can be seen as worse (for example, "I feel sorry for those who don't believe the same things I do"). People also tend to have more negative stereotypes about out-groups ("they are lazy"). In-groups and out-groups help to explain some negative human behaviors like exclusion and bullying. When certain groups of people are defined as different, they may also be seen as inferior (when people assume that their in-group is the best, everyone in the out-group is somehow less); therefore, in-groups may engage in sexism, racism, ethnocentrism, heterosexism, and other such behaviors. (These ideas are discussed in more detail below.)

A **reference group** is a standard measure that people compare themselves to. For example, peers who are also studying for the MCAT might be a reference group for you. This is a group you might compare yourself to. What are the people in this group studying? What classes are they taking? When are they taking the exam? To which medical schools are they applying? An individual can have multiple reference groups, and these different groups may convey different messages. For example, you might view your friends in class who are all taking the MCAT as one reference group, and your older sibling, who is in medical school, and his or her medical school friends as another reference group.

Furthermore, there are descriptions of **group size**. The number of people present within the group has consequences for group relations. The smallest social group, known as the **dyad**, contains two members. Dyadic interaction is often more intimate and intense than that in larger groups because there is no outside competition. However, the small size also requires active cooperation and participation from both members to be stable. In some cases of dyads, such as within marriages, there are laws that enforce the strength of the pair. Dyads can involve equal relationships, such as with monogamous romantic partners, or unequal relationships, such as with master-servant relationships. The next largest group, known as the **triad**, contains three members. In the dyad, there is a single relationship, but in the triad, there are three relationships, one between each pair of members. For this reason, triads can be more or less stable. It is possible for the group to become more stable because there is an additional person to mediate tension; it is possible for the group to become less stable because it is an observed rule that two people will tend to unite, causing conflict with the final group member. Triads can also be equal or unequal, then, and a common example of hierarchical triads involves groups where there is a single dominant member, such as in an MCAT tutoring group (one tutor and two students).

People who exist in the same space but do not interact or share a common sense of identity make up an **aggregate**. For example, an MCAT study group that meets after class regularly at a coffee shop to prepare for the exam is a group. All of the people that frequent that coffee shop on a regular basis (but do not interact or share a common identity) are an aggregate. Similarly, people who share similar characteristics but are not otherwise tied together would be considered a **category**. All of the people studying for the MCAT this year make up a category of people.

Bureaucracy is a term used to describe an administrative body and the processes by which this body accomplishes work tasks. Bureaucracies rise from an advanced division of labor in which each worker does his or her small task. These tasks are presided over and coordinated by managers. Bureaucracies can be a very efficient way to complete complicated tasks because each member of the organization has a specific role. A major theory of bureaucracy was developed by sociologist Max Weber, who considered bureaucracy to be a necessary aspect of modern society. Weber outlined the following characteristics of an ideal bureaucracy:

1. It covers a fixed area of activity
2. It is hierarchically organized
3. Workers have expert training in an area of specialty
4. Organizational rank is impersonal, and advancement depends on technical qualification, rather than favoritism
5. Workers follow set procedures to increase predictability and efficiency

One major concept related to bureaucracy is rationalization. Rationalization describes the process by which tasks are broken down into component parts to be efficiently accomplished by workers within the organization. Because the workers follow set procedures in completing tasks, it is easy to predict the outcome of the process. Manufacturers have taken advantage of these aspects of bureaucracy when designing production processes. One of the first manufacturers to popularize this process was Henry Ford, who implemented assembly lines in his automobile plants. Ford rationalized the process of building a car by breaking it down into component parts and assigning the assembly of each part to a worker. In this way, he was able to have cars efficiently assembled and each car was exactly the same as the ones coming before and after it. Sociologist George Ritzer studied a similar process—the design of McDonalds restaurants to produce food quickly, and to produce uniform products across all franchises. He describes the rationalization of fast food production as **McDonaldization**. This process has four components that reflect the principles of bureaucracy: efficiency, calculability (assessing performance through quantity and/or speed of output), predictability, and control (automating work where possible in order to make results more predictable).

While a bureaucracy, in its ideal form, may be the most efficient way to accomplish complicated tasks, this organizational form can have several drawbacks. First, because workers follow set procedures, this can cause the organization to struggle when adapting to challenges that require it to change its way of coordinating tasks. Second, workers may become overly attached to their individual task and lose sight of the organizational mission as a whole. Third, workers may become overly attached to the set procedures and not respond flexibly to new challenges on an interpersonal level.

One paradoxical feature of organizations is that, although they may be founded to tackle new challenges in revolutionary ways, as their organizational structure becomes more complex, it also becomes more conservative and less able to adapt. Thus, revolutionary organizations inevitably become less revolutionary as their organizational structures develop and become entrenched. This pattern is known as the **Iron Law of Oligarchy**. Oligarchy means rule by an elite few, and it comes about through the very organization of the bureaucracy itself. Bureaucracies depend on increased centralization of tasks as one moves up the hierarchy. That is, there are many layers of managers in a bureaucracy, each one responsible for coordinating (centralizing) a set of tasks. The individuals who are responsible for coordinating the coordinators have the most power, and those individuals become an oligarchy at the top of the organizational structure. Furthermore, these oligarchs become specialized at their task (management), just as other members of the organization become specialists in their tasks. As discussed above, one downside to bureaucracy is that workers will fight to maintain control over their task and their established way of carrying it out. Thus, managers defend their position at the top of the organizational structure, thereby entrenching the oligarchy.

Social Facilitation

Social psychology seeks to understand how people influence each other through their interactions. The most basic level of experience between members of society is "mere presence." **Mere presence** means that people are simply in each other's presence, either completing similar activities or apparently minding their own business. For example, the task of grocery shopping usually involves the mere presence of other shoppers, without direct engagement. What's fascinating is that it turns out the mere presence of others has a measurable effect on an individual's performance.

People tend to perform simple, well-learned tasks better when other people are present. For example, people can do simple math problems more quickly and run slightly faster when in the presence of others. People's color preferences are even stronger when they make judgments in the presence of others (a task that has no competitive influence). This finding has been called the **social facilitation effect**, and it may help explain why some of us study in the library (in the presence of others) or walk faster when in the presence of other pedestrians. However, the social facilitation effect only holds true for simple or practiced tasks. The presence of others can impair performance when completing complex or novel tasks. Thus, people do not complete complex math problems as quickly and may have a harder time navigating in novel environments when others are present.

The prevailing explanation for these phenomena involves arousal. The presence of others stimulates arousal, which serves to activate our dominant responses (the practiced responses that come most easily to us). When completing tasks that are easy and well-practiced, these dominant responses are exactly what is called for; thus performance improves with arousal stimulated by the presence of others. When completing tasks that are more complex or novel, the dominant responses are likely to be incorrect for the situation; thus performance declines with arousal, and in the presence of others. A basketball player who is a good, well-practiced shooter will experience an improvement in performance when there is an audience, because making baskets is his or her dominant response. A player who does not often shoot the ball will suffer with an audience, because shooting is not his or her dominant response.

There are other factors that also impact one's performance in the presence of others. Overwhelming fear of evaluation reduces performance even on behaviors that were previously automatic, because self-consciousness and doubt can lead to overanalysis. Athletes struggle if they tend to overthink their body movements at critical times. Distraction is also a factor, with the presence of others sometimes serving to divert our attention from tasks. This can be due to external events, such as things others are doing, or internal events, such as our thoughts of what others might be thinking or doing.

Deindividuation

When situations provide a high degree of arousal and a very low sense of responsibility, people may act in startling ways, surprising both to themselves at a later time and to others who know them closely. In these situations, people may lose their sense of restraint and their individual identity in exchange for identifying with a group or mob mentality, a situation called **deindividuation**. Its effects can be seen in examples ranging from atrocious acts during wartime to mosh pits at concerts. Deindividuation is a lack of self-awareness and is the result of a disconnection of behavior from attitudes.

The confluence of several factors create the ideal conditions for deindividuation to occur. These factors include

- group size: larger groups create a diminished sense of identity and responsibility, and may allow people to achieve anonymity by getting "lost in the crowd."
- physical anonymity: using facepaint, masks, or costumes (or communicating anonymously online) makes one less identifiable.
- arousing activities: rather than beginning with a frenzy, deindividuating circumstances usually start with arousing activities that escalate.

The bottom line is that factors that reduce self-awareness increase a sense of deindividuation. This can further include social roles (as evidenced by Zimbardo's prison study) and the use of alcohol, which serves to disinhibit and reduce self-consciousness.

Bystander Effect

The **Kitty Genovese** case involved the stabbing of a woman in New York City late at night. Although details of the case are more complicated, the incident was highlighted because of the perceived lack of effort of neighbors to help her while she cried for help. After her murder was discovered, detectives interviewed her neighbors and found that many of them had heard her cries for help, but no one had called the police. Time and again, the reason provided for a lack of action was that everyone assumed someone else had already called the police. Research spawned by this event revealed what is known as the **bystander effect**: the finding that a person is less likely to provide help when there are other bystanders. This occurs because the presence of bystanders creates a diffusion of responsibility—the responsibility to help does not clearly reside with one person in the group. When faced with circumstances in which one is the only individual available to assist, one may be more likely to act. Interestingly, the likelihood that someone will stop to help is inversely correlated with the number of people around; therefore, if you ever find yourself in a life-threatening emergency, you would be better off in a small town with a few folks around than in the middle of Times Square with thousands of people around.

Social Loafing

The bystander effect involves a diffusion of responsibility when in the presence of others. Taken further, this effect extends to circumstances in which people are working together toward common goals. In these situations, there is a tendency for people to exert less effort if they are being evaluated as a group than if they are individually accountable, a phenomenon called **social loafing**. It is something that you may have experienced in your everyday life, and does not necessarily mean that the "loafer" is someone who is lazy or irresponsible. For example, as an audience member in a small group of five, you are likely to clap louder for a presenter than if you were in an audience of 500 people. This is thought to occur because there can be less pressure on individuals as parts of a group on some tasks, leading to a tendency to take a little bit of a free ride, getting the benefit from the group while putting less effort in than one might on one's own.

Social facilitation and social loafing are both responses to the group situation and the task at hand. Which one tends to occur is based in part on evaluation. When being part of a group increases concerns over evaluation, social facilitation occurs. When being part of a group decreases concerns over evaluation, social loafing occurs. In order to fight against the threat of social loafing, companies in which people work in groups often use measures of group performance (for example, a store's total revenue) as well as of individual performance (for example, individual sales).

Group Polarization

We've seen how groups can influence one's performance, either by facilitating or hindering it based on circumstances. But how does group influence affect beliefs and opinions? It turns out that groups tend to intensify the preexisting views of their members—that is, the average view of a member of the group is accentuated. This tendency is called **group polarization**. It does NOT indicate that the group becomes more divided on an issue, but rather, suggests that the entire group tends toward more extreme versions of the average views they initially shared before discussion.

Group polarization occurs at every level in society—in families, schools, political parties, communities, and such. Consider a political debate on whether a wetland area should be converted into a shopping center. Although they likely each initially held a belief in the importance of conserving the wetlands, members of an environmental political party who interact with each other end up adopting a more extreme stance toward conservation than previously held by the average member. Similarly, members of another political party that focuses on the importance of jobs would emphasize this focus even more after discussions within the group. Thus, each group adopts a more extreme stance than its initial position. This creates more divisiveness between the two groups. When you consider the group polarization phenomenon together with the fact that people tend to preferentially interact with like-minded people, you can see why group negotiations are so difficult.

There are two reasons why group polarization occurs. The first is **informational influence**; in group discussion, the most common ideas to emerge are the ones that favor the dominant viewpoint. This serves to persuade others to take a stronger stance toward this viewpoint and provides an opportunity to rehearse and validate these similar opinions, further strengthening them. In fact, just thinking about an opinion for a couple of minutes can strengthen your support of it, because we tend to mostly think of facts that support it. The second reason is **normative influence**, which is based on social desirability, that is, wanting to be accepted or admired by others. If you want to identify with a particular group, then you may take a stronger stance that you initially would have in order to better relate with and internalize the group's belief system. The influence of **social comparison** (evaluating our opinions by comparing them to those of others) extends far beyond high school.

Groupthink

Pressure not to "rock the boat" in a group by providing a dissenting opinion can lead to what is known as groupthink. Although **groupthink** is a state of harmony within a group (because everyone is seemingly in a state of agreement), it can lead to some pretty terrible decisions. Groupthink manifests in a group when certain factors come together. Groups that are at risk tend to be overly friendly and cohesive, isolated from dissenting opinions, and have a directive leader whose decisions everyone tends to favor.

There are certain symptoms that are often clues to the presence of groupthink.

- The group is overly optimistic of its capabilities and has unquestioned belief in its stances—an overestimation of "might and right."
- The group becomes increasingly extreme by justifying its own decisions while demonizing those of opponents.
- Some members of the group prevent dissenting opinions from permeating the group by filtering out information and facts that go against the beliefs of the group (a process called **mindguarding**).
- There is pressure to conform, and so individuals censor their own opinions in favor of consensus, which creates an illusion of unanimity.

Stigma and Deviance

Deviance can be defined as a violation of society's standards of conduct or expectations. Deviant behavior can range from being late to an interview to smuggling drugs. In the United States, there are many groups who are classified as deviants, including drug pushers and gang members. However, more harmless groups can also be labeled deviants, including the obese and the mentally ill. Deviance can even involve positive acts, for example, Rosa Parks and other African Americans who refused to sit in the back of the bus were acting deviantly in an attempt to change norms they saw as unfair.

Society often devalues deviant members by assigning demeaning labels, called **stigma**. Entire groups may be labeled based on physical or behavioral qualities. For example, the term "fob" (for "fresh off the boat") has been used to refer to recent immigrants. Once these identities have been assigned, they can follow individuals and affect their lives based on the reactions other people have when they discover the labels. How might your behavior toward an individual change (for example, how likely would you be to hire the person) if you learned that he or she carried the label "felon"?

Conformity and Obedience

Behavior can often be contagious; for example, have you ever walked past someone on the street who is staring up at something on a tall building or in the sky? If you have never had this experience, try it and see what happens—more than likely other people around you will also start looking up. People, as social creatures, tend to do what others are doing. This can have an interesting impact on behavior. There are two well-known experiments that sought to investigate the influence of conformity and obedience.

Solomon Asch wanted to test the effects of **group pressure** (or **peer pressure**) on individuals' behavior, so he designed a series of simple experiments where subjects would be asked to participate in a study on visual perception. In the experiment, subjects were asked to determine which of three lines was most similar to a comparison line (in the experiment, there was one line that was clearly identical to the comparison line and the other two were clearly longer). When subjects completed this task alone, they erred less than 1% of the time. When subjects were placed in a room with several other people that they thought were also participating in the study, but were actually **confederates** (meaning that they were part of the experiment), the results were quite different. On the first few tests, all of the confederates responded correctly. However, after a little while the confederates began all choosing one of the incorrect lines. What's interesting is that Asch found that more than one third of subjects conformed to the group by answering incorrectly. They chose to avoid the discomfort of being different, rather than trust their own judgment in answering. The phenomenon of adjusting behavior or thinking based on the behavior or thinking of others is called **conformity**.

Another commonly referenced experiment is **Stanley Milgram**'s study involving fake shocks. The participants in this study believed that they were in control of equipment that delivered shocks to a student who was attempting to pass a memory test. No shocks were actually used. A researcher was in the room and directed the participant to administer increasing levels of shock to this student, a confederate, by turning a dial whenever he or she answered incorrectly. The only contact the participant had with the student was to hear the student's voice from the other room. When shocks were given at particular levels, the participants would hear moans, shouts of pain, pounding on the walls, and after that, dead silence. Milgram found that participants in the study were surprisingly obedient to the researcher's demands that they continue to administer the shocks. Out of 40 subjects, few questioned the procedure before reaching 300 volts and 26 of the subjects continued all the way to the maximum 450 volts. The experiment speaks to the power of authority and the discomfort that being disobedient invokes.

There are three ways that behavior may be motivated by social influences

1) *Compliance*: compliant behavior is motivated by the desire to seek reward or to avoid punishment. There is likely to be a punishment for disobeying authority. Compliance is easily extinguished if rewards or punishments are removed.

2) *Identification*: identification behavior is motivated by the desire to be like another person or group. A participant who conformed in Asch's experiment likely did not want to be disapproved of for choosing a different answer than the rest of the group. Identification endures as long as there is still a good relationship with the person or group being identified with and there are not convincing alternative viewpoints presented.

3) *Internalization*: internalized behavior is motivated by values and beliefs that have been integrated into one's own value system. Someone who has internalized a value not to harm others may have objected to the shocks administered in Milgram's study. This is the most enduring motivation of the three.

When the motivation for compliance is desire for the approval of others and to avoid rejection, this is called **normative social influence**. With normative social influence, people conform because they want to be liked and accepted by others. This often leads to public compliance, but not necessarily private acceptance of social norms. **Informational social influence** is the process of complying because we want to do the right thing and we feel like others "know something I don't know." Informational social influence is more likely to apply to new situations, ambiguous situations, or when an obvious authority figure is present.

There are several factors that influence conformity.

1) *Group Size:* A group doesn't have to be very large, but a group of 3-5 people will elicit more conformity than one with only 1-2 people.

2) *Unanimity:* There is a strong pressure not to dissent when everyone else agrees. However, if just one person disagrees, others are more likely to voice their real opinions.

3) *Cohesion:* An individual will more likely be swayed to agree with opinions that come from someone within a group with whom the individual identifies.

4) *Status:* Higher-status people have stronger influence on opinions.

5) *Accountability:* People tend to conform more when they must respond in front of others rather than in closed formats in which they cannot be held accountable for their opinions.

6) *No Prior Commitment:* Once people have made public commitments, they tend to stick to them. For example, once someone has taken a pledge to become a fraternity brother, he is more likely to follow the norms of that group.

7.3 SOCIAL INTERACTION AND SOCIAL BEHAVIOR

All social interactions take place within social structures, which are composed of five elements: statuses, social roles, groups (previously discussed), social networks, and organizations. These five elements are developed through the process of socialization, discussed earlier. Social interactions include things like expressing emotion, managing others' impressions of you, communicating, and other social behaviors.

Social Structures

Statuses and Roles

Status is a broad term in sociology that refers to all the socially defined positions within a society. These can include positions such as "president," "parent," "resident of Wisconsin," and "Republican." Needless to say, one person can hold multiple statuses at the same time. Some of these statuses may place someone in a higher social position while others may imply a lower position. For example, Kobe Bryant is a professional basketball player, a high social position. He also entered the NBA after high school and therefore did not complete a college education, putting him in a low social position (for this measure) compared to those with college diplomas. One's **master status** is the one that dominates the others and determines that individual's general position in society. For Kobe Bryant, it is safe to say that his status as a basketball player dominates the others. To illustrate this point, even fans of Kobe have likely spent little time considering his other statuses (father, husband, citizen). Sometimes the master status is not one the individual prefers; someone with a disability may be strongly identified by others as holding that status, with less attention paid to her other statuses, which she may find more important and fulfilling.

Statuses may be ascribed or achieved. **Ascribed statuses** are those that are assigned to a person by society regardless of the person's own efforts. For example, gender and race are ascribed statuses. **Achieved statuses** are considered to be due largely to the individual's efforts. These can include statuses such as "doctor," "parent," and "Democrat."

Roles

Social roles are expectations for people of a given social status. It is expected that doctors will possess strong medical knowledge and be intelligent. Role expectations can also come with ascribed statuses. There may be an expectation that a female is more likely to be a babysitter than a male. Roles help contribute to society's stability by making things more predictable.

However, roles can also be sources of tension in multiple ways. **Role conflict** happens when there is a conflict in society's expectations for *multiple statuses* held by the same person (for example, a male nurse or a gay priest). **Role strain** is when a *single status* results in conflicting expectations. For example, a homosexual man may feel pressure to avoid being "too gay" and also "not gay enough." **Role exit** is the process of disengaging from a role that has become closely tied to one's self-identity to take on another. Some examples include the transition from high school student to more independent college student living on campus with peers. Another would be transitioning from the workforce to retirement. These transitions are difficult because they involve the process of detaching from something significant, as well as embarking on something new and unknown.

Networks and Organizations

Networks

Think about the people you know. Now think about the people that those people know. As you keep extrapolating out to more distant connections, you can get a sense of your **social network**. A social network is a web of social relationships, including those in which a person is directly linked to others as well as those in which people are indirectly connected through others. Facebook is a popular online social network. Social networks are often based on groups that individuals belong to. Network ties may be weak, but they can be powerful resources in meeting people (for example, using a network like LinkedIn to find a job).

Organizations

Large, more impersonal groups that come together to pursue particular activities and meet goals efficiently are called **organizations**. They tend to be complex and hierarchically structured. Formal organizations can include businesses, governments, and religious groups. Organizations serve the purpose of increasing efficiency, predictability, control, and uniformity in society. They also allow knowledge to be passed down more easily, so that individual people become more replaceable. As an example, consider going to a McDonald's. Because this corporation is an organization, one may expect a particular experience and menu options regardless of who is actually working at that particular restaurant.

There are three types of organizations. **Utilitarian organizations** are those in which members get paid for their efforts, such as businesses. **Normative organizations** motivate membership based on morally relevant goals, for example, Mothers Against Drunk Driving (MADD). **Coercive organizations** are those for which members do not have a choice in joining (for example, prisons). Like groups, organizations both are influenced by statuses and roles and help define statuses and roles.

Social Interactions

Expressing and Detecting Emotion

The physiological basis of emotion was discussed in Chapter 4. Emotion is also vital in explaining how we react to situations and others. Emotions arise based on our (typically unconscious) appraisals of situations. The ability to quickly appraise situations using emotion has evolutionary significance: if we hear something and feel fearful, we might have the opportunity to escape a threatening situation faster than if we were to wait to see what was causing the noise, and then make a decision about whether it would be a good idea to escape. Some emotional responses, such as likes, dislikes, and fears, involve no conscious thought. More complex emotions, like hatred, love, guilt, and happiness, can have important influences on our memories, expectations, and interpretations. Take a simple example: if you are having an awful day and are in a really crummy mood when your mother calls you, you might have an expectation that she is calling to nag you about something, even when she is actually calling for some other reason.

We detect emotion in others using clues: their body language, tone and pitch in their voices, and expression in their faces, which can display an incredibly impressive array of emotion that humans are precisely wired to detect (Chapter 4). For example, through experiments it was determined that if we glimpse a face for a mere tenth of a second, we can accurately judge the emotion it portrays. The eyes and mouth are the two areas of the face that convey the most emotion: we can detect fear and anger in the eyes and happiness in the mouth. Some of our facial muscles can actually betray our emotions if we are trying to conceal our feelings. For example, lifting the inner part of the eyebrow conveys distress or concern. Raising the eyebrows and pulling them together conveys fear. Muscles in the eyes and cheeks convey happiness through smiling. Some people are more sensitive to emotional cues than others, and introverts are better at reading others' emotions, while extroverts are generally easier to read.

Gender Shapes Expression

Some studies suggest that women surpass men at reading emotional cues. Women's greater sensitivity to nonverbal cues perhaps explains their greater emotional literacy, or ability to describe their emotions. Men tend to describe emotions in simpler ways, while women are generally capable of describing more complex emotions. Women also demonstrate greater emotional responsiveness in positive and negative situations, with the one exception being anger. Anger is the one emotion that seems to be considered by most a "masculine" emotion. For example, when shown pictures of a gender-neutral face that was either smiling or angry, people were more likely to assume the face was male if it was angry, and female if it was smiling. **Empathy**, the ability to identify with others' emotions, is relatively equal between the sexes. Both men and women can "put themselves in someone else's shoes" and feel that person's pain or elation. But women are more likely than men to *express* empathy by crying or reporting genuine distress at another's misfortune. In studies, women tend to experience emotional events more deeply, with greater brain activation in the areas that process emotion, and are better able to remember emotional events later.

Culture Shapes Expression

Culture provides an additional filter for interpreting emotion. In other cultures, common emotions like fear and happiness are expressed in ways that Americans may find difficult to interpret. Gestures (movements of the hands and body that are used to express emotion) vary widely between cultures. For example, the use of a thumbs-up sign indicates to an American that things are "okay," but is used as an insult in some other cultures, whereas the extension of just the middle finger expresses anger or discourtesy in America, but is a neutral symbol in several other cultures. Certain facial expressions, however, seem to be universal; babies and blind people make the same universal emotional expressions with their faces. While cultures do share universal facial expressions, the degree to which emotion is expressed is influenced by culture. Cultures that promote individuality (such as Western cultures) also encourage emotional expressiveness. Like many other facets of human interaction, emotion is best understood by considering its biological, psychological, and sociological aspects.

Impression Management

In sociology and psychology, **impression management** or **self-presentation** is the conscious or unconscious process whereby people attempt to manage their own images by influencing the perceptions of others. This is achieved by controlling either the amount or type of information, or the social interaction. People construct images of themselves, and want others to see them in certain lights. There are multiple impression management strategies that people employ. Assertive strategies for impression management include the use of active behaviors to shape our self-presentations, such as talking oneself up and showing off flashy status symbols to demonstrate a desired image. Defensive strategies for impression management include avoidance or self-handicapping. **Self-handicapping** is a strategy in which people create obstacles and excuses to avoid self-blame when they do poorly. It is easier to erect external hindrances to explain our poor performance than to risk considering or having others consider an internal characteristic to be the cause of a poor performance. A classic example is the student who loudly lets everyone know before an exam that she did not study. Her strategy is such that if she receives a poor grade on the exam, it can't be blamed on her intelligence (an internal characteristic that is likely an important element of her self-esteem), but must rather be blamed on an external factor, the fact that she didn't study.

Front Stage Versus Back Stage Self

The **dramaturgical perspective** in sociology stems from symbolic interactionism and posits that we imagine ourselves as playing certain roles when interacting with others. This perspective uses the theater as a metaphor for the way we present ourselves; we base our presentations on cultural values, norms, and expectations, with the ultimate goal of presenting an acceptable self to others. Dramaturgical theory suggests that our identities are not necessarily stable, but dependent on our interactions with others; in this way, we constantly remake who we are, depending on the situations we are in. Social interaction can be broken into two types: front stage and back stage. In the **front stage**, we play a role and use impression management to craft the way we come across to other people. In the **back stage**, we can "let down our guard" and be ourselves. For example, the way you dress and behave at work (front stage) is potentially very different than your dress and behavior at home (back stage).

Verbal and Nonverbal Communication

Nonverbal communication involves all of the methods for communication that we use that do not include words. Because humans are inherently visual creatures, a majority of these cues are visual, but we employ other cues as well. Nonverbal communication includes gestures, touch, body language, eye contact, facial expressions, and a host of finer subtleties. The act of communicating verbally also employs a lot of nonverbal cues, such as pitch, volume, rate, intonation, and rhythm. In a society in which written communication is exploding in popularity (for example, emails and text messaging), we also employ nonverbal cues in our writing, such as emoticons, use of capitalization and punctuation, and spacing. Consider the following three text messages. Each uses the same three words, yet they each express slightly different ideas:

OH MY GOD!!!!!

Oh. My. God.

Oh my... God?

Animal Signals and Communication

Effective communication is important for non-human animals, as well. Animals that live in social groups must be able to convey information about food, territory, dominance hierarchies, mating, and predators in order to ensure social harmony and survival. Unlike humans, who rely heavily upon visual cues and language to communicate, animals employ a wider range of signal modalities.

Visual cues are employed by animals that communicate predominantly during the daytime, and to other animals that have acute vision. For example, many organisms advertise that they are poisonous[1] by employing warning colors. **Warning colors** are bright colors meant to advertise to predators that an organism is toxic or noxious. Bright colors such as orange and red are rare in nature, and most organisms that are brightly colored are either toxic or mimicking a toxic organism. For example, the monarch butterfly feeds on the milkweed plant. Milkweed contains toxins that the monarch sequesters, making the monarch toxic to birds: if a bird eats a monarch it will get sick and often vomit. This is beneficial to the monarch species because vomiting is a form of conditioning that is acquired rather rapidly and is quite resistant to extinction. (Can you think of something that you will never eat again because you once vomited after eating it?) This is an important evolutionary adaptation, since vomiting usually indicates that something poisonous has been ingested. Therefore, if a bird eats a monarch butterfly and becomes sick, it will never eat another monarch again. The viceroy butterfly does not eat milkweed, and is not toxic. However, it has adapted over time to mimic the coloring of the monarch butterfly, thus benefiting from the monarch's protection from predators; this evolutionary adaptation is called **mimicry**.

Organisms use bright colors for other types of communication as well. For example, some organisms use bright colors to attract mates (like the red-breasted robin) or to communicate information to others in their species about territory (for example, the Carolina anole, a type of lizard, extends its brightly colored throat fan and bobs its head in a characteristic manner to communicate information about territory to other males of its species).

Many animals also employ auditory communication. Sounds can be manipulated in many ways to communicate information, and many animals are bound to their social groups by characteristic patterns of sounds (such as whale songs or birdsong). A given species may also employ a variety of songs or calls to communicate. For example, certain bird species will emit a pure-tone alarm noise that warns their neighbors of danger. The nature of the pure-tone makes it difficult for a predator to locate the bird that made the call. This same species can employ a completely different sound for mating purposes, for which it is important to locate the source of the sound, and with it a potential mate. Bats employ a very sophisticated system of echolocation, which also serves as a form of self-communication. By emitting a high-frequency sound and then detecting its echo off potential prey, bats are able to hunt very precisely at night without the use of visual cues.

Chemical signals are also an important part of animal communication. While chemical signals may operate on a much slower scale than visual and auditory communication, they can last much longer (a fact put to good use by police dogs). The term for chemical messengers employed by animals to communicate with each other is **pheromones**. Pheromones can be employed within a given species to attract mates. Furthermore, some social insects employ a wide range of pheromones; for example, ants release alarm pheromones, death pheromones, and food pheromones (this last explains the perfectly organized line of ants that visit your picnic—as soon as one ant has found a promising food source, it releases food pheromones along its trail back to the anthill, so that other ants can follow the trail straight to the food source).

Lastly, many animals also communicate through touch or movement. Many organisms engage in mating dances to attract members of the opposite sex (oftentimes also employing visual cues, such as the

---

[1] The organisms mentioned here are obviously not *consciously* employing any of these techniques; rather their coloring and other signal modalities are the results of millennia of natural selection. In the above example, the organisms with the brightest colors were the least likely to get eaten (i.e., if one organism was eaten once, the predator learned to associate the color with the toxic taste or adverse reaction and was much less likely to eat the organism's brother as well as other brightly colored butterflies, thus ensuring the survival and passing on of the trait for bright color).

gorgeous plumage of the male peacock or the odd blue feet of the blue-footed booby), and/or engage in ritualized dominance displays. The honeybee, another insect with impressive social organization, has been well-studied for its elaborate communication. Honeybees engage in specific dances to communicate information about the locations of food sources.

Social Behavior

Social behavior occurs between members of the same species within a given society. Communication occurs between members of the same species, but not usually between different species. Specific social behaviors include attraction, aggression, attachment, and social support.

Attraction between members of the same species is a primary component of love, and explains much about friendship, romantic relationships, and other close social relationships. Researchers in social psychology are particularly interested in studying human attraction because it helps to explain how much we like, dislike, or hate others. Research into human attraction has found that the following three characteristics foster attraction: proximity, physical attractiveness, and similarity.

Proximity (geographic nearness) is the most powerful predictor for friendship. Think of the people you consider your closest friends. How many of them shared a grade school classroom or a neighborhood with you growing up? How many people from your freshman dorm or living situation do you still consider to be close friends? People are more inclined to like, befriend, and even marry others from the same class, neighborhood, or office. People prefer repeated exposure to the same stimuli; this is known as the **mere exposure effect**. With certain exceptions, familiarity breeds fondness. This partially explains the common affinity for celebrities, and the fact that many people vote based on name recognition alone, regardless of whether or not they know much about a candidate. The tendency to like those in close proximity probably has an evolutionally foundation; for our ancestors, the familiar faces were likely the ones that could be trusted.

Appearance also has a powerful impact on attraction. Physical attractiveness is an important predictor of attraction; in fact, studies show that people rate physically attractive people higher on a number of characteristics and traits, indicating that physically attractive people are somehow more likeable. While many aspects of attractiveness vary across cultures, some appear to be culturally universal, such as youthful appearance in women (perhaps reflecting a biological constraint of fertility), and maturity, dominance, and affluence in men. Humans also tend to prefer average, symmetrical faces. Attractiveness is also influenced by personality traits; people believed to have positive personality traits are judged more attractive.

Similarity between people also impacts attraction. Friends and partners are likely to share common values, beliefs, interests, and attitudes. The more alike people are, the more their liking for each other endures over time.

Aggression

While attraction is an important unifying force in society, aggression is the opposite; a potentially destructive force to social relations. **Aggression** is broadly defined as behavior that is forceful, hostile, or attacking. In sociology, aggression is considered something that is intended to cause harm or promote social dominance within a group. Aggression can be communicated verbally or by actions or gestures. While aggression is employed for a variety of reasons by humans today (competitive sports, war, getting ahead at

7.3

work), in non-human animals it is generally employed as a means for protecting resources, such as food, territory, and mates. Indeed, aggression was likely employed for similar reasons by prehistoric humans, and as our society evolved, we began using aggression in additional ways.

Aggression is considered an innate instinct, but biology and society can influence aggression. There are three types of predictors for aggressive behavior: genetic, neural, and biochemical. Identical twin studies suggest that there is some genetic predisposition towards aggressiveness; if one twin has a temper, the other tends to as well. Humans and other animals are naturally wired both to inhibit and to produce aggressive behavior. While no particular locus in the brain controls aggression, certain areas are thought to facilitate aggression, while other areas (in the frontal lobe) inhibit aggression. Many biochemical factors can alter the neural control of aggression. Alcohol, for example, can lower aggression inhibition, making someone more aggressive while drunk. Animals also tend to exhibit less aggression when they are castrated[2].

Many psychological and social factors are thought to trigger aggression in humans. The **frustration-aggression principle** suggests that when someone is blocked form achieving a goal, this frustration can trigger anger, which can lead to aggression. Other frustrating stimuli, such as physical pain, unpleasant odors, and hot temperatures can also lead to aggression. Aggression is more likely to occur in situations in which prior experience has somehow promoted aggression. For example, if a child acts aggressively toward another child and ends up getting what she wants (lunch money, for example), she is more likely to behave in an aggressive manner in the future. People who are ostracized are also more likely to behave aggressively, which may partially explain some of the mass shootings that have occurred in schools and public spaces. While it would be a mistake to oversimplify the roots of aggression, it seems clear that biology, experience, and society combine to provide the fodder for aggression.

Social Support

Social support is a major determinant of health and wellbeing for humans and other animals. Family relationships provide comfort, and close relationships are predictive of health outcomes. Happily married people live longer, healthier lives, regardless of age, sex, and race. People who have social support have been shown to engage in healthier behaviors; they are less likely to smoke, more likely to exercise, and report a better capacity to cope with adversity and stress. Interestingly, social support is not confined to human-human interactions. People with dogs or other pets also reap some of the benefits of social support.

Biological Explanations of Social Behavior in Animals

Many animals also exhibit a wide range of social behavior. Some species (such as ants, bees, and wasps) engage in highly organized and hierarchical social behaviors, with each individual playing a specific role within the group. Most mammals also engage in social behavior, and many interesting phenomena have been elucidated by studying how mammals interact with members of their own species.

---

[2] Though castration does not *completely* remove aggression, as territorial battles between "fixed" housecats illustrate.

Foraging Behavior

Foraging behavior describes the search for and exploitation of food resources by animals. Securing food can come at a high energetic cost, which is an important consideration for organisms; the amount of energy it requires a lion to track, chase, and kill an antelope, or the amount of energy it takes an antelope to search for and graze upon enough foliage to sustain itself matters greatly to that organism's patterns of behavior. Ethologists believe that organisms employ learning behavior in the search for food. Since an organism's environment is constantly changing, it is important that foraging behavior is adaptable. Many organisms employ observational learning of older members in the group to learn behaviors such as knowing what is safe to eat.

Mating Behavior and Mate Choice

Mating behavior involves the pairing of opposite-sex organisms for the purposes of reproduction and the propagation of genes. Mating behaviors include courtship rituals, copulation, the building of nests, and the rearing of offspring for specified periods of time. For animals, mating strategies include random mating, disassortive mating, and assortative mating. In random mating, all members of a species are equally likely to mate with each other, meaning that there are no spatial, genetic, or behavioral limitations to mating. This ensures the largest amount of genetic diversity, and protects against genetic drift and bottle-necking. Assortative mating is a nonrandom mating pattern in which individuals with similar genotypes or phenotypes mate with one another more frequently than would be expected with random mating. In negative assortative mating, also known as disassortative mating, individuals with more disparate traits mate more frequently than would be expected with random mating.

Inclusive Fitness and Altruism

The **inclusive fitness** of an organism is defined by the number of offspring the organism has, how it supports its offspring, and how its offspring support others in a group. The inclusive fitness theory proposes that an organism can improve its overall genetic success through altruistic social behaviors. An **altruistic behavior** is one that helps ensure the success or survival of the rest of a social group, possibly at the expense of the success or survival of the individual. For example, the ground squirrel, a social mammal that lives in dens underground, will sound an alarm call if it sees a predator near the group. The alarm call does two things: first, it alerts the rest of the group to danger, and second, it calls the predator's attention to the particular squirrel that makes the noise. Therefore, in many instances alerting the group results in the demise of the individual that sounded the alarm. Even though the alerter has not survived to reproduce, it has helped promote the survival of the rest of the clan, many of whom are probably close genetic relatives. In this way, the altruistic behavior of the ground squirrel has increased its own inclusive fitness by ensuring the survival of its siblings and other genetic relatives.

Applying Game Theory

Evolutionary **game theory** is used to try and predict large, complex systems, such as the overall behavior of a population. Evolutionary game theory has been used to explain many complex and challenging aspects of biology, such as how altruistic behaviors work in the context of Darwinian natural selection. While it may seem that large groups of animals and large crowds of people are too complex to accurately predict behavior, game theory suggests that it might be possible to do so. This type of analysis might be useful, for instance, in predicting the behavior of a large crowd of people in an enclosed space during a disaster. While this field is still emerging, due to social constraints on our behavior, it may be quite possible to accurately predict behavior in complex living systems in the future.

Chapter 7 Summary

- Self-concept or self-identity is the sum of an individual's understanding of him or herself, including physical, psychological, and social attributes.

- Personal identity includes personal attributes (such as age, disability status, ethnicity/race) while social identity consists of social definitions (religion, gender, occupation).

- Self-efficacy is a belief in one's own competence and effectiveness, while self-esteem is an individual's overall evaluation of worth.

- Those with an internal locus of control believe they are able to influence outcomes through their own effort; those with an external locus of control believe outcomes are controlled by outside forces.

- Symbolic interactionism proposes that the mind and self emerge through the social process of communication and the use of cultural symbols.

- Socialization is the process by which people learn the norms, values, attitudes, and beliefs necessary to become proficient members of society.

- Norms are spoken or unspoken rules and expectations for the behavior in society. Mores are norms that are highly important for the benefit of society and so are often strictly enforced.

- Agents of socialization include the following: family, school, peer group, the workplace, religion/government, and mass media/technology.

- Cultural assimilation occurs when an individual forsakes their own culture to completely adopt another culture; amalgamation occurs when majority and minority groups combine to form a new group.

- Multiculturalism or pluralism endorses equal standing for all cultural traditions within a society.

- A subculture is a segment of society that shares a distinct pattern of traditions and values that differs from that of the larger society.

- Kohlberg described six stages of moral development; most adults reach stage 4, but few reach stage 6.

- In order to determine if behavior can be attributed to internal or external causes, consistency, distinctiveness, and consensus must be considered.

- The fundamental attribution error occurs when people tend to underestimate the impact of the situation and overestimate the impact of a person's character or personality on observed behavior.

- The self-serving bias is the tendency to attribute our successes to ourselves and our failures to others or to the external environment.

- The optimism bias is the belief that bad things happen to other people, but not to us; the just world phenomenon is a tendency to believe that the world is fair and people get what they deserve.

- A false consensus occurs when we assume that everyone else agrees with what we do (even though they may not); a projection bias happens when we assume others have the same beliefs we do.

- Stereotypes are oversimplified ideas about groups of people, based on character-istics (race, gender, sexual orientation, religion, disability).

- Prejudice refers to the thoughts, attitudes, and feelings someone holds about a group that are not based on actual experience. Discrimination is prejudiced treat-ment of someone based on their membership in a specific social group.

- An illusory correlation is when a relationship is perceived between variables (typi-cally people, events, or behaviors) even when no such relationship exists.

- A self-fulfilling prophecy occurs when stereotypes lead to behaviors that affirm the original stereotypes; stereotype threat refers to a self-fulfilling fear that one will be evaluated based on a negative stereotype.

- Ethnocentrism is the tendency to judge people from another culture by the stan-dards of one's own culture, while cultural relativism judges another culture based on its own standards.

- A group is a collection of any number of people (as few as two) who regularly interact and identify with each other, sharing similar norms, values, and expectations.

- Primary groups are usually smaller and include those with whom the individual engages with, in person, in long-term, emotional ways; secondary groups are larger and more impersonal, and are usually of short duration.

- An in-group is a group that an individual belongs to and believes to be an integral part of who they are; an out-group is a group that an individual does not belong to.

- The social facilitation effect occurs when people perform simple, well-learned tasks better when other people are present.

- Deindividuation occurs in situations that provide a high degree of arousal and a very low sense of responsibility, when people lose their sense of restraint and their individual identity in exchange for identifying with a group or mob mentality.

- The bystander effect describes the finding that a person is less likely to provide help when there are other bystanders.

- Social loafing is the tendency for people to exert less effort if they are being evaluated as a group than if they are individually accountable.

- Group polarization occurs when the average view of a member of the group is accentuated or enhanced by group membership.

- Groupthink is a phenomenon that occurs within a group when the desire for harmony or conformity in the group results in a consensual perspective without much thought of alternative viewpoints.

- Deviance is a violation of society's standards of conduct or expectations.

- Behavior is motivated by social influences when there is: compliance, identification, and internalization.

- Several factors influence conformity, including: group size, unanimity, cohesion, status, accountability, and lack of prior commitment.

- Status is a broad term in sociology that refers to all the socially defined positions within a society.

- Social roles are expectations for people of a given social status.

- Impression management or self-presentation is the conscious or unconscious process whereby people attempt to manage their own images by influencing the perceptions of others.

- The dramaturgical perspective posits that we imagine ourselves as playing certain roles when interacting with others in society.

CHAPTER 7 FREESTANDING PRACTICE QUESTIONS

1. Agent(s) of socialization include:

   I. parents.
   II. teachers.
   III. friends.

   A) I only
   B) I and II
   C) II and III
   D) I, II, and III

2. Eli studies really hard for his chemistry class but keeps getting poor scores on quizzes and lab assignments. Eventually, he begins to feel like nothing he does will improve his performance in chemistry. When faced with future chemistry assignments, Eli doesn't even bother trying because he feels destined to fail at chemistry. This can best be described as:

   A) learned helplessness.
   B) an internal locus of control.
   C) incongruity.
   D) the fundamental attribution error.

3. If one of the members of a group of monkeys warns the others of an impending attack by a lion by making a lot of noise, jumping up and down, and waving its arms, thus drawing the lion's attention, this can best be defined as an act of:

   A) social isolation.
   B) exclusive fitness.
   C) role-playing.
   D) altruism.

4. When new members of a society eventually become indistinguishable from the rest of society, adopting the language, norms, and customs, which process has occurred?

   A) Multiculturalism
   B) Amalgamation
   C) Assimilation
   D) Groupthink

5. A researcher randomly surveys people asking them how they found out about their most recent job, either through an acquaintance or through a close friend. The researcher concluded that the results proved the social network theory, which suggests:

   A) more respondents found their jobs from an acquaintance rather than a close friend.
   B) more respondents found their jobs from a close friend rather than an acquaintance.
   C) half of the respondents found their jobs from an acquaintance while the other half of the respondents found their jobs from a close friend.
   D) a majority of respondents found their jobs on their own.

6. A doctor does a check up on a 40-year-old patient and talks to him in a serious and professional manner. A few moments later, the same doctor goes to a different room to do a routine check up on a 5-year-old patient. The doctor makes funny faces throughout the check-up in order to make the patient laugh. This scenario is most closely related to which concept?

A) Deviance
B) Impression management
C) Conflict theory
D) Symbolic interactionism

7. George Herbert Mead explains that the final step to forming a self is through the ability of seeing oneself. This ability to examine oneself leads to the idea that individuals have two aspects of self: the "I" and the "Me." Which of the following is true about the "I" and the "Me?"

I.   The "I" is the observer while the "Me" is the observed.
II. The "I" prevents the "Me" from violating social norms in a particular setting.
III. It is possible for an individual to reflect on the "I" and the "Me."

A) I only
B) II only
C) I and II only
D) I and III only

8. Despite having a stake in an upcoming election, a citizen eligible to vote declines to go to the polls, declaring that her vote is too small to make a difference and she knows her candidate will win anyway. Her behavior is most demonstrative of which of the following?

A) Social loafing theory
B) Opponent-process theory
C) Regression to the mean
D) Group polarization

CHAPTER 7 PRACTICE PASSAGE

When people want to establish a new form of identity, they undergo an exiting process to transition from their ex-role to their new role. The exiting process from their ex-role will be satisfied once society gives acknowledgement to the individual's change in identity. This is a difficult transition because society has already set expectations for the individual based on their ex-role. Through a series of interviews of people who have undergone role exiting, ranging from ex-nuns to ex-convicts, researchers found several issues that individuals encounter in the process of creating new roles.

The first issue that individuals face is the presentation of self. Individuals use external and internal indicators to publicly show others that they would like to be treated differently from their past selves. For example, transsexuals, who identify with a gender that is opposite of their biological sex, alter their clothes and mannerisms based on what they believe society considers acceptable of the sex they want to convey in their new role. It is the responsibility of others in society to recognize the individual's new identity through the newly acquired props and mannerisms the individual employs.

Social reaction is another issue for those exiting an old role and assuming a new one. During the exiting process, individuals are affected by reactions they receive from society based on their ex-role. Role exits are either socially desirable (such as being a drug user turning into an ex-drug user) or socially undesirable (such as being a doctor and turning into an ex-doctor). People continue to hold positive or negative expectations about the old role that an individual is trying to break away from as they continue through the exiting process. However, the more society expects certain behaviors from an individual, the more likely the individual will act in a way they are expected to act. For instance, if parents and teachers continue to treat a student like a delinquent, it is likely that the student will continue to misbehave because he is fulfilling the role assigned. The presentation of self and social reaction to the ex-role together determine the difficulty of adapting to the new role for the individual.

Another challenge is the change of friendship networks for the individual. People who shift identities are inclined to distance themselves from their old peers in order to be surrounded with a network that would encourage and facilitate their new role. For example, individuals who are married surround themselves with other married couples. However, if they became "ex-spouses," they are likely to begin associating with single people and fellow divorcées because their interactions with other married couples are different and uncomfortable. Additionally, while in their old role, individuals formed bonds with other people. After role-exiting, individuals have to manage their relationships with people who continue to be a part of their ex-role as well as those who are part of their new role.

Finally, individuals face role residuals, which can also be known as "hangover identity." This concept describes the number of aspects that persist for an individual from their ex-role even after completing the exiting process to their newly formed identity. Overall, the more involved an individual was in his former role, the more likely he is to have a higher role residual compared to someone who was not as committed to his previous role.

Source: Adapted from H.R.F. Ebaugh, *Becoming an Ex: The Process of Role Exit.* ©1988 by The University of Chicago Press

1. Which of the following theories best describes the process of presentation of self in creating an ex-role?

   A) Social facilitation
   B) Dramaturgy
   C) Social support
   D) Peer pressure

2. Which of the following scenarios describes the self-serving bias?

   A) An employee who receives a bonus believes this reward was well-deserved because of how hard she worked and all of the extra hours she put in to her job.
   B) A man who is ignored by a salesperson at a high-end suit store believes the salesperson is just a rude jerk.
   C) A survey finds that most people think that attractive celebrities are good people.
   D) An employee receives a promotion and feels lucky to have been "in the right place at the right time."

3. Based on the passage, which of the following types of social identities do transsexuals try to express through their self-presentation?

    I. Sexual orientation
   II. Gender
  III. Biological sex

A) I only
B) II only
C) III only
D) II and III

4. A felon fails to find a job because potential employers are aware of his role as a convict. Which of the following concepts best describes this social reaction?

A) Social stigma
B) Social support
C) False consensus
D) Socialization

5. All of the following are ways that an individual's behavior may be motivated by social influences, EXCEPT:

A) compliance.
B) identification.
C) aggregation.
D) internalization.

6. Which of the following individuals would most likely experience "hangover identity?"

A) A biological male who identifies as a female, but has not yet begun the transition to the female gender.
B) An alcoholic who was sober for six months and then relapsed.
C) Someone who was married for six weeks and then gets a divorce.
D) A recent retiree who worked at the same company for 45 years, had a tight group of friends at work, participated in the company Thursday night bowling league, and volunteered with her colleagues every holiday season in a neighborhood soup kitchen.

SOLUTIONS TO CHAPTER 7 FREESTANDING PRACTICE QUESTIONS

1. **D**   Item I is true: family, including parents, are considered agents of socialization (choice C can be eliminated). Item II is true: educators, like teachers, are agents of socialization (choice A can be eliminated). Item III is true: peers and friends are also agents of socialization (choice B can be eliminated; choice D is correct).

2. **A**   Learned helplessness occurs when someone tries hard but fails repeatedly at a task. Eventually, the individual believes that they have no control over the outcome, develops an external locus of control (choice B is wrong), and stops trying (choice A is correct). Incongruity refers to the idea that the real self has fallen short of the ideal self; while this may pertain to the situation described in the question stem, there is not enough evidence to assume that succeeding in chemistry is part of Eli's idealized self (choice C is wrong). The fundamental attribution error occurs when an individual attributes the actions of others (not themselves) to their personalities (choice D is wrong).

3. **D**   When a social organism behaves in such a way as to benefit the group (such as the monkey attempting to warn the others about the lion by making noise, jumping, and waving its arms), even at a potential cost to itself (because the lion has now noticed the monkey), it is demonstrating altruistic behavior (choice D is correct). *Inclusive* fitness is defined by an organism improving its genetic success by helping others with similar genes to survive; exclusive fitness is not an element of social interaction among animals (choice B is wrong). Social isolation does not explain the behavior of the monkey in relationship to the rest of the group (choice A is wrong), nor does role-playing, which explains how individuals (humans) take on expected roles within groups (choice C is wrong).

4. **C**   Assimilation occurs when a new member alters her own culture in order to adapt to the dominant culture. When new members of society eventually become indistinguishable from the rest of society, assimilation has occurred (choice C is correct). Multiculturalism is the belief that different cultures can live harmoniously without feeling the need to adjust or adapt to the dominant culture (choice A is wrong). Amalgamation occurs when the two cultures combine to form a new culture, different from both of the original cultures (choice B is wrong). Groupthink is the likelihood for people within the predominant group to establish a consensual perspective without much thought of alternative viewpoints (choice D is wrong).

5. **A**   The social network theory posits that people's networks are important and necessary for the spread of ideas and resources; there is much strength in weak ties because weak ties allow the sharing of new resources to a vast network. It is more likely for participants to find jobs through an acquaintance (weak tie) compared to a close friend (strong tie; choice A is correct). Although having strong ties has an advantage to people's networks, there is a sense of redundancy with the information and resources provided; generally people's strong ties have information that the person is already aware of since they are a part of the same cluster (choice B is wrong). Since the researcher concluded that the results "proved the social network theory," it wouldn't make sense for the results to be half and half (choice C is wrong), nor would it make sense that most respondents found their jobs on their own (choice D is wrong).

6. **B** Impression management is the concept of expressing parts of one's self, depending on the person on the receiving end of the interaction. The doctor conveys this by acting differently towards the 40-year-old patient and the 5-year-old patient (choice B is correct). Deviance occurs when an individual is violating social norms. It is socially acceptable for the doctor to act professional with the adult and silly with the child (choice A is wrong). Conflict theory is the belief that inequality exists due to an uneven distribution of power and resources in society; this theory is unrelated to the scenario described in the question (choice C is wrong). Symbolic interactionism describes the way people interact and respond towards others based on how the individual interprets the interaction itself. The interpretation of social symbols are usually defined through the individual's own social process. In comparison to impression management, symbolic interactionism is not most closely related to the scenario and does not fully explain the doctor's differing behaviors between the two patients (choice D is wrong).

7. **A** Item I is true: the "I" is the aspect of the self that allows individuals to evaluate the other part of the self that is the "Me" (choice B can be eliminated). Item II is false: the "Me" is responsible for preventing the "I" from responding to society in a way that will violate social norms (choice C can be eliminated). Item III is false: although it is possible to reflect on the "Me," it is not possible to directly reflect on the "I" since the "I" is the part of the self that is doing the reflecting (choice D can be eliminated and choice A is correct).

8. **A** According to social loafing theory, people working in groups will exert less effort when they are not held individually accountable, downplaying the importance of their own contribution while assuming that someone else will take up the slack. Because the citizen described does have a stake in the election, but decides not to vote because she believes her vote won't make a difference (she assumes that the candidate will win because everyone else will vote for that candidate), her behavior can best be explained by social loafing (choice A is correct). The opponent-process theory has to do with color perception, not group behavior (choice B is wrong) and regression to the mean is a statistical phenomenon, not a social one (choice C is wrong). Group polarization describes the phenomenon whereby a group's views become more extreme; it does not explain the scenario presented in the question stem (choice D is wrong).

SOLUTIONS TO CHAPTER 7 PRACTICE PASSAGE

1. **B** In the second paragraph, the mention of "props" is a strong indicator that dramaturgy is implicated, which is the concept that individuals' lives are a stage and they use the appropriate props to portray their respective roles (choice B is correct). Social facilitation is the idea that an individual will perform better on tasks because of the presence of other people; this concept does not apply to the process of presentation of self (choice A is incorrect). Social support involves having a strong network system to assist the individual in their time of need; this does not best explain the process of presentation of self (choice C is incorrect). Peer pressure is the influence of peers to encourage individuals to conform to the norms of their society; the passage implies that the individuals choose to change themselves as opposed to being pressured into doing so (choice D is incorrect).

2. **A** Self-serving bias occurs when we attribute our successes to ourselves and our failures to external factors; the employee who attributes her promotion to her own hard work is the best example of the self-serving bias (choice A is correct). Self-serving bias does not attribute success to external factors like luck (choice D is wrong). The man who believes a salesperson is a rude jerk after he is ignored by the salesperson is committing a fundamental attribution error, by attributing the salesperson's actions to some internal element of personality (choice B is wrong). The physical attractiveness stereotype explains why people tend to believe that attractive people are also "good" people (choice C is wrong).

3. **B** Item I is false: sexual orientation describes an individual's sexual attraction and preference; while this is a social identity, transsexuals are not attempting to convey information about their sexual preference through presentation of self (choice A can be eliminated). Item II is true: gender is a social identity; transsexuals express their self-perceived gender through the use of outward indicators. The passage specifies that transsexuals use clothing and a change in behavior to adjust to gender norms of society (choice C can be eliminated). Item III is false: biological sex is not a social identity; rather, it is based on human biology. The passage example focuses on the act of presenting the individuals' self through props and characteristics rather than body parts (choice D can be eliminated and choice B is correct).

4. **A** Social stigma is the negative association that others have about an individual based on their past selves, which distinguishes them from the rest of society; ex-felons have a high social stigma since their former role as a convict is greatly disapproved of in society (choice A is correct). Social support describes close relationships people have with each other, typically within a family; the scenario presented in the question stem does not demonstrate social support (choice B is incorrect). A false consensus occurs when an individual believes that everyone else agrees with what they do; like social support, false consensus has no relevance to the scenario (choice C is incorrect). Socialization is the process of creating an individual identity based on what the individual learns from society's norms, values, and customs; socialization does not explain the social reaction to the ex-felon (choice D is incorrect).

5. **C** There are three ways that an individual's behavior may be motivated by social influences. Compliance is a desire to seek rewards or avoid punishment (choice A is a motivating factor and can be eliminated). Identification is the desire to be like another person or group (choice B is a motivating factor and can be eliminated). Internalization happens when values and beliefs are intergrated into a person's own value system and then drives their behavior (choice D is a motivating factor and can be eliminated). However, aggregation is not a term in sociology; an *aggregate* describes people who exist in the same space but do not share a common sense of identity (choice C is not a motivating behavior and is the correct answer choice).

6. **D** A "hangover identity" (also known as a role residual) can occur when several aspects persist for an individual from their ex-role even after completing the exiting process to their newly formed identity. According to the final paragraph, "the more involved an individual was in his former role, the more likely he is to have a higher role residual compared to someone who was not as committed to his previous role." Therefore, a newly retired individual who worked at the same company for a long time and was very involved with her coworkers would be most likely to experience "hangover identity" upon transitioning into her new role as retiree (choice D is correct). A biological male who has not begun the process of transitioning to female has not yet abandoned his former role (choice A is wrong), and neither the alcoholic nor the person married were committed to their roles for a significant amount of time (choices B and C are wrong).

Chapter 8
Social Structure

Humans live within societies and human behavior is best understood when considering the impact of the individual on the collective as well as the impact of the collective on the individual. By understanding social structures we can better understand the individual. Social structure, culture, and demographic factors also play an important role in an individual's health. Social stratification and inequality affect all societies across the globe, and afford power and privilege to some while denying it from others.

8.1 SOCIOLOGY: THEORETICAL APPROACHES

A **society** can be defined as the group of people who share a culture (discussed more in depth later in this chapter) and live/interact with each other within a definable area. **Sociology** attempts to understand the behavior of groups. Sociology is the study of how individuals interact with, shape, and are subsequently shaped by, the society in which they live. Cultural influences are important in understanding individuals, and sociologists consider both the actions of individuals and patterns of behavior in groups.

In order to understand how individuals behave in society, and how society impacts individuals, **three** main sociological frameworks have been developed, as well as numerous additional theories, some of which are introduced below. These broad frameworks, or theories, are used by sociologists to understand the behavior of societies.

A distinction can be made between the sociological theories in regards to their level of an analysis. **Macro-sociologists** are interested in large-scale structural considerations. Macro-level theories focus on the effects on structures on individual actions; interests include the mechanisms through which structures explain patterns of behavior. **Micro-sociologists** are interested in small-scale individual considerations. Micro-level theories focus on the effects of individuals on the social structure; interests include the mechanisms through which millions of individual interactions create an overall social impression. The concepts of social behavior and structures are interrelated: individuals impact structures and structures impact individuals.

Presented in this section are the three classical or traditional theoretical perspectives: the functionalist, conflict, and interactionist theories; and four more modern or recent perspectives: the feminist, social constructionist, rational choice, and social exchange theories. In addition to those discussed in depth here, there is an increasing collection of modern theories, such as the critical, field, and positivist theories. Furthermore, sociological tradition includes a number of subfields (for example, criminology) and interacts with many subjects in an interdisciplinary fashion (for example, social psychology), introducing additional theories discussed elsewhere in this book.

Functionalism (also known as Structural Functionalism)

The oldest of the main theories of sociology, **functionalism** is a view that conceptualizes society as a living organism with many different parts and organs, each of which has a distinct purpose. The approach focuses on the social functions of different structures by seeing what they contribute to society at large. For example, the contribution of our lungs to the body is to orchestrate the exchange of air. Similarly, we can think about the function of schools, churches, hospitals, and other social structures. Just like organs function interdependently to help the organism survive, social structures work together to sustain society. Similarly, just as an organism can thrive, evolve and grow, or become disease-addled and die, so can society.

Émile Durkheim, considered the father of sociology, was the pioneer of modern social research and established the field as separate and distinct from psychology and political philosophy. Durkheim was a major proponent of functionalism, and believed that modern societies were more complex than primitive societies, where people might be held together because they were all quite similar, sharing a common language, values, and symbols. In modern society, he argued, people might be quite dissimilar, but still relied upon each other to make the society function. Durkheim proposed that complex societies involved many different but interdependent parts working together to maintain stability, a type of **dynamic equilibrium**.

Healthy societies would be able to achieve and maintain this equilibrium, unhealthy ones would not. Durkheim further believed that society should always be viewed holistically—as a collective of social facts, rather than individuals. Social facts are the elements that serve some function in society, such as the laws, morals, values, religions, customs, rituals, and rules that make up a society.

There is a distinction in the functionalist framework made between manifest and latent functions. **Manifest functions** are the intended and obvious consequences of a structure, while **latent functions** are unintended or less recognizable consequences, and can be considered beneficial, neutral, or harmful. For example, the manifest function of a hospital may be to promote health in the populace, and a latent function may also be to reduce crime by creating more jobs in a community. It should be noted that not all of the effects of social structures are good. A social dysfunction is a process that has undesirable consequences, and may actually reduce the stability of society. For example, the hospital may also increase an income gap between medical professionals in the community and others or create racial tensions through unfair hiring practices.

While functionalism was the prevailing theory in sociology in the 1950s, many sociologists began to argue that it was unable to account for the many rapid sociological advances taking place in the 1960s and 1970s; though this theory is still considered useful in some respects, other theories have been developed to better explain sociological functions at a macro level.

Conflict Theory

Unlike the functionalist perspective, which emphasizes the harmony of parts, **conflict theory** views society as a competition for limited resources. According to conflict theory, society is a place where there will be inequality in resources; therefore, individuals will compete for social, political, and material resources like money, land, power, and leisure. Furthermore, social structures and institutions will reflect this competition in their degree of inherent inequality; certain groups and people will be able to amass more resources than others. Those with the most power and influence will maintain their positions of power by suppressing the advancement of others. This tension does not have to be violent, but could occur as negotiations, debates, and disputes. The theory focuses on those aspects that are functional for one group in society, but dysfunctional for another. For example, inequality in pay for women vs. men continues to be a source of tension in American society. Conflict theory often considers the discrepancies between dominant and disadvantaged groups.

Karl Marx, who is closely identified with this theory, looked at the economic conflict between different social classes. Marx argued that societies progress through class struggle between those who own and control production and those who labor and provide the manpower for production. He believed that capitalism produced internal tensions that would ultimately lead to self-destruction of capitalist society, to be replaced by socialism. **Ludwig Gumplowicz** expanded upon Marx's ideas by proposing that society is shaped by war and conquest, and that cultural and ethnic conflicts lead to certain groups becoming dominant over other groups. **Max Weber** agreed with Marx that inequalities in a capitalist system would lead to conflict, but he did not believe that the collapse of capitalism was inevitable; rather, he argued that there could be more than one source of conflict, such as conflict over inequalities in political power and social status. Weber also argued that there were several factors that moderated people's reaction to inequality, such as agreement with authority figures, high rates of social mobility, and low rates of class difference. Along with Émile Dukheim, Karl Marx and Max Weber are considered the three founding fathers of sociology.

More recently, conflict theory has been applied to inequalities between groups based on race and gender. Conflict theory has been used to explain the forces at work in maintaining a system of inequality that continues to oppress women and minority groups.

The major criticism of conflict theory is that it focuses too much on conflict and does not recognize the role of stability within society. Conflict theory (a) ignores the non-forceful ways in which people and groups reach agreement, (b) approaches society more from the perspective of those who lack power, and (c) focuses on economic factors almost exclusively as the sole issue for conflict within society.

Symbolic Interactionism

While the first two perspectives look at society from a macro (zoomed-out) perspective, **symbolic interactionism** starts at the micro (close-up) level and sees society as the buildup of these everyday typical interactions. Influenced by the work of George Herbert Mead (see section 7.1 for more details), this theory examines the relationship between individuals and society by focusing on communication, the exchange of information through language and symbols. Symbolic interactionism is particularly interested in the symbols that people use to contribute values and beliefs to others. For example, dress codes at the workplace can communicate a sense of whether the setting is casual or formal. The presence of bike lanes may communicate the values of a community. All of these small social changes combined create our overall impression of society. Symbolic interactionism sees the individual as active in shaping her society, instead of as merely being acted upon by society.

This theory analyzes society by addressing the subjective meanings that people impose upon objects, events, and behaviors. Subjective meaning is important, because people behave based on what they *believe to be true*, whether or not it actually is true. Therefore, society is constructed through human interpretation; people interpret one another's behaviors, and these interpretations form a social bond. Symbolic Interactionism holds the principal of *meaning* to be the central aspect of human behavior: (1) humans ascribe *meaning* to things and act toward those things based on their ascribed meaning; (2) *language* allows humans to generate meaning through social interaction with each other and society; (3) humans modify meanings through an interpretive *thought* process.

A specific type of interactionist philosophy is called the **dramaturgical approach**. As the name suggests, this assumes that people are theatrical performers and that everyday life is a stage. Just as actors project a certain on-screen image, people in society choose what kind of image they want to communicate verbally and non-verbally to others. For example, a college student who lands a coveted internship downtown will project a different image while at her internship than she will in class, and an even different image still when hanging out with her friends at a bar, or visiting her family in her childhood home. For more detail on dramaturgy, see Chapter 7. The primary criticism of this perspective is that research may not be objective and that the theory is focused too narrowly on symbolic interaction.

Feminist Theory

The feminist theory is concerned with the social experiences of both men and women and the differences between these experiences (for example, manhood versus womanhood and masculine versus feminine). Feminist sociologists strive to understand both the social structures contributing to gender differences (macro-level questions) and the effects of gender differences on individual interactions (micro-level questions). This approach is related to the concept of feminism, but feminism is better described as a collection of social movements with the purpose of establishing men and women as equals in terms of social rights, roles, statuses, and so forth. Because gender is a social construct, rather than some innate difference between people, sociologists are interested in the processes that create gender inequalities (more on gender in section 8.3). The feminist perspective uses this understanding to strive for a gender balance using techniques such as presenting the powerful contributions women have made to the world to gain the public's attention.

The feminist perspective sometimes extends to the idea of active oppression in which both individuals and structures maintain inequalities. Micro-level oppression can occur as the result of authoritative principles that allow men to restrict women. The use of violence in families is an example of this. Macro-level oppression can occur when economic, political, and other social structures permit the domination of women. The driving ban for women in Saudi Arabia is a high-profile modern example of this. Feminist theory can also extend to questions of intersectionality. These theorists are interested in the unique experiences of women of different classes, ethnicities, races, and so forth.

There is also intersection with numerous academic disciplines, concerning experts such as communication scholars, economists, epistemologists, historians, legal theorists, philosophers, political theorists, religious scholars, social geographers, and even artistic scholars. For example, an expert in politics might be interested in the historical fight for legal rights for women in terms of economic independence (the right to own properties), political representation (women's suffrage), and even their own bodies (reproductive rights). It is also of concern that women are underrepresented in politics. The **glass ceiling** is an invisible barrier that limits opportunities for the promotion of women in professional contexts. In most professional fields, women receive less power and prestige and are sometimes even prevented from progressing in position. This contributes to the gender **wage gap** in which men and women report consistent differences in income. For example, female doctors report lower salaries than male doctors, even when controlling for specialties. Further areas of interest to feminists include female bodies, language, motherhood, objectification, power, reproduction, and violence.

Rational Choice and Social Exchange Theories

Economic considerations also have a place in the sociological tradition. **Economics** is a social science concerned with resources, whether goods or services, and their production, distribution, and consumption by both individuals and groups (for example, corporations). Capitalist societies, in particular, are built on competition and thus economics influences social behavior. The related rational choice and social exchange models are both built on the premise that opportunities for profit motivate and drive human behavior; this behavior is goal-oriented. **Cost-benefit analysis** is an important component of the decision-making process; individuals make rational economic decisions to minimize costs and maximize benefits (cost-effective decisions). Economic theories assume that behaviors are utilitarian. The word "rational" refers to the idea that people accept that which will give them more and reject that which will give them less. There is thus a degree of self-interest in rational decisions. Both rational choice and exchange theories have similar assumptions, such as the assumption that individuals have possible alternatives and the freedom of choice to make decisions about these alternatives. Furthermore, although these theories are rooted in economic ideas, the processes still operate within the common social structure and are considered social norms.

The **rational choice theory** is concerned with decisions made between multiple courses of actions. This perspective argues that there is a simple instrumental reason for all choices: it provides the greatest reward at the lowest cost. In particular, rational choice is more concerned with measurable resources, such as information, money, and time (extrinsic costs), than subjective emotions, such as guilt (intrinsic costs). For example, students preparing for the MCAT must consider the most rational choice for their particular interest: a score that will earn them an acceptance to medical school. Rational choice theorists would argue that you chose the Princeton Review books for test preparation because it offered the greatest rewards (information) for the lowest costs (stress). The central premise is that all choice is rational with the specific intention to increase personal advantages and decrease personal disadvantages. It is not possible to have all that we want but we can make rational decisions to get the greatest overall satisfaction. For example, the rational choice model of voting states that election decisions are made based on which candidate offers the greatest personal benefits to the voter, although it does require some information about the potential effects of each alternative. Despite the action being political in nature, it is likened to a consumer choice. The rational choice theory allows scholars to model patterns of behavior, which thus allows the possibility of predicting future outcomes.

The related **social exchange theory** is concerned with decisions regarding multiple opportunities for interaction. The rational choice perspective explains that we assign different values to different courses of action and prefer the action with the greatest personal benefit. The social exchange perspective explains that decisions regarding interactions are similar; we assign punishments (costs) and rewards (benefits) to interactions and relationships and prefer those with the greatest personal benefits. While social exchanges are calculated and negotiated, their costs and rewards do not have to be economic in nature. People prefer approving interactions better than disapproving interactions just as we prefer credit over debt. Thus, rewards are those things with positive values; these benefits can be economic but can also be physical (a hug), psychological (support), or even subtle gestures (a smile). In contrast, punishments are those things with negative values; again, these costs can be economic but can also be physical (a shove), psychological (abandonment), or even subtle gestures (a frown). The subjective nature of the costs and benefits means that this perspective becomes more complicated but also more flexible.

According to this perspective, social exchange involves the exchange of resources: material or non-material, economic or social. In line with the goal of minimum costs and maximum benefits, the worth of a social interaction is measured according to the simple equation:

Profit from the interaction = rewards of the interaction – punishments of the interaction

The direction of the results (positive or negative) determines whether the interaction will occur. This equation also relates to reinforcement principles. Interactions with known positive worth based on past experiences will be continued and those with known negative worth will be discontinued. For example, couples considering whether to continue their marriage or file for divorce would consider the gains and losses associated with each choice, such as appearance, conversation, and intelligence, in order to make a rational decision that allows the most gratification. In fact, studies of interpersonal relationships are commonly applied by the social exchange model, but they can also be applied in other contexts, such as business research and parenting research. In all exchanges, the best relationships result from interactions with mutual benefits. It might seem as though economic perspectives present people as self-centered. However, individuals in relationships are often dependent on their partners; with the proper balance, interactions can reach equilibrium where partners complement one another in their give and take.

These theories have received similar criticism. In particular, descriptions of social behavior as mathematical calculations fail to consider additional influences in the complex process of decision-making. Thus, while the theories have useful properties, sociologists often pose additional questions. Furthermore, the rational choice model argues that all social realities are the result of individual actions and interactions, known as **methodological individualism**. Most sociologists agree that micro-level factors influence our perceived realities; however, this staunch viewpoint does not leave room to consider large-scale structures.

Social Constructionism

Social constructionism argues that people actively shape their reality through social interactions—it is therefore something that is constructed, not inherent. A major focus of social constructionism is to uncover the ways in which individuals and groups participate in the construction of their perceived social reality. A **social construct** is a concept or practice that is a construct of a group; essentially, everybody in society agrees to treat a certain aspect a certain way regardless of its inherent value. For example, money in itself is worthless—merely a piece of paper or metal—but because people have agreed that it is valuable, it has agreed-upon value. A social construct is something that isn't, necessarily, inherently true in nature.

Possibly one of the best examples of social construction is the institution of marriage. It is something that exists completely within the realm of human society and contains its own specific rules, morals, expectations, etc. Society has created certain ideas about how marriage is supposed to look, as well as how it is supposed to be fulfilled by individuals.

A major focus of social constructionists is the study of how individuals and groups participate in the construction of society and social reality. Social construction is a dynamic, ongoing process, which must be maintained, reaffirmed, and passed along to future generations. As you can possibly determine, a vast amount of our culture is socially constructed (in that it has a set of rules that are determined by societies whims, and trends). Rules and norms are not overarching, undeniable truths, but are created concepts. For example, there is some argument that gender and categories of sexual orientation are social constructs.

In actuality, there is evidence that sexual preference may be more of a fluid concept that exists on a continuum. Additionally, dating and marriage are socially constructed concepts, with the general trend in American society being that a man tends to be older than a woman in a heterosexual couple. This is a tendency that has been negotiated through social interactions. While these things are often taken for granted, social constructionism focuses on the social process (rather than the biological process) that drives the formation of these concepts that people may assume to be "real."

Theoretical Approach	Level of Analysis	Founder and Theorists
Functionalism	Macro-	Émile Durkheim
Conflict Theory	Macro-	Karl Marx Ludwig Gumplowicz Max Weber
Symbolic Interactionism	Micro-	George Herbert Mead
Feminist Theory	Both levels possible	–
Rational Choice Theory	Micro-	–
Social Exchange Theory	Micro-	–
Social Constructionism	Micro-	–

Table 1 Overview of Sociological Theoretical Approaches

8.2 SOCIAL INSTITUTIONS

Social institutions are complexes of roles, norms, and values organized into a relatively stable form that contribute to social order by governing the behavior of people. Social institutions provide predictability and organization for individuals within a society and mediate social behavior between people. Social institutions provide harmony, and allow for specialization and differentiation of skills. Examples of social institutions in the U.S. include our educational systems, family, religions, government, and health care systems.

Family

The family, in all of its many different forms, is part of all human cultures. A family may be defined as a set of people related by blood, marriage, adoption, or some other agreed-upon relationship that signifies some responsibility to each other. Over history, families have tended to serve five functions

1) Reproduction and the monitoring of sexual behavior
2) Protection
3) Socialization—passing down norms and values of society
4) Affection and companionship
5) Social status—social position is often based on family background and reputation

One way of conceptualizing family is to distinguish **nuclear family**, consisting of direct blood relations, and **extended** family, in which grandparents, aunts, uncles, and others are included. Across cultures and even within a culture, the members of the family that typically live together may vary.

The extension of a family through marriage can occur in many different ways. **Monogamy** refers to a form of marriage in which two individuals are married only to each other. **Polygamy** allows an individual to have multiple wives or husbands simultaneously. Throughout world history, polygamy has actually been more common than the monogamous relationships currently considered the norm in the U.S. There are two subtypes of polygamy. **Polygyny** refers to a man married to more than one woman while **polyandry** refers to a woman married to more than one man.

Marriage itself can have many different motivations. In the United States, it is popular for "love at first sight" and romance to be idealized as the basis of a strong marriage. Therefore, dating multiple people before getting married is common. However, in other cultures these feelings may be secondary or even perceived of as misleading. In societies with arranged marriages, parents or community figures are thought to have a better understanding of what makes a successful relationship and love is thought of as something that develops following the formation of a relationship. In others, assisted marriages are common, in which parents provide children with possible mates, out of which the child can choose. In choosing a mate, **endogamy** refers to the practice of marrying within a particular group. **Exogamy** refers to a requirement to marry outside a particular group, with it being the norm in almost all cultures to prohibit sexual relationships between certain relatives.

How we think about who we are related to is referred to as **kinship**. Kin do not have to live together, and kin is considered a cultural group rather than a biological one. Kinship groups may include extended family and members of the community or friends (like godparents and close family friends that are referred to as "aunts" and "uncles"). If kin groups involve both the maternal and paternal relations, this is called **bilateral descent**. Preference for paternal and maternal relations is called **patrilineal** and **matrilineal** descent, respectively.

Families may differ in terms of who has the power and authority to make decisions. In some families, each individual is given power over certain tasks, such as cooking, shopping, working, cleaning, and finances. There are three types of authority patterns based on gender. In a **patriarchy**, men have more authority than women and in a matriarchy, women have more authority than men. In an **egalitarian family**, spouses are treated as equals and may be involved in more negotiation when making decisions.

There are many alternatives to the traditional family that consists of a husband and wife with their 2.1 children, a dog, and a white picket fence in a middle-income neighborhood. A few of the differences seen in the United States are described as follows:

1) *Cultural differences:* many cultures emphasize the importance of extended family, often living with grandparents, cousins, and the like. In some cases, "kin" who are non-blood related members of the community may be considered part of the family.

2) *Divorce:* The divorce rate has generally risen in the United States due to several factors. First, there is a growing social and religious acceptance of divorce. Second, more and more opportunities are becoming available for women to succeed autonomously making divorce a real possibility. Third, the financial and legal barriers to divorce have lessened over time as it has become more common. This has opened the door to more nontraditional family structures, such as remarried and blended families, as well as single parent homes.

3) *Cohabitation:* there has been a large increase, especially among couples in their 20s and 30s in living together without getting married. These couples may be in a transitional phase heading toward marriage, or may choose not to get married at all. Sometimes these couples will have children and do many of the same things "traditionally" married couples do (like buy property and have a joint checking account) but remain legally unmarried.

4) *Lesbian and gay relationships:* Despite the Supreme Court ruling in 2015 to legalize same-sex marriage nationwide, there is still an ongoing debate about whether gay and lesbian couples *should* be allowed to marry and whether they *should* be allowed to raise a child. Research studies have not supported the assertion that children of gay couples have worse outcomes; however, gay and lesbian couples are still subject to discrimination. Nevertheless, lesbian and gay couples might also engage in all of the same behaviors that a "traditionally" married couple might, including property ownership and raising children.

Both individual and group experiences can threaten the strength of families. For example, the loss of a child can have negative effects for partner relationships. **Family violence** is a more dramatic example in which one member of the family is directly responsible for the threat through their mistreatment of another person, often in an attempt to gain power, leaving the target fearful and powerless. There are many aspects to violence: the harm can be threatened or actual, self-directed or other-directed, physical or non-physical, an isolated event or a repeating occurrence, and so on. **Child abuse** involves violence directed toward a child target. There are four categories of child abuse: physical abuse, emotional abuse, sexual abuse, and neglect. **Domestic abuse**, also referred to as dating abuse or spousal abuse, involves violence directed toward one partner of an intimate relationship, where the abuser is the second partner. **Elder abuse** involves violence directed toward an older target. The added element in elder abuse is that there is an expectation of trust from the older person, which is violated in the course of violence. The consequences of abuse are serious, ranging from lifelong mental health problems (such as post-traumatic stress disorder) and difficulties with social functioning (such as substance abuse) to death. Violence has effects for both the target and others with an awareness of the abuse, such as an older child who tries to intervene in the case of spousal abuse. Abuse has been linked to alcohol consumption, mental illness, and certain social conditions.

Education

Educational institutions have both manifest (stated) and latent (hidden) functions. Their manifest functions are to systematically pass down knowledge and to give status to those who have been educated. For example, patients trust doctors mainly because of the conferral of an awarded degree and subsequent licensure. This degree and licensure represents an agreed-upon amount of information, skills, and training acquired in order to practice medicine (something that was actually not always the case in the U.S.!). Latent functions are just as important; they include socialization, serving as agents of change, and maintaining social control.

As a social institution, schools transmit aspects of the dominant culture. School plays a role in teaching the dominant language and literature, holidays and traditions, historical figures and events, and exposes people to existing beliefs. This is not an entirely objective process and involves a significant degree of interpretation. Were the American colonists pioneers in a fight for independence or were they ungrateful rebels who did not appreciate Britain's guidance and protection? Schooling also helps maintain the current social norms by training students on discipline expected in institutions like the workplace, training for particular vocations, and even redirecting students to fit norms (for example, guidance counselors may steer male and female students into different traditional roles).

While many forms of student socialization are intentional (manners, learning to talk only when called on, learning to work independently), there are other lessons learned in school that may not be stated on the teacher's lesson plan. These lessons are known as the **hidden curriculum**. Students may be aware of the hidden curriculum because it can come into conflict with the manifest (stated) curriculum. For example, medical educators know that medical students experience a conflict between the stated values of their curriculum and the lived reality of hospital work they encounter during their third and fourth years. While students may have learned about the sanctity of patient care during their lectures, they often encounter hospital staff whose actions inadvertently teach them that patients are nuisances.

However, the existence of schools also allows for new, distinct ideas to form. College campuses allow for discussion through the blending of many different people and ideas. International students, LGBT students, and students of all different political beliefs have a common ground in which ideas can transform. Social change can also be implemented intentionally through changes in the school curriculum, for example, education about drug use or diversity is often a part of schooling.

Schooling, however, does not offer an equal opportunity to all. Certain benefits such as small class size, excellent teachers, and the availability of the latest technology and resources, are based on the socioeconomic status of the school district for public schools. The option of private school is only really an option for those in the higher income brackets. Access to higher education, a key factor in getting a good job, is also highly dependent on family income, as well as other factors (like whether or not children were encouraged by parents to apply to college, know where to find information about applying for loans, understand the process of applying to college, and so forth). Level of education then continues to be influential in terms of power, respect, and social standing. Our education system has often been criticized as one that serves to maintain or widen socioeconomic and privilege gaps. This is accomplished through the processes of educational segregation and stratification.

These processes lead to an informal type of **educational segregation**, the widening disparity between children from high-income neighborhoods and those from low-income neighborhoods. Since public schools receive funding from local taxes, and those schools located in wealthier neighborhoods receive more money—and arguably have better teachers—and are thus able to provide a stronger education to students.

Additionally, in wealthier neighborhoods, parents have the time and resources to be more involved, and would potentially intervene if there were something occurring at the school that they did not agree with (for example, if one of the teachers was doing a poor job, the parents would be more likely to get involved). On the other hand, children in poorer neighborhoods have public schools that are poorly funded, and teachers that may not get enough resources to do their job well. Consequently, poorer schools have higher teacher turnover, employ worse teachers (often the school is stuck with whomever they can get to fill the position), and provide a worse education to students (a fact that has been demonstrated by standardized test scores—though arguably not the best measure—for decades). Children from poorer neighborhoods also tend to have parents who do not have time to get involved in their education, often because both parents are working, sometimes more than one job, or a single parent is working one or more jobs to support the family. Even if conditions at the school are reprehensible, parents likely don't have the time to intervene, and even if they did intervene, they likely don't have many options for instigating change. Therefore, children from poorer neighborhoods:

- tend to attend poorer schools and are more likely than children from wealthier neighborhoods to receive poorer educations.
- either drop out of school before graduation or graduate with no intention of attending college; if they do pursue a college education, they are more likely than children from wealthier neighborhoods to pursue a vocational degree or an associate's degree.
- are far less likely than children from wealthier neighborhoods to pursue a four-year college degree, and even more unlikely to pursue education beyond college, like a graduate or medical degree.
- are more likely to end up with lower-paying jobs, and perpetuate the cycle of poverty for themselves, while children from wealthier neighborhoods are more likely to go to college, possibly even pursue an advanced degree beyond college, and end up with higher-paying jobs, perpetuating their own cycle of wealth.

However, it is not merely the misfortune of being born into a poor family or living in a poor neighborhood that can affect students' schooling trajectories—teachers can greatly affect students' achievement. Research has shown that teachers tend to quickly form expectations of individual students, and once they have formed these expectations, they tend to act toward the student with these expectations in mind. If the student accepts the teacher's expectations as reasonable, the student will begin to perform in accordance with them, as well. This is known as **teacher expectancy theory**. Teacher expectancy is often praised as something that helps children exceed their own expectations of themselves—this is the ideal of education. However, teachers are not free of stereotypes, and their expectations can have the effect of underestimating students. When these students then perform to meet their teacher's low expectations of them, they reinforce the teacher's stereotypes and simultaneously miss out on the opportunities for upward mobility education can provide.

Therefore, while education has long been touted as the path to upward mobility in the U.S., and there are certainly many exceptions (children from poor neighborhoods who become doctors and children from wealthy neighborhoods who drop out of high school), as a social institution education actually serves to reinforce and perpetuate social inequalities. This is known as **educational stratification**: a social arrangement—living in different areas, having parents with different levels of involvement, being able or unable to pay for private or higher education—that becomes entrenched through educational segregation and is reproduced in new generations of children, such that the children's educational achievements mirror those of their parents.

Religion

Organized religion is a social institution involving beliefs and practices. These practices are based on objects and ideas that are recognized as sacred, or extraordinary and worthy of reverence. The MCAT may include information regarding the forms of religious organizations, common information on the five major world religions, and the social functions of religion. The forms of religious organizations include the following:

1) **Ecclesia:** a dominant religious organization that includes most members of society, is recognized as the national or official religion, and tolerates no other religions. It is often integrated into political institutions, and people do not choose to participate but are born into the social institution. Examples of countries with this social structure are Sweden (Lutheranism is the official state religion) and Iran (Islam is the official state religion).

2) **Church:** a type of religious organization that is well-integrated into the larger society. Church membership tends to occur by birth, but most churches allow people to join. Congregations are typically concerned both with the sacred and ordinary aspects of life and have well-stipulated rules and regulations. Churches may be tied to the state (state church) or independent of it (denomination). An example in the U.S. is the Catholic Church.

3) **Sect:** a religious organization that is distinct from that of the larger society. Sects are often formed from breaking away from larger religious institutions. Over time, some sects may develop into churches. Membership may be by birth or through conversion. Sects may withdraw from the larger society to practice their beliefs and may be fairly exclusive. Examples of sects in the U.S. include the Mormon community and the Amish community.

4) **Cult / New religious movement:** a religious organization that is far outside society's norms and often involves a very different lifestyle. Cult members have a bad reputation and are quickly judged by society to be "crazy," but remember that many of the world's dominant religions including Christianity, Islam, and Judaism, started as cults. Examples of cults in the U.S. include the Branch Davidians and Heaven's Gate.

From a functionalist standpoint, religion can create social cohesion (as well as dissent), social change (as well as control), and provide believers with meaning and purpose. Social cohesion is often experienced by members of religious groups due to the system of shared beliefs and values that it provides. Religious communities can be a source of emotional, spiritual, and material support in difficult times. However, religion can also be a source of social dissent, as a history of violence between religious factions indicates. Religion can be a vehicle for social change. Teachings such as the Protestant work ethic have a profound impact on how members live their lives. Liberation theology refers to the use of the church in a political effort against various social issues, such as poverty and injustice. However, religious principles can also be used as a means of social control, to create laws and regulations, attribute social statuses, and determine gender roles. Religion is a powerful social institution that can influence members of society in different ways depending on the context.

Religion and social change has been a major research topic. Religion can prompt social change as mentioned above, but there are also cases where it must respond to social change (such as with **modernization**, the transformation from traditional social structures to more "rational" or economics-driven ones). Modern societies are often more complex; social structures become more bureaucratic and institutions become more specialized. Religion is often moved from the public sphere to the private sphere as it becomes a separate institution. There is an ideological component to modernization. The term "modern" often has positive connotations; modern things are seen as attractive and up-to-date. The term "traditional" often has negative connotations; traditional things are seen as less attractive and out-of-date. The classical sociologists predicted that as societies became more modern, there would be a decline in religious practice in favor of more rational thought. Thus, modernization has contributed to the loss of close identification with traditional religious beliefs and practices. **Secularization** is the process through which religion loses its social significance in modern societies. For the individual, there is a decline in religious observance. For the societies, there is a decline in the public influence of religious leaders. However, evidence of secularization is contested and even in the United States, religious factors continue to influence economics and politics. **Fundamentalism** is a second response to modernist societies in which there is strong attachment to traditional religious beliefs and practices. There is a strict adherence to basic religious doctrines resulting from a literalist interpretation of these texts. Fundamentalists argue that religion should be an integral part of social life. Thus, fundamentalist groups are often concerned with political issues such as abortion and same-sex marriage. There are fundamentalist movements in all religions; for example, the Westboro Baptist Church or Muslim Brotherhood.

A very brief overview of the five major world religions is as follows:

1) **Christianity** is the largest single faith in the world, with about 30% of the population across the globe identifying as Christian, though there are multiple denominations. About 80% of people in the United States identify as Christian and although church and state are legally separate, many social and political matters reference God. Christianity is monotheistic (one God), and its followers also believe in prophets (Jesus as the Son of God), an afterlife, and a judgment day.

2) **Islam** is the second largest religion in the world. Its followers are known as Muslims, and it is estimated that between 20–25% of the world's population is Muslim. It is also monotheistic (Allah), and its followers believe in prophets (with the final one being Mohammad), an afterlife, and judgment day. Muslim governments often do not separate religion and state and often religion dictates law in Muslim countries. Muslim cultures vary in their norms, with issues such as the veil worn by women being cultural rather than religious.

3) **Hinduism** developed in India and is a polytheistic religion (many gods) practiced by about 14% of the world's population, although there are major deities such as Shiva and Vishnu. Hinduism also includes a belief in reincarnation, or rebirth after death.

4) **Buddhism** developed based on the teachings of Siddhartha, later known as Buddha, in India. Buddhists believe in overcoming cravings for physical or material pleasures primarily through meditative practices.

5) **Sikhism** is a monotheistic religion that is practiced by roughly 0.35% of the world's population. Sikh's believes in one god and the teachings of the ten Gurus.

6) **Judaism** is also monotheistic and formed the historical basis for Christianity and Islam. Jews believe that God formed a covenant with Abraham and Sarah, and that if certain rules were followed (the Ten Commandments), God would bring paradise to Earth. Jews make up about 0.22% of the world's population, and modern Israel is a Jewish state that tightly intertwines religion and law.

There are many individual differences among people who consider themselves members of a particular religion. **Religiosity** refers to the extent of influence of religion in a person's life. Some may be very devout, with the extreme form being **fundamentalists**, who adhere strictly to religious beliefs. Others may adhere more to the beliefs of the religion without the rituals or to the rituals without the beliefs. Still others may define themselves by some sort of religion but do not practice their religion actively or attend any formal religious events (for example, someone with Jewish parents might define themselves as Jewish but not celebrate any Jewish holidays, attend synagogue, or otherwise practice Judaism in any way).

Government and Economy

Our political and economic structures both influence and are influenced by social structure. Power structures are a fundamental part of both politics and economics (consider the Marxist theories discussed in section 8.1). Governments across the world derive their power from different places. The United States government is one based on **rational-legal authority**, legal rules and regulations are stipulated in a document like the Constitution. Many corporations, including health care organizations, work within this structure and are often organized in a similar way. Other governments around the world may derive power from **traditional authority**, power due to custom, tradition, or accepted practice. Still other leaders may be powerful due to **charismatic authority**, the power of their persuasion. Martin Luther King, Jr. was a charismatic leader whose voice was the source of his power.

Traditional governance was often uncentralized (bands and tribes), but modern governance is often more centralized (states). Historical examples of governance also include supranational governments in which independent nations made political alliances (empires). Political sociologists are interested in the relationship between the government and the people; these scholars are concerned with the organization of governments in terms of the distribution of power and the effects of this distribution on social control. **Aristarchic governments** are controlled by a small group of people, selected based on specific qualifications, with decision-making power; the public is not involved in most political decisions. Aristarchies include **aristocracies** (those ruled by elite citizens, like those with noble births) and **meritocracies** (those ruled by the meritorious, like those with a record of meaningful social contributions). **Autocratic governments** are controlled by a single person, or a selective small group, with absolute decision-making power. Autocracies include **dictatorships** (those ruled by one person) and **fascist governments** (those ruled by a small group of leaders). **Monarchic governments** are controlled by a single person, or a selective small group, who inherited their leadership role, like kings and queens. There are both absolute and constitutional monarchies, in which leaders are limited through formal constitutions.

There are also concerns of how the leadership is elected. **Authoritarian governments** consist of unelected leaders; the public might have some individual freedoms but have no control over representation. Authoritarianisms include **totalitarianism** (those in which unelected leaders regulate both public and private life through coercive means of control). **Democratic governments** consist of elected leaders; the public has some degree of political decision-making power through either direct decisions or representation. Democracies include **direct democracies** (governments in which there is direct public participation) and **representative democracies** (governments in which there is indirect public participation through the election of representatives). Democratic structures are common in the Western world, such as in the United States, where most of the population is granted the right to vote through public elections, although there might not be an equal distribution of this decision-making power (for example, minorities have been denied the right to vote in the past). This often results in the formation of **political parties**, formal groups of people that share the same principle political beliefs and organize with a common purpose of ensuring governance that supports these principles through appropriate policies. **Oligarchic governments** are less clear as leaders can be elected or unelected; the public might have the power to elect representation, but people have little influence in directing decisions and social change. Oligarchies are controlled by a small group of people with shared interests; for example, theocracies are governments ruled by religious elite.

Finally, the structure of governments can be studied. **Republican governments** consider their countries to be public concerns and are thus democratic in nature, meaning that the people have the supreme power in these societies. **Federalist governments** include a governing representative head that shares power with constituent groups. There is the division between the central government, or the federal government, and the constituent governments, or the state, provincial, and local governments. **Parliamentary governments** include both executive and legislative branches that are interconnected; members of the executive branch (ministers) are accountable to members of the legislature. **Presidential governments** also include organizing branches, as well as a head of state.

Other political concepts include **anarchy**, which refers to societies without a public government; here, there is a common implication of "lawlessness." **Economics** is concerned with the production, distribution, and consumption of resources, both goods and services. Most economic structures fit into one of four categories: command, market, mixed, or traditional. In **command economies**, also known as **planned economies**, economic decisions are based on a plan of production and the means of production are often public (state owned); these include socialism and communism. In **market economies**, economic decisions are based on the market ("supply and demand") and the means of production are often private; these include laissez-faire and free market economies. **Mixed economies** blend elements of command and market economies with both public and private ownership. There are various forms of mixed economics; for example, in some societies, there is public oversight, and even funding, of private production, such as in the United States. **Traditional economies** consider social customs in economic decisions; this practice is most common in rural areas and often involves bartering and trading.

In addition to deriving power from rational-legal authority, our political and economic system is influenced greatly by capitalist ideals, although the United States is not purely capitalist. **Capitalism** is an economic system in which resources and production are mainly privately owned, and goods/services are produced for a profit. The driving force in capitalist societies is the pursuit of personal profit. It is thought that the advantages of capitalism are that it benefits the consumer by allowing for competition, which theoretically promotes higher quality and lower price of goods and services. Capitalism is also thought to emphasize personal freedom, by limiting government restrictions and regulations.

On the other hand, **socialism** is an economic system where resources and production are collectively owned. Socialism includes a system of production and distribution designed to satisfy human needs (good/services are produced for direct use instead of for profit). Private property is limited and government intervenes to share property amongst all. The driving force in socialist societies is collective goals; everyone is given a job and everyone is provided with what they need to survive. In socialist societies, the economy is usually centrally controlled and run by the government. **Communism** is a specific socialist structure in which there is common ownership of the means of production, but also the absence of currencies, classes, and states, based on shared economic, political, and social ideologies.

Most nations incorporate both capitalist and socialist ideas. **Welfare capitalism** is a system in which most of the economy is private with the exception of extensive social welfare programs to serve certain needs within society. Most countries in Western Europe demonstrate welfare capitalism because most of their economies are based on capitalist principles, but universal health care is provided by the state. **State capitalism** is a system in which companies are privately run, but work closely with the government in forming laws and regulations. In the United States, most businesses are privately owned, but the government runs many operations, such as schools, the postal service, museums, and the military. However, most hospitals and other health care providers, as well as insurance companies, remain privately run in the U.S. (though this may be changing).

Numerous trends have led to the economic system that currently exists. Notably, the Information Revolution has been followed by a deindustrialization. Instead of focusing on tangible products, the emphasis has shifted to intangible products, such as information technology and services. This has changed the focus from factory work to work that can be done almost anywhere, and emphasizes literacy over mechanical skills. This shift has led to a focus on **professions**, highly esteemed white-collar occupations that require a great deal of education.

The **division of labor** occurs as societies become so complex that it is not possible for an individual to meet all of his or her needs alone, such as happened with the rise of capitalism. Different occupations emerge as a response; these occupations are specialized to serve a specific social need (for example, doctors can treat medical problems and mechanics can address our automobile issues). Because individuals no longer participate in all of the activities required for survival, there is an increase in interdependence. The division of labor has had both positive and negative consequences for social order; for example, it has increased the rate of production but it has also decreased the similarities in social experience among individuals, contributing to class differences. Thus, the division of labor is about more than economic interests.

Durkheim contributed to our current understanding of the division of labor and differentiated between two forms of social solidarity in relation to economic approaches. **Mechanical solidarity** allows society to remain integrated because individuals have common beliefs that lead to each person having the same fundamental experience. Individuals share a **collective conscience**, which presumes the existence of a greater social order that guides individual actions through shared beliefs, morals, and values. This is common in primitive, traditional societies, like agricultural societies. **Organic solidarity** allows society to integrate through a division of labor, which leads to each person having a different personal experience; thus, each movement is distinguishable and separate. This is common in advanced, modern societies, like industrial societies, and often occurs as the concentration of people in a given area grows.

Health and Medicine

Medicine is the social institution that governs health and illness, particularly with respect to diagnosis, treatment, and prevention of illness. The **delivery of health care** in the United States is accomplished by teams of health-care providers with different training backgrounds and specialty areas, such as physicians and nurses of all specialties, physical and occupational therapists, dentists, hospitalists, social workers, community health workers, caregivers, pharmacists, alternative medicine providers, and rehabilitative therapists—to name only a few! The delivery of health care is organized into different levels: primary, secondary, and tertiary care. Primary care describes the care provider responsible for ongoing preventative care or disease management, or community-based care (such as an urgent care center). Secondary care includes acute care (emergency department), as well as specialty care, which is often received following a referral from a primary care provider. Tertiary care is a very specialized form of health care. It is based on consultations with specialist care providers and often occurs in hospitals or care facilities designed just for the purpose of caring for patients with a limited set of conditions. Examples of tertiary care include cancer hospitals, burn centers, and palliative care (end-of-life care) facilities. It is also important to remember that community centers and agencies can provide para-medical care, such as patient education, in-home care work, and public health outreach.

Society plays a large role in defining health/illness and acceptable health care practices. For example, societies differ in the degree of emphasis that they put on physical health versus mental health. In many nations, ADHD and depression are not considered illnesses and are not treated. The United States has experienced the spread of the **medical model of disease**, which emphasizes physical or medical factors as being the cause of all illness. Because the medical model characterizes all illness as having a physiological or pathological basis, the medical profession has been able to reframe many conditions as disease states based on the success of empirical treatment or the hope that scientific research will eventually expose the underlying cause of disease. The process by which a condition comes to be reconceptualized as a disease with a medical diagnosis and a medical treatment is known as **medicalization**. When medicalization results in medical explanations for social problems, the physician can act as the expert on a variety of issues including child development, criminality, drug addiction, and depression—issues that were formerly part of the expertise of other professions, such as the church or the legal profession. However, the medical model is only one way of understanding illness, and it does not always describe illness from the patient's point of view.

An alternate way of understanding illness is known as the **social model of disease**. The social model of disease emphasizes the effect one's social class, employment status, neighborhood, exposure to environmental toxins, diet, and many other factors can have on a person's health. While someone working from the perspective of the medical model might look for the *ultimate* cause of a person's illness (for example, pneumonia resulting from exposure to the bacterium *streptococcus pneumoniae*), someone working from the social model would be attuned to a more *proximate* cause—something about the patient's life circumstances that put him/her at greater risk of exposure to the bacterium. Although the medical model remains the dominant form of clinical reasoning in medical care, there has been an emphasis on the biopsychosocial aspects of medical care (hence the presence of this material on the MCAT). This model aims to take into consideration the psychological, social, and cultural factors that influence health, including perception of illness, beliefs about health, community practices, etc. that may affect emotional states, medication compliance, and a multitude of other health-related outcomes.

The social model of disease, as discussed above, postulates that social pressures create the conditions for health and illness. The field that studies how social organization contributes to the prevalence, incidence and distribution of disease across and within populations is known as **social epidemiology**. Being low-income can predispose individuals to conditions that limit individuals' ability to eat healthy food, exercise, get enough sleep, and avoid the long-term effects of severe stressors. First, low-income individuals often work multiple jobs to try to make ends meet and provide for their children. This type of work schedule does not leave much time for exercise and can contribute to obesity among low-income populations. Second, some low-income neighborhoods are not safe for adults or children to exercise outside. In addition, the climate may not allow for outdoor exercise even in safe neighborhoods, and low-income people are often not able to afford gym memberships. Third, low-income people who work many jobs often sacrifice sleep to do so. Under conditions of sleep deprivation, the body is unable to regulate leptin, a satiety hormone. When leptin levels are low, individuals do not feel sated after eating, and may consume more food as a result. Lack of sleep may also contribute to difficulties in coping with stressors. Fourth, very low-income neighborhoods are often food deserts. A **food desert** is an area where healthy, fresh food is difficult to find because there are no proper grocery stores (a liquor store or convenience store may be the only option in a food desert). Because of a lack of grocery stores, people in lower-income neighborhoods are more likely to eat high-calorie foods that have low nutritional value, such as fast food. In addition to being readily available, these foods are fast and inexpensive, important attributes for low-income people who are trying to support themselves and their families on very little disposable income, all while working several jobs. Last, living paycheck-to-paycheck is extremely stressful. The effects of chronic stress on the body take their toll as poor health: low infant birth weight, high blood pressure, overweight, and cognitive deficits, to name only a few.

Health care needs vary by population. On a macroscopic level, there are disparities in the distribution of disease across the world. In the United States (as is the case in many high-income nations), there is a focus on treating (and to some degree preventing) chronic conditions such as obesity, heart disease, and cancer. However, in lower-income nations, the focus is on treating more acute illnesses; this is largely because the threat is more immediate (particularly in areas that have minimal access to vaccinations, antibiotics, and clean water), and the incidence of chronic illness is much lower.

Being ill impacts not only the patient, but also the patient's social networks. Two main sociological concepts describe what illness can be like for a patient. One concept, the sick role, describes society's response to illness. The second concept, illness experience, explains the patient's subjective experience of illness.

The **sick role** is a concept developed by American sociologist Talcott Parsons. According to this concept, when a person is ill, he or she is not able to be a contributing member of society. Being ill, from Parsons' point of view, is a type of deviance. For others to take up the extra work in this person's absence they must consider the person's illness to be legitimate—they must sanction this person's deviance by exempting him/her from normal social roles and by not blaming the person for his or her illness. In return, the person must fulfill the role obligations of an ill person: the person should seek medical care and the person should make a sincere attempt to get well.

However, the sick role concept does not always hold up empirically. Other sociologists have pointed out the limitations of this role for those with chronic disease, stigmatized diseases, and "lifestyle" diseases. For example, if a person is suffering from a condition about which little is known, such as fibromyalgia, others may not accept that the person is actually ill and not confer the legitimation of the sick role. Second, the sick role concept was developed to describe acute illness and cannot explain chronic illness, where a person has good days and bad days, and often must carry on with normal life despite poor health. A person with chronic illness also cannot fulfill the social obligation to get well that the sick role imposes. Last, although one of the rights of the patient according to the sick role concept is that individuals should not be blamed for their illness, sometimes people are blamed for their poor health. This is particularly the case when others see the person's disease as a result of their lifestyle (for example, cirrhosis as a result of chronic alcohol consumption).

Other research has examined the type of doctor-patient relationship the sick role concept implies. The sick role implies a passive patient and an authoritative physician. Not only does this ignore the ways that gender, race, age, class, and other social variables affect the doctor-patient relationship, it also ignores the patient's subjectivity. Perhaps the patient rejects the passivity of the sick role. Perhaps the patient does not want to be seen as sick at all. Research on **illness experience** therefore takes the patient's subjective experience of illness as its main concern. When studying illness experience, sociologists are not just interested in the meanings people give to their illness, but also how the experience of being ill affects patients' daily lives—their ability to work, spend time with friends and family, and cultivate their selves. Illness experience is particularly important to consider in light of chronic disease. With a chronic disease a patient can have no reasonable expectation of getting better; thus she or he must adjust normal daily life to fit the constraints of the illness. This process can be isolating and destabilize one's sense of self, which is largely founded on the activities of normal life, hobbies and work, and one's relationships. Self-concept and daily activities reinforce each other, so illness experience encompasses both the individual's understanding of his or her condition as well as the material impact being ill has on that person's daily life.

8.3 CULTURE AND DEMOGRAPHICS

Culture

Culture simply refers to a shared way of life, including the beliefs and practices that a social group shares. Although cultures can vary a great deal, they are composed of some common elements. **Symbolic culture** consists of symbols that are recognized by people of the same culture. Symbols convey agreed-upon meaning, can communicate the values and norms of the culture, and include rituals, gestures, signs, and words that help people within a society communicate and understand each other. Some examples of symbols in the United States include the following:

- the Statue of Liberty, meant to symbolize independence and equal opportunity
- "ummm" as the sound someone makes when he or she is thinking
- a nod, a gesture indicating the affirmative
- a band on the ring finger of the left hand indicating marriage (or engagement, if the ring has a diamond)
- a red octagon at an intersection, signifying that a driver needs to stop

Symbols and rituals can differ between cultures, for example, some cultures celebrate the life of a deceased relative with a party while others mourn at a more somber funeral.

Language and the alphabet it is based on are really just formal systems of symbols that allow people to communicate. **Language** (discussed in Chapter 4) is a symbolic system that is codified for communication. Letters in an alphabet (or characters in other cultures) have specific meaning, and are combined to form words (which also have agreed-upon meaning) and words combine for sentences. Language evolves constantly, and is vital for shaping ideas about who we are relative to each other in society. The **Sapir-Whorf hypothesis** asserts that people understand their world through language and that language, in turn, shapes how we experience our world.

While symbolic elements of culture involve values and norms, **material culture** involves physical objects or artifacts. This includes clothing, hairstyles, food, and the design of homes. The importance placed on material objects can reflect the culture's values; for example, the American dream often includes a car, a symbol of mobility and independence. In contrast, **non-material culture** is specific to social thoughts and ideas, such as values (described below).

Popular culture is a phrase used to describe features of culture that appeal to the masses, often those communicated through mass media such as radio and television. This is distinguished from **high culture**, which describes those features often limited to the consumption of the elite, like the ballet or opera. However, because the elite tend to control the outlets for popular culture, some non-mainstream groups have denounced it for reasons such as its consumerist nature. Popular culture has its own **cultural icons**, which are signs that represent their meaning in a given culture. The cross is representative of the Christian religion; in a similar fashion, the single crystal-encrusted glove is representative of Michael Jackson and can be called *iconic*.

While comparing different cultures is useful for noticing differences, some anthropologists assert that there are also some cultural **universals**—patterns or traits that are common to all people. Cultural universals tend to pertain to basic human survival and needs, such as securing food and shelter, and also pertain to events that every human experiences, including birth, death, and illness. Despite these very important similarities that unite us all, cultural differences are far more common than cultural universals.

Two of the most crucial elements of culture are its values and beliefs. People within a given culture tend to share common values and beliefs. **Values** can be defined as a culture's standard for evaluating what is good or bad, while **beliefs** are the convictions or principles that people hold. Values often define how people in a society should behave, but they may not actually reflect how people do behave. For example, in the U.S., open-mindedness and tolerance are considered to be values, yet examples of racism and homophobia abound. In order to promote societal values, laws, sanction, or rewards may be in place to encourage behavior in line with social values and discourage behavior counter to social values. For example, it is against the law to discriminate based on race, color, religion, sex, or national origin when making employment decisions. **Norms** (discussed in more detail in Chapter 7) are the visible and invisible rules of social conduct within a society. Norms help define what types of behaviors are acceptable and in accordance with a society's values and beliefs.

Culture and Social Groups

Sociobiology is a study of how biology and evolution have affected human social behavior. Primarily, it applies Darwin's principle of natural selection to social behavior, suggesting there is a biological basis for many behaviors. That is, particular social behaviors persist over generations because they are adaptive for survival. For example, sexual behavior may vary by gender because men have a lower investment in reproduction than women, who have to carry the baby for nine months. Aggression may also manifest in different ways in society based on biological drives, with men committing more violent crimes than women. Sociobiologists would argue that biological predisposition is influenced by social factors. An aggressive individual may learn to channel these tendencies away from socially unacceptable acts (for example, assault) and toward socially accepted activities (for example, cage-fighting).

Scientists also believe that the origins of culture lie in human evolution. Through time, humans in various societies evolved the ability to categorize and communicate human experience through the use of symbols (as discussed above). As these codified systems for communication were learned and taught to future generations, they began to develop independently of human evolution. While people living in different areas will likely develop their own unique cultures, culture can still be taught and learned. Therefore, anthropologists consider culture to be not just a product of human evolution, but a complement to it; it is a means of social adaptation to the natural world.

Social Construction and Transformation

Cultural diffusion is the transfer of elements of culture—social ideas and processes such as religious traditions—from one social group to another. This contributes to cultural similarities between different societies. Diffusion can also occur within a single culture, leading to some similarities in beliefs even in different levels of societies (such as among different classes). It can be direct or indirect, or sometimes even forced, as with cultural imperialism. The rate of diffusion has increased as a result of modern conveniences that offer opportunities for cross-cultural communication, like modern media and transportation.

This is important for **cultural competence** or effective interactions between people from different cultures. For example, in medicine, the diffusion of cultural understanding—which leads to effective communication—is an important element in reducing disparities in health and health care. **Cultural transmission** is the process through which this information is spread across generations, or the mechanisms of learning. For example, a meme is an element of culture that spreads from person to person; cultural transmission is concerned with how this occurs. Learning is a social process that occurs through individual experiences in which we attach different meanings to different things; we then learn to remember and respond to these meanings. Much transmission occurs through socialization processes.

Social construction suggests that our realities are produced and reproduced; elements of culture are not static. In some cases, **social change** occurs, in which societies experience a change in state. This can be subtle, like with the development of new linguistic phrases, or radical, like with **revolutions**, which involve fundamental changes and social restructuring. Transformative social changes, such as technological innovations, often challenge our understanding of the world because there is no social consensus about the new innovation; the creation of new social rules "lags" behind. This is described as **cultural lag**. The period of cultural lag can cause social problems, such as protests, because the process of adaption is difficult. The foundational work on cultural lag explained that material culture changes much faster than non-material culture, which often resists change. For example, medical advancements in surgical procedures now provide the option of permanent contraception (such as vasectomies for men and tubal ligations for women). These options raise serious ethical questions about reproduction that did not concern past generations. The technologies progressed (social change), but the new rules are still less clear.

When individuals experience changes, such as social changes, that necessitate a period of adjustment, there is often **transition shock**. When this disorientation is the result of an individual being subjected to alternative cultures and foreign environments, such as through leisure travel or permanent relocation, it is called **culture shock**. This is a real experience that involves deeper emotions than homesickness; it challenges an individual's assumptions about their social surroundings. Different cultures have different cuisines, fashions, languages, signs, etc., and individuals must grow accustomed to all of these changes. For example, the transition to medical school causes a definite reaction for most students; there is a feeling of "information overload" as the result of exposure to unfamiliar content and the disruption of people's previous schedules. **Reverse culture shock** involves the same experiences but upon an individual's return to their initial environment.

Sociocultural evolution is a set of theories describing the processes through which societies and cultures have progressed over time. Both individual behavior and social structures experience continuous transformation in response to their complex needs. Sociologists argue that these changes are the result of social factors, such as social interactions, rather than biological factors. Thus, sociocultural evolution is less concerned with the evolution of human bodies, but instead questions how human minds have evolved for us to succeed as beings with natural social tendencies. Historical studies have revealed a lot of societies throughout time, but today, there exist just a couple hundred as the result of natural growths and declines. Two modern theories of sociocultural evolution, *modernization* and *sociobiology*, are discussed previously.

POPULATION STUDIES

Human **population** is the collection of people in a defined geographical area, and also refers to the number of people in the area. Population studies are interested in demographic shifts and can be quite complex. There is periodic population growth and population decline as a result of a plethora of factors including birth rates, death rates, and migration rates. The world as a whole is experiencing a period of population growth (the annual growth rate is 1.2%) that is predicted to continue for many decades. Much of this growth is attributed to advances in agricultural production (the green revolution) and innovations in medicine that have contributed to changes in birth and death rates. In contrast, studies of population decline are often concerned with great reductions in population as a result of catastrophes, such as epidemics and massacres, or widespread social changes (such as rural flight). Population growth and decline are measured using the **population growth rate**: the rate of population change in a specified time period, reported as a percent of the initial population (positive rates indicate increases and negative rates indicate decreases).

There are concerns with population increases and decreases both. For example, in societies experiencing growth, there is concern of reaching **overpopulation**, at which point there are more people than can be sustained; in societies experiencing decline, there are concerns about maintaining economic success. The total possible population that can be supported with relevant resources and without significant negative effects in a given area is referred to as the **carrying capacity**. Populations tend to increase and decrease until **population equilibrium** is met at this maximum load.

Population projections are estimates of future populations made from mathematical extrapolations of previous data. Traditional projections are based on birth rates, death rates, and migration rates, and thus do not consider unpredicted effects on population, like the chance of catastrophes. The global population reached seven billion in 2011. Experts project an increase in this population until at least 2050 with upper estimates ranging from 9 to 11 billion despite decreases in worldwide fertility rates. The projections suggest that the greatest contributions will be made in less-developed regions. In fact, nine countries are expected to contribute to more than half of the world's population; these countries are underdeveloped regions, including China and India, with the exception of the United States where international migration rates are an important consideration. In contrast, in some developed regions, the death rate exceeds the birth rate, which coupled with the increasing life expectancies suggests population declines; however, migration is expected to balance this (an unchanged population). Last, there are projected declines in some countries, such as the Eastern European countries where there are high death rates and high emigration rates as the result of devastating genocides.

Population distributions—in particular, age and sex distributions—are sometimes represented through graphical illustrations called **population pyramids** (Figure 1). These representations create age- and sex-specific groups (cohorts) using either total population (the number of people in each group) or percentages (the percentage of the total population in each group). The x-axis represents the population and y-axis separates men and women with the tradition positioning males on the left and females on the right. This creates a clear and distinct shape that describes the social structure. For example, an expansive population pyramid is wide at the base, representing a high birth rate and a high death rate. Thus, population pyramids can help predict population trends and determine the social needs for dependents, such as children and people of retirement age.

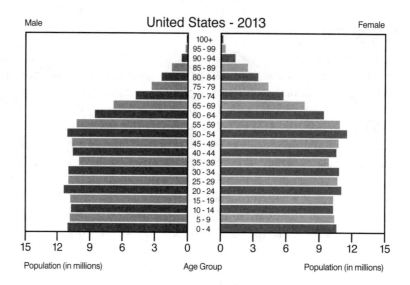

Figure 1 Population Pyramid: Birth Rates, Death Rates, and Migration Rates are the Main Determinants of Changes in Population

Fertility and Mortality

Birth rates and death rates are often reported through statistical measures. The **crude birth rate** (CBR) is the annual number of births per 1,000 people in a population. Experts consider crude birth rates of 10-20 to be low and those of 40-50 to be high. Worldwide, Japan has the lowest birth rate and Niger has the highest birth rate. The **crude death rate** (CDR) is the annual number of deaths per 1,000 persons in a population. Experts consider crude death rates below 10 to be low and those above 20 to be high. World-wide, death rates are highest in sub-Saharan African nations. The **rate of population change** is the difference between the crude birth rate and crude death rate. There are also **age-specific birth rates** and **age-specific death rates**, which are the annual number of births or deaths per 1,000 persons in an age group.

Regarding increases in population, in broad terms, **fertility** is the ability of a woman to reproduce and **fecundity** is the potential reproductive capacity of a woman. The **general fertility rate** is the annual number of births per 1,000 women in a population. The more complicated measure of **total fertility rate** predicts the total number births per single woman in a population with the assumption that the woman experiences the current recorded age-specific fertility rates and reaches the end of her reproductive life. Most women are capable of reproduction between the ages of 15 and 45 ("childbearing years"). The **replacement fertility rate** is the fertility rate at which the population will remain balanced, and **sub-replacement fertility** indicates that the birth rate is less than the death rate, thus the population size will not be sustained. The **population-lag effect** refers to the fact that changes in total fertility rates are often not reflected in the birth rate for several generations. This is the result of **population momentum**, in which the children produced during periods of higher fertility rates reproduce; there are more women of reproductive age and thus more births overall, regardless of the number of births per women. Because crude birth rates do not consider age or sex differences, fertility rates offer a clearer idea of demographic trends. For example, fertility rates have increased in the older age groups as women pursue education and participate in the labor force at greater rates, thus beginning reproduction later in life. There are countries around the world with policies to regulate population growth and decline through policing births, such as China's one child policy. Numerous social considerations, such as education, race, socioeconomic status, and even geographical location, have effects on fertility rates.

Regarding decreases in population, **mortality** refers to the death rate in a population, and this also includes both general and specific measures. This is distinguished from **morbidity**, which refers to the nature and extent of disease in a population; the **prevalence rate** measures the number of individuals experiencing a disease and the **incidence rate** measures the number of new cases of a disease. Reference to death rates in medicine often concern the **case fatality rate**, which measures deaths as the result of a set diagnosis or procedure, sometimes specific to the beginning or late stages. The current leading cause of death worldwide is ischemic heart disease, but there are also variations in causes of death by location; for example, age-related issues are a major cause of death in developed countries while malnutrition is a major cause of death in developing countries. There is an inverse correlation between a nation's crude death rate and its gross domestic product (GDP). The crude death rate is not sensitive to factors with a natural correlation to death, such as age structure. Thus, there are two additional common and reliable indicators of important qualities of life: the infant mortality rate and life expectancy. The **infant mortality rate** is the annual number of deaths per 1,000 infants under one year of age. This rate is lowest in European countries, such as Iceland, at a low of 5 and highest in the sub-Saharan regions of Africa, such as Sierra Leone, at a high of 170. **Life expectancy** is the number of years that an individual at a given age can expect to live at present mortality rates. Estimates of global life expectancies range from 36 to 79 years; Malawi has the lowest life expectancy and Canada, Iceland, Sweden, and Switzerland have the highest life expectancies.

Developed regions tend to have lower birth rates and death rates. Factors contributing to decreasing crude birth rates include access to contraception, costs associated with raising a child, and other social changes. For example, teenage births are at a historical low in the United States and an increasing number of older couples are choosing to postpone reproduction, or to not reproduce at all. Factors contributing to decreasing crude death rates include improvements in agriculture, medicine, and sanitation. Historic examples of dramatic population declines include the European Black Death and the Great Irish Famine, which is less problematic in the modern world. However, it is also possible for there to be slight increases in the death rate as the prevalence of preventable diseases increases due to poor fitness and nutrition and other poor health behaviors, like substance abuse.

Migration

In addition to birth rates and death rates, population is also determined through rates of **migration**, the geographical movement of individuals, families, or other small or large groups of people. Migration implies the intention of permanent relocation ("settling down") and is thus distinct from non-permanent movement. For example, non-permanent travel for leisure, pilgrimage, or seasonal reasons and **nomadism**, which is a traditional method of continuous travel in search of natural resources as a method of sustenance ("hunting and gathering"), are not considered migration because there is no intention to settle. Migration is often a movement of long distances, but this varies. **External migration**, also referred to as cross-border or international migration, involves migration to another nation. Motivations for external migration are often economic or political in nature. **Internal migration** involves migration to another region of the same nation. Motivations for internal migration are often more economic in nature as individuals pursue better opportunities, such as education. **Voluntary migration** is the result of internal factors (a personal decision). **Involuntary**

8.3

migration, or forced migration, is the result of external factors that pose a threat to the individual in their initial environments and are often a form of social control, such as ethnic cleansing. Those who migrate to unsettled areas are **settlers** and those who migrate to settled areas as a result of displacement are **refugees**. More complicated is **colonization**, which involves migration to settled areas in which dominance is exerted over the foreign state. There is often exploitation of the indigenous peoples with the use of harsh tactics such as the "divide and conquer" of territories, as well as a disregard for existing social structures. This has been transformative in the structures of societies around the world, such as the United States where the original inhabitants, the Native Americans, are often marginalized. **Immigration** involves entering a new area and these people are called immigrants (and can be either legal or illegal residents); **emigration** involves leaving an old area and these people are called emigrants. For example, there is a high rate of emigration from Mexico and a high rate of immigration to the United States. There is also a high rate of illegal immigration, which has disadvantages for both the migrant individual and their new home. **Reverse migration**, or return migration, is the return of individuals to their former homes.

There are numerous historical theories describing the reasons for migration and its effects. Everett Lee, a popular theorist, differentiated between push and pull factors in migration. **Push factors** are those things that are unattractive about an area and "push" people to leave. Push factors are often economic, political, or religious in form: active oppression of social groups; additional forms of prejudice and discrimination, such as housing discrimination; insufficient access to social resources, such as education, or social services to meet basic needs, such as shelter; widespread inequalities, such as health disparities; etc. There are also more extreme examples, such as destructive violence or natural disasters. For example, as a result of the large-scale **genocide**, or mass execution with the intention of eliminating a specific social group, there was a high rate of emigration from Bosnia in the 1990s. **Pull factors** are those things that are attractive about an area and "pull" people there. These are the opposite of push factors and often include positive opportunities for economic, political, or religious freedom and success. The interaction between push and pull factors contributes to the rates of migration. Migration also has an impact on the nation to which people move; for example, the cultural infiltration of new ideas.

Urban Growth, Decline, and Renewal

Internal migration includes the movement between rural and urban areas. The spatial distribution of individuals and social groups is an interest of **social geography**. **Urbanization** refers to the growth of urban areas (as people move from rural to urban areas) as the result of global change. Urbanization is tied to **industrialization**, the process through which societies transform from agrarian to industrial in nature, and industrialized countries have more people living in urban areas than non-industrialized countries do. The global urbanization rate is roughly 50%, and approximately 80% of the U.S. population lives in urban areas (including cities and suburbs). People move to urban areas for a variety of reasons, predominantly for the opportunities for economic advancement that cities provide. Cities tend to offer many employment opportunities, as well as being places where money and wealth are localized. Furthermore, people can access more social services in cities. This is related to **rural flight**, or rural exodus, which studies the migration from rural areas to urban areas from the other perspective. Emigration from rural areas is often related to a decreasing emphasis on agricultural processes. The widespread social changes associated with industrialization and urbanization during the eighteenth and nineteenth centuries are responsible for the start of the sociological tradition as a separate subject following the scientific method. The oldest theories were developed in an attempt to process these broad historical changes.

In contrast to urban growth, suburbanization leads to urban decline. **Suburbanization** refers to population growth on the fringes of urban areas (as people move from urban areas to suburban areas). The **suburbs** are residential satellite communities located in the peripheral regions of major urban centers that are often connected to the cities in some fashion. In the United States, more people live in the suburbs than in the cities, but individual suburbs tend to be less populated than cities. **White flight** is a historical example of suburbanization that involved the migration of whites from cities to more racially homogenous suburbs. Migration to these metropolitan regions is an example of **urban sprawl**, or the migration of people from urban areas to otherwise remote areas. The negative effects of urban sprawl include **urban blight**, which occurs when less functioning areas of large cities degrade as a result of urban decline. These forms of migration can thus lead to desolate properties, such as condemned houses, and the resulting dangerous conditions can contribute to an increase in crime levels in blighted areas. Those who remain in the blighted areas are often poor and have less access to social amenities and opportunities.

Gentrification refers to the renovation of urban areas (as people move from rural or suburban areas back to urban areas) in a process of urban renewal. Gentrification is often specific to the introduction of wealthier residents to the cities who then help to restore the existing infrastructure, which alters the region's demographics and economics. For example, the conversion of old industrial buildings to high end "loft-style" housing options brings new business to the area to serve the new middle class population. Gentrification is a form of **urban renewal**, or the redevelopment of urban areas. This causes much social change with both positive and negative effects; for example, it can increase the tax base, but it can also lead to the displacement of the original local people. Urban renewal can be a mechanism for reform or a mechanism for control (for example, eminent domain).

Theories of Population Change

There are multiple theories of population change. **Demographic transition** (DT) is the transition from overall higher to overall lower birth and death rates as a result of a country's development from a pre-industrial to industrial framework due to both economic and social changes; thus, both fertility and mortality rates decrease as in the transition from an agricultural to a manufacturing society. This has long-term effects, such as a stable population. The model includes specific stages of transition and, in general, developed countries are further along in this transition than developing countries but most countries have started to experience changes in crude birth rate and crude death rate. However, the model is limited; for example, it does not consider additional social factors that affect birth rates, like religious influences.

Thomas Robert Malthus argued that population is the result of available resources for sustenance, such as productive farmland. Humans are inclined to reproduce and thus population growth is often exponential, especially during times of excess. However, **Malthusianism** states that the possible rate of population increase exceeds the possible rate of resource increase. This perspective resulted as a criticism of utopian views, explaining that the rules of nature make it impossible for population to increase unchecked without serious distress due to insufficient resources. These negative effects subject the lower classes, in particular, to poor living conditions. Malthus described two forms of checks on population growth: **positive checks** that raise the death rate, like disease, disasters, hunger, and wars, and **preventative checks** that lower the birth rate, like abstinence, birth control, late marriage, and same-sex relationships. A **Malthusian Catastrophe** occurs when the means of sustenance are not enough to support the population, resulting in population reduction through actual or predicted famine. **Neo-Malthusianism** is a movement based on these principles that advocates for population control in order to reduce the negative effects of population strain, such as environmental effects. Malthus found controlled populations to be more stable in terms of economics and standards of living in particular.

Demographics in U.S. Society

Demography is the study of human population dynamics, including the size, structure, and distribution of a population, and changes in the population over time due to birth, death, and migration. An analysis of the demographics of a given society can provide powerful information about many sociological phenomena. Demographic data are largely derived from censuses, and focus on specific indicators of changes, like birth and death (also known as mortality) rates.

As of 2013, the U.S. population was approximately 316,710,000, making it the third most populous country in the world. The U.S. population consists of approximately 155.6 million females and 151.4 million males. At age 85 and older, women outnumber men by 2 to 1. The median age is 36.8 years; people under the age of 20 make up roughly one-fourth of the U.S. population and people over age 65 make up about one-eighth of the U.S. population.

Race and ethnicity are important elements of the U.S. population. For the purposes of the U.S. census, race refers to the biological, anthropological, or genetic origin of an individual, and includes the following categories: White, Black or African American, American Indian or Alaska Native, Asian, and Native Hawaiian or Other Pacific Islander. Unlike race, ethnicity is a socially defined concept referring to whether or not people identify with each other based on shared social experience or ancestry. The only two ethnicities queried on the U.S. census is "Hispanic or Latino" or "not Hispanic or Latino." According to the 2010 U.S. census, the population breaks down as follows:

U.S. Census Race Category	% of Population
White, not Hispanic or Latino	63%
White, Hispanic or Latino	9%
Black/African American	12%
Asian American	5%
American Indian/Alaskan Native	1%
Native Hawaiian/Pacific Islander	0.2%
Some other race	6%
People who identify as two or more races	3%

Table 2 Breakdown of U.S. Population by Race (according to U.S. Census data, 2010)

In 2009, approximately 13% of the population was foreign-born, including approximately 11 million noncitizens. Latin America accounts for just over half of all of the people who are foreign-born in the U.S., so is thus the largest source of both legal and illegal immigration to the U.S. The net migration rate is roughly 4.3 immigrants per 1,000 people. According to various studies, by the year 2042, people who identify as "White, not Hispanic or Latino" will no longer make up the majority of the population. While estimates vary, the percentage of the population that identifies as gay, lesbian, or bisexual is roughly 2%.

In regards to population studies, there has been a rapid decline in the total global fertility rate; this is of particular concern in the U.S. where the average women has less than two children, which is below the population replacement level. To be specific, the current replacement fertility rate is set at 2.1; as of 2012, the estimated fertility rate for American females was 1.88 (sub-replacement fertility). The mortality rate in the U.S. is just below the global rate of around 8 (per 1000 people). The infant mortality rate experienced a 50%

decrease in 20 years and is now approximately 7 (per 1000 live births). The current life expectancy at birth is 78 years on average (75 years for males and 80 years for females). The current migration rates (external migration) have caused increases in population despite low birth rates and death rates (although population growth is nonetheless near a historical low). There are also examples of internal migration. There have been historic migrations from the eastern states to the western states (expansion), as well as the migration of African Americans from the rural south to the urban north as a result of racial conflict. The **Great Migration** is an example of a domestic reverse migration. During this period, there was an increase in black migration to the now urban South as racial relations improved. Because the North had started to deindustrialize, the opportunities for work prompted this migration to specific areas of the South, such as Georgia.

Demographic Structure

Researchers often use aggregate statistics to provide a demographic profile of a specific population (based on region or time). Demographics often focus on subsets of the population with the intent of describing the shared characteristics of members of these subsets. Demographic information has some practical uses—for example, advertising strategies use demographics to address specific audiences—but critics argue that these uses are limited because of the generalizations made. In essence, demographics describe social groups rather than individuals.

Minorities are those demographic groups that receive differential treatment though processes of prejudice and discrimination due to their shared characteristics. These groups have lower statuses than other groups, and are thus considered inferior. It is important to note that despite the title, these groups are termed minorities not for their size but instead for their disparate social experiences and the description holds regardless of population size. Thus, despite the gender and sex distributions being near equal in most societies, women are sometimes considered minorities because of their perceived status as inferior and subordinate to men. The **dominant groups** are those with the social power to assign these labels.

Demographic measures discussed below include age, gender, race and ethnicity, sexual orientation, and immigration status. However, there are many more examples of demographic interest, such as disabilities, languages, and socioeconomic characteristics (education, employment status, income, wealth, et cetera).

Age

People's position between birth and death, and subsequent position changes over time, is measured through **age**. In Western societies, the most common use is numerical age, a chronological measurement that begins at birth (thus babies are age 0 at birth). This is distinguished from measures of prenatal development, such as gestational age, although some societies do consider this period (thus babies are age 9 months at birth if full-term). Years are the most common units of measurement for age, but months or even weeks are also used in certain situations, such as with infants. The most basic categories of age are described in the following ranges:

- **Juveniles (infants, children, preadolescents, and adolescents):** 0-19 years
- **Early adults:** 20-39 years
- **Middle adults:** 40-59 years
- **Late adults:** 60+ years

8.3

However, additional descriptions are also used (for example, those aged 13-18 are called teenagers). **Age cohorts** are an example of statistical cohorts in which a group of subjects share the characteristic of age. These groups are used in longitudinal studies, also called **cohort studies**, which conduct research for extended periods of time to better understand the different perspectives of those in the cohort and those in the general population. Generational cohorts, or **generations**, are groups of people born in the same period. These distinct generations share specific experiences that become representative of the group (a popular example is Generation X). Demographic age profiles describe populations in terms of age groups. Populations with a proportionate distribution are the most stable. **Population aging** occurs when there is a disproportionate amount of older people in a population. This raises concerns such as health-care demands and provider shortages. **Ageism** is prejudice or discrimination against a person based on age, often against older people. Because most objective measures of age are not functional, subjective measures can be used to determine how old someone feels. For example, self-reported measures of health, and age-related health problems, are correlated with outcomes.

The concept of aging has both biological and social components. *Social aging* reflects the biological changes in a multidimensional process in which individuals experience complex emotional and social changes. Factors including active engagement, interpersonal relationships, personal control, and social support contribute to optimal aging and predict objective and subjective measures of well-being in adults. There are serious social implications of an aging population. Economic consequences of a rising median age include increased requirements for pension liabilities, retirement packages, and worker's compensation. In contrast, an increase in children leads to greater demands for social resources such as education. Furthermore, younger people are more likely to contribute to social changes, such as the creation of new technologies or the push for political changes.

The social significance of aging is considerable. For example, children and adults have different legal rights. Individuals receive different roles and statuses, as well as greater social opportunities, at certain milestones, such as the age of consent, drinking age, retirement age, smoking age, and voting age. These are sometimes called **rites of passages**; these rituals reflect important life transitions and also include more personal changes such as marriage. Further social conventions include age-regulated admission to rated movies and discounts for children and seniors. The courts also consider age in cases of criminal prosecution; the defense might argue that juveniles are not liable for their crimes due to a lack of social experiences and responsibilities.

There are theories that explain the social construction of age. These perspectives argue that perceptions of age are not inherent but instead social creations based on cultural customs, traditions, and values. Eastern cultures tend to respect older people for their experiences and wisdom. Western cultures, however, tend to see aging as undesirable. It is thus common to take measures to control appearances and impressions, such as cosmetic surgeries. The response to aging parents exemplifies these cultural differences. Retirement homes are more popular in developed societies and public perceptions of these resources are accepting; in less modern societies, it is expected that children will care for their parents and assisted living options might be seen as disrespectful.

Gender

Sex is a biological characteristic that is assigned at birth and permanent in most cases; it is based on chromosomes, external genitalia, gonads, and hormones. Thus, categories of sex are male (XY) and female (XX). The third sex, albeit rare, is intersex. This classification is applicable when a single sex cannot be identified. Biological differences between men and women include the fact that in the process of reproduction, it is women who experience menstruation (if not pregnant) or gestation, birth, and lactation (if pregnant). **Gender** is a social characteristic (a social construction) that is learned and flexible; it is based on behavioral role expectations. Thus, categories of gender are masculine and feminine. Following the example of reproduction, social differences between men and women exist from conception and include the trend of decorating nurseries for expected male babies in blue and expected female babies in pink. Developed societies often discuss gender in dichotomous terms, where masculine and feminine are opposites, but in some societies, there are third genders, such as two-spirits, and neither male nor female individuals are held in high regard in some traditional Native American tribes.

Gender is thought to be influenced by both nature and nurture. In terms of nature, biological measures can have behavioral effects (for examples, hormones influence emotions). The natural sciences are interested in the consequences of biological differences between men and women on gender. In some cases, genetic abnormalities (such as the XXY chromosomal abnormality in Klinefelter's syndrome) might cause unexpected presentations when compared to the assumptions made from one's biological sex. In terms of nurture, our social surroundings have a profound effect on the development of our gender identities. The social sciences—including **gender studies** (men's studies, women's studies, and LGBT studies)—are interested in the consequences of social processes. Gender is not an inherent fact but a social construction learned through gender socialization. During this process, multiple agents of socialization are responsible for the transmission of distinct gender roles to men and women. **Gender roles** describe the social and behavioral expectations for men and women. These expectations are internalized and become connected to our self-identities (how we think about ourselves) and thus influence our behaviors. **Gender expression** is the external manifestation of these roles. Gender roles are dependent on the cultural-historical context. For example, gender roles tend to be less influential in the middle and upper classes when compared to the working class.

Gender is also political in that it is subject to social control. Thus, the gendered experiences have been produced and reproduced in patriarchal societies through social structures, at times through formal means, in accordance to different values, such as religious doctrines, as well as the notion of biological differences. **Sexism** is prejudice or discrimination against a person based on gender or sex, often against women. Despite revolutionary social changes, there continues to be a flawed perception of the genders in which men are viewed as dominant and women are viewed as subordinate; men are the reference group and women are the "other" group in continuous reference to men. Men and women are both different and unequal in the social resources afforded; it is an unfortunate truth that women are marginalized and afforded less power at birth and fewer opportunities throughout their lifetime to gain power. A classic example of gender inequalities concerns the institution of marriage. Most coverage of marriage presents it as a reflection of commitment and emotion; however, there are also practical concerns. In entering a marriage, women receive an increased number of responsibilities. The well-known concept of the gendered division of labor in the household reflects the expectation that women will be subordinate to men. It further limits the representation of women in the public sphere, which also limits the opportunities women have for the reasoning processes that society values. These disparate experiences are an interest of the previously discussed Feminist Theory.

Gender roles are those behaviors that are considered appropriate or proper for men and women. Gendered behaviors that follow social conventions are approved while those that do not are disapproved; thus, deviation from gender roles tends to create social disorder. **Transsexual** individuals have gender identities that are inconsistent with their biological sex divisions. Popular culture often equates this with cross-dressing and drag performances. There is much prejudice and discrimination against transsexual communities. Modern technologies allow the pursuit of anatomical realignment through sex reassignment surgeries when the difference between one's gender and sex is causing impaired functioning.

In some cases, social structures contribute to the separation of the genders, known as **gender segregation**, for economic, political, religious, or social reasons. This can be problematic because it often separates people based on apparent biological distinctions rather than gender identities and is thus better described as **sex segregation**. The mechanism of segregation varies; it can be complete or partial, enforced through informal social processes or formal policies, and involve a spatial separation or other social separation (such as the historical exclusion of women from participation in certain occupations). Gender segregation is often controversial, but in some cases, it has had some positive outcomes. For example, in Europe, educational establishments are often single-gendered, which is thought to improve results.

Race and Ethnicity

Race and ethnicity are related concepts that are of much interest to sociologists because of their importance in human interactions; however, it is important to first understand the distinction between these two demographic characteristics. **Race** is a description of a distinct social group based on certain shared characteristics. These shared characteristics are often inherited biological traits (and thus manifest in physical appearances), but can also be cultural, ethnic, and geographical in nature. According to the U.S. Census, the currently accepted race categories include Black/African American, White, Asian, American Indian/Alaska Native, Native Hawaiian/Other Pacific Islander, and "Other." **Ethnicity** is also a description of a distinct social group based on certain shared characteristics. These shared characteristics include common ancestral, cultural, geographical, historical, linguistic, and/or national experiences, and members of the same ethnic group often share similar appearances, cuisines, fashions, ideologies, languages and dialects, and so forth. The five largest ethnic groups are as follows: (1) Han Chinese, (2) Hindustani people, (3) Arabs, (4) Bengalis, and (5) Russians. This shows the distinction of ethnicities from nationalities. For example, Arab populations originate in the Arabian Peninsula, which includes several modern nations with the current five largest populations being in (1) Egypt, (2) Algeria, (3) Iraq, (4) Sudan, and (5) Morocco. In the reverse direction, in addition to Arab populations, Egypt also includes ethnic minorities, such as the Beja, Berber, Dom, and Nubian peoples. Discussion of ethnicities is thus more complex. **Ethnogenesis** is a social process that results in the creation of separate ethnicities. Historical examples of this include the development of small sub-ethnic groups, **tribes**, into independent ethnic groups. Those ethnic groups founded in the same population share close features, such as related languages; this is exemplified in the Balkans. Thus, it can be suggested there is a racial component to ethnogensis, and this is not incorrect; however, the shared identities, and thus the requirements needed for membership in an ethnic group, are more specific than with race. Furthermore, the concept of race often has an emotional component that is not present in the classification of ethnic groups.

Both races and ethnicities are social constructs. Members of the same racial or ethnic group do not share identities for the mere fact of similarities in determined characteristics. The shared identities are instead formed on the basis of shared historical and social experiences. It is not the common origin that forms the group but the shared consciousness of the common origin, and the meanings ascribed to that specific origin. There are cultural, religious, and traditional influences on the creation, and the reinforcement, of these identities. For example, both demographics, while imprecise, have contributed to the collective differentiation of people through hierarchies. This resulted in different social experiences with the historical mistreatment of minorities. For example, the historical definition of race as a genetic concept promoted the idea that there were also other differences between racial groups, such as differences in intelligence, which was then used to oppress people. Modern research provides no evidence for the taxonomic significance of race as all people are part of the same species and subspecies (*Homo sapiens sapiens*). Despite the fact that this has been discredited, prejudice and discrimination on the basis on race and ethnicity continues in modern societies. The Holocaust, for example, occurred less than a century ago. Prejudices and actions that discriminate based on race, or hold that one race is inferior to another, are called **racism**. While the exact definitions of "race," "ethnicity," and "racism" have been subject to much debate over the years, racism tends to be seen when the dominant or majority group (usually white) holds a prejudice or engages in discrimination, whether intentional or not, against non-dominant or minority groups (usually not white). Sometimes racism is used to describe discrimination on an ethnic or cultural basis, independent of whether these differences are described as racial. The confusion largely stems from confusion about the definitions of the terms "race" and "ethnicity." Ethnocentrism is a related concept that describes biases that result when people look at issues from the perspective of a particular cultural background. It is often whites who are said to be ethnocentric in sociological studies, but this is not absolute.

Michael Omi and Howard Winat's **racial formation perspective** offers another explanation of the social construction of race, explaining that race is not genetic but constructed through economic, political, and social forces that have the social control to create categories of race, and ascribe social meanings to these categories. This perspective was created with the purpose of deconstructing race in its modern form. Its arguments thus differ from traditional race theories in that race is seen as a complex and fluid social construct, rather than a concrete and static characteristic, enforced through both micro- and macro-level social processes. In contrast to other theories that do not present race as an exclusive social construct, the racial formation perspective argues that without these processes, the differences in biological features are meaningless. For example, there was an increase in race consciousness during the recent presidential elections in the United States. This perspective might argue that this consciousness was not the result of a candidate's pigmentation (which is alone meaningless); instead, it happened because the political success of President Obama disrupted our racial expectations for politicians. This violation, and the subsequent discussion, served to reinforce racial labels through important social structures such as the media. The scholars also argue that race is a fundamental and pervasive component of social structure in the United States. Thus, race is both constructed and made important through processes of social learning.

Racialization, or **ethnicization**, is the social process in which the dominant group ascribes racial or ethnic identities, perceived or real, to groups that do not otherwise relate to the labels. These processes are used as forms of social control, often as a part of imperialism or nationalism. Historical examples of racialization and ethnicization have resulted in the eventual self-identification of these groups with the ascribed race or ethnicity. For example, an example of religious racialization involves the development of a shared Jewish culture. Judaism is a religion, and while religions do promote to common behaviors, the outside identification of Jews as an ethnic group contributed to nationalism that ended in the development of modern Israel as an official Jewish state.

Related, but separate, concepts include citizenship, nationality, national origin, and religion.

Sexual Orientation

Sexual orientation describes the direction of a person's romantic or sexual attraction or behavior. It is important to note that these categories are crude descriptions of attractions or behaviors not of people themselves (this becomes more nuanced, such as with transsexual individuals). There are three main sexual orientations

- **Heterosexual**: The orientation toward the opposite gender or sex
- **Homosexual**: The orientation toward the same gender or sex
- **Bisexual**: The orientation toward both genders or sexes

Bisexual identities do not necessitate an equal attraction toward both genders and sexes; in some cases, there is a distinct, but not exclusive, sexual preference toward one gender or sex. Bisexual communities include those who are **pansexual** and attracted to people irrespective of gender or sex. Recent research suggests a fourth sexual orientation (asexual) but this is contended because others argue that it is actually the absence of a traditional sexual orientation. **Asexuality** involves the lack of sexual attraction. This is different from the decision to be abstinent or celibate for personal reasons, such as religious beliefs. In fact, those with no or little sexual attraction sometimes participate in sexual behavior nonetheless for reasons like reproduction. Sexual orientation exists along a continuum, with the extremes being exclusive attraction to the opposite gender or sex (heterosexual) and exclusive attraction to the same gender or sex (homosexual). The Kinsey Scale, also called the Heterosexual-Homosexual Rating Scale, is shown below.

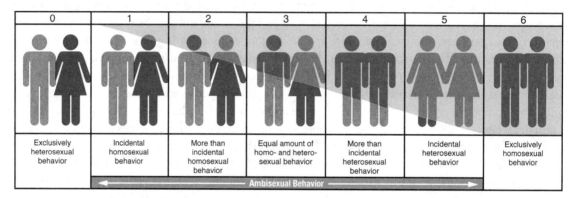

Figure 2   Kinsey Scale of Sexual Behavior

Demographics of sexual orientation can be unclear for reasons such as vague selection criteria. Despite the fact that sexual orientation is often thought to be independent of social influences, in societies that do not offer rights to non-heterosexual persons, it is possible that people do not feel comfortable with public identification of this characteristic. Furthermore, much research on romantic relationships involves marriage, which might be limited to heterosexual couples. **Heterosexism** is prejudice or discrimination against a person based on their sexual orientation toward the same sex (for example, homophobic attitudes). **Heteronormative beliefs** consider heterosexual to be the preferred sexual orientation, and often enforce strict gender roles. The prejudice and discrimination against non-heterosexual individuals can be political, economic, religious, or social in nature (see the section on social stratification and inequalities for a relevant discussion of power, prestige, and privilege in Section 8.4). There are sometimes public sanctions, such as formal policies, reinforcing these beliefs. This has led to modern social movements for the recognition of legal rights, such as adoption rights, marriage rights, and health-care rights for same-sex couples. For example, the controversial "Don't Ask, Don't Tell" was repealed in 2010. There are sometimes heterosexual allies who reject prejudice and discrimination through supporting equal civil rights regardless of sexual orientation. There are also differences between the non-heterosexual groups. For example, there is much discussion about the disparate experiences of the white gay male and those with other non-heterosexual identities; these individuals, based on their other demographics, are often afforded more social resources (for example, educated, middle class, white men).

There is also discussion of the complex social construction of sexual orientation. Despite the fact that non-heterosexual behaviors have existed for centuries, it is sometimes argued that specific social identities did not exist to represent these behaviors before recently. In the past, non-heterosexual behaviors described the specific sexual act (for example, sodomy). The modern state has been instrumental in the creation of these identities. Perceptions of sexualities also differ around the world. For example, considering non-verbal communication, it is common in some cultures to kiss same-sex friends as a greeting, but this same behavior might be seen as indicative of a romantic relationship, rather than a friendship in some Western cultures. Furthermore, while sexual orientation is an individual characteristic, sociologists are interested in the social structures that develop around the concept. For example, homosexual communities have created divisions and separate identities for men and women (gay and lesbian). There are specific social structures for which membership is limited based on sexual orientation. LGBTQ (lesbian, gay, bisexual, transgender, and queer or questioning) communities in the United States, for example, include self-designated non-heterosexual or non-cisgender individuals.

There is much debate about the causes of sexual orientation, including both biological theories that consider factors like genetics and hormones and environmental theories that consider factors like parenting. There is some argument that non-heterosexual behavior is unnatural for certain reasons (for example, it does not permit reproduction). However, research suggests that sexual orientation is a human characteristic that is generally resistant to change, leading some to argue that non-heterosexual behavior can be natural. Furthermore, there is no substantive scientific evidence to support the argument that sexual orientation can be changed through interventions.

Sexual orientation is one component of the more nuanced discussion of sexual identities, which includes more variants (as well as none at all). Non-binary sexual identities include androphilic, gynephilic, and polysexual.

Immigration Status

Immigration was introduced above as the migration of people to a new area. Immigration status is another common demographic measure. In the past, the United Nations estimated the international migrant population to be near 3 percent of the total world population. Most of these migrants moved to developed countries. European countries host the most immigrants worldwide (around 70 million); North American countries host the second most (around 45 million). Recent research recorded that the highest percentage of respondents (23 percent) in a study who identified as being interested in migration named the United States as their preferred destination. This can be attributed in part to the **American Dream**, an ideological construct that offers individuals the opportunities for happiness and success with the proper amount of determination. This central promise has contributed to the rise in migration to the U.S. in the search for a better life with enhanced personal freedoms.

The United States has had four main periods of immigration, based on the social context, as well as the distinct demographics (ethnicities, nationalities, and races) of the migrants.

1) **The seventeenth and eighteenth centuries:** During this period, English colonists migrated to the U.S. (the colonial period). Indentured servants also migrated through this process, accounting for more than half of all immigrants from Europe during the period.

2) **The mid-nineteenth century:** During this period, the most migrants came from northern Europe.

3) **The early twentieth century:** During this period, the most migrants came from southern and Eastern Europe. For example, Jewish refugees moved to the U.S. in flight from the Nazi regime during World War II. The peak of European migration was 1907, after which the social context of the U.S. made conditions less suitable for immigration. The Great Depression, for example, led to a period of higher national emigration rates than immigration rates (this occurred in the early 1930s).

4) **The late twentieth century (post-1965) to the present:** During this period, the majority of migrants have been from Asia and Latin America. The top five leading countries of origin are (1) Mexico, (2) People's Republic of China, (3) Philippines, (4) India, and (5) Cuba. In general, most immigrants are women in the 15 to 35 age range. It is common for people to migrate to areas with similar populations (such as areas populated with people of their ethnic background). Thus, immigration is often to selective regions; 70 percent of foreign-born people in the U.S. reside in seven states (California, Florida, Illinois, New Jersey, New York, Pennsylvania, and Texas). The rates of immigration during this period have been unprecedented. For example, the decade with the historical highest rate of immigration was from 1990 to 2000; between 10 and 11 million legal and illegal immigrants entered the U.S. during this phase. There are now more than 37 million legal immigrants and an estimated 1.5 million illegal immigrants living in the U.S.

The United States has restrictive legal limits on immigration. There are current quotas based on origin, and these limits do not consider populations (thus the maximum number of visas offered is the same for all countries). **Immigration controls** are formal policies that define and regulate who has the right to settle in an area. This is important because it restricts legal immigration, and increases the need for economic and political resources to ensure an individual's success in migrating. This is an area of concern because it creates a disadvantage for poor migrants, often those same people who are exploited for cheap labor. Today, most legal immigration is granted on the basis of family reunification (this accounts for two-thirds of all cases), employment skills, and humanitarian reasons. Historically, immigration decisions have been made for other reasons, such as ethnic selection. In some cases, the U.S. government has granted amnesties for undocumented immigrants. The presence of illegal immigrants presents definite challenges in describing the complex demographics of the U.S.

The shared experiences of immigrants are of concern to sociologists. These individuals are often mistreated, and in some cases their rights are violated, in the immigration process. Immigrants are also a common target of prejudice and discrimination. For example, as mentioned above, in the aftermath of 9/11, there was an increase in hate crimes. Public attitudes, in general, are more positive toward established migrants (such as the Polish and Italian communities) and more negative toward recent migrants (such as Hispanic communities). For these reasons, there are often intersections between immigration status and race and ethnicity, as well as social class for the reasons discussed above. There is also a distinction in the public opinion of legal and illegal immigrants, often fueled by media coverage of migration. Furthermore, immigrant status can have implications for social functioning due to the differences in the social conventions of developing and developed countries. For example, arranged marriages are more common in the East than in the West which requires immigrants to reconcile these practices with the accepted traditions of their new homes.

DEMOGRAPHIC SHIFTS AND SOCIAL CHANGE

Globalization

Modern advancements in telecommunications and transportation have contributed to the rates of **globalization**, the process of increasing interdependence of societies and connections between people across the world. **Telecommunications**, in particular, use modern technologies to ease the challenges of communication across distances, and like most information and communication technologies, contribute to the integration of economical, political, and social processes worldwide. In response to an increase in global competition, multinational corporations and transnational companies have formed in order to gain the benefits of cooperation and pursue new investment opportunities. This is made possible through new technologies that ease the challenges of international communication, such as videoconferences for business, as well as the possibilities for international exchange of resources through automatic electronic transactions. **Economic interdependence** can be thought of as the division of labor on a global scale; countries might have the demand for products without the internal means of production. For example, the United States is dependent on other countries for some natural resources, like oil. These new markets can pose concerns. The example of **outsourcing** involves the contracting of third parties for specific operations. This can be domestic or foreign, but the financial savings associated with foreign outsourcing have made it a focus of much opposition.

Politics are also an important component of globalization. The increased opportunities for international communication contribute to an increased awareness of relevant global issues through the diffusion of knowledge. This has lead to the development of international organizations, like the popular intergovernmental organization known as the United Nations. **Non-governmental organizations** (NGOs) are those organizations without an official government affiliation with the intention of contributing to the lessening of global issues. Médecins Sans Frontières (MSF), or Doctors Without Borders, is a good example of an international humanitarian NGO; MSF is committed to lessening global inequalities in health. Thus, globalization eases borders and allows international cooperation in the fight for human rights.

There are also cultural consequences of globalization as the sharing of cultures leads to more foreign choices, such as cuisines and media options. In some cases, this interchange can lead to the disintegration of local culture as new ideas are welcomed. Furthermore, globalization contributes to rates of migration, thus changing the demographics of an area. This can also create environmental challenges, such as air pollution resulting from increased transportation. Two dramatic examples of resulting social changes in globalization are civil unrest and terrorism. Periods of **civil unrest**, or civil disorder, involve forms of collective behavior in which there is public expression of the group's concern, often in response to major social problems, like with political demonstrations and protests. This can have serious consequences for societies, such as the destruction of public properties and the interruption of important services. **Terrorism** involves the use of violence with the intention to create fear in the target communities. There is no single form of terrorism: it can be committed for ideological, nationalistic, political, religious, or other reasons. The defining characteristic of terrorist acts is indiscriminate violence; thus, terrorism involves violence directed toward non-combatants. The United States experienced a series of terrorist attacks on September 11, 2001, and this is one of the most-discussed examples of terrorism in the world. The result of the extremist organization known as Al Qaeda, this is the deadliest terrorist attack recorded. The aftermath of these attacks, including the Global War on Terrorism, have had serious domestic and international consequences, such as an increase in hate crimes committed against American Muslims.

Perspectives on globalization are varied, and some of the positives and negatives of three main aspects of globalization (economic, political, and sociocultural globalization) are discussed above. Let's expand upon these contrasting perspectives using the example of the political consequences. Proponents consider the positive consequences of globalization. As mentioned above, processes of globalization offer greater democratic representation of less-developed countries as a result of new political institutions. These international bodies are often concerned with human issues, such as environmental issues, like chlorofluorocarbon (CFC) emissions and nuclear proliferation, and promote international cooperation in addressing these issues, such as researching alternative energies and conservation. There are some in favor of organized world governments to address the needs of world citizens. Opponents consider the negative consequences of globalization. In contrast to the arguments of democratic globalization, critics believe it contributes to the disintegration of democratic values. The economic issues inherent in globalization, such as the concentration of economic power in developed countries, contribute to oppressive politics; thus, globalization is not seen as a contributor to social cohesion but to social control.

Social Movements

The section on collective behavior introduces social movements as a method of achieving social change. In this sense, social movements are a reflection of public dissatisfaction and a collective to response economic, political, or social issues. This necessitates the existence of two opposing groups: those who support the current social structure and those who support change. For example, the social issue of abortion has created two distinct social movements: pro-choice and pro-life. It is common that social movements arise when the formal means of participation, like voting, do not address the concerns of the public. For this reason, much social movement is seen as the people's opposition to those in power, and in particular those who have vested interests so strong that there is resulting corruption at the expense of the public. The processes involved in social movements might contribute to an intermediate disruption of social order, but the purpose is to protect the core values of modern societies: civil rights, freedom, justice, protection, etc. Thus, the most successful social movements are the result of critical social problems that violate these central values. This makes the concern relevant to the general population and necessitates that the issue must be resolved through progressive social change.

There has been an unprecedented increase in the use of public participation to challenge existing social structures and facilitate positive changes in modern times (consider the increased freedoms for minorities, for example). This is often seen as a function of the founding principles of democracies, such as the freedom of speech, as well as a result of the related processes of industrialization and urbanization. **Relative deprivation** has also been suggested as a contributing factor. Relative deprivation refers to the conscious experience of individuals or groups that do not have the resources needed for the social experiences and services that are seen as appropriate to their social position. In essence, there is a feeling of being entitled to more than what one has in their current situation, based on relative, not absolute, standards. This perceived deprivation can be economic, political, or social. Relative deprivation can also contribute to social deviance.

The organization of social movements varies, but the most successful movements tend to have strong leadership. These often charismatic leaders help create allied communities of consensus, and later have coordinating roles. The overall organization might be loose but there is nonetheless a divide between those who support the cause (insiders) and those who do not (outsiders). Popular social movements are often supported through the efforts of multiple social movement organizations. For example, People for the Ethical Treatment of Animals (PETA) is a single organization that participates in the broader social movement for animal rights and its members are part of an even larger group of advocates.

The use of telecommunications is one of the most important strategies used in modern social movements. The Internet, and social networking in particular, has made it easier to accomplish the successful formation of groups, and provides an effective means of directing efforts once these groups are formed. The rapid dissemination of information through the Internet contributes to the success of activist groups in educating the masses. For example, the Internet group known as Anonymous describes itself as an "Internet gathering" and its followers, called Anons, have take collective action against injustices, often recognized through their use of identifiable Guys Fawkes masks. The power of Internet communication as a means of activism is so strong that it considered a contributing factor in the increase of government censorship online.

Furthermore, peaceful, rather than violent, social movements are often more successful in gaining the public's support. This is more in line with the principle concept of social movements: protecting central beliefs (such as peace), which are here used to its advantage. It is also less threatening, which allows more people to participate because it is more difficult for the movement to be discredited; for example, peaceful action has a lower chance of leading to arrest. Movements that are violent in nature ("rebellions") are often self-destructive.

8.4 STRATIFICATION, HEALTH, AND HEALTH CARE DISPARITIES

Stratification and Inequality

Social stratification refers to the way that people are categorized in society; people can be categorized by race, education, wealth, and income (among other things). People with the most resources comprise the top tiers of the stratification while people with the least resources comprise the bottom tiers. Social stratification is a system that not only serves to define differences (or inequalities) but also serves to reinforce and perpetuate them. The **caste system** describes a closed stratification where people can do nothing to change the category that they are born into. On the other hand, the **class system** considers both social variables and individual initiative; the class system groups together people of similar wealth, income, education, etc. but the classes are open, meaning that people can strive to reach a higher class (or fall to a lower one). However, a person's upward social mobility is constrained; a person's class position affords them only a certain amount of resources. Individuals can supplement these resources with different forms of capital gained from social institutions, such as education. A **meritocracy** is another stratification system that uses merit (or personal effort) to establish social standing; this is an idealized system—no society solely stratifies based on effort. Most sociologists define stratification in terms of socioeconomic status. **Socioeconomic status** (SES) can be defined in terms of power (the ability to get other people to do something), property (sum of possessions and income) and prestige (reputation in society), because these three concepts tend to (but not always) be related in U.S. society. Though these stratifications vary, the U.S. is roughly divided into the following social classes:

- Upper Class: the top 3% of the population who earn millions to billions in annual income; people in the upper class tend to possess a large amount of power, property, and prestige. Furthermore, it is estimated that the top 1% of the population, the "super rich," earns 5% of the income

- Middle Class: the 40% of the population who earns $46,000 up to the cut-off for the "upper class" (definitions here vary)
- Working Class: the 30% of the population who earns between $19,000 and $45,000
- Lower Class: the 27% of the population who earn less than $18,000

Inequality persists in U.S. society for a multitude of reasons. For one, those with the most power, property, and prestige are highly motivated to maintain their status also have the power and means to control and protect the system that keeps them at the top and others at the bottom. The super-rich not only own most of the companies and factories, but they also are capable of influencing legislature by supporting certain politicians and lobbying or advocating (often with their pocketbooks) for tax laws and other rules that will help them maintain their money and power, even at the expense of other people. Inequality also exists because it is ingrained in our society; we believe in the American Dream (if you work hard you can succeed!). Inequality also persists because people are socialized to accept their position in life; wealthy parents socialize their children to expect wealth and power and prestige while poor parents socialize their children to expect the same level of income that their parents make. The education system in the U.S. then serves to reinforce inequalities (see discussion on Education above).

Social mobility refers to the ability to move up or down within the social stratification system. **Upward mobility** refers to an increase in social class; in America, we applaud examples of upward mobility because everyone wants to believe that it is possible to achieve the American Dream. **Downward mobility** refers to a decrease in social class. **Intergenerational mobility** occurs when there is an increase or decrease in social class between parents and children within a family, and **intragenerational mobility** describes the differences in social class between different members of the same generation. For example, Mark Zuckerberg's sister is quite possibly in a very different social class than her brother, the founder of Facebook (a millionaire by age 30).

While individuals may be aware of their individual class standing in a strictly social or economic sense, sociologists also use specific terms to describe how aware individuals are of others who share their class and what effect this may have on social and economic life. Karl Marx theorized that capitalism would divide society into two classes: those who owned the means of production (the Bourgeoisie) and those who worked for the owners (the proletariat). As the owners buy up the means of production from small business owners, more and more people will be forced into the proletariat. As the proletariat grows larger and larger, members of that class will develop a new awareness of their status as workers—an individual's active awareness of his/her membership in a social class is called **class consciousness**. However, not all individuals gain this awareness of class relations. Members of the Bourgeoisie take capitalism for granted instead of seeing it is a historically situated (and transient) economic system. Meanwhile, members of the proletariat can have a **false consciousness** when they do not recognize the state of class relations under capitalism. This can happen when members of the proletariat believe strongly in meritocracy and economic rationality. Those with false consciousness fail to realize that faith in meritocracy can work against their class interests by hiding the consequences of the existing relations of production—exploitation of workers by the Bourgeoisie.

Social reproduction refers to the structures and activities in place in a society that serve to transmit and reinforce social inequality from one general to the next. Cultural capital and social capital are two mechanisms by which social reproduction occurs. **Cultural capital** refers to the non-financial social assets that promote social mobility. Education is an excellent example of cultural capital; an education gives someone the potential to be upwardly mobile (though there are a lot of reasons why inequalities in U.S.

educational system might actually partially prevent someone from becoming upwardly mobile, as well). **Social capital** refers to the potential for social networks to allow for upward social mobility. For example, if a young women comes from an upper middle-class family and wants to become a doctor, her mom might introduce her to a friend who is a doctor, who can give her some advice and set her up with a shadowing opportunity. Alternatively, if a young man comes from a poor neighborhood and wants to become a doctor, he might not know of anyone who is in the health-care field, and may not have any friends who are even planning on attending college. Social capital is a powerful way to tap into vast networks of resources, but can also serve to reinforce inequalities already present in society.

Power (the ability to get other people to do something) and **prestige** (reputation in society) are two related components of socioeconomic status in U.S. society. Both power and prestige rely on privilege, a less often discussed aspect of social life. **Privilege** is a set of unearned benefits one receives because of some attribute largely outside of their control, like one's gender, race, class, sexual identity, citizenship status, or ability. For example, many social institutions assume that all of their users are heterosexual. This can include tax benefits for married couples, hospital visitation rights, child custody, and routine health exams. Heterosexual individuals navigate these institutions without finding it odd that they fill out generic forms with entries for "mother" and "father," have people make assumptions that their spouse is of the opposite sex, or (for women) are asked if they are using contraception during safer sex discussions. Non-heterosexuals, however, do not experience the privilege of navigating social institutions that are built around their needs; they must constantly explain and educate, facing possible discrimination in the process. In a more literal example, able-bodied people have the privilege to navigate the built environment as they please, but a wheelchair user may have to take a more circuitous route to find an elevator, or may not be able to participate in certain activities at all. Overall, people who lack privilege cannot take certain things for granted, face disadvantage, and must put extra work into navigating social institutions.

When social scientists study privilege, they conceptualize different privileged identities (whiteness, maleness, heterosexuality, ablebodiedness, and so forth) as intersecting with each other and affording individuals advantage in a non-additive way. Likewise, different disadvantaged identities (non-white, non-male, non-heterosexual, disabled, et cetera) can intersect and afford individuals a compounded disadvantage. There are also situations where one form of privilege (for example, whiteness) can mitigate a disadvantaged identity (for example, disability). This analytical approach, which seeks to highlight the ways different identities intersect within individuals and social groups to produce unique social positions, is called **intersectionality**. Sociologists conducting intersectional analyses assert that, for example, the social position of a black lesbian cannot be understood by considering her blackness and then her non-heterosexuality; rather, the unique social position of black lesbian must be considered in its own right. Identities, whether privileged or disadvantaged, do not combine additively and should not be considered in isolation.

A person's social position shapes his or her life chances; as discussed above, people navigate social institutions differently based on his or her social position. When individuals can navigate social institutions with ease, they do not experience these institutions as constraining. However, when less-privileged individuals try to navigate the same social institutions, they run up against resistance or may not be able to navigate the institution at all. Different users' experience with the same institution is therefore stratified, and a disparity exists between those who easily navigate the institution and those who cannot or do so with difficulty. Health care is a very significant institution in U.S. society, and there are notable disparities between groups who can access the health care they need and those who cannot. One of the major factors that affects access is one's ability to pay for health care. Because health care must be bought just like other goods, the same socioeconomic gradient that affects individuals' ability to buy goods affects their ability to pay for health care. For this reason, we can consider the effect of a **socioeconomic gradient**

8.4

in health. However, this socioeconomic gradient transcends the ability to pay for medical care and extends to the conditions in which people live. One's socioeconomic status also affects where one can live and corresponds to the type of work one does. Lower paid work, such as unskilled manual labor, is often dirty, dangerous, and difficult (the 3 Ds). This type of work may predispose laborers to injury or ill health, all while affecting their ability to pay for their health care.

Global stratification compares the wealth, economic stability, and power of various countries. A comparison across the globe highlights the worldwide patterns of **global inequality:**

- certain countries hold a majority of the resources
- access to resources among countries seriously impacts other social factors, such a mortality
- the burden of inequality is placed on certain segments of the population

For example, the poorest people in the wealthiest countries (such as the U.S.) are far better off than the poorest people in the poorest countries. Likewise, women and racial and ethnic minorities often bear the brunt of unequal distributions of resources. High-income countries include the U.S., Canada, and many western European countries. Low-income countries include India, Nigeria, and China, among several others. In these countries, women are disproportionately affected by poverty. Poverty is defined as being either relative or absolute. **Relative poverty** is the inability to meet the average standard of living within a society whereas **absolute poverty** is the inability to meet a bare minimum of basic necessities, including clean drinking water, food, safe housing, and reliable access to health care.

Health and Health Care Disparities

On a broader scale, **social epidemiology** is the study of the distribution of health and disease across a population, with the focus on using social concepts to explain patterns of health and illness in a population. Many factors influence the accessibility and availability of health care across various social groups. **Health care disparities** include the population-specific differences in the presence of disease, health outcomes, and quality of health care across difference social groups. Social epidemiology can help to explain some of the health care disparities that exist across multiple social constructs, including gender, race, and class.

Gender

Historically, medical research, treatment, and pharmacological studies have been conducted on men. Some studies suggest that over 90% of medical research was conducted on male subjects only, and that the findings were extrapolated to women. Women were traditionally excluded from medical research for a number of reasons, including: the female menstrual cycle (and subsequent menopause) presented a fluctuating variable affecting her physiology (and might therefore impact the results of a drug study, for example), females might become pregnant (and virtually no medical research is conducted on pregnant women), and studies that included both male and female subjects were generally considered to be more difficult to conduct. For all of these reasons, medical research was conducted predominantly on men, and the results were then assumed to be similar for women. We are now seeing that this is not a responsible or ethical way to conduct research. For example, women and men are roughly equally likely to experience a heart attack, but women and men experience heart attack symptoms differently; men tend to experience "crushing" chest pain, but women are more likely to experience abdominal pain, indigestion, difficulty breathing, or fatigue. The fact that most early heart attack studies were conducted almost entirely in men led to a general misperception that women would experience the same symptoms as men, which is in fact not the case. Furthermore, there exists a disparity between how women and men are treated for heart disease, likely due to a **gender bias** (when women and men receive different treatment for the same disease or illness) and a lack of information. For example, women tend to be treated less aggressively than men for heart disease, primarily because studies on men have set the standard for detection and treatment of heart disease.

Drug dosing provides another example of the potentially deleterious effects of conducting medical research in men and extrapolating information to women. Recently, the Food and Drug Administration (FDA) pulled a popular prescription sleep aid from the market because women were experiencing drowsiness and impairment the morning following prescribed usage that was leading to an increase in car accidents. Further testing demonstrated that the recommended dosage was too high for women; a costly mistake that could have been prevented had drug-dosage studies been conducted on both women and men before the drug was approved.

Race and Social Class

While race and social class (or socioeconomic status) are two very different social constructs, when discussing health and health care disparities, it makes sense to look at these two factors together, partially because in the U.S. a large proportion of minority groups are also socioeconomically disadvantaged. Large health-care disparities exist between minorities and whites in the U.S. For example, infant mortality rates are almost twice as high for African Americans as they are for white people, disease risk for cancer, heart disease, and diabetes is higher for African Americans than for white people, and studies suggest that Hispanics receive 60% inferior health care than non-Hispanics. Access to health care and accurate health information is a large part of the problem. Lower-income areas (with larger proportions of minorities) have fewer health care facilities, and a lack of health insurance prevents many lower-income people from seeking regular or preventative health care. Typically, once an uninsured person makes it into the health care system, a problem that was potentially treatable has developed into a much larger (and much more expensive) problem, thus perpetuating the cycle of avoiding the doctor until it is, or is almost, too late.

Chapter 8 Summary

- A society is defined as the group of people who share a culture and live/interact with each other within a definable area.

- Functionalism is a sociological theory that conceptualizes society as a living organism with many different parts and organs, each of which has a distinct purpose; Émile Durkheim was a major proponent of functionalism.

- Manifest functions are the intended and obvious consequences of a structure; latent functions are unintended or less recognizable consequences of a structure.

- Conflict theory views society as a place where there will be inequality in resources, therefore individuals will compete for social, political, and material resources like money, land, power, and leisure; Karl Marx, a proponent of conflict theory, advocated for socialism.

- Symbolic interactionism examines the relationship between individuals and society by focusing on communication, the exchange of information through language and symbols

- The dramaturgical approach suggests that people in society choose what kind of image they want to communicate verbally and nonverbally to others.

- Social constructionism argues that people actively shape their reality through social interactions; it is therefore something that is constructed, not inherent.

- Social institutions are a complex of roles, norms, and values organized into a relatively stable form that contributes to social order by governing the behavior of people. They provide predictability and organization for individuals within a society, and mediate social behavior between people.

- Social institutions include family, education, organized religion, government and economy, and medicine.

- Culture simply refers to a shared way of life, including the beliefs and practices that a social group shares.

- Symbolic culture consists of symbols that carry a particular meaning and are recognized by people of the same culture.

- Material culture involves the physical objects that are particular to that culture.

- Values can be defined as a culture's standard for evaluating what is good or bad, while beliefs are the convictions or principles that people hold.

- Demography is the study of human population dynamics, including the size, structure, and distribution of a population, and changes in the population over time due to birth, death, and migration.

- Residential segregation refers to the separation of groups into different neighborhoods; separation most often occurs due to racial differences, ethnic differences, and/or socioeconomic differences.

- Environmental injustice refers to the fact that people in poorer communities are more likely to be subjected to negative environmental impacts to their health and well-being.

- Social stratification refers to the way that people are categorized in society; people can be categorized by race, education, wealth, and income (among other things).

- The two most common systems for categorizing people in a society are the class system (allows mobility between classes) and the caste system (unchangeable). A meritocracy is a stratification system that uses merit (or personal effort) to establish social standing; this is an idealized system—no society solely stratifies based on effort.

- Social mobility refers to the ability to move up or down within the social stratification system; upward mobility refers to an increase in social class while downward mobility refers to a decrease in social class.

- Intergenerational mobility occurs when there is an increase or decrease in social class between parents and children within a family, and intragenerational mobility describes the differences in social class between different members of the same generation.

- Social reproduction refers to the structures and activities in place in a society that serve to transmit and reinforce social inequality from one generation to the next.

- Cultural capital refers to the non-financial social assets that promote social mobility and social capital refers to the potential for social networks to allow for upward social mobility.

- Global stratification compares the wealth, economic stability, and power of various countries.

- Relative poverty is defined as an inability to meet the average standard of living within a society, while absolute poverty is the inability to meet a bare minimum of basic necessities, including clean drinking water, food, safe housing, and reliable access to health care.

- Many important disparities exist in both the U.S. and global health care systems, include gender disparities, race disparities, and disparities due to social class.

CHAPTER 8 FREESTANDING PRACTICE QUESTIONS

1. Social institutions include all of the following, EXCEPT:

A) Social networks
B) Families
C) Schools
D) Churches

2. Joy lives in a neighborhood where 40% of the population is obese. Almost half of the adults in her neighborhood are unemployed and rely on food stamps. There are no grocery stores within a ten block radius of where Joy lives, but there are many fast-food chains. The economic and social situation in Joy's neighborhood could be described as:

    I. a food desert.
   II. absolute poverty.
  III. relative poverty.

A) I only
B) II only
C) I and II
D) I and III

3. A country where the economy is profit-driven and privately-owned, but public services like health care and education are state-funded, would be considered:

A) socialist.
B) capitalist.
C) collectivist.
D) welfare capitalist.

4. A study finds that lower-income Hispanic women from a specific urban community located near a factory are more than twice as likely to develop a rare form of cancer than women in the general population. This finding could be potentially attributed to all of the following, EXCEPT:

A) class-dependent health care disparities.
B) environmental injustice.
C) gender-dependent health care disparities.
D) ethnicity-dependent health care disparities.

5. Which of the following is NOT a macro theory of sociology?

A) Functionalism
B) Conflict theory
C) Feminist theory
D) Symbolic interactionism

6. Which of the following is FALSE about Émile Durkheim's functionalism?

A) Functionalism is less concerned about the interactions of small groups.
B) Functionalism involves the idea that society is similar to an organism.
C) Functionalism encourages people to actively change the status quo of society for their own benefit.
D) Functionalism believes that once one part of an institution changes, it will always affect the other parts of the institution.

CHAPTER 8 PRACTICE PASSAGE

Historical data on life expectancies for the wealthy show that, since the Sanitary Act in the nineteenth century, mortality rates have decreased. The human life span has continued to increase over time, as countries have modernized. Among all of the age groups, decreases in infant mortality rates are the most dramatic because infant exposure to environmental pathogens is a huge factor affecting their mortality. In recent years, the elderly age group has begun to demonstrate an increase in life expectancy compared to the infant age group, which is beginning to demonstrate little or no change over time. Figure 1 displays the rise of modern life expectancy for the different age groups in the United States from 1900 to 2000.

Life Expectancy in the United States, 1900 to 2000							
Gender	**Age**	**1900**	**1920**	**1940**	**1960**	**1980**	**2000**
Male	0	43.9	62.4	65.3	75.9	77.3	77.5
	15	32.4	34.0	40.5	55.8	68.9	71.3
	35	28.3	27.3	23.5	28.4	38.4	41.4
	55	19.9	23.5	28.2	33.9	34.2	35.9
	75	5.2	5.7	3.3	3.8	4.5	4.9
Female	0	40.3	42.9	50.2	69.8	75.8	75.9
	15	34.5	39.1	40.3	58.3	60.3	69.3
	35	30.9	27.4	35.9	46.7	43.4	49.7
	55	23.4	24.2	29.6	32.3	36.8	34.3
	75	5.8	3.2	4.3	5.9	6.1	6.4

Figure 1   Life Expectancy in Years for Various Age Groups Between 1900-2000

Generally, females have higher life expectancy rates than males in modern societies. There is biological evidence that shows that women are more impervious to pathogens compared to men. For example, some theorize that the X-chromosome and hormonal mechanisms influence the efficiency of the immune system. There is also psychosocial evidence that supports this finding. Women in pre-modern societies have a higher mortality rate due to sexist practices, which can lead to neglect or even infanticide of female infants. Figure 2 displays the gender mortality ratio of men and women in the United States from 1900 to 2000. Gender mortality ratio is the male to female proportion in death rates.

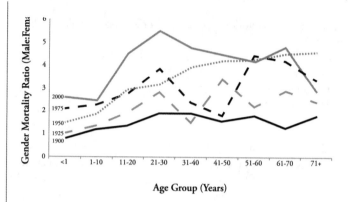

Figure 2   Gender Mortality Ratio in the United States Between 1900-2000

In pre-modern societies, there are high mortality rates due to poverty and governmental persecution. Most people in pre-modern societies believe that daily oppression is beyond their control, and that they have no choice but to accept their fate. On the other hand, people in modern societies believe that they can proactively strive for change when facing a difficult situation. Alex Inkeles was a sociologist who administered interviews to over 6,000 men from Argentina, Chile, India, Israel, Nigeria, and Pakistan to prove that modernization changes the personality structure of people. Inkeles discovered that during the course of modernization, individuals became more involved with the steps necessary to improve their society.

Source: Adapted from Leonard A. Sagan, *The Health of Nations: True Causes of Sickness and Well-Being.* ©1987 by Basic Books, Inc.

1. According to Figure 1, what is true about life expectancy in the United States?

A) In recent years, the life expectancy for infants has plateaued for both sexes.
B) Age 35 is the ideal age to accurately determine the expectancy of life for both sexes.
C) In 1980, males at age 55 had a higher life expectancy compared females at age 55.
D) At the age of 75, life expectancy consistently increased over time for both sexes.

2. Suppose that in a pre-modernist society, a lower-class woman tries to join a conversation among a group of upper-class men. As a result, the men ridicule the woman. This scenario most accurately portrays:

A) prejudice against the in-group.
B) prejudice against the out-group.
C) discrimination against the in-group.
D) discrimination against the out-group.

3. Suppose that a pre-modernist moves up from the lower class to the upper class because the government recognized his skills as a craftsman. Which of the following is true about this pattern of social mobility?

   I.   The pre-modernist experienced
        intergenerational mobility.
   II. The pre-modernist experienced
        intragenerational mobility.
   III. This pre-modern society practiced meritocracy.

A) I only
B) II only
C) I and III only
D) II and III only

4. According to Figure 2, at what age do the mortality rates of males widely differ from the mortality rates of females in 1925?

A) 21–30
B) 31–40
C) 41–50
D) 51–60

5. Poor people in pre-modern societies are forced to live in a place where they lack food, water, and shelter for them to survive. Which of the following most closely defines the struggles that lower class pre-modernists faced?

A) Absolute poverty
B) Social change
C) Relative poverty
D) Global inequality

6. Which ideology best describes Alex Inkeles's findings?

A) Traditional theory, in which society is observed at its current state in order to learn and understand its systems.
B) Critical theory, in which people continually evaluate and change society in order to attain progress.
C) Functionalism, in which the interdependence of institutions strives to maintain stability in a society.
D) Conflict theory, in which the inequality between classes ultimately forces change on a society.

SOLUTIONS TO CHAPTER 8 FREESTANDING PRACTICE QUESTIONS

1. **A** Social institutions are complexes of roles, norms, and values organized into a relatively stable form that contribute to social order by governing the behavior of people. Families, schools, and churches are all examples of social institutions (choices B, C, and D can be eliminated), while social networks are not (choice A is not a social institution and is the correct answer choice).

2. **D** Item I is true: a food desert refers to an area, typically in a highly populated lower-income urban environment, where healthy, fresh food is difficult to find. Joy's neighborhood does not have an nearby grocery store but does have a plethora of fast-food restaurants, therefore it would arguably qualify as a food desert (choice B can be eliminated). Item II is false: absolute poverty is the inability to meet a bare minimum of basic necessities, including clean drinking water, food, safe housing, and reliable access to health care; the scenario described is not absolute poverty (choice C can be eliminated). Item III is true: relative poverty is defined as an inability to meet the average standard of living within a society; due to the fact that so many in her neighborhood are unemployed, this scenario is arguably describing relative poverty (choice A can be eliminated and choice D is correct).

3. **D** Welfare capitalism refers to a system of government where most of the economy is private with the exception of extensive social welfare programs to serve certain social needs within society (such as health care and education; choice D is correct). Socialism is an economic system where resources and production are collectively owned. Socialism includes a system of production and distribution designed to satisfy human needs; good/services are produced for direct use instead of for profit (choice A is wrong). Capitalism is an economic system in which resources and production are mainly privately owned, and goods/services are produced for a profit; strict capitalism does not include state-funded public services (choice B is wrong). Collectivism is an economic or social outlook that emphasizes interdependence between people; a profit-driven economy would not be a part of a collectivist country (choice C is wrong).

4. **C** Gender-dependent health care disparities highlight differences in the treatment and outcomes between men and women; because this question relates lower-income Hispanic women to women in the general population, there is no evidence that the disparity is based on gender because no comparison is made to men (this finding is not attributable to choice C, so it is the correct answer choice). Class-dependent health care disparities are based on socioeconomic difference between classes and ethnicity-dependent health care disparities are based on ethnic difference between groups; because this question relates lower-income Hispanic women to women in the general population, it is possibly that this disparity exists due to either class and/or ethnicity (the finding could be attributable to either choices A or D. so both choices can be eliminated). Environmental injustice refers to the fact that people in poorer communities are more likely to be subjected to negative environmental impacts to their health and well-being; because these women live near a factory, this health care disparity could be the results of environmental injustice (the finding could be attributable to choice B, so it can be eliminated).

5. **D** Macro theories concern interactions between groups of people, while micro-level theories are concerned with interactions between individuals. Symbolic interactionism, which is concerned with the way individuals use symbols to communicate in society, is the only micro-level theory listed (choice D is not a macro-level theory and is the correct answer choice). Functionalism explains how social processes work on a broad scale. It considers the function and purpose of large groups within society, e.g., churches, schools, hospitals, and the like, and is considered a macro-level theory (choice A can be eliminated). Conflict theory explains society based on constant competition between groups for limited resources and is considered a macro-level theory (choice B can be eliminated). Feminist theory is concerned with inequality between the genders (whole groups of people) rather than inequalities between particular individuals (choice C is a macro-level theory and can be eliminated).

6. **C** Functionalism discourages people from changing the norm because it emphasizes the idea of stability through the universal agreement to abide by the norms of society (choice C is false and therefore, the correct answer). Functionalism focuses on society as a whole rather than the individual aspects of society (choice A is true and can be eliminated). Organic solidarity is an idea within functionalism that compares society to an organism (choice B is true and can be eliminated). Functionalists believe that if one part of the system changes, then the rest of the system will have to adjust to the dysfunction until social stability can be restored (choice D is true and can be eliminated).

SOLUTIONS TO CHAPTER 8 PRACTICE PASSAGE

1. **A** According to Figure 1, for both males and females at the age of 0, life expectancy 1980–2000 has not increased significantly; therefore, this figure illustrates that the life expectancy of infants has plateaued (choice A is correct). There is not enough information given in the passage or the figure to determine the age that is most ideal for accurately calculating life expectancy (choice B is wrong). In 1980, males at the age of 55 had a lower life expectancy rate (34.2) than females (36.8; choice C is wrong). Between the years 1900–2000, life expectancy rates at age 75 decreased for females in 1920 and for males in 1940 (choice D is wrong).

2. **D** Discrimination is the mistreatment of others based on their perceived differences in characteristics and social position. The men view the woman as an out-group member because they do not identify themselves as being in the same group as her based on their status and gender (choice D is correct and choice C is wrong). Prejudice leads to discrimination. It is the positive or negative attitude that people have about another group of people based on their perceptions of them. The scenario does not closely relate to the concept of prejudice because the men have already committed the action of discrimination against the woman by mocking her (choice A and choice B are wrong).

3. **D** Item I is false: intergenerational mobility is the mobility across generations. This usually occurs when the child has a higher or lower social class than their parents (choices A and C can be eliminated). Note that both remaining answer choices include Item II so it must be true: unlike intergenerational mobility, intragenerational mobility is the mobility within the generation for an individual. The pre-modernist moved up in social class within his lifetime. Item III is true: meritocracy is the system in which power and prestige are given to those who have the skills to be appointed in the upper class. The pre-modernist gained mobility through his craftsmanship skills (choice B can be eliminated and choice D is correct).

4. **C** By following the gender mortality ratio in 1925, ages 41-50 have a mortality ratio of roughly 3.4, meaning that for every 1 female who dies, 3.4 males die within this age range; therefore, this is the highest mortality ratio between men and women (choice C is correct). Although ages 21-30 have the highest ratio in 2000, the same trend does not apply for the year 1925 (choice A is wrong). Ages 31-40 show gender mortality ratio at its lowest in 1925 (choice B is wrong). Although ages 51-60 have a high gender mortality ratio in 1975, it is not the same case for 1925 (choice D is wrong).

5. **A** Absolute poverty is defined as the capacity of necessary living resources that individuals are able to attain; poor pre-modernists have no choice but to live in a society that they struggle to acquire those necessities (choice A is correct). Social change is the adjustment of social systems that can occur over a period of time; pre-modernists in poverty were less likely to participate in creating social changes because of their fatalistic point of view (choice B is wrong). Relative poverty is when there is a reference point of the group of people in comparison to another group of people based on their socioeconomic status and living conditions; the question stem is closely related to absolute poverty because it focuses more on the physical resources needed for survival (choice C is wrong). Global inequality can be eliminated as an answer because the question does not go into the inequalities in a global perspective (choice D is wrong).

6. **B** According to the last paragraph, "Inkeles discovered that during the course of modernization, individuals became more involved with the steps necessary to improve their society".
Critical theory as defined in the answer choices is most applicable to the scenario described
in the passage (choice B is correct). Traditional theory is focused on learning and understanding a given society rather than proactively making change, as Inkeles described in his
study (choice A is wrong). Functionalism strives for stability and prompts people to stay
with the status quo; furthermore, Inkeles does not make any conclusions about "institutions" (choice C is wrong). Conflict theory involves the power struggle between classes;
there is no information in the passage that supports the idea that class struggle was one of
Inkeles' discoveries (choice D is wrong).

Psychology and Sociology Glossary

After each entry, the section number in the *MCAT Psychology & Sociology Review* text where the term is discussed is given.

absolute poverty
The inability to meet a bare minimum of basic necessities, including clean drinking water, food, safe housing, and reliable access to health care. [**Section 8.4**]

acetylcholine (ACh)
The neurotransmitter used at the neuromuscular junction, throughout the parasympathetic nervous system, and by the preganglionic neurons of the sympathetic nervous system. [**Section 3.2**]

acetylcholinesterase
The enzyme that breaks down acetylcholine in the synaptic cleft. [**Section 3.2**]

achieved status
Those statuses that are considered to be due largely to an individual's efforts. [**Section 7.3**]

acquisition
In classical conditioning, the process of learning the association between a conditioned stimulus and response. [**Section 5.1**]

action potential
A localized change in a neuron's membrane potential that propagates away from its point of origin. Action potentials are all-or-none processes mediated by the opening of voltage-gated Na^+ and K^+ channels when the membrane is brought to threshold potential; opening Na^+ channels causes characteristic depolarization, while opening K^+ channels repolarizes the membrane. [**Section 3.1**]

activation-synthesis theory
The theory that dreams are simply byproducts of brain activation during REM sleep. Suggests that the content of dreams is not purposeful or meaningful. [**Section 4.3**]

actor-observer bias
The tendency to blame our actions on the situation and blame the actions of others on their personalities. [**Section 7.2**]

addiction
A compulsion to perform an act repeatedly; can consist of a psychological dependence and/or a physical dependence as evidenced by drug addiction withdrawal. [**Section 4.3**]

adrenal cortex
The outer region of the adrenal gland. The adrenal cortex produces cortisol in response to long-term (chronic) stress and aldosterone in response to low blood pressure or low blood osmolarity. [**Section 3.6**]

adrenal medulla
The inner region of the adrenal gland, the adrenal medulla is part of the sympathetic nervous system and releases epinephrine (adrenaline) and norepinephrine into the bloodstream when stimulated. Epinephrine and norepinephrine prolong and enhance the effect of sympathetic stimulation on the body. [**Section 3.4**]

adrenocorticotropic hormone (ACTH)
A tropic hormone produced by the anterior pituitary gland that targets the adrenal cortex, stimulating it to release cortisol and aldosterone. [**Sections 3.6 & 4.5**]

affect
A person's visible emotion in the moment. [**Section 6.3**]

affirmative action
Policies that take factors like race or sex into consideration to benefit underrepresented groups in admissions or job hiring decisions; these policies have been used to benefit those believed to be current or past victims of discrimination. [**Section 7.2**]

aggregate
People who exist in the same space but do not interact or share a common sense of identity. [**Section 7.2**]

aggression
Behavior that is forceful, hostile, or attacking. In sociology, aggression is considered something that is intended to cause harm or promote social dominance within a group. [**Section 7.3**]

Ainsworth, Mary
Famous for her "strange situation experiments" where mothers would leave their infants in an unfamiliar environment to see how they would react. Studies suggested a distinction between securely attachment infants and insecurely attached infants. [Section 5.3]

algorithm
A step-by-step detailing aid to problem solving. [Section 4.2]

alpha waves
Low amplitude, high frequency brain waves present in a relaxed state. Alpha waves are the first indicator that a person is ready to drift off to sleep. [Section 4.3]

altruism
A behavior that helps ensure the success or survival of the rest of a social group, possibly at the expense of the success or survival of the individual. [Section 7.3]

Alzheimer's disease
The most prevalent form of dementia, this disease is characterized behaviorally by an inability to form new memories, known as anterograde amnesia. [Section 6.3]

amalgamation
Occurs when majority and minority groups combine to form a new group. [Section 7.1]

amygdala
Almond-shaped structure deep within the brain that orchestrates emotional experiences. [Section 4.4]

anal stage
The second of Freud's five psychosexual stages, in this stage the child seeks sensual pleasure through control of elimination. [Section 6.1]

anterior pituitary gland
Also known as the adenohypophysis, the anterior pituitary is made of glandular tissue. It makes and secretes six different hormones: FSH, LH, ACTH, TSH, prolactin, and growth hormone. The anterior pituitary is controlled by releasing and inhibiting factors from the hypothalamus. [Section 3.6]

anterograde amnesia
An inability to form new memories. [Sections 5.4 & 6.3]

antisocial personality disorder
A psychological disorder characterized by a history of serious behavior problems beginning in adolescence, including significant aggression against people or animals, deliberate property destruction, lying or theft, and serious rule violation. [Section 6.3]

anxiety disorder
Anxiety is an emotional state of unpleasant physical and mental arousal; a preparation to fight or flee. In a person with an anxiety disorder, the anxiety is intense, frequent, irrational (out of proportion), and uncontrollable; it causes significant distress or impairment of normal functioning. [Section 6.3]

aqueous humor
A thin, watery fluid found in the anterior segment of the eye (between the lens and cornea). The aqueous humor is constantly produced and drained, and helps bring nutrients to the lens and cornea, as well as remove metabolic wastes. [Section 3.5]

Asch, Solomon
Conducted research on conformity and group pressure by placing subjects in a room with several confederates (the subjects believed the confederates to be fellow study subjects) and observing the behavior of the subject when the confederates provided clearly wrong answers to questions. [Section 7.2]

ascribed status
Those statuses that are assigned to a person by society regardless of the person's own efforts. [Section 7.3]

assimilation
The process in which an individual forsakes aspects of his or her own cultural tradition to adopt those of a different culture. Generally, this individual is a member of a minority group who is attempting to conform to the culture of the dominant group. [Section 7.1]

associative learning
Process of learning in which one event, object, or action is directly connected with another. Two general categories include classical and operant conditioning. [**Section 5.1**]

attenuation model of selective attention
Model of selective attention in which the mind has an attenuator, like a volume knob, that can tune up inputs to be attended and tune down unattended inputs, rather than totally eliminating them. Accounts for the cocktail party effect. [**Section 4.2**]

attitude
A person's feelings and beliefs about other people or events around him or her, and his or her behavioral reactions based on those underlying evaluations. [**Section 6.4**]

attribution theory
A theory that attempts to explain how individuals view behavior—both our own behavior and the behavior of others—by attributing behavior to either internal or external causes. [**Section 7.2**]

auditory cortex
The area of the temporal lobe responsible for processing sound information. [**Section 3.5**]

auditory tube
Also known as the Eustachian tube, the auditory tube connects the middle ear cavity with the pharynx. It functions to equalize middle ear pressure with atmospheric pressure so that pressure on both sides of the tympanic membrane is equal. [**Section 3.5**]

authoritarian parenting
Parenting style in which parents impose strict rules that are expected to be followed unconditionally in an attempt to control children. This style is demanding and often relies on punishment. [**Section 5.3**]

authoritative parenting
Parenting style that places limits on behavior and consistently follows through on consequences, but also expresses warmth and nurturing and allows for two-way communication between parents and children. [**Section 5.3**]

autonomic nervous system (ANS)
The division of the peripheral nervous system that innervates and controls the visceral organs (everything but the skeletal muscles). It is also known as the involuntary nervous system and can be subdivided into sympathetic and parasympathetic branches. [**Section 3.4**]

availability heuristic
Mental shortcut of making judgments on the frequency of something occurring based on how readily it is available in our memories. [**Section 4.2**]

avoidance learning
The process by which one learns to perform a behavior in order to ensure that a negative or aversive stimulus will not be present. [**Section 5.1**]

avoidant personality disorder
A psychological disorder characterized by feelings of inadequacy, inferiority, and undesirability, and a preoccupation with fears of criticism. [**Section 6.3**]

axon
A long projection of the cell body of a neuron down which an action potential can be propagated. [**Section 3.1**]

Babinski reflex
In response to the sole of the foot being stroked, a baby's big toe moves upward or toward the top surface of the foot and the other toes fan out. [**Section 5.3**]

back stage
In the dramaturgical perspective, this is where we can "let down our guard" and be ourselves, as opposed to the "front stage," where we are playing a role for others. [**Section 7.3**]

Bandura, Albert
Famous for his Bobo doll studies that demonstrated observational learning; also pioneered the idea of the importance of self-efficacy in promoting learning. [**Section 5.1**]

baroreceptor
A sensory receptor that responds to changes in pressure; for example, there are baroreceptors in the carotid arteries and the aortic arch that monitor blood pressure. [Section 3.5]

basal nuclei
Also known as basal ganglia, these structures in the brain help to smooth coordinated movement by inhibiting excess movement. [Section 3.4]

basilar membrane
The flexible membrane in the cochlea that supports the organ of Corti (the structure that contains the hearing receptors). The fibers of the basilar membrane are short and stiff near the oval window and long and flexible near the apex of the cochlea. This difference in structure helps the basilar membrane to transduce pitch. [Section 3.5]

behavioral genetics
Study of the role of inheritance in interacting with experience to determine an individual's personality and behaviors. [Section 5.2]

behavioral therapy
This type of therapy uses conditioning to shape a client's behaviors in the desired direction. [Section 6.1]

behaviorism
According to this perspective, personality is a result of learned behavior patterns based on a person's environment. Behaviorism is deterministic, proposing that people begin as blank slates and that environmental reinforcement and punishment completely determine an individual's subsequent behavior and personalities. [Section 6.1]

beliefs
The convictions or principles that people within a culture hold. [Section 8.2]

belief bias
A tendency to draw conclusions based on what one already believes rather than sound logic. [Section 4.2]

belief perseverance
The maintenance of beliefs even in the face of evidence to the contrary. [Section 4.2]

bilateral descent
A system of lineage in which the relatives on the mother's side and father's side are considered equally important. [Section 8.2]

biofeedback
Means of recording and feeding back information about subtle autonomic responses to an individual in an attempt to train the individual to control previously involuntary responses (for example, muscle tension, heart rate, respiratory rate). [Section 4.5]

bipolar disorder
A psychological disorder characterized by cyclic mood episodes at both extremes or "poles," depression and mania. In bipolar I disorder, a person has experienced at least one manic or mixed episode. In bipolar II disorder, the manic phases are less extreme. [Section 6.3]

bipolar neuron
A neuron with a single axon and a single dendrite, often projecting from opposite sides of the cell body. Bipolar neurons are typically associated with sensory organs. [Section 3.1]

body dysmorphic disorder
A psychological disorder characterized by a preoccupation with a slight physical anomaly or imagined defect in appearance, often involving the face, hair, breasts, or genitalia. [Section 6.3]

borderline personality disorder
A psychological disorder characterized by enduring or recurrent instability in impulse control, mood, and image of self and others. Impulsive and reckless behavior, together with extreme mood swings, reactivity, and anger, can lead to unstable relationships and to damage both of the person with the disorder and of others in his or her life. [Section 6.3]

bottom-up processing
A type of sensory processing that begins with the sensory receptors and works up to the complex integration of information occurring in the brain; note that the brain in fact uses a combination of bottom-up processing and top-down processing. [Section 3.5]

Broca's area
Region of the brain located in the left hemisphere of the frontal lobe and involved with speech production. Damage to this part of the brain results in Broca's aphasia, where individuals know what they want to say but are unable to express it verbally. [Section 4.6]

bystander effect
The fact that a person is less likely to provide help when there are other people around. [Section 7.2]

Cannon-Bard Theory
Theory of emotion that asserts that the physiological and cognitive aspects of emotion occur simultaneously and collectively lead to the behavioral reaction. [Section 4.4]

capitalism
An economic system in which resources and production are mainly privately owned and goods/services are produced for a profit. [Section 8.2]

caste system
A closed social stratification where people can do nothing to change the category that they are born into. [Section 8.4]

catatonic-type schizophrenia
A psychological disorder characterized by psychosis in the form of catatonic behavior (including extremely retarded or excited motor activity). [Section 6.3]

category
People who share similar characteristics but are not otherwise tied together as a group. [Section 7.2]

Cattell, Raymond
A psychologist interested in personality, who used factor analysis with hundreds of surface traits to identify which traits were related to each other. By this process, he identified sixteen source traits, and by factor analysis reduced fifteen of these into five global factors: extroversion, anxiety, receptivity, accommodation, and self-control. [Section 6.1]

central executive
Part of Alan Baddeley's model of working memory that oversees the visuospatial sketchpad, phonological loop, and episodic buffer. Responsible for shifting and dividing attention. [Section 4.2]

central nervous system
The subdivision of the nervous system consisting of the brain and spinal cord. [Section 3.4]

central route
Cognitive route of persuasion based on the content and deeper aspects of an argument. [Section 5.2]

cerebellum
The region of the brain that coordinates and smoothes skeletal muscle activity. [Section 3.4]

cerebral cortex
A thin (4 mm) layer of gray matter on the surface of the cerebral hemispheres. The cerebral cortex is the conscious mind, and is functionally divided into four lobes: the frontal lobes, parietal lobes, temporal lobes, and occipital lobes. [Section 3.4]

cerebrospinal fluid (CSF)
A clear fluid that circulates around and through the brain and spinal cord. CSF helps to physically support the brain and acts as a shock absorber. It also exchanges nutrients and wastes with the brain and spinal cord. [Section 3.4]

charismatic authority
A form of leadership where devotion is reliant upon an individual with exceptional charisma (persuasiveness, charm, and ability to connect with people). [Section 8.2]

chemical synapse
A type of synapse at which a chemical (a neurotransmitter) is released from the axon of a neuron into the synaptic cleft, where it binds to receptors on the next structure (either another neuron or an organ). [Section 3.2]

chemoreceptor
A sensory receptor that responds to specific chemicals. Some examples are gustatory (taste) receptors, olfactory (smell) receptors, and central chemoreceptors (which respond to changes in cerebrospinal fluid pH). [Section 3.5]

choroid
The darkly-pigmented middle layer of the eyeball, found between the sclera (outer layer) and the retina (inner layer). [Section 3.5]

chunking
Memory technique in which information to be remembered is organized into discrete groups of data. This clustering allows more information to be remembered overall. [Section 5.4]

church
In sociology, a type of religious organization that is well-integrated into the political and economic structures of society, and it attempts to provide an all-encompassing worldview for followers. [Section 8.2]

ciliary muscle
Muscle that helps focus light on the retina by controlling the curvature of the lens of the eye. [Section 3.5]

circadian rhythm
The waxing and waning of alertness throughout the 24-hour day. [Section 4.3]

class system
A social stratification where people are grouped together by similar wealth, income, education, and the like, but the classes are open, meaning that people can strive to reach a higher class (or fall to a lower one). [Section 8.4]

classical conditioning
Process in which two stimuli are paired in a way that changes a response to one of them. [Section 5.1]

cochlea
The curled structure in the inner ear that contains the membranes and hair cells used to transduce sound waves into action potentials. [Section 3.5]

cocktail party effect
Phenomenon of information of personal importance from previously unattended channels "catching" one's attention. [Section 4.1]

coercive organizations
Organization in which members do not have a choice in joining. [Section 7.3]

cognitive behavioral therapy (CBT)
A type of therapy that addresses thoughts and behaviors that are maladaptive by using goal-oriented and systematic techniques. [Section 6.1]

cognitive dissonance theory
A theory that explains that we feel tension ("dissonance") whenever we hold two thoughts or beliefs ("cognitions") that are incompatible, or when attitudes and behaviors don't match. When this occurs, we try to reduce this unpleasant feeling of tension by making our views of the world match how we feel or what we've done. [Section 6.4]

cognitive psychology
Tradition of psychology that focuses on the brain, cognitions, and thoughts as mediating learning and stimulus-response behaviors. [Section 5.1]

concrete operational stage
Piaget's third stage of his developmental theory where children aged 7 to 11 learn to think logically and learn the principle of conservation as well as mathematical concepts. [Section 4.2]

conditioned response
A previously unconditioned response to an unconditioned stimulus that has become a learned response to a conditioned stimulus. [Section 5.1]

conditioned stimulus
An originally neutral stimulus that is paired with an unconditioned stimulus until it can produce the conditioned response without the unconditioned stimulus being present. [Section 5.1]

cones
Photoreceptors in the retina of the eye that respond to bright light and provide color vision. [Section 3.5]

confederates
In psychological and social research, a confederate is a person who is working with the experimenter and posing as a part of the experiment, but the subjects are not aware of this affiliation. [Section 7.2]

confirmation bias
A tendency to search only for information that confirms a preconceived conclusion. [Section 4.2]

conflict theory
A theory that views society as being in competition for limited resources. According to conflict theory, society is a place where there will be inequality in resources, therefore individuals will compete for social, political, and material resources like money, land, power, and leisure. [Section 8.1]

conformity
The phenomenon of adjusting behavior or thinking based on the behavior or thinking of others. [Section 7.2]

consciousness
Awareness of self, internal states, and the environment. [Section 4.3]

conversion disorder
A psychological disorder characterized by a change in sensory or motor function that has no discernible physical or physiological cause, and which seems to be significantly affected by psychological factors. The symptoms of conversion disorder begin or worsen after an emotional conflict or other stressor. [Section 6.3]

cornea
The clear portion of the tough outer layer of the eyeball, found over the iris and the pupil. [Section 3.5]

corpus callosum
The largest bundle of white matter (axons) connecting the two cerebral hemispheres. [Section 3.4]

cortisol
This steroid hormone is released during chronic stress; it shifts the body's use of fuel from glucose toward fats and proteins, thus "sparing" glucose for the brain's use. Prolonged release of cortisol is associated with suppressed immunity and increased susceptibility to illness. [Sections 3.6 & 4.5]

crude birth rate
The annual number of live births per thousand people in a population. [Section 8.3]

crude death rate
The annual number of deaths per thousand people in a population. [Section 8.3]

cult (also known as a new religious movement)
A religious organization that is far outside society's norms and often involves a very different lifestyle. [Section 8.2]

culture
A shared way of life, including the beliefs and practices that a social group shares. [Section 8.3]

cultural capital
The non-financial social assets that promote social mobility. [Section 8.4]

cultural relativism
Judging another culture based on its own cultural standards. [Section 7.2]

cultural universals
Patterns or traits that are common to all people; cultural universals tend to pertain to basic human survival and needs, such as securing food and shelter, and also pertain to events that every human experiences, including birth, death, and illness. [Section 8.3]

cyclothymic disorder
A psychological disorder that is similar to bipolar disorder but the moods are less extreme. A person with cyclothymic disorder has experienced cyclic moods, including many hypomanic episodes, as well as many episodes of depressed mood that are milder than a major depressive episode for at least two years. [**Section 6.3**]

death instinct
According to psychoanalytic theory, the death instinct drives aggressive behaviors fueled by an unconscious wish to die or to hurt oneself or others. [**Section 6.1**]

deindividuation
An explanation of people's startling and often uncharacteristic behavior when situations provide a high degree of arousal and a very low sense of responsibility. [**Section 7.2**]

delusion
A false belief that is not due to culture, and is not relinquished despite evidence that it is false. [**Section 6.3**]

demography
The study of human population dynamics, including the size, structure, and distribution of a population, and changes in the population over time due to birth, death, and migration. [**Section 8.3**]

dendrite
A projection off the cell body of a neuron that receives nerve impulses from a different neuron and sends the impulse to the cell body. Neurons can have one or several dendrites. [**Section 3.1**]

dependent personality disorder
A psychological disorder characterized by a need to be taken care of by others and an unrealistic fear of being unable to take care of himself or herself. [**Section 6.3**]

depersonalization disorder
A psychological disorder characterized by a recurring or persistent feeling of being cut off or detached from one's body or mental processes, as if observing one's self from the outside. [**Section 6.3**]

depolarization
The movement of the membrane potential of a cell away from the resting potential to a more positive membrane potential. [**Section 3.1**]

depressant
Class of drugs that depress or slow down neural activity, includes alcohol, barbiturates (tranquilizers), and opiates. [**Section 4.3**]

depth of processing
The idea that information that is thought about at a deeper level is better remembered. [**Section 5.4**]

deviance
A violation of society's standards of conduct or expectations. [**Section 7.2**]

Diagnostic and Statistical Manual of Mental Disorders (DSM)
The universal authority on the classification and diagnosis of psychological disorders; the current latest edition is the fifth edition of the DSM (the DSM-5). [**Section 6.3**]

diencephalon
The portion of the forebrain that includes the thalamus and hypothalamus. [**Section 3.4**]

difference threshold (also called the just noticeable difference, or JND)
This threshold is the minimum noticeable difference between any two sensory stimuli 50% of the time. [**Section 3.5**]

discrimination (scientific)
Occurs when the conditioned stimulus is differentiated from other stimuli. [**Section 5.1**]

discrimination
Unjust treatment of a group, based on group characteristics (such as age, sex, race, ethnicity, disability). [**Section 7.2**]

dishabituation
The restoration to full strength of a response to a stimulus that had previously become weakened through habituation. [**Section 5.1**]

disorganized-type schizophrenia
A psychological disorder that is characterized by psychosis in the form of flat or inappropriate affect, disorganized speech, and disorganized behavior. [Section 6.3]

dissociative amnesia
A psychological disorder characterized by at least one episode of suddenly forgetting some important personal information, usually related to severe stress or trauma. [Section 6.3]

dissociative disorder
A psychological disorder characterized by a person's thoughts, feelings, perceptions, memories, or behaviors being separated from conscious awareness and control, in a way that is not explainable as mere forgetfulness. [Section 6.3]

dissociative fugue
A psychological disorder where someone suddenly goes on a journey, during which he or she cannot recall personal history prior to the journey. [Section 6.3]

dissociative identity disorder
A psychological disorder characterized by alternating between two or more distinct personality states (or identities), only one of which interacts with other people at any one time. [Section 6.3]

divided attention
The ability to focus on multiple tasks simultaneously. [Section 4.1]

downward mobility
A decrease in social class. [Section 8.4]

dramaturgical approach
Assumes that people are theatrical performers and that everyday life is a stage; just as actors project a certain on-screen image, people in society choose what kind of image they want to communicate verbally and nonverbally to others. Also called the dramaturgical perspective. [Sections 7.3 & 8.1]

drive
An urge originating from a physiological discomfort such as hunger, thirst, or sleepiness. Drives can be useful for alerting an organism that it is no longer in a state of homeostasis, an internal state of equilibrium. [Section 6.2]

Drive Reduction Theory
A theory about the impact of motivation on human behavior that suggests that a physiological need (a drive) creates an aroused state that motivates the organism to reduce that need by engaging in some behavior. [Section 6.2]

dual coding hypothesis
A hypothesis that it is easier to remember words with associated images than either words or images alone. [Section 5.4]

Durkheim, Émile
Considered the father of sociology and a major proponent of functionalism, Émile Durkheim was the pioneer of modern social research and established the field of sociology as separate and distinct from psychology and political philosophy. [Section 8.1]

dynamic equilibrium
In sociology, a dynamic equilibrium occurs when complex societies contain many different but interdependent parts working together to maintain stability. [Section 8.1]

dyssomnias
Broad category of disorders involving abnormalities in the amount, quality, or timing of sleep. Includes insomnia, narcolepsy, and sleep apnea. [Section 4.3]

dysthymic disorder
A psychological disorder characterized as a less intense, chronic form of depression. A person with dysthymic disorder has felt milder symptoms of depression most days for at least two years, with symptoms never absent for more than two months, and without experiencing a major depressive episode. [Section 6.3]

ecclesia
A dominant religious organization that includes most members of society, is recognized as the national or official religion, and tolerates no other religions. [Section 8.2]

echoic memory
Memory for sound, which lasts for about 3-4 seconds. [Section 5.4]

effector
The organ that carries out the command sent along a particular motor neuron. [Section 3.3]

efferent neurons
A neuron that carries information (action potentials) away from the central nervous system; a motor neuron. [Section 3.3]

egalitarian family
A family system where spouses are treated as equals and may be involved in more negotiation when making decisions. [Section 8.2]

ego
According to Freud's psychoanalytic theory, the ego is ruled by the reality principle, and uses logical thinking and planning to control consciousness and the id (the unconscious driving force ruled by the pleasure principle). [Section 6.1]

ego defense mechanisms
To cope with this anxiety and protect the ego, all people develop ego defense mechanisms that unconsciously deny or distort reality. Ego defense mechanisms are therefore normal, and become unhealthy only when taken to extremes. [Section 6.1]

elaboration likelihood model
Model that explains when people may be persuaded by just the content of an argument, and when they may be persuaded by more superficial characteristics such as the appearance of the person delivering the message or the length of the argument. [Section 5.2]

Electra complex
This complex occurs during the phallic stage (the third of Freud's five psychosexual stages) when a female child is sexually attracted to her father and hostile toward her mother, who is seen as a rival. [Section 6.1]

electrical synapse
A type of synapse in which the cells are connected by gap junctions, allowing ions (and therefore the action potential) to spread easily from cell to cell. [Section 3.2]

electroencephalogram (EEG)
Recording of electrical impulses in the brain. [Section 4.3]

electromyogram (EMG)
Recording of skeletal muscle movements. [Section 4.3]

electrooculogram (EOG)
Recording of eye movements. [Section 4.3]

empathy
The ability to identify with others' emotions. [Section 7.3]

encoding
The process of transferring sensory information into the memory system. [Section 5.4]

endocrine gland
A ductless gland that secretes hormones into the blood. [Section 3.6]

endocrine system
A system of ductless glands that secrete chemical messengers (hormones) into the blood. [Section 3.6]

endogamy
The practice of marrying within a particular group. [Section 8.2]

environmental injustice
When people in poorer communities are more likely to be subjected to negative environmental impacts to their health and well-being. [Section 8.4]

epinephrine
A hormone produced and secreted by the adrenal medulla that prolongs and increases the effects of the sympathetic nervous system. [**Section 3.4**]

episodic buffer
Part of Alan Baddeley's model of working memory that interacts with information in long-term memory. [**Section 4.2**]

episodic memory
Autobiographical memory for information of personal importance. [**Section 5.4**]

EPSP
Excitatory postsynaptic potential; a slight depolarization of a postsynaptic cell, bringing the membrane potential of that cell closer to the threshold for an action potential. [**Section 3.2**]

Erikson, Erik
Erikson extended Freud's theory of developmental stages in two ways. Erikson added social and interpersonal factors, to supplement Freud's focus on unconscious conflicts within a person. And Erikson delineated additional developmental stages and conflicts in adolescence and adulthood, to supplement Freud's focus on early childhood. Erikson's stages include: trust vs. mistrust, autonomy vs. shame and doubt, initiative vs. guilt, industry vs. inferiority, identity vs. role confusion, intimacy vs. isolation, generativity vs. stagnation, and integrity vs. despair. [**Section 6.1**]

escape learning
Through operant conditioning, this is the process of learning to engage in a particular behavior in order to get away from a negative or aversive stimulus. [**Section 5.1**]

estrogen
The primary female sex hormone. Estrogen stimulates the development of the female secondary sex characteristics during puberty, maintains those characteristics during adulthood, stimulates the development of new uterine lining after menstruation, and stimulates mammary gland development during pregnancy. [**Section 3.6**]

ethnicity
A socially defined concept referring to whether or not people identify with each other based on shared social experience or ancestry. [**Section 8.3**]

ethnocentrism
The tendency to judge people from another culture by the standards of one's own culture. [**Section 7.2**]

executive functions
Higher order thinking processes that include planning, organizing, inhibition, and decision-making. [**Section 4.4**]

exocrine gland
A gland that secretes its product into a duct, which ultimately carries the product to the surface of the body or into a body cavity. An example of exocrine glands are sweat glands. [**Section 3.6**]

exogamy
A requirement to marry outside a particular group, with it being the norm in almost all cultures to prohibit sexual relationships between certain relatives. [**Section 8.2**]

explicit (or declarative) memory
Memories that can be consciously recalled, such as factual knowledge. [**Section 5.4**]

external locus of control
The belief that one does not have control over outcomes, but they are controlled by outside forces. [**Section 7.1**]

extinction
In classical conditioning, the unpairing of the conditioned and unconditioned stimuli, accomplished by introducing the conditioned stimulus repeatedly in the absence of the unconditioned stimulus. [**Section 5.1**]

false consensus
Occurs when we assume that everyone else agrees with what we do (even though they may not). [**Section 7.2**]

false memory
Inaccurate memory created by the power of imagination or suggestion. [**Sections 4.3 & 5.4**]

feature detection theory
A theory of visual perception that proposes that certain neurons fire for individual and specific features of a visual stimulus, such as shape, color, line, movements, etc. [Section 3.5]

fecundity
The potential reproductive capacity of a female in a population. [Section 8.3]

feral children
Neglected or abandoned children who grow up without human contact or care; much of our knowledge about socialization comes from these individuals who were not socialized. [Section 7.1]

filter model
Model of selective attention that suggests that information from a sensory buffer is put through a filter that allows only selected inputs through. [Section 4.1]

Five-Factor Model (Costa and McCrae's Five-Factor Model)
A model developed to explain personality using five overarching personality traits, which include: extroversion, neuroticism, openness to experience, agreeableness, and conscientiousness. [Section 6.1]

fixed-interval schedule
Reinforcement schedule in which reward is offered after a set period of time has passed. [Section 5.1]

fixed-ratio schedule
Reinforcement schedule in which reward is offered after a set number of instances of a behavior. [Section 5.1]

folkways
Norms that are more informal, yet shape everyday behavior (styles of dress, ways of greeting). [Section 7.1]

food desert
An area, typically in a highly populated lower-income urban environment, where healthy, fresh food is difficult to find. [Section 8.2]

foot-in-the-door phenomenon
A strategy that involves enticing people to take small actions, and then gradually asking for larger and larger commitments. [Section 6.4]

formal operational stage
Piaget's fourth stage of his developmental theory from age 12 to adulthood. During this stage, people learn abstract and moral reasoning. [Section 4.2]

Freud, Sigmund
An Austrian neurologist who is considered the founding father of psychoanalytic theory. [Section 6.1]

front stage
In the dramaturgical perspective, this is where we play a role and use impression management to craft the way we come across to other people. [Section 7.3]

frustration-aggression principle
This principle suggests that when someone is blocked from achieving a goal, this frustration can trigger anger, which can lead to aggression. [Section 7.3]

functional fixedness
A tendency to perceive the functions of objects as fixed and unchanging. [Section 4.2]

functionalism (also known as structural functionalism)
The oldest of the main theories of sociology, this theory conceptualizes society as a living organism with many different parts and organs, each of which has a distinct purpose. [Section 8.1]

fundamental attribution error
When we tend to underestimate the impact of the situation and overestimate the impact of a person's character or personality on their behavior. [Section 7.2]

fundamentalists
People who observe strict adherence to religious beliefs. [Section 8.2]

Gage, Phineas
Famous case of a man who suffered damage to his prefrontal cortex after a railroad tie blasted through his head. His symptoms, due to damage to this area, included impulsivity, an inability to stick to plans, and an inability to demonstrate empathy. [Section 4.4]

game theory
A theory used to try and predict large, complex systems, such as the overall behavior of a population. [Section 7.3]

ganglion
A clump of gray matter (unmyelinated neuron cell bodies) found in the peripheral nervous system. [Section 3.4]

gender bias in medicine
Occurs when women and men receive different treatment for the same disease or illness. [Section 8.4]

general fertility rate
The annual number of live births per 1000 women of childbearing age within a population. [Section 8.3]

general intelligence
Foundational base of intelligence that supports more specialized abilities. [Section 5.2]

generalization
In classical conditioning, the process by which stimuli similar to a conditioned stimulus also become conditioned stimuli that elicit the conditioned response. [Section 5.1]

generalized anxiety disorder (GAD)
A psychological disorder characterized by tension or anxiety much of the time about many issues, but without the presence of panic attacks. [Section 6.3]

generalized other
When a person tries to imagine what is expected of them from society, they are taking on the perspective of the generalized other. [Section 7.1]

genital stage
The fifth of Freud's five psychosexual stages, this stage begins in adolescence, when sexual themes resurface and a person's life/sexual energy fuels activities such as friendships, art, sports, and careers. [Section 6.1]

genotype
The genetic makeup of an organism. [Section 5.2]

gestalt psychology
A theory that the brain processes information in a holistic manner; specifically, for visual information, the brain tends to make assumptions in order to detect the whole, instead of serially processing all of the individual parts. [Section 3.5]

global inequality
The extent to which income and wealth is distributed in an uneven manner among the world's population. [Section 8.4]

global stratification
A comparison of the wealth, economic stability, and power of various countries. [Section 8.4]

glucagon
A peptide hormone produced and secreted by the alpha cells of the pancreas. It primarily targets the liver, stimulating the breakdown of glycogen, thus increasing blood glucose levels. [Section 3.6]

gonadotropins
Anterior pituitary tropic hormones; follicle stimulating hormone (FSH) and luteinizing hormone (LH) stimulate the gonads (ovaries and testes) to produce gametes and to secrete sex steroids. [Section 3.6]

gray matter
Unmyelinated neuron cell bodies and short unmyelinated axons. [Section 3.4]

group
A collection of any number of people (as few as two) who regularly interact and identify with each other, sharing similar norms, values, and expectations. [Section 7.2]

group polarization
The phenomenon where groups tend to intensify the preexisting views of their members until the average view is more extreme than it initially was. [Section 7.2]

group pressure (or peer pressure)
Pressure exerted by a group that causes one to change behaviors, values, attitudes, or beliefs. [Section 7.2]

groupthink
A phenomenon where, within a group, the desire for harmony or conformity results in an easy consensus, even if the final decision is not the best one. [Section 7.2]

growth hormone
A hormone released by the anterior pituitary that targets all cells in the body. Growth hormone stimulates whole body growth in children and adolescents, and increases cell turnover rate in adults. [Section 3.6]

Gumplowicz, Ludwig
Expanded upon Marx's ideas about conflict theory by proposing that society is shaped by war and conquest, and that cultural and ethnic conflicts lead to certain groups becoming dominant over other groups. [Section 8.1]

gustatory receptors
Chemoreceptors on the tongue that respond to chemicals in food. [Section 3.5]

habit
Action that is performed repeatedly until it becomes automatic. [Section 5.1]

habituation
A decrease in response to a stimulus after repeated presentations. [Section 5.1]

hair cells
Sensory receptors found in the inner ear. Cochlear hair cells respond to vibrations in the cochlea caused by sound waves, and vestibular hair cells respond to changes in position and acceleration (used for balance). [Section 3.5]

hallucination
A false sensory perception that occurs while a person is conscious (not during sleep or delirium). [Section 6.3]

hallucinogens
Class of drugs also known as psychedelics that distort perceptions in the absence of any sensory input, creating hallucinations or altered sensory perceptions; includes LSD and marijuana. [Section 4.3]

halo effect
A tendency to believe that people have inherently good or bad natures, rather than looking at individual characteristics. [Section 7.2]

Harlow, Harry and Margaret
Researchers known for their controversial experiments with monkeys in which they showed that baby monkeys are drawn to mothers that provide comfort rather than simply food. Also showed that monkeys raised in isolation developed severe mental and social deficits. [Section 5.3]

health care disparities
The population-specific differences in the presence of disease, health outcomes, and quality of health care across different social groups. [Section 8.4]

heuristics
Mental shortcuts used for problem-solving. Using heuristics sometimes sacrifices accuracy for speed. [Section 4.2]

hippocampus
Brain structure located in the medial temporal lobe of the brain and plays a key role in forming memories. Damage to this part of the brain can lead to an inability to form new memories, or anterograde amnesia. [Section 4.4]

histrionic personality disorder
A psychological disorder characterized by a strong desire to be the center of attention, and seeking to attract attention through personal appearance and seductive behavior. [Section 6.3]

humanistic psychology
A psychological perspective developed partially in response to Freud's psychoanalytic theory, which emphasizes an individual's inherent drive toward self-actualization. Carl Rogers is most associated with humanistic psychology. [Section 6.1]

hypnotism
Structured social interaction in which an individual is instructed to focus attention a particular way, relax, and let go. Hypnotized individuals may be more susceptible to accepting suggestions. [Section 4.3]

hypochondriasis
A psychological disorder characterized by a preoccupation with the fear of having a serious illness. [Section 6.3]

hypophysis
The pituitary gland. [Section 3.6]

hypothalamus
Brain structure located above the brain stem that is involved in many autonomic processes including body temperature, hunger, thirst, fatigue, and sleep. It is also involved in the physiological aspects of emotion, including sweating and increased heart rate.
[Sections 3.6 & 4.4]

iconic memory
The brief photographic memory for visual information, which decays in a few tenths of a second. [Section 5.4]

id
According to Freud's psychoanalytic theory, the largely unconscious id is the source of energy and instincts. Ruled by the pleasure principle, the id seeks to reduce tension, avoid pain, and gain pleasure. It does not use logical or moral reasoning, and it does not distinguish mental images from external objects. According to Freud, young children function almost entirely from the id.
[Section 6.1]

ideal self
Constructed out of life experiences, societal expectations, and admirable traits from role models. The ideal self is the person you ought to be, while the real self is the person you actually are. [Section 7.1]

identity formation (or individuation)
The development of a distinct individual personality. [Section 7.1]

illusory correlation
A perceived relationship between two things (people, events, or behaviors), even when none exists. [Section 7.2]

implicit (or procedural) memory
Memory that involves conditioned associations and knowledge of how to do something. [Section 5.4]

impression management or self-presentation
The conscious or unconscious process whereby people attempt to manage their own images by influencing the perceptions of others. This is achieved by controlling the amount or type of information or the social interaction. [Section 7.3]

in-group
A group that an individual belongs to and believes to be an integral part of who they are. [Section 7.2]

incentive theory
A theory that suggests that incentives (objects and events in the environment that either help induce or discourage certain behaviors) motivate human behavior. [Section 6.2]

inclusive fitness
A theory that suggests that cooperation among organisms (including altruistic behaviors) promotes genetic success, meaning that even if not all of the organisms survive to reproduce, some of their genes will still be passed to the next generation. [Section 7.3]

incongruity
The emotional result when the real self falls short of the ideal self. [Section 7.1]

infantile amnesia
A lack of explicit memory for events that occurred before the age of roughly 3.5 years. While people are unable to recall memories from this part of their life, learning and memory do still occur. The reason for infantile amnesia is unknown. [Section 5.3]

information-processing models
Models for cognition that assume that information from the environment is processed by our computer-like minds through a series of steps including attention, perception, and storage into memory. [Section 4.2]

informational social influence
The process of complying because we want to do the right thing and we feel like others "know something I don't know." [Section 7.2]

insecure attachment
Style of relating to others that forms when an infant has caregivers who are inconsistently responsive or unresponsive to needs. In Ainsworth's experiments, insecurely attached infants were found to be less likely to explore their surroundings in the presence of their mother. They may be extremely upset or demonstrate indifference when the mother returned to the room. [Section 5.3]

insight learning
Sudden flash of inspiration that provides a solution to a problem. The "Aha!" moment where previously learned ideas or behaviors are suddenly combined in unique ways. [Sections 4.2 & 5.1]

insomnia
Most common sleep disorder, characterized by difficulty falling or staying asleep. [Section 4.3]

instinct
Behaviors that are unlearned and present in fixed patterns throughout a species. [Section 6.2]

institutional discrimination
Refers to unjust and discriminatory practices employed by large organizations that have been codified into operating procedures, processes, or institutional objectives. [Section 7.2]

instrumental conditioning
See operant conditioning. [Section 5.1]

intellectual disability
Classification for individuals who have an IQ below 70 and functional impairment in their everyday lives. Previously called "mental retardation." [Section 5.2]

intelligence
The ability to learn from experience, problem-solve, and use knowledge to adapt to new situations. [Section 5.2]

intergenerational mobility
A change (increase or decrease) in social class between parents and children within a family. [Section 8.4]

internal locus of control
The belief of an individual that she is able to influence outcomes through her own efforts and actions. [Section 7.1]

interneuron
A neuron found completely within the central nervous system. Interneurons typically connect sensory and motor neurons, especially in reflex arcs. [Section 3.3]

intragenerational mobility
Describes the differences in social class between different members of the same generation. [Section 8.4]

IPSP
Inhibitory postsynaptic potential; a slight hyperpolarization of a postsynaptic cell, moving the membrane potential of that cell further from threshold. [Section 3.2]

iris
A pigmented membrane found just in front of the lens of the eye. In the center of the iris is the pupil, a hole through which light enters the eyeball. The iris regulates the diameter of the pupil in response to the brightness of light. [Section 3.5]

James-Lange Theory
Theory of emotion that claims that emotional experience is the result of physiological and behavioral responses. [Section 4.4]

351

just world phenomenon
The tendency to believe that the world is fair and people get what they deserve. When bad things happen to others, it is the result of their actions or their failure to act, and when good things happen to us, it is because we deserved it. [Section 7.2]

justification of effort
When people modify their attitudes to match their behaviors, specifically those involving effort. [Section 6.4]

K-complex
Large and slow wave with a duration of a half second that occurs in Stage 2 sleep. [Section 4.3]

kinship
Familial relationships including blood ties, family ties, and common ancestry. [Section 8.2]

Kohlberg's stages of moral development
Six identifiable developmental stages of moral reasoning, which form the basis of ethical behavior. The pre-conventional (level 1) contains the first stage (obedience and punishment orientation) and second stage (self-interest orientation). The conventional (level 2) contains the third stage (interpersonal accord and conformity) and fourth stage (authority and social-order maintaining orientation). The post-conventional (level 3) contains the fifth stage (social contract orientation) and sixth stage (universal ethical principles). [Section 7.1]

language
A symbolic system that is codified for communication. [Section 4.2]

language acquisition
The process by which infants learn to understand and speak their native language. [Section 4.6]

language acquisition device
Innate feature unique to the human mind that allows people to gain mastery of language from limited exposure during sensitive developmental years in early childhood, as hypothesized by Noam Chomsky. [Section 4.6]

latency stage
The fourth of Freud's five psychosexual stages; in this stage sexual interest subsides and is replaced by interests in other areas such as school, friends, and sports. [Section 6.1]

latent content
According to Freud, the unconscious drives and wishes that are difficult to express and underlie dreams. [Section 4.3]

latent functions
The unintended or less recognizable consequences or a social structure; can be considered beneficial, neutral, or harmful. [Section 8.1]

latent learning
Learning this takes place in the absence of any observable behavior to show that it has occurred. This learning can later manifest and be demonstrated as observable behavior when it is required. [Section 5.1]

learned helplessness
A condition where one has learned to behave helplessly, failing to respond even though there are opportunities to avoid unpleasant circumstances or gain positive rewards. [Sections 4.5 & 7.1]

libido
According to psychoanalytic theory, the libido is the life instinct, which drives behaviors focused on survival, growth, creativity, pain avoidance, and seeking pleasure. [Section 6.1]

life expectancy
The number of years that an individual at a given age can expect to live at present mortality rates. [Section 8.3]

linguistic relativity hypothesis
Asserts that the language one speaks determines their thoughts and perceptions of the world. [Section 4.6]

long-term memory
Information that is retained long-term, potentially indefinitely; it is believed to have an infinite capacity. [Section 5.4]

long-term potentiation
A persistent increase in synaptic strength between two neurons that occurs following brief periods of their stimulation. Leads to increase sensitivity of neurons recently stimulated. Believed to play a role in learning and the consolidation of memory from short-term memory to long-term memory. [Section 5.1]

looking glass self
The idea that a person's sense of self develops from interpersonal interactions with others in society and the perceptions of others. According to this idea, people shape their self-concepts based on their understanding of how others perceive them. [Section 7.1]

luteinizing hormone (LH)
A tropic hormone produced by the anterior pituitary gland that targets the gonads. In females, LH triggers ovulation and the development of the corpus luteum during the menstrual cycle; in males, LH stimulates the production and release of testosterone. [Section 3.6]

major depressive disorder
A psychological disorder characterized by one or more major depressive episodes, where a person has felt worse than usual for most of the day, nearly every day, for at least two weeks. [Section 6.3]

manic episode
An experience of an abnormal euphoric, unrestrained, or irritable mood, with at least three of the following symptoms: grandiose, exaggerated, or delusional self-esteem, high energy with little need for sleep, increased talkativeness and pressured speech, poor judgment; increased psychomotor and goal-directed activity, and distractibility with flight of ideas or racing thoughts. [Section 6.3]

manifest content
According to Freud, the overt storylines of dreams. [Section 4.3]

manifest functions
The intended and obvious consequences of a social structure. [Section 8.1]

Marx, Karl
Closely identified with conflict theory, Marx argued that societies progress through class struggle between those who own and control production and those who labor and provide the manpower for production. He believed that capitalism produced internal tensions which would ultimately lead to self-destruction of capitalist society, to be replaced by socialism. Karl Marx, along with Émile Durkeim and Max Weber, is considered a founding father of sociology. [Section 8.1]

Maslow's Hierarchy of Needs
Abraham Maslow sought to explain human behavior by creating a hierarchy of needs (demonstrated by a pyramid). At the base of this pyramid are physiological needs, or the basic elements necessary to sustain human life. In order, the rest of the needs include: safety, love and belongingness, esteem, and self-actualization. Lower level needs must be met before higher level needs. [Section 6.2]

master status
The one status that dominates the other statuses and determines that individual's general position in society. [Section 7.3]

material culture
Consists of the physical objects that are particular to a culture, which helps to explain the relationship between artifacts and social relations. [Section 8.3]

matriarchy
A social system where females (especially mothers within families) are the primary authority figures. [Section 8.2]

matrilineal descent
A system of lineage in which the relatives on the mother's side are considered most important; an individual belongs to their mother's lineage. [Section 8.2]

mechanoreceptor
A sensory receptor that responds to mechanical disturbances, such a shape changes (being squashed, bent, pulled). Mechanoreceptors include touch receptors in the skin, hair cells in the ear, muscle spindles, and others. [Section 3.5]

meditation
Mindfulness technique for training attention in a particular way; may involve intense focus on one object of attention or broad attention to a field of awareness. [**Section 4.3**]

medulla oblongata
The portion of the hindbrain that controls respiratory rate and blood pressure, and specialized digestive and respiratory functions such as vomiting, sneezing, and coughing. [**Section 3.4**]

melatonin
Hormone produced by the pineal gland that affects sleep/wake cycles and seasonal functions. [**Section 4.3**]

meninges
The protective connective tissue wrappings of the central nervous system (the dura mater, arachnoid mater, and pia mater). [**Section 3.4**]

mental retardation
See *intellectual disability*. [**Section 5.2**]

mental set
A tendency to fixate on ideas and solutions that have worked in the past, even if they may not apply to the current situation. [**Section 4.2**]

mere exposure effect
The phenomenon where people develop a preference for things because they have been exposed to them (sometimes repeatedly). [**Section 7.3**]

mere presence
The most basic level of "interaction" between individuals; when people are simply in each other's presence, either completing similar activities or just minding their own business. [**Section 7.2**]

meritocracy
A social stratification where people's social standings are judged based on merit (or personal effort) alone; this is an idealized system—no society solely stratifies based on effort. [**Section 8.4**]

method of loci
A memory device that involves imagining moving through a familiar place, such as your home, and in each place, leaving a visual representation of a topic to be remembered. [**Section 5.4**]

midbrain
The portion of the brain responsible for visual and auditory startle reflexes. [**Section 3.4**]

Milgram, Stanley
Conducted research on obedience where he asked subjects to administer a shock to what they thought was another subject (but was just an actor), and he monitored the degree of subjects' compliance or obedience. [**Section 7.2**]

Mindfulness-based stress reduction (MBSR)
Protocol involving mindfulness meditation shown to be effective for helping individuals with pain, stress, and anxiety. [**Section 4.3**]

mindguarding
When some members of the group prevent dissenting opinions from permeating the group by filtering out information and facts that go against the beliefs of the group; this tends to lead to groupthink. [**Section 7.2**]

mirror neurons
Neurons that fire when a particular behavior or emotion is observed in another. May be responsible for vicarious emotions and a foundation for empathy. [**Section 5.1**]

misinformation effect
A tendency to misremember an event, particularly when misleading information is presented between the event and the mental encoding of the event. [**Section 5.4**]

mnemonic
Any memory technique use to promote the retention and retrieval of information. [**Section 5.4**]

modeling
Mechanism behind observational learning in which an observer sees a behavior being performed by another person. This model is utilized to allow the observer to later imitate the behavior. [Section 5.1]

monogamy
A form of marriage in which two individuals are married only to each other. [Section 8.2]

mood
A person's sustained internal emotion that colors his or her view of life. [Section 6.3]

mood-dependent memory
When learning occurs during a particular emotional state, it is most easily recalled when one is again in that emotional state. [Section 5.4]

mood disorder
A psychological disorder characterized by a persistent pattern of abnormal mood serious enough to cause significant personal distress and/or significant impairment to social, occupational, or personal functioning. [Section 6.3]

mores
Norms that are highly important for the benefit of society and so are often strictly enforced. Mores are generally (but not always) formal norms. [Section 7.1]

moro reflex
Startle reflex. In response to a loud sound or sudden movement, and infant will startle; the baby throws back its head and extends its arms and legs, cries, then pulls the arms and legs back in. This reflex is present at birth, and lasts until about six months. [Section 5.3]

mortality
The death rate in a population. [Section 8.3]

multiculturalism (also known as pluralism)
A perspective that endorses equal standing for all cultural traditions. It promotes the idea of cultures coming together in a true melting pot, rather than in a hierarchy. [Section 7.1]

multipolar neuron
A neuron with a single axon and multiple dendrites; the most common type of neuron in the nervous system. [Section 3.1]

myelin
An insulating layer of membranes wrapped around the axons of almost all neurons in the body. Myelin is essentially the plasma membranes of specialized cells. In the peripheral nervous system they are Schwann cells and in the CNS they are oligodendrocytes. [Section 3.1]

narcissistic personality disorder
A psychological disorder characterized by feelings of grandiosity, with fantasies of beauty, brilliance, and power. [Section 6.3]

narcolepsy
Sleep disorder in which the individual experiences periodic, overwhelming sleepiness during waking periods that usually last less than five minutes. [Section 4.3]

negative feedback
A biological process that works by maintaining stability or homeostasis; a system produces a result, which feeds back to stop the system and maintain the result within tightly controlled bounds. [Section 6.2]

negative punishment
The removal of a positive or rewarding stimulus following a behavior. Tends to decrease the likelihood of that behavior. [Section 5.1]

negative reinforcement
The removal of a negative or aversive stimulus following a behavior. Tends to increase the frequency of that behavior. [Section 5.1]

neural plasticity
A process that refers to the malleability of the brain's pathways and synapses based on behavior, the environment, and neural processes. [Section 5.4]

neuron
The basic functional and structural unit of the nervous system. The neuron is a highly specialized cell designed to transmit action potentials. [Section 3.1]

neurotransmitter
A chemical released by the axon of a neuron in response to an action potential that binds to receptors on the postsynaptic cell and causes that cell to either depolarize slightly (EPSP) or hyperpolarize slightly (IPSP). Examples are acetylcholine, norepinephrine, GABA, dopamine, and others. [Section 3.2]

neutral stimulus
A stimulus that does not elicit any intrinsic response in the absence of outside interference (conditioning). [Section 5.1]

night terror
Usually occur during Stage 3 sleep, unlike nightmares. The individual may sit up or walk around, babble, and appear terrified, although none of it is remembered the next morning. [Section 4.3]

nociceptors
Pain receptors. Nociceptors are found everywhere in the body except the brain. [Section 3.5]

nodes of Ranvier
Gaps in the myelin sheath of the axons of peripheral neurons. Action potentials can "jump" from node to node, thus increasing the speed of conduction (saltatory conduction). [Section 3.1]

nonassociative learning
Learning that occurs in the absence of associating specific stimuli or events. Two types are habituation and sensitization. [Section 5.1]

nonverbal communication
Involves all of the methods for communication that we use that do not include words. [Section 7.3]

norepinephrine (NE)
The neurotransmitter used by the sympathetic division of the autonomic nervous system at the postganglionic (organ-level) synapse. [Section 3.2]

normative social influence
When the motivation for compliance is a desire for the approval of others and to avoid rejection. [Section 7.2]

normative organizations
An organization where membership is based on morally relevant goals. [Section 7.3]

norms
The visible and invisible rules of social conduct within a society. Norms help define what types of behaviors are acceptable and in accordance with a society's values and beliefs. Formal norms are generally written down; laws are examples of formal norms. Informal norms are generally understood but are less precise and often carry no specific punishments. [Sections 7.1 & 8.3]

nucleus accumbens
Structure located in the brainstem and part of the dopaminergic reward pathway. Releases dopamine in response to many drugs, contributing to addictive behavior. [Section 4.3]

object permanence
The understanding that things continue to exist once they are out of sight. [Section 4.2]

observational learning (or vicarious, social learning)
A type of learning that occurs when a person watches another person's behavior and its consequences, thereby learning rules, strategies, and expected outcomes in different situations. [Section 6.1]

obsessive-compulsive disorder (OCD)
A psychological disorder characterized by obsessions (repeated, intrusive, uncontrollable thoughts or impulses that cause distress or anxiety), compulsions (repeated physical or mental behaviors that are done in response to an obsession or in accordance with a set of strict rules, in order to reduce distress or prevent something dreaded from occurring), or both. [Section 6.3]

obsessive-compulsive personality disorder (OCPD)
A psychological disorder characterized by accumulation of money or worthless objects. [Section 6.3]

Oedipus complex
This complex occurs during the phallic stage (the third of Freud's five psychosexual stages) when a male child is sexually attracted to his mother and hostile toward his father, who is seen as a rival. [Section 6.1]

olfactory receptors
Chemoreceptors in the upper nasal cavity that respond to odor chemicals. [Section 3.5]

operant conditioning
Also known as instrumental conditioning. A form of associative learning based on consequences, in which rewards increase the frequency of behaviors associated with them and punishments decrease their frequency. [Section 5.1]

optic disk
The "blind spot" of the eye, this is where the axons of ganglion cells exit the retina to form the optic nerve. There are no photoreceptors in the optic disk. [Section 3.5]

optic nerve
The nerve extending from the back of the eyeball to the brain that carries visual information. The optic nerve is made up of the axons of the ganglion cells of the retina. [Section 3.5]

optimism bias
The belief that bad things happen to other people, but not to us. [Section 7.2]

oral stage
The first of Freud's five psychosexual stages, in this stage the child seeks sensual pleasure through oral activities such as sucking and chewing. [Section 6.1]

organ of Corti
The structure in the cochlea of the inner ear made up of the basilar membrane, the auditory hair cells, and the tectorial membrane. The organ of Corti is the site where auditory sensation is detected and transduced to action potentials. [Section 3.5]

organization
A large group, more impersonal than a network, that comes together to pursue particular activities and meet goals efficiently. [Section 7.3]

ossicles
The three small bones found in the middle ear (the malleus, the incus, and the stapes) that help to amplify the vibrations from sound waves. The malleus is attached to the tympanic membrane and the stapes is attached to the oval window of the cochlea. [Section 3.5]

out-group
A group that an individual does not belong to. [Section 7.2]

outer ear
The portion of the ear consisting of the pinna and the external auditory canal. The outer ear is separated from the middle ear by the tympanic membrane (the eardrum). [Section 3.5]

oval window
The membrane that separates the middle ear from the inner ear. [Section 3.5]

overconfidence
An overestimation of the accuracy of one's knowledge and judgments. [Section 4.2]

pain disorder
A psychological disorder characterized by clinically important pain whose onset or severity seems significantly affected by psychological factors. [Section 6.3]

palmar grasp reflex
In response to stroking a baby's palm, the baby's hand will grasp. This reflex lasts a few months. [Section 5.3]

panic disorder
A psychological disorder that is characterized by panic attacks, which can be cued by certain situations, but are more often uncued or "spontaneous," occurring frequently and unexpectedly. [Section 6.3]

parallel processing
A system whereby many aspects of a stimulus are processed simultaneously instead of in a step-by-step or serial fashion. [Section 3.5]

paranoid personality disorder
A psychological disorder characterized by mistrust and misinterpretation of others' motives and actions, and suspicion of harm or betrayal. [Section 6.3]

paranoid-type schizophrenia
A psychological disorder characterized by psychosis is in the form of hallucinations and/or delusions, usually relating to a certain theme. [Section 6.3]

parasomnia
Abnormal behaviors during sleep, including somnambulism and night terrors. [Section 4.3]

parasympathetic nervous system (PNS)
The division of the autonomic nervous system known as the "resting and digesting" system. It causes a general decrease in body activities such as heart rate and blood pressure, an increase in blood flow to the GI tract, and an increase in digestive function. Because the preganglionic neurons all originate from either the brain or the sacrum, it is also known as the *craniosacral* system. [Sections 3.4 & 4.4]

parathyroid hormone
A hormone produced and secreted by parathyroid glands that increases serum calcium levels. It targets the bones (stimulates osteoclasts), the kidneys (increases calcium reabsorption), and the small intestine (increases calcium absorption). [Section 3.6]

Parkinson's disease
A movement disorder caused by the death of cells that generate dopamine in the basal ganglia and substantia nigra, two subcortical structures in the brain. Among the symptoms are a resting tremor (shaking), slowed movement, rigidity of movements and the face, and a shuffling gait. [Section 6.3]

patriarchy
A social system where males are the primary authority figures, and where fathers hold authority over women and children in a family. [Section 8.2]

patrilineal descent
A system of lineage in which the relatives on the father's side are considered most important; an individual belongs to their father's lineage. [Section 8.2]

Pavlov, Ivan
Famous for naming and describing the process of classical conditioning by training dogs to salivate to the sound of a ringing bell. [Section 5.1]

penis envy
Occurs during the phallic stage (the third of Freud's five psychosexual stages), when a female realizes she does not have a penis. [Section 6.1]

peptide hormone
A hormone made of amino acids (in some cases just a single, modified amino acid). Peptide hormones are generally hydrophilic and cannot cross the plasma membranes of cells, thus receptors for peptide hormones must be found on the cell surface. An exception is thyroxine, which is hydrophobic enough to enter the cells easily. Binding of a peptide hormone to its receptor usually triggers a second messenger system within the cell. [Section 3.6]

peripheral nervous system
All the parts of the nervous system except for the brain and spinal cord. [Section 3.4]

peripheral route
Cognitive route of persuasion that involves more superficial or secondary characteristics of an argument or an orator. [Section 5.2]

permissive parenting
Parenting style that creates few rules and demands and little discipline. Parents are warm and loving toward their children, but very lenient and allow their children to be in charge. [Section 5.3]

person-situation controversy (also known as the trait versus state controversy)
This controversy stems from a disagreement about the degree to which a person's reaction in a given situation is due to their personality (trait) or is due to the situation itself (state). [Section 6.1]

personal identity
A distinct sense of self, including personally-defined attributes. [Section 7.1]

personality
The nuanced and complex individual pattern of thinking, feeling, and behavior associated with each person. [Section 6.1]

personality disorder
A psychological disorder characterized by an enduring, rigid set of personality traits that deviates from cultural norms, impairs functioning, and causes distress either to the person with the disorder or to those in his or her life. [Section 6.3]

personality trait
A generally stable predisposition toward a certain behavior. [Section 6.1]

phallic stage
The third of Freud's five psychosexual stages, in this stage the child seeks sensual pleasure through the genitals. [Section 6.1]

phenotype
The observable characteristics and traits of an organism. [Section 5.2]

pheromone
A chemical signal that causes a social response in members of the same species. [Section 3.5]

phobia
A strong unreasonable fear that almost always causes either general anxiety or a full panic attack. [Section 6.3]

phonological loop
Part of Alan Baddeley's model of working memory that allows for the repetition of verbal information to aid with encoding it into memory. [Section 4.2]

photoreceptor
A receptor that responds to light. [Section 3.5]

physical attractiveness stereotype
A specific type of halo effect bias; people tend to rate attractive individuals more favorably for personality traits and characteristics than they do those who are less attractive. [Section 7.2]

Piaget, Jean
Developmental psychologist who formulated a four-stage theory of development for children. [Section 4.2]

pineal gland
Region of the brain responsible for the production of melatonin, a hormone that influences sleep/wake cycles and seasonal functions. [Section 4.3]

polyandry
A form of marriage in which a woman is married to more than one man. [Section 8.2]

polygamy
A form of marriage in which an individual may have multiple wives or husbands simultaneously. [Section 8.2]

polygyny
A form of marriage in which a man is married to more than one woman. [Section 8.2]

polysomnography (PSG)
Multimodal technique for measuring physiological processes during sleep, including EEG, EMG, and EOG. [Section 4.3]

positive punishment
The introduction of a negative or aversive stimulus following a behavior. Tends to decrease the likelihood of that behavior. [Section 5.1]

positive reinforcement
Reward immediately following a behavior. Tends to increase the frequency of that behavior (for example, praise). [Section 5.1]

positive transfer
When old information facilitates the learning of new information. [Section 5.4]

post-traumatic stress disorder (PTSD)
Disorder characterized by three clusters of symptoms: re-experiencing of the traumatic event through flashbacks or nightmares, hypervigilance to one's surroundings, and avoidance of situations related to the stressful event. [Sections 4.5 & 6.3]

posterior pituitary gland
Also known as the neurohypophysis, the posterior pituitary is made of nervous tissue (neurons) and stores and secretes two hormones made by the hypothalamus: oxytocin and ADH. The posterior pituitary is controlled by action potentials from the hypothalamus. [Section 3.6]

postganglionic neuron
In the autonomic division of the PNS, a neuron that has its cell body located in an autonomic ganglion (where a preganglionic neuron synapses with it), and whose axon synapses with the target organ. [Section 3.4]

prefrontal cortex
Anterior part of the frontal lobes of the brain involved in complex behaviors such as planning, sequencing, social responses, and decision making. Directs behavioral aspects of emotion including approach and avoidance behaviors. Damage to this area may lead to inappropriate social behavior, impulsivity, and trouble with initiation. [Section 4.4]

preganglionic neuron
In the autonomic nervous division of the PNS, and neuron that has its cell body located in the CNS, and whose axon extends into the PNS to synapse with a second neuron at an autonomic ganglion (the second neuron's axon synapses with the target organ). [Section 3.4]

prejudice
The thoughts, attitudes, and feelings someone holds about a group that are not based on actual experience; a prejudgment or biased thinking about a group and its members. [Section 7.2]

preoperational stage
Piaget's second stage in his developmental theory from ages 2 to 7. During this stage, children learn pretend play and the idea that a symbol can represent something else. They remain egocentric in this stage. [Section 4.2]

primacy effect
A tendency to better recall the first items on a list. [Section 5.4]

primary groups
Groups that play a more important role in an individual's life (often meeting emotional needs); these groups are usually smaller and include those with whom the individual engages with in person, in long-term, emotional ways. [Section 7.2]

primary reinforcers
Unconditioned consequences that are innately satisfying or desirable. May be biologically driven. [Section 5.1]

priming
An effect of implicit memory whereby exposure to a given stimulus "primes" or prepares the brain to respond to a later stimulus. [Section 5.4]

principle of aggregation
The idea that an attitude affects a person's aggregate or average behavior, but cannot necessarily predict each isolated act. [Section 6.4]

prison study (also known as the Stanford prison study)
A psychological experiment conducted by Philip Zimbardo designed to elucidate the extreme effects of role-playing on human behavior. 24 male students were isolated and asked to plays the roles of prisoners and guards; the participants adapted to their roles well beyond Zimbardo's expectations. The "guards" enforced extreme measures, including psychological torture, and many of the "prisoners" passively accepted psychological abuse and readily harassed other "prisoners" who attempted to prevent it. [Section 6.4]

proactive interference
A type of memory interference that occurs when previously learned information interferes with the recall of information learned more recently. [Section 5.4]

progesterone
A steroid hormone produced by the corpus luteum in the ovary during the second half of the menstrual cycle. Progesterone maintains and enhances the uterine lining for the possible implantation of a fertilized ovum. It is the primary hormone secreted during pregnancy. [Section 3.6]

projection bias
Occurs when we assume others have the same beliefs we do, due to our tendency to look for similarities between ourselves and others. [Section 7.2]

prolactin
A hormone secreted by the anterior pituitary that targets the mammary glands, stimulating them to produce milk. [Section 3.6]

proprioceptor
A receptor that responds to changes in the body position, such as stretch on a tendon, or contraction of a muscle. The receptors allow us to be consciously aware of the position of our body parts. [Section 3.5]

prospective memory
Remembering to do something in the future. [Section 5.4]

psychoanalytic theory
According to this theory, personality is shaped by a person's unconscious thoughts, feelings, and memories. Classical psychoanalytic theory was developed by Sigmund Freud. [Section 6.1]

psychoanalytic therapy
This therapy approach uses various methods to help a patient become aware of his or her unconscious motives, and to gain insight into the emotional issues and conflicts that are causing difficulties. [Section 6.1]

psychological disorder (or psychological illness or mental illness)
A set of behavioral and/or psychological symptoms that are not in keeping with cultural norms, and that are severe enough to cause significant personal distress and/or significant impairment to social, occupational, or personal functioning. [Section 6.3]

psychological fixation
According to Freud, adult personality is largely determined during the first three psychosexual stages. If parents either frustrate or overindulge the child's expression of sensual pleasure at a certain stage so that the child does not resolve that stage's developmental conflicts, the child becomes fixated at that stage, and will, as an adult, continue to seek sensual pleasure through behaviors related to that stage. [Section 6.1]

psychosexual stages
According to Freud's psychoanalytic theory, individuals progress through five psychosexual stages, one corresponding to the part of the body that is the focus of sensual pleasure. The five stages are the oral stage, anal stage, phallic stage, latent stage, and genital stage. [Section 6.1]

punishment
In operant conditioning, a consequence that decreases the likelihood that a preceding behavior will be repeated. Types include positive and negative punishment. [Section 5.1]

pupil
A hole in the center of the iris of the eye that allows light to enter the eyeball. The diameter of the pupil is controlled by the iris in response to the brightness of light. [Section 3.5]

race
The biological, anthropological, or genetic origin of an individual, and includes the following U.S. Census categories: White, Black or African American, American Indian or Alaska Native, Asian, and Native Hawaiian or Other Pacific Islander. [Section 8.3]

racism
Prejudices and discriminatory actions that are based on race (or ethnicity), or hold that one race (or ethnicity) is inferior to another. [Section 7.2]

rapid eye movement (REM)
Bursts of quick eye movements present in the last stage of sleep. [Section 4.3]

rational-legal authority
A form of leadership that is organized around rational legal rules. [Section 8.2]

recall
Retrieving information from memory. Free recall involves retrieval without any cues, whereas cued recall prompts retrieval with a cue.
[Sections 4.2 & 5.4]

recency effect
A tendency to recall the last items presented in a list. [Section 5.4]

reciprocal determinism
A reciprocal interaction between a person's behaviors (conscious actions), personal factors (cognitions, motivations, personality), and environmental factors. [Section 5.2]

recognition
Retrieving information from memory with the use of cues, such as a multiple-choice format. [Sections 4.2 & 5.4]

reference group
A group that serves as a standard measure that people compare themselves to, such as a peer group. [Section 7.2]

reflex
Automatic behaviors that occur without thinking. [Section 5.3]

reflex arc
A relatively direct connection between a sensory neuron and a motor neuron that allows an extremely rapid response to a stimulus, often without conscious brain involvement. [Section 3.3]

rehearsal
Technique of repeating verbal information in one's phonological loop to promote the encoding of sensory information into memory. [Section 5.4]

reinforcement
A consequence that increases the likelihood that a preceding behavior will be repeated. Two types are positive and negative reinforcement. [Section 5.1]

reinforcement schedule
The frequency and regularity with which rewards are offered. Schedules can be based on a number of target behaviors (ratio) or on a time interval (interval). Types include fixed-ratio, variable-ratio, fixed-interval, and variable-interval. [Section 5.1]

relative poverty
An inability to meet the average standard of living within a society. [Section 8.4]

relative refractory period
The period of time following an action potential when it is possible, but difficult, for the neuron to fire a second action potential, due to the fact that the membrane is further from threshold potential (hyperpolarized). [Section 3.2]

relearning
The process of learning material that was originally learned. [Section 5.4]

religiosity
The extent that religion influences a person's life. [Section 8.2]

REM stage
Final stage of sleep characterized by rapid eye movements (REM) and beta waves, which are seen in individuals when they are awake. Despite these wave patterns, however, the sleeper is paralyzed aside for small twitches, leading to the descriptions of this stage as "paradoxical sleep." This is generally when dreams occur. [Section 4.3]

replacement level fertility
The number of children that a woman or couple must have in order to replace the number of the people in the population who die. [Section 8.3]

representativeness heuristic
A mental shortcut where one judges the likelihood of things based on typical mental representations or examples of those things. [Section 4.2]

residential segregation
The separation of groups into different neighborhoods; separation most often occurs due to racial differences, ethnic differences, and/or socioeconomic differences. Residential segregation is not based on laws, but rather enduring social patterns, which are attributed to suburbanization, discrimination, and personal preferences. [Section 8.4]

residual-type schizophrenia
A psychological disorder where the acute phase of schizophrenia has resolved and the criteria for schizophrenia are no longer met, but some symptoms are still present in milder forms. [Section 6.3]

resource model of attention
States that attention is a limited resource. If multiple tasks do not exceed this limit, they can be done simultaneously. If they do, then they interfere with each other and are difficult to do simultaneously. [Section 4.1]

retention interval
The amount of time elapsed since information was learned and when it must be recalled. [Section 5.4]

reticular formation
Also known as the Reticular Activating System. Structures in the brainstem that are important for alertness and arousal (as in wakefulness). [Section 4.3]

retina
The innermost layer of the eyeball. The retina is made up of photoreceptors, bipolar cells, and a layer of ganglion cells. [Section 3.5]

retroactive interference
A type of memory interference that occurs when newly learned information interferes with the recall of information learned previously. [Section 5.4]

retrograde amnesia
Occurs when one is unable to recall information that was previously encoded. [Section 5.4]

rods
Photoreceptors in the retina of the eye that respond to dim light and provide us with black and white vision. [Section 3.5]

Rogers, Carl
Considered the founder of the humanistic psychology perspective, Carl Rogers pioneered the person-centered approach to therapy. [Sections 6.1 & 7.1]

role conflict
Occurs when there is a conflict in society's expectations for multiple statuses held by the same person (for example "male" and "nurse"). [Section 7.3]

role exit
The process of disengaging from a role that has become closely tied to one's self-identity to take on a new role. [Section 7.3]

role strain
Occurs when a single status results in conflicting expectations (for example a homosexual man may feel pressure to avoid being "too gay" and also "not gay enough"). [Section 7.3]

rooting reflex
In response to touching or stroking one of a baby's cheeks, the baby will turn its head in the direction of the stroke and open its mouth to "root" for a nipple. [Section 5.3]

saltatory conduction
A rapid form of action potential conduction along the axon of a neuron in which the action potential appears to jump from one node of Ranvier to another node of Ranvier. [Section 3.1]

sanctions
Rewards and punishments for behaviors that are in accord with or against norms. [Section 7.1]

Sapir-Whorf hypothesis
This hypothesis asserts that people understand their world through language and that language, in turn, shapes how people experience their world. [Section 8.3]

scapegoat
The people or group who are unfairly blamed for something, or at whom displaced aggression is directed. [Section 7.2]

Schachter-Singer Theory
Theory of emotion that asserts that the experience of physiological arousal occurs first and is followed by a conscious cognitive interpretation or appraisal that allows for the identification of the experienced emotion. [Section 4.5]

schemas
Mental frameworks or blueprints that shape and are shaped by experience. [Sections 4.2 & 5.4]

schizoaffective disorder
A psychological disorder characterized by the combination of mood and psychotic symptoms: in this disorder, both the symptoms of schizophrenia and a major depressive, manic, or mixed episode are experienced for at least one month. [Section 6.3]

schizoid personality disorder
A psychological disorder characterized by little interest or involvement in close relationships, even those with family members. [Section 6.3]

schizophrenia
A psychological disorder that is chronic and incapacitating and is characterized by psychosis and material impairment in social, occupational, or personal functioning. [Section 6.3]

schizophreniform disorder
A psychological disorder characterized by symptoms of schizophrenia present for a period of one to six months, during which the symptoms may or may not have interfered with functioning. [Section 6.3]

schizotypal personality disorder
A psychological disorder characterized by several traits that cause problems interpersonally, including constricted or inappropriate affect; magical or paranoid thinking; and odd beliefs, speech, behavior, appearance, and perceptions. [Section 6.3]

Schwann cell
One of the two peripheral nervous system supporting (glial) cells. Schwann cells form the myelin sheath on axons of peripheral neurons. [Section 3.1]

sclera
The white portion of the tough outer layer of the eyeball. [Section 3.5]

secondary group
A larger and more impersonal group than a primary group, which usually interacts for specific reasons for relatively short periods of time; these groups serve pragmatic needs. [Section 7.2]

secondary reinforcers
Conditioned reinforcers that are learned through their direct or indirect relationship with primary reinforcers. For example, money is a secondary reinforcer; it is not innately rewarding but we have learned that it can provide access to primary reinforcers. [Section 5.1]

sect
A religious organization that is distinct from the parent religion from which it was formed. [Section 8.2]

secure attachment
A style of relating to others that forms when an infant has caregivers who are sensitive and responsive to needs. In Ainsworth's experiments, securely attached infants were found to be willing to explore surroundings in the presence of the mother. They were upset but consolable when the mother left and then returned to the room. [Section 5.3]

selective attention
The process by which one input is selected to focus on out of the field of possibilities in the environment. [Section 4.1]

selective priming
Being predisposed to observe something because it has previously been encountered frequently or is expected. [Section 4.1]

self-actualization (or actualizing tendency)
According to humanistic psychology, individuals have an innate drive to maintain and enhance themselves, or realize their human potential, as long as no obstacle intervenes. [Section 6.1]

self-concept (or self-identity)
Broadly defined as the sum of an individual's knowledge and understanding of his- or herself, including physical, psychological, and social attributes, which can be influenced by the individual's attitudes, habits, beliefs, and ideas. [Sections 6.1 & 7.1]

self-consciousness
Awareness of one's self. [Section 7.1]

self-efficacy
The belief in one's own competence and effectiveness. [Section 7.1]

self-esteem
One's overall self-evaluation of one's self-worth. [Section 7.1]

self-fulfilling prophecy
When stereotypes lead a person to behave in such a way as to affirm the original stereotypes. [Section 7.2]

self-handicapping
A strategy in which people create obstacles and excuses to avoid self-blame when they do poorly. [Section 7.3]

self-reference effect
The tendency to better remember information relevant to ourselves. [Section 5.4 & 7.1]

self-schemas
The beliefs and ideas people have about themselves. [Section 7.1]

self-serving bias
The tendency to attribute our successes to ourselves and our failures to others or the external environment. [Section 7.2]

semantic memory
Memory for factual information. [Section 5.4]

semicircular canals
Three loop-like structures in the inner ear that contain sensory receptors to monitor balance. [Section 3.5]

sensitization
An increase in the strength of a response with repeated presentations of a stimulus. [Section 5.1]

sensorimotor stage
First stage of Piaget's developmental theory from birth to age 2 where babies learn object permanence and demonstrate stranger anxiety. [Section 4.2]

sensory memory
The initial recording of sensory information in the memory system; sensory memory is a very brief snapshot that quickly decays. [Section 5.4]

serial position effect
Includes the primacy and recency effect. When information is presented serially (in a list format), individuals are more likely to recall the first and last items presented. [Section 5.4]

shaping
In operant conditioning, the process of reinforcing intermediate, proximal behaviors until a final, desired behavior is achieved. [Section 5.1]

short-term memory
Memory that is limited in duration and in capacity. [Sections 5.1 & 5.4]

signal detection theory
A theory that attempts to predict how and when someone will detect the presence of a given sensory stimuli (the "signal") amidst all of the other sensory stimuli in the background (considered the "noise"). There are four possible outcomes: a hit (the signal is present and was detected), a miss (the signal was present but not detected), a false alarm (the signal was not present but the person thought it was), and a correct rejection (the signal was not present and the person did not think it was). [Section 3.5]

Skinner, B.F.
Coined the term "operant conditioning." Skinner is famous for his "Skinner box" in which he used reinforcements to shape animal behavior. [Section 5.1]

sleep apnea
Sleep disorder in which the individual intermittently stops breathing during sleep and may wake up gasping for breath. [Section 4.3]

sleep cycle
One sleep cycle consists of progression through sleep stages 1 through 4 in sequence, followed by an ascension from 4 back to 1 and then a transition into REM sleep. Typically takes about ninety minutes. [Section 4.3]

sleep spindle
Bursts of waves present in stage 2 sleep. [Section 4.3]

social behaviorism
The idea that the mind and self emerge through the process of communicating with others. [Section 7.1]

social capital
The potential for social networks to allow for upward social mobility. [Section 8.4]

social cognition
The ability of the brain to store and process information regarding social perception. [Section 7.2]

social cognitive perspective
According to this perspective, personality is formed by a reciprocal interaction among behavioral, cognitive, and environmental factors. [Sections 5.2 & 6.1]

social construct
A social mechanism or practice that is constructed by society; essentially, everybody in society agrees to treat a certain aspect a certain way regardless of its inherent value. [Section 8.1]

social constructionism
A sociological theory that argues that people actively shape their reality through social interactions; it is therefore something that is constructed, not inherent. Social constructionism looks to uncover the ways in which individuals and groups participate in the construction of their perceived social reality. [Section 8.1]

social cues
Verbal or nonverbal hints that guide social interactions. [Section 6.1]

social dysfunction
A process that has undesirable consequences, and may actually reduce the stability of society. [Section 8.1]

social epidemiology
The study of the distribution of health and disease across a population, with the focus on using social concepts to explain patterns of health and illness in a population. [Section 8.4]

social facilitation effect
The phenomenon that describes how people tend to perform simple, well-learned tasks better when other people are present. [Section 7.2]

social facts
The elements that serve some function in society, such as the laws, morals, values, religions, customs, rituals, and rules that make up a society. [Section 8.1]

social identity
The social definitions of self, including race, religion, gender, occupation, and the like. [Section 7.1]

social institutions
A complex of roles, norms, and values organized into a relatively stable form that contributes to social order by governing the behavior of people. Social institutions provide predictability and organization for individuals within a society, and mediate social behavior between people. [Section 8.2]

social loafing
The phenomenon where people tend to exert less effort if they are being evaluated as a group than if they are individually accountable. [Section 7.2]

social mobility
The ability to move up or down within the social stratification system. [Section 8.4]

social network
A web of social relationships, including those in which a person is directly linked to others as well as those in which people are indirectly connected through others. [Section 7.3]

social perception
The ability to understand others in our social world; the initial information we process about other people in order to try to understand their mindsets and intentions. [Section 7.2]

socialism
An economic system where resources and production are collectively owned. Socialism includes a system of production and distribution designed to satisfy human needs (good/services are produced for direct use instead of for profit). [Section 8.1]

socialization
The process through which people learn to be proficient members of society; a lifelong process where people learn the attitudes, values, and beliefs that are reinforced by a particular culture. [Section 7.1]

social phobia
An unreasonable, paralyzing fear of feeling embarrassed or humiliated while one is watched by others, even while performing routine activities such as eating in public or using a public restroom. [Section 6.3]

social reproduction
The structures and activities in place in a society that serve to transmit and reinforce social inequality from one generation to the next. Cultural capital and social capital are two mechanisms by which social reproduction occurs. [Section 8.4]

social roles
Expectations for people of a given social status. [Section 7.3]

social stratification
The way that people are categorized in society; people can be categorized by race, education, wealth, and income (among other things). [Section 8.4]

social support
The perception that one is cared for and part of a social network; supportive resources can be tangible or emotional. [Section 7.3]

society
A group of people who share a culture and live/interact with each other within a definable area. [Section 8.1]

sociobiology
The study of how biology and evolution have affected human social behavior. Primarily, it applies Darwin's principle of natural selection to social behavior, suggesting there is a biological basis for many behaviors. [Section 8.3]

socioeconomic status (SES)
Often defined in terms of power (the ability to get other people to do something), property (sum of possessions and income) and prestige (reputation in society), because these three concepts tend to (but not always) be related in U.S. society. [Section 8.4]

sociology
The study of how individuals interact with, shape, and are subsequently shaped by, the society in which they live. [Section 8.1]

soma
The cell body of a neuron. [Section 3.1]

somatization disorder
A psychological disorder characterized by a variety of physical symptoms over an extended time period, including: pain, gastrointestinal symptoms, sexual symptoms, and pseudoneurological symptoms. [Section 6.3]

somatoform disorder
A psychological disorder characterized primarily by physical symptoms and concerns, which may mimic physical (somatic) disease. However, the symptoms are not explainable medically and do not improve with medical treatment. [Section 6.3]

somnambulism
Sleepwalking. [Section 4.3]

source monitoring error
A specific type of error of recollection where a memory is incorrectly attributed to the wrong source. [Section 5.4]

source traits
The factors underlying human personality and behavior. [Section 6.1]

spatial summation
Integration by a postsynaptic neuron of inputs (EPSPs and IPSPs) from multiple sources. [Section 3.2]

specific phobia
A persistent, strong, and unreasonable fear of a certain object or situation. Specific phobias are classified into four types depending on the types of triggers they involve, including: situational type, natural environment type, blood-injection-injury type, and animal type. [Section 6.3]

spontaneous recovery
In classical conditioning, a reoccurrence of a previously extinct conditioned response in the presence of a conditioned stimulus. Often occurs after a period of time has passed since the initial extinction of the response. [Section 5.1]

spotlight model
Model for visual attention, with a spotlight representing one's attention and its ability to unlock from a current target, move focus, and lock onto a new target. [Section 4.1]

spreading activation theory
A theory of information retrieval that involves a search process where specific nodes are activated, which leads to the activation of related nodes, and so on. A node does not become activated until it receives input signals from its neighbors that are strong enough to reach a response threshold. The effect of input signals is cumulative: the response threshold is reached by the summation of input signals from multiple nodes. [Section 5.4]

state
Situational factors that can influence personality and behavior; states are unstable, temporary, and variable. [Section 6.1]

state capitalism
A system in which companies are privately run, but work closely with the government in forming laws and regulations. [Section 8.2]

status
A sociological term that refers to all the socially defined positions within a society. [Section 7.3]

stereotypes
Oversimplified ideas about groups of people, based on characteristics (race, gender, sexual orientation, religion, disability). Stereotypes can be positive or negative. [Section 7.2]

stereotype threat
Refers to a self-fulfilling fear that one will be evaluated based on a negative stereotype. [Section 7.2]

steroid hormone
A hormone derived from cholesterol. Steroids are generally hydrophobic and can easily cross the plasma membrane of cells, thus receptors for steroids are found intracellularly. Once the steroid binds to the receptor, the receptor-steroid complex acts to regulate transcription in the nucleus. [Section 3.6]

stigma
Extreme disapproval of a person or group based on the person or groups actual or perceived deviance from society. [Section 7.2]

stimulants
Class of drugs that speed up body functions and neural activity. Includes caffeine, nicotine, cocaine, and amphetamines. [Section 4.3]

stranger anxiety
Developmentally typical anxiety displayed by children from approximately eight to twelve months of age toward close contact with strangers. May be expressed by crying and clinging to familiar caregivers. [Section 5.3]

subculture
A segment of society that shares a distinct pattern of traditions and values that differs from that of the larger society. [Section 7.1]

sucking reflex
In response to anything touching the roof of the baby's mouth, it will begin to suck. [Section 5.3]

summation
The integration of input (EPSPs and IPSPs) from many presynaptic neurons by a single postsynaptic neuron, either temporally or spatially. Summation of input can either stimulate the postsynaptic neuron and possibly lead to an action potential, or it can inhibit the neuron, reducing the likelihood of an action potential. [Section 3.2]

superego
According to Freud's psychoanalytic theory, the superego inhibits the id and influences the ego to follow moralistic rather than realistic goals. Based on societal values as learned from one's parents, the superego makes judgments of right and wrong and strives for perfection. The superego seeks to gain psychological rewards such as feelings of pride and self-love, and to avoid psychological punishment such as feelings of guilt and inferiority. [Section 6.1]

symbolic culture
Consists of symbols that carry a particular meaning and are recognized by people of the same culture. These symbols can communicate the values and norms of the culture. [Section 8.3]

symbolic interactionism
A micro-level theory in sociology, which examines the relationship between individuals and society by focusing on communication, the exchange of information through language and symbols. Symbolic interactionism suggests that the mind and self emerge through the social process of communication or use of symbols. [Sections 7.1 & 8.1]

sympathetic nervous system (SNS)
Subdivision of the autonomic nervous system directing what is known as the "fight or flight" response to prepare the body for action. It increases heart rate, blood pressure, and blood sugar levels and directs the adrenal glands to release stress hormones. [Sections 3.4 & 4.5]

synapse
A neuron-to-neuron, neuron-to-organ, or muscle cell-to-muscle cell junction. [Section 3.2]

synaptic cleft
A microscopic space between the axon of one neuron and the cell body or dendrites of a second neuron, or between the axon of a neuron and an organ. [Section 3.2]

telencephalon
The cerebral hemispheres. [Section 3.4]

temperament
Dispositional emotional excitability. Tends to be fairly stable through the life span. [Section 4.4]

temporal summation
Summation by a postsynaptic cell of input (EPSPs or IPSPs) from a single source over time. [Section 3.2]

thalamus
The central structure of the diencephalon of the brain. The thalamus acts as a relay station and major integrating area for sensory impulses. [Section 3.4]

thermoreceptor
A receptor that responds to changes in temperature. [Section 3.5]

theta waves
Waves of low to moderate intensity and intermediate frequency present during stage 1 of sleep. [Section 4.3]

tonic neck reflex
In response to its head being turned to one side, a baby will stretch out its arm on the same side and the opposite arm bends up at the elbow. This reflex lasts about six to seven months. [Section 5.3]

top-down processing
A type of information processing that occurs when the brain applies experience and expectations to interpret sensory information; note that the brain in fact uses a combination of bottom-up processing and top-down processing. [Section 3.5]

traditional authority
A form of leadership where power is due to custom, tradition, or accepted practice. [Section 8.2]

trait
Internal, stable, and enduring aspects of personality that should be consistent across most situations. [Section 6.1]

trial and error
Strategy of problem-solving that involves trying different alternatives sequentially until success is achieved. [Section 4.2]

tropic hormone
A hormone that controls the release of another hormone. [Section 3.6]

tympanic membrane
The membrane that separates the outer ear from the middle ear. The tympanic membrane is also known as the eardrum. [Section 3.5]

unconditioned response
A response that automatically follows an unconditioned stimulus, without necessitating learning and conditioning to create the link. [Section 5.1]

unconditioned stimulus
A stimulus that elicits an unconditioned response automatically, without necessitating learning and conditioning to create the link. [Section 5.1]

undifferentiated-type schizophrenia
A psychological disorder characterized by the basic criteria for schizophrenia, but symptoms that do not fit into one of the other subtypes. [Section 6.3]

universal emotions
Six major emotions that appear to be universal across cultures: happiness, sadness, surprise, fear, disgust, and anger. [Section 4.4]

universal grammar
Basic rules of language, presumed to be innate, that allow the human mind to gain mastery of language from limited exposure during sensitive developmental years in early childhood. [Section 4.6]

upward mobility
An increase in social class. [Section 8.4]

urbanization
The growth of urban areas (as people move from rural to urban areas) as the result of global change. Urbanization is tied to industrialization, and industrialized countries have more people living in urban areas than non-industrialized countries do. [Section 8.3]

utilitarian organization
An organization in which members get paid for their efforts, such as businesses. [Section 7.3]

vagus nerves
Cranial nerve pair X. The vagus nerves are very large mixed nerves (they carry both sensory input and motor output) that innervate virtually every visceral organ. They are especially important in transmitting parasympathetic input to the heart and digestive smooth muscle. [Section 3.4]

values
A culture's standard for evaluating what is good or bad. [Section 8.3]

variable-interval schedule
Reinforcement schedule in which reward is offered after an unpredictable time interval. [Section 5.1]

variable-ratio schedule
Reinforcement schedule in which reward is offered after an unpredictable number of occurrences of a behavior. [Section 5.1]

visual cortex
The area of the occipital lobe responsible for processing visual information. [Section 3.5]

visuospatial sketchpad
Part of Alan Baddeley's model of working memory that allows for the repetition of visuospatial information (images) to aid with encoding it into memory. [**Section 4.2**]

vitreous humor
A thick, gelatinous fluid found in the posterior segment of the eye (between the lens and the retina). The vitreous humor is only produced during fetal development and helps maintain intraocular pressure (the pressure inside the eye). [**Section 3.5**]

walking/stepping reflex
In response to the soles of a baby's feet touching a flat surface, they will attempt to "walk" by placing one foot in front of the other. This reflex disappears around six weeks and reappears around 8-12 months when a baby learns to walk. [**Section 5.3**]

Weber, Max
Weber agreed with Marx's ideas about conflict theory, but he did not believe that the collapse of capitalism was inevitable; rather, he argued that there could be more than one source of conflict, such as conflict over inequalities in political power and social status. Max Weber, along with Émile Durkeim and Karl Marx, is considered a founding father of sociology. [**Section 8.1**]

Weber's law
This law pertains to sensory perception and dictates that two stimuli must differ by a constant proportion in order for their difference to be perceptible. [**Section 3.5**]

welfare capitalism
A system in which most of the economy is private with the exception of extensive social welfare programs to serve certain needs within society. [**Section 8.2**]

Wernicke's area
The area of the brain, located in the posterior section of the temporal lobe in the language-dominant hemisphere of the brain (left for most people), that is involved with the comprehension of speech and written language. Individuals with damage to this area are unable to understand language and produce nonsensical sounds with the same rhythm and syntax as speech. [**Section 4.6**]

white matter
Myelinated axons. [**Section 3.4**]

withdrawal
An uncomfortable and often painful experience that may accompany the discontinuing of a drug. Withdrawal is immediately alleviated if the user takes the substance (thus reinforcing the addiction) or dissipates slowly over time (as is the case with detoxification). [**Section 4.3**]

working memory
Short-term memory for information in immediate awareness. According to Alan Baddeley, working memory consists of four components: a central executive, a phonological loop, a visuospatial sketchpad, and an episodic buffer. [**Section 4.2**]

Yerkes-Dodson Law
Law that describes an upside down U-shaped relationship between arousal and performance. It asserts that a moderate level of arousal creates optimal performance. Too little arousal leads to complacency and too much arousal can be overwhelming. [**Section 4.4**]

Zimbardo, Philip
A psychologist best known for his prison study, which elucidated the extreme effects of role-playing on human behavior. A group of 24 male students were isolated and asked to plays the roles of prisoners and guards; the participants adapted to their roles well beyond Zimbardo's expectations. The "guards" enforced extreme measures, including psychological torture, and many of the "prisoners" passively accepted psychological abuse and readily harassed other "prisoners" who attempted to prevent it. [**Section 6.4**]

NOTES

International Offices Listing

China (Beijing)
1501 Building A,
Disanji Creative Zone,
No.66 West Section of North 4th Ring Road Beijing
Tel: +86-10-62684481/2/3
Email: tprkor01@chol.com
Website: www.tprbeijing.com

China (Shanghai)
1010 Kaixuan Road
Building B, 5/F
Changning District, Shanghai, China 200052
Sara Beattie, Owner: Email: sbeattie@sarabeattie.com
Tel: +86-21-5108-2798
Fax: +86-21-6386-1039
Website: www.princetonreviewshanghai.com

Hong Kong
5th Floor, Yardley Commercial Building
1-6 Connaught Road West, Sheung Wan, Hong Kong
(MTR Exit C)
Sara Beattie, Owner: Email: sbeattie@sarabeattie.com
Tel: +852-2507-9380
Fax: +852-2827-4630
Website: www.princetonreviewhk.com

India (Mumbai)
Score Plus Academy
Office No.15, Fifth Floor
Manek Mahal 90
Veer Nariman Road
Next to Hotel Ambassador
Churchgate, Mumbai 400020
Maharashtra, India
Ritu Kalwani: Email: director@score-plus.com
Tel: + 91 22 22846801 / 39 / 41
Website: www.score-plus.com

India (New Delhi)
South Extension
K-16, Upper Ground Floor
South Extension Part–1,
New Delhi-110049
Aradhana Mahna: aradhana@manyagroup.com
Monisha Banerjee: monisha@manyagroup.com
Ruchi Tomar: ruchi.tomar@manyagroup.com
Rishi Josan: Rishi.josan@manyagroup.com
Vishal Goswamy: vishal.goswamy@manyagroup.com
Tel: +91-11-64501603/ 4, +91-11-65028379
Website: www.manyagroup.com

Lebanon
463 Bliss Street
AlFarra Building - 2nd floor
Ras Beirut
Beirut, Lebanon
Hassan Coudsi: Email: hassan.coudsi@review.com
Tel: +961-1-367-688
Website: www.princetonreviewlebanon.com

Korea
945-25 Young Shin Building
25 Daechi-Dong, Kangnam-gu
Seoul, Korea 135-280
Yong-Hoon Lee: Email: TPRKor01@chollian.net
In-Woo Kim: Email: iwkim@tpr.co.kr
Tel: + 82-2-554-7762
Fax: +82-2-453-9466
Website: www.tpr.co.kr

Kuwait
ScorePlus Learning Center
Salmiyah Block 3, Street 2 Building 14
Post Box: 559, Zip 1306, Safat, Kuwait
Email: infokuwait@score-plus.com
Tel: +965-25-75-48-02 / 8
Fax: +965-25-75-46-02
Website: www.scorepluseducation.com

Malaysia
Sara Beattie MDC Sdn Bhd
Suites 18E & 18F
18th Floor
Gurney Tower, Persiaran Gurney
Penang, Malaysia
Email: tprkl.my@sarabeattie.com
Sara Beattie, Owner: Email: sbeattie@sarabeattie.com
Tel: +604-2104 333
Fax: +604-2104 330
Website: www.princetonreviewKL.com

Mexico
TPR México
Guanajuato No. 242 Piso 1 Interior 1
Col. Roma Norte
México D.F., C.P.06700
registro@princetonreviewmexico.com
Tel: +52-55-5255-4495
+52-55-5255-4440
+52-55-5255-4442
Website: www.princetonreviewmexico.com

Qatar
Score Plus
Office No: 1A, Al Kuwari (Damas)
Building near Merweb Hotel, Al Saad
Post Box: 2408, Doha, Qatar
Email: infoqatar@score-plus.com
Tel: +974 44 36 8580, +974 526 5032
Fax: +974 44 13 1995
Website: www.scorepluseducation.com

Taiwan
The Princeton Review Taiwan
2F, 169 Zhong Xiao East Road, Section 4
Taipei, Taiwan 10690
Lisa Bartle (Owner): lbartle@princetonreview.com.tw
Tel: +886-2-2751-1293
Fax: +886-2-2776-3201
Website: www.PrincetonReview.com.tw

Thailand
The Princeton Review Thailand
Sathorn Nakorn Tower, 28th floor
100 North Sathorn Road
Bangkok, Thailand 10500
Thavida Bijayendrayodhin (Chairman)
Email: thavida@princetonreviewthailand.com
Mitsara Bijayendrayodhin (Managing Director)
Email: mitsara@princetonreviewthailand.com
Tel: +662-636-6770
Fax: +662-636-6776
Website: www.princetonreviewthailand.com

Turkey
Yeni Sülün Sokak No. 28
Levent, Istanbul, 34330, Turkey
Nuri Ozgur: nuri@tprturkey.com
Rona Ozgur: rona@tprturkey.com
Iren Ozgur: iren@tprturkey.com
Tel: +90-212-324-4747
Fax: +90-212-324-3347
Website: www.tprturkey.com

UAE
Emirates Score Plus
Office No: 506, Fifth Floor
Sultan Business Center
Near Lamcy Plaza, 21 Oud Metha Road
Post Box: 44098, Dubai
United Arab Emirates
Hukumat Kalwani: skoreplus@gmail.com
Ritu Kalwani: director@score-plus.com
Email: info@score-plus.com
Tel: +971-4-334-0004
Fax: +971-4-334-0222
Website: www.princetonreviewuae.com

Our International Partners

The Princeton Review also runs courses with a variety of
partners in Africa, Asia, Europe, and South America.

Georgia
LEAF American-Georgian Education Center
www.leaf.ge

Mongolia
English Academy of Mongolia
www.nyescm.org

Nigeria
The Know Place
www.knowplace.com.ng

Panama
Academia Interamericana de Panama
http://aip.edu.pa/

Switzerland
Institut Le Rosey
http://www.rosey.ch/

All other inquiries, please email us at
internationalsupport@review.com